MW00612393

SAT Reading and Writing Prep

A Workbook with 600+ Questions & Explanations

SAT Reading and Writing Prep: A Workbook with 600+ Questions & Explanations

This publication was written and edited by the team at Ivy Global.

Editor-in-Chief: Corwin Henville

Producers: Lloyd Min and Junho Suh

Editors: Alex Emond, Grace Bueler, Mark Mendola, Sacha Azor

Contributors: Thea Bélanger-Polak, Stephanie Bucklin, Nathan Létourneau, Bessie Fan, Ian Greig, Elizabeth Hilts, Lei Huang, Geoffrey Morrison, Ward Pettibone, Arden Rogow-Bales, Kristin Rose, Nathan Tebokkel, Sarah Boivin, and Isabel Villeneuve

About the Publisher

Ivy Global is a pioneering education company that delivers a wide range of test prep and consulting services.

E-mail: publishing@ivyglobal.com
Website: http://www.ivyglobal.com

Edition 1.1 – Copyright 2020 by Ivy Global. All rights reserved.

SAT is a registered trademark of the College Board, which is not affiliated with this book.

Contents

Introduction
Chapter1

Section 1
About This Book

Welcome, students, parents, and teachers! This book is designed to prepare students for the SAT exam, a standardized exam created and administered by the College Board, which is required by many colleges and universities in the United States as part of the admissions process.

The goal of this book is to provide practice drills to help students improve their SAT score by targeting specific skills. There are 119 unique question types on the SAT and this book includes a set of drills for every single type of Reading and Writing question. Detailed answer explanations are also included for those drills. This book does not, however, include instructional content outside of the answer explanations, nor does it include a practice test. For practice tests, we recommend purchasing the Ivy Global SAT 6 Practice Tests book (ivy.gl/6PT) for the best available practice tests. For further instruction, we recommend Ivy Global's comprehensive SAT Guide which can be found at ivy.gl/satguide or contacting us for experienced tutoring help at ivyglobal.com/sat/tutoring.

How to Begin

We recommend using this book after taking a practice test and scoring it with our free Cloud scoring tool. Free practice tests can be found online at prep.ivyglobal.com and detailed scoring analysis for those exams at cloud.ivyglobal.com.

In addition to receiving a score, scoring a practice test on Cloud will provide you with detailed analysis of your test performance broken down by question type like the following example:

Reading Questions Breakdown					
Category/Topic		Correct	Incorrect	Omitted	Total
Information and Ideas		26	10	0	36
Direct Information (IE)		2	1	0	3
Vocabulary in Context (IW)		6	4	0	10
Describing Relationships (IR)		2	1	0	3
Implied Information (II)		6	1	0	7
Main Ideas (IT)		0	1	0	1
Finding Evidence (IC)		7	2	0	9
Similar Situation (IA)		3	0	0	3

This information will allow you to identify the types of questions that could use improvement. You can then look up those question types with the table of contents in this book and practice!

For additional resources to help you in your studies, please visit us at ivyglobal.com/study. Good luck studying!

 For additional resources, please visit **ivyglobal.com/study**.

Ivy Global

Reading
Chapter 2

Ivy Global

Section 1
Information and Ideas

Questions in the Information and Ideas domain test your ability to extract information from a passage. You will need to find specific details to answer questions that are directly addressed in the passage, reason about implications and analogous situations, look for evidence that supports specific ideas, identify and summarize main ideas, recognize relationships between characters and events, and decode the meaning of challenging words and phrases..

"Finding Evidence" questions contribute to the "Command of Evidence" cross-test score, and "Vocabulary in Context" questions contribute to the "Vocabulary in Context" cross-test score.

There are 8 specific question types in this domain:

Development			
IE	Direct Information	IT	Main Ideas
II	Implied Information	IS	Summarizing
IA	Similar Situation	IR	Describing Relationships
IC	Finding Evidence	IW	Vocabulary in Context

Direct Information

Part 1

Direct Information questions require you to correctly answer direct factual questions about information stated in the passage. They may require you to quickly locate factual information in the passage, including names, dates, or quantities. They may also require you to correctly interpret complex sentences or challenging vocabulary and select a choice that correctly paraphrases that information.

DIRECTIONS

Every passage or paired set of passages is accompanied by a number of questions. Read the passage or paired set of passages, then use what is said or implied in what you read and in any given graphics to choose the best answer to each question.

Question 1

This passage is adapted from *Sylvie and Bruno* by Lewis Carroll. First published in 1889.

All the people cheered again, and one man, who was more excited than the rest, flung his hat high into the air, and shouted (as well as I could
Line make out) "Who roars for the Sub-Warden?"
5   Everybody roared, but whether it was for the Sub-Warden, or not, did not clearly appear: some were shouting "Bread!" and some "Taxes!", but no one seemed to know what it was they really wanted.
All this I saw from the open window of the
10   Warden's breakfast-saloon, looking across the shoulder of the Lord Chancellor, who had sprung to his feet the moment the shouting began, almost as if he had been expecting it, and had rushed to the window that commanded the best view of the
15   marketplace.
"What can it all mean?" he kept repeating to himself.

 1

According to the passage, the narrator witnesses the cheering

A) while seated on a bench close to the crowd.

B) while standing outside the Warden's breakfast-saloon.

C) while looking out an open window of a building.

D) while having a heated argument with the Lord Chancellor.

Question 2

This passage is adapted from "Beyond the Sweetness of Sugar" by Duane Mellor and Nenad Naumovski. ©2016 by Duane Mellor and Nenad Naumovski.

One of the simplest ways to make food less hospitable to bacteria is to remove water. This is known as reducing the water activity. Something
Line that is completely dry has a water activity of 0 (a
5   relatively small number of foods have this rating), while water has an activity of 1, with table sugar sitting at around 0.2. Reducing the water activity

in food below 0.70 can seriously limit bacteria growth.

10   This is exactly what making jam does. Firstly, the fruit is heated with sugar and pectin (a type of fibre). This helps to break down tough cell walls and sterilizes the mixture.

2

The author of the passage explains that reducing the water activity to below 0.7 in foods leads to

A) reduced growth of bacteria in the food.

B) dryness in the food.

C) overgrowth of bacteria in the food.

D) change in the texture and shape of the food.

Question 3

This passage is adapted from "Why It's Time to Take Children's Books Seriously" by Catherine Butler. ©2016 by Catherine Butler.

    Once a generation, it seems, a cri de coeur goes out, in which a representative of the world of children's literature speaks with revelatory
Line authority to the literary establishment and makes it
5 reassess the place of children's books. In 1968, the Times Literary Supplement invited Alan Garner, the author of The Owl Service, to write about his approach. Garner argued that children are the most rewarding and demanding readers, pointedly
10 saying of his next book: "If it is good enough, it will probably be for children." Likewise, in 1996, Philip Pullman began his Carnegie Medal acceptance speech by declaring: "There are some themes, some subjects, too large for adult
15 fiction; they can only be dealt with adequately in a children's book."

3

The passage indicates that children's literature

A) should be reassessed once a generation for inappropriate themes.

B) is difficult to write because child readers are so demanding.

C) should have its place reconsidered since it can contain large themes.

D) is the subject of much controversy in the world of literature.

Question 4

This passage is adapted from "Is Your Nervous System a Democracy or a Dictatorship When Controlling Your Behavior?" by Ari Berkowitz. ©2016 by Ari Berkowitz.

    For some behaviors, a single nerve cell acts as a dictator, triggering an entire set of movements via the electrical signals it uses to send messages.
Line (We neurobiologists call those signals action
5 potentials, or spikes.) Take the example of touching a crayfish on its tail; a single spike in the lateral giant neuron elicits a fast tail-flip that vaults the animal upward, out of potential danger. These movements begin within about one
10 hundredth of a second of the touch.

4

According to the author, what is a significant characteristic of nerve cells?

A) They primarily help animals react to danger.

B) They can be produced in one one hundredth of a second.

C) They are assigned to specific parts of the body.

D) They communicate messages that trigger movements.

Question 5

This passage is adapted from Hard Times by Charles Dickens. First published in 1905.

Mr. Gradgrind walked homeward from the school in a state of considerable satisfaction. It was his school, and he intended it to be a model.
Line He intended every child in it to be a model—just
5 as the young Gradgrinds were all models.

There were five young Gradgrinds, and they were models every one. They had been lectured at, from their tenderest years; coursed, like little hares. Almost as soon as they could run
10 alone, they had been made to run to the lecture-room. The first object with which they had an association, or of which they had a remembrance, was a large black board with a dry Ogre chalking ghastly white figures on it.

5

The passage indicates that Mr. Gradgrind considered all of his children models because they

A) had begun their studies at a young age.

B) enjoyed going to school and attending lectures and classes.

C) were the children of the school principal.

D) excelled in the most difficult subjects in school.

Question 6

This passage is adapted from "Americans Think National Parks are Worth $92 Billion, but We Don't Fund Them Accordingly" by Linda J. Bilmes and John Loomis. ©2016 by Linda J. Bilmes and John Loomis.

Using methods similar to the way federal agencies analyze proposed regulations, we conducted a peer-reviewed economic study to
Line estimate what the national parks are worth to
5 Americans. We asked a representative sample of more than 700 households how much they would pay in increased taxes to preserve those assets for themselves and their grandchildren.

Our results showed that Americans put a total
10 value of $92 billion per year on our national parks, monuments, seashores, and recreation areas. This represents the amount respondents would pay to preserve the parks ($62 billion) and their programs ($30 billion)—whether they actually
15 visit the parks or not. Ninety-five percent said that protecting national parks for future generations was important, and 81 percent were willing to pay higher federal taxes to ensure that the park system was protected and preserved.

6

Based on the passage, which choice best describes Americans' responses to the economic study?

A) They would pay increased taxes because they want to protect the wildlife in the parks.

B) They would pay increased taxes to preserve the parks and support preservation programs for generations to come.

C) They would not pay increased taxes because there is already enough tax money going into the preservation of parks and programs.

D) They would not pay increased taxes because they believe that the valuation of the parks is too high.

Question 7

This passage is adapted from "Remind Me Again, What is Thalidomide and How Did It Cause So Much Harm?" by Arthur Daemmrich. ©2015 by Arthur Daeemrich.

Thalidomide was first synthesized in March 1954 by chemists at Chemie Grünenthal (Grünenthal), a small pharmaceutical and fine
Line chemical manufacturer in northwestern Germany.
5 Laboratory and animal test results were first published in 1956 and showed the drug had a low toxicity. Standard toxicity tests at the time involved dosing mice until half of the population died. This determined a "lethal dose 50", or LD50,
10 level. For thalidomide, no toxic effects were found at even 5,000 milligrams per kilogram of body

weight in mice. Others tests in mice and rats, including cardiac, blood pressure, respiratory, urine secretion, temperature, and basal metabolic

15 rate showed no harmful effects.

7

Which of the following does the author report about the drug thalidomide?

A) Thalidomide is non-toxic and safe for human use.

B) The LD50 level of thalidomide was 5000 milligrams per kilogram of body weight in mice.

C) Thalidomide was first produced by chemists in March 1954.

D) Thalidomide did not affect blood pressure or blood sugar of mice and rats.

Question 8

This passage is adapted from "Do Fish Have Feelings? Maybe" by Sonia Rey Planellas. ©2016 by Sonia Rey Planellas.

The fish brain is small and organized differently from that of mammals. But it also has structures with the same evolutionary origin
Line as parts of the mammal brain that play a key
5 role in generating emotions (the amygdala) and supporting learning (the hippocampus). If these areas are damaged, we see similar behavioral effects in fish and mammals, suggesting they serve a similar function.

10   There's also a huge amount of research that clearly shows fish have impressive learning capacities and use these to support a whole range of sophisticated behaviors. Many species of fish can perform complicated feats of navigation by

15 remembering mental maps. Others can work out how likely they are to win fights with other fish by observing and remembering potential rivals' previous battles. And some even make and use tools such as an anvil for cracking open bivalve

20 mollusk shells.

8

Which of the following did the author NOT mention in regards to fish brain structure and function?

A) Fish have brain structures comparable to those in mammals.

B) Fish can effectively learn new tasks through use of the amygdala.

C) Fish have the brain capacity to store memories.

D) The brains of fish are not organized in the same way as the brains of mammals.

Question 9

This passage is adapted from The Man in the Iron Mask by Alexandre Dumas. First published in the late 1840s.

On a bed of green serge, similar in all respect to the other beds in the Bastile, save that it was newer, reposed a young man. According to custom,
Line the prisoner was without a light.
5   Near the bed a large leathern armchair, with twisted legs, sustained his clothes. A little table—without pens, books, paper, or ink—stood neglected in sadness near the window; while several plates, still unemptied, showed that the

10 prisoner had scarcely touched his evening meal. Aramis saw that the young man was stretched upon his bed, his face half concealed by his arms. The arrival of a visitor did not cause any change of position; either he was waiting in expectation, or

15 was asleep.

Aramis lighted the candle from the lantern, pushed back the armchair, and approached the bed with an evident mixture of interest and respect. The young man raised his head. "What is it?" said he.

The passage describes the man's prison cell as all of the following EXCEPT:

A) neglected and filthy.

B) dark and lonesome.

C) bare and unadorned.

D) dim and subdued.

Question 10

This passage is adapted from "New Plastic-Munching Bacteria Could Fuel a Recycling Revolution" by Mark Lorch. ©2016 by Mark Lorch.

Plastics are polymers, long thin molecules made of repeating (monomer) building blocks. These are cross-linked to one another to build a
Line durable, malleable mesh. Most plastics are made
5 from carbon-based monomers, so in theory they are a good source of food for microorganisms.

But unlike natural polymers (such as cellulose in plants), plastics aren't generally biodegradable. Bacteria and fungi co-evolved with natural
10 materials, all the while coming up with new biochemical methods to harness the resources from dead matter. But plastics have only been around for about 70 years. So microorganisms simply haven't had much time to evolve the necessary
15 biochemical tool kit to latch onto the plastic fibers, break them up into the constituent parts, and then utilize the resulting chemicals as a source of energy and carbon that they need to grow.

Which of the following does the author say about microorganisms breaking down plastic?

A) Microorganisms can only break down biodegradable, natural matter.

B) Microorganisms can break down plastic materials, but not completely.

C) Microorganisms cannot latch onto matter that is dead, such as plastic.

D) Microorganisms can evolve to break down new materials.

Question 11

This passage is adapted from The Mysterious Affair at Styles by Agatha Christie. First published in 1920.

I had been invalided home from the Front; and, after spending some months in a rather depressing Convalescent Home, was given a month's sick
Line leave. Having no near relations or friends, I was
5 trying to make up my mind what to do, when I ran across John Cavendish. I had seen very little of him for some years. Indeed, I had never known him particularly well. He was a good fifteen years my senior, for one thing, though he hardly looked
10 his forty-five years. As a boy, though, I had often stayed at Styles, his mother's place in Essex.

We had a good yarn about old times, and it ended in his inviting me down to Styles to spend my leave there.
15 "The mater will be delighted to see you again—after all those years," he added.

"Your mother keeps well?" I asked.

"Oh, yes. I suppose you know that she has married again?"
20 I am afraid I showed my surprise rather plainly. Mrs. Cavendish, who had married John's father when he was a widower with two sons, had been a handsome woman of middle-age as I remembered her. She certainly could not be a day less than
25 seventy now. I recalled her as an energetic, autocratic personality, somewhat inclined to charitable and social notoriety, with a fondness for opening bazaars and playing the Lady Bountiful. She was a most generous woman, and possessed a

30 considerable fortune of her own.

"Rotten little bounder too!" John said savagely. "I can tell you, Hastings, it's making life jolly difficult for us."

11

In the passage, the author answers all of the following questions EXCEPT:

A) How did the narrator run into John Cavendish?

B) Why was the narrator home from the war? *sick leave*

C) How did the narrator know John Cavendish?

D) What was the narrator's opinion of John Cavendish's mother?

Question 12

This passage is adapted from "Is technology making your attention span shorter than a goldfish's?" by Martin Thirkettle and Graham Pike. ©2015 by Martin Thirkettle and Graham Pike.

The increasing number of distractions in our world is partly due to the new and ever-evolving ways in which advertisers can put their message
Line in front of us—and the "increasingly immersive"
5 techniques they'll use once the message is there. Realizing this helps us understand that our attention is a resource being fought over by advertisers.

12

According to the passage, increased distractions are a result of

A) new and evolving advertising methods competing for attention.

B) additional work that must be done in people's careers.

C) novel modes of entertainment that compete for audiences.

D) increased interest in content-based advertisements.

Question 13

This passage is adapted from "Does a planet need plate tectonics to develop life?" by Craig O'Neill. ©2016 by Craig O'Neill.

Plate tectonics may be a phase in the evolution of planets that has implications for the habitability of exoplanets, according to new research
Line published this month in the journal Physics of
5 the Earth and Planetary Interiors. Two of the things that make Earth unique in our solar system are that it has plate tectonics—with the surface broken up into a number of tectonic plates that drift around, moving continents and causing
10 earthquakes—and life.

13

According to the passage, what causes earthquakes?

A) The drifting of tectonic plates

B) The rotation of planets

C) The evolution of life

D) The heat of the solar system

Question 14

This passage is adapted from Aunt Jane's Nieces by Edith Van Dyne. First published in 1906.

Professor De Graf was sorting the mail at the breakfast table.

"Here's a letter for you, Beth," said he, and
Line tossed it across the cloth to where his daughter sat.
5 The girl raised her eyebrows, expressing surprise. It was something unusual for her to receive a letter. She picked up the square envelope between a finger and thumb and carefully read the inscription, "Miss Elizabeth De Graf, Cloverton,
10 Ohio." Turning the envelope she found on the reverse flap a curious armorial emblem, with the word "Elmhurst."

14

Beth expresses surprise when she is tossed the letter because

A) it had been a long time since she last received word from Elmhurst.

B) Beth did not usually receive letters addressed to her.

C) her father usually forbade her from reading letters addressed to her directly.

D) it was unusual to receive a letter with the armorial emblem.

Question 15

This passage is adapted from "From kitsch to Park Avenue: the cultural history of the plastic pink flamingo" by Annie Dell'Aria. ©2015 by Annie Dell'Aria.

In the postwar era, cheap, sturdy, and versatile plastics were becoming an increasingly popular
Line material for mass-produced commercial products, 5 from Tupperware to Model 500 rotary phones. Design historian Jeffrey Meikle discusses how this era was referred to as "a new Rococo marked by extravagance, excess, and vulgarity." Many design and cultural critics pilloried plastic for its ability
10 to easily depart from established design principles, though consumers and manufacturers kept the craze going.

15

According to the author, the introduction of cheap plastics into the market contributed to

A) the trend of consumers becoming manufacturers.

B) a design style of extravagance, excess, and vulgarity.

C) mass production of commercial products.

D) preservation of established design principles.

Question 16

This passage is adapted from "How computer science was used to reveal Gauguin's printmaking techniques" by Marc Walton. ©2015 by Marc Walton.

Professor Oliver Cossairt, of the Department of Computer Science and Electrical Engineering at Northwestern University, specializes in an area of research known as computational imaging—
Line essentially, a merging of computer science with 5 photography. In particular, Cossairt's research has focused on developing cameras capable of visualizing information beyond the limits of what the human eye can perceive. To better discern artist Paul Gauguin's printmaking methods,
10 Cossairt helped implement photometric stereo, a simple computer vision technique first devised in 1980 as a way to digitally render real objects.

16

Based on the passage, which of the following was a cause of Cossairt's development of photometric stereo?

A) To help further his career at the university

B) To help merge computer science and photography

C) To help expose Gauguin forgeries

D) To analyze Gauguin's artistic methods

Question 17

This passage is adapted from The Governess by Julie M. Lippmann. First published in 1916.

"Hello, Nan!"

"Heyo, Ruthie!"

"Where are you going?"

Line
    "Over to Reid's lot."

5 "Take me?"

"No, Ruthie, can't."

The little child's lip began to tremble. "I think you're real mean, Nan Cutler," she complained.

Nan shook her head. "Can't help it if you do,"

10 she returned, stoutly, and took a step on.

"Nannie," cried the child eagerly, starting after her and clutching her by the skirt, "I didn't mean that! Truly, I didn't. I think you're just as nice as you can be. Do please let me go with you. Won't

15 you?"

Nan compressed her lips. "Now, Ruth, look here," she said after a moment, in which she stood considering, "I'd take you in a minute if I could but the truth is—oh, you're too little."

17

The narrator describes Nan's refusal to allow Ruthie to join her as primarily inspiring Ruthie to

A) run away in tears.

B) redouble her pleads to go. *keeps asking*

C) insult Nan's appearance.

D) beg to spend time with Nan.

1. (C) is the correct answer. The narrator claims they were witnessing this scene "from the open window of the Warden's breakfast-saloon.". (A) and (B) are incorrect because they suggest that the narrator was outside, rather than inside, the breakfast-saloon. (D) is incorrect because the passage nowhere indicates that the narrator was having an argument with the Lord Chancellor, only that he/she was viewing the scene "across the shoulder of the Lord Chancellor."

2. (A) is the correct answer. The passage indicates that "reducing the water activity in food below 0.70 can seriously limit bacteria growth." (B) is incorrect because although it could be factually true, the passage never mentions this, nor does it focus on this particular effect of water reduction. This answer choice is therefore irrelevant. (C) is incorrect because the passage does not ever suggest an overgrowth of bacteria due to reduction of water activity; rather, it promises to limit the growth of bacteria. (D) is incorrect because while it may also be factually true, the passage never indicates nor discusses this fact.

3. (C) is the correct answer. The focus of the passage is how children's authors call for us to "reassess the place of children's books." The quote from Philip Pullman communicates the idea that "there are some themes, some subjects, too large for adult fiction; they can only be adequately dealt with in a children's book." This suggests that children's literature is a more adequate setting—more so than adult literature—to present large themes and subjects, and is one reason he thinks the genre should be regarded differently than it is. (A) is incorrect because the passage nowhere indicates that themes in children's literature are inappropriate for young readers, nor does it state that that children's books should be reassessed for this reason. (B) is incorrect because the passage does not claim that children's literature is too difficult to write. The passage only states that children are "rewarding and demanding readers." (D) is incorrect because while it may be factually true, there is no mention of controversy in the passage.

4. (D) is the correct answer. The first sentence describes nerve cells as dictators, "triggering an entire set of movements via the electrical signals it uses to send messages." Nerve cells send messages using electrical signals, which in turn trigger physical movements in specific parts of the body. (A) is incorrect because although the passage solely cites the example of the "lateral giant neuron" in crayfish, it is incorrect to assume that helping animals react to danger is the primary function of nerve cells. (B) is incorrect because the passage states that movements are elicited within one hundredth of a second of stimulation; the passage does not discuss nerve cell production or reproduction. (C) is incorrect because the passage does not discuss the specific connections between nerve cells and body parts.

5. (A) is the correct answer. The passage indicates that the Gradgrind children were trained from a very young age to go to lectures and classes without being asked. Mr. Gradgrind had rigorously disciplined them in their schooling, which is why he saw them as models—ideal students, even—at his school. (B) is incorrect because the passage never states that they enjoyed going to school. (C) is incorrect because although this answer choice is factually true, the passage does not indicate this as the reason why Mr. Gradgrind viewed his children as models. (D) is incorrect because the passage does not mention the children excelling in any of their studies.

6. (B) is the correct answer. The passage indicates that "ninety-five percent said that protecting national parks for future generations was important." Almost all responses from the study said they would pay increased taxes, and cited this reason for their decision. (A) is incorrect because the passage does not discuss protecting wildlife. (C) is incorrect because the passage reports that most Americans would in fact pay increased taxes to preserve parks. (D) is incorrect because the passage does not suggest that Americans believe this; in fact, almost all of the sampled Americans said that "protecting national parks for future generations was important."

7. (C) is the correct answer. The first sentence indicates that the drug was first synthesized—that is, produced—in March 1954. (A) is incorrect because although the passage states that the drug had "low toxicity" and "no toxic effects", the author does not report that it is safe for human use. (B) is incorrect because the author reported that "no toxic effects were found even at 5,000 milligrams per kilogram of body weight in mice." Since LD50 is the mark at which half the population dies, this answer choice is incorrect. Furthermore, the LD50 level for thalidomide was never reported in the passage. (D) is incorrect because the author never mentions blood sugar tests nor the results.

8. (B) is the correct answer. The author mentions that fish do indeed have "impressive learning capacities," which are attributable to the hippocampus. The amygdala plays the role of generating emotions; it is the hippocampus that allows for sophisticated learning. (A) is incorrect because the author does mention that the fish brain "has structures with the same evolutionary origin as parts of the mammal brain…they serve a similar function." (C) is incorrect because the author mentions that fish can remember mental maps and can remember potential rivals' previous battles. (D) is incorrect because in the first sentence, the author mentions that "the fish brain is small and organized differently from that of mammals."

9. (A) is the correct answer. The passage never indicates that the room is filthy or dirty in any way. (B) is incorrect because the passage does indicate that the room is "without a light" and that the prisoner is alone in his cell. (C) is incorrect because the room is described as bare and untouched: "A little table—without pens, books, paper or ink—stood neglected in sadness near the window." (D) is incorrect because the room is described as dim and subdued in the first paragraph.

10. (D) is the correct answer. The author indicates that given the required time, microorganisms like bacteria can "evolve the necessary biochemical tool kit to latch onto the plastic fibers, break them up into the constituent parts, and then utilize the resulting chemicals as a source of energy and carbon that they need to grow." In other words, microorganisms cannot break down plastic yet, but they certainly are capable of doing so in the future. (A) is incorrect because the author states that microorganisms can break down matter that is not traditionally biodegradable, such as plastic; they simply have not yet developed the means to do so. (B) is incorrect because the passage nowhere states that microorganisms can only partially break down plastic. Rather, it suggests that given the necessary time, microorganisms will evolve the necessary biochemical methods to break down plastic. (C) is incorrect because microorganisms can in fact "harness the resources from dead matter."

11. (A) is the correct answer. The passage mentions that the narrator "ran across John Cavendish," but gives no other explanation of how they met. (B) is incorrect because the passage states the narrator "had been invalided home from the Front" and spent some time in a Convalescent Home recovering. (C) is incorrect because the passage mentions that, as a boy, the narrator spent time at Styles, John's mother's home in Essex. (D) is incorrect because the narrator gives a description of Mrs. Cavendish, noting she had been "a handsome woman of middle-age" and describing her as an "energetic, autocratic personality."

12. (A) is the correct answer. The passage notes that increasing distractions are "partly due to the new and ever-evolving ways in which advertisers can put their message in front of us," including immersive techniques, which advertisers use to fight for consumer attention. (B) and (C) are incorrect because they are not mentioned in the passage. (D) is incorrect because the passage does not indicate that consumers are more interested in advertisements, nor that these advertisements are content-based.

13. (A) is the correct answer. The passage notes that plate tectonics moves continents and causes earthquakes, which may be a precursor to the development of life. (B) is incorrect because the rotation of planets is not mentioned. (C) is incorrect because the evolution of life is not linked to earthquakes, except that the creation of life may also be linked to tectonic plates. (D) is incorrect because solar systems are not specifically discussed in the passage, except to note Earth is unique within ours.

14. (B) is the correct answer. Beth expressed surprise because it was "unusual for her to receive a letter." (A) is incorrect because there is no indication that Elmhurst is a person or a place, nor is there indication that she had received word from Elmhurst before. (C) is incorrect because there is no indication that she was forbidden from reading letters addressed to her. (D) is incorrect because the passage does not indicate that it was unusual to receive a letter with an emblem.

15. (B) is the correct answer. The author indicates that this cheap and versatile plastic was used in an era of mass-produced products characterized by "extravagance, excess, and vulgarity." (A) is incorrect because the passage does not indicate that consumers ever became manufacturers. (C) is incorrect because the author only indicates that plastics were used in the mass production of commercial products, not that the plastics themselves led to this production. (D) is incorrect because the passage describes a departure from established design principles, not an adherence.

16. (D) is the correct answer. The passage mentions that Cossairt "helped implement photometric stereo" in order "to better discern Gauguin's printmaking methods," or in other words, to analyze Gauguin's artistic methods. (A) is incorrect because the passage makes no mention of Cossairt attempting to further his career. (B) is incorrect because even though he did so, merging computer science and photography was not a specific goal of Cossairt's; the only goal of Cossairt's mentioned is understanding Gauguin's printmaking methods. (C) is incorrect because the passage makes no mention of forgeries or exposing them.

17. (B) is the correct answer. After first calling Nan mean, Ruthie starts after her and begs Nan to "please let me go with you." (A) is incorrect because Ruthie stays and pleads with Nan, and does not flee. (C) is incorrect because Ruthie does not insult Nan's appearance; she only calls her mean. (D) is incorrect because Ruthie begs to go with Nan to Reid's specifically, not just to spend time with Nan.

Implied Information
Part 2

Implied Information questions require you to draw reasonable inferences using information in a passage. They may require you to interpret euphemisms or other forms of indirect communication between characters. They may also require you to reason about what is implied about perspectives, relationships, or hypothetical situations not described in the passage.

DIRECTIONS

Every passage or paired set of passages is accompanied by a number of questions. Read the passage or paired set of passages, then use what is said or implied in what you read and in any given graphics to choose the best answer to each question.

Question 1

This passage is adapted from "Technology changes how authors write, but the big impact isn't on their style" by Matthew Kirschenbaum. ©2016 by Matthew Kirschenbaum.

Sitting at a typewriter, we are always in the present moment as the carriage trundles forward character by character, line by line. Word
Line processing, by contrast, allowed writers to grasp
5 a manuscript as a whole, a gestalt. The entire manuscript was instantly available via search functions. Whole passages could be moved at will, and chapters or sections reordered. The textual field became fluid and malleable, a potentially
10 infinite expanse, or at least limited only by the computer's ever-expanding memory.

The result was a new kind of control over writing space, a sentiment shared by early adopters of the technology otherwise as different
15 from one another as National Book Award winner Stanley Elkin and queen of the vampires Anne Rice. "Once you really get used to a computer and you get used to entering the information from that keyboard, things happen in your mind,
20 I mean, you change as a writer. You're able to do things that maybe you never would have thought of doing before," concluded Rice. Elkin extolled his renewed appreciation for plot after acquiring a word processor in 1979: "Plots have become very
25 interesting to me," he told an interviewer at the time. "You put the machine into the search mode,

and you find what the reference was earlier, and you can begin to use these things as tools, or nails, in putting the plot together."
30 What Elkin and Rice are describing, each in their own way, is what composition theorists like Christina Haas have called the "sense of the text." It means the mental model of the words on the page (or screen) and how the writer perceives
35 his or her relationship to them. Word processing, as the testimony of countless writers suggests, profoundly altered their sense of the text, both in terms of how they approached their writing and what they thought possible. But all of that is a far
40 cry from "style," typically defined as an author's individual word choices and sentence structures or arrangements.

The passage most strongly suggests that

A) computers have had no influence on the writing process.

B) style and plot are largely distinct elements of writing.

C) it is always better to write on a computer than on a typewriter.

D) the typewriter and the computer are more similar than most people believe.

Question 2

This passage is adapted from "New helium microscope reveals startling details without frying the sample" by Ivy Shih. ©2016 by Ivy Shih.

The helium atom beam's energy is less than 0.1 electron volts, far lower than the 100,000 electron volt beam used by electron microscopes
Line and the roughly 1 electron volt energy of a typical
5 chemical bond.
"Imagine the helium atoms as a great big soft ball that bounces off the outermost electrons on the sample surface. It doesn't get close to the atom core through the first layer," Dastoor said.
10 If the beam has too much energy, it runs the risk of breaking chemical bonds and damaging the sample. This is why many samples can only be viewed once, or very few times, under a conventional electron microscope.

The passage most strongly suggests that using a helium-based microscope would have what advantage over using a conventional electron microscope?

A) Scientists could view samples more times with a helium-based microscope than they can with an electron microscope.

B) Helium-based microscopes would be less expensive to build than electron microscopes.

C) Only helium-based microscopes can achieve the highest levels of magnification currently available.

D) It would take considerably less energy to run a helium-based microscope than it would to run an electron microscope.

Question 3

This passage is adapted from "The Crux" by Charlotte Perkins Gilman. First published in 1911.

"But who is Morton Elder, and what has he done?" asked Mrs. Williams as soon as she could be heard.
Line This lady now proved a most valuable asset.
5 She was so new to the town, and had been so immersed in the suddenly widening range of her unsalaried duties as "minister's wife," that she had never even heard of Morton Elder.
A new resident always fans the languishing
10 flame of local conversation. The whole shopworn stock takes on a fresh luster, topics long trampled flat in much discussion lift their heads anew, opinions one scarce dared to repeat again become almost authoritative, old stories flourish freshly,
15 acquiring new detail and more vivid color.
Mrs. Lane, seizing her opportunity while the sisters gasped a momentary amazement at anyone's not knowing the town scapegoat, and taking advantage of her position as old friend and
20 near neighbor of the family under discussion, swept into the field under such headway that

even the Foote girls remained silent perforce; surcharged, however, and holding their breaths in readiness to burst forth at the first opening.

3

The passage most strongly implies that Morton Elder is

A) a newcomer to the town.

B) willfully ignorant of village customs.

C) notorious among local residents.

D) respected by the minister's wife.

Question 4

This passage is adapted from "Why does using a period in a text message make you sound insincere or angry?" by Lauren Collister. ©2016 by Lauren Collister

Though periods can still signal the end of a sentence in a text message, many users will omit them (especially if the message is only
Line one sentence long). This tendency now subtly
5 influences how we interpret them.

Because text messaging is a conversation that involves a lot of back-and-forth, people add fillers as a way to mimic spoken language. We see this with the increased use of ellipses, which can
10 invite the recipient to continue the conversation. The period is the opposite of that—a definitive stop that signals, as linguistics professor Mark Liberman has explained, "This is final, this is the end of the discussion." For some, this can appear
15 angry or standoffish.

Earlier this year, psychologist Danielle Gunraj tested how people perceived one-sentence text messages that used a period at the end of the sentence. Participants thought these text messages
20 were more insincere than those that didn't have a period. But when the researchers then tested the same messages in handwritten notes, they found that the use of a period didn't influence how the messages were perceived.

4

The passage most strongly implies that using an ellipsis in a text message

A) is unprofessional and should be avoided.

B) rarely affects how a text message is received.

C) is uncommon among regular phone users.

D) does not come across as unfriendly.

Question 5

This passage is adapted from "Enough with the spoiler alerts! Plot spoilers often increase enjoyment" by Alan Jern. ©2016 by Alan Jern.

It may come as a surprise that being exposed to a spoiler could cause someone to enjoy a film even more. One possible explanation has to do
Line with the psychological concept of "fluency." The
5 more fluent something is—whether it's a story, a song, or a face—the easier it is to process and understand. And many psychology studies have shown that the easier something is to process, the more likely people are to like it.
10 One way that fluency can make a story more enjoyable is that it reduces the need to make (possibly incorrect) inferences about where the story is going or what a character is thinking or feeling. You've probably experienced this when
15 listening to music. The first time you hear a song, you might not think it's anything special. But after the song becomes more familiar and you can anticipate how it will unfold, you realize that you really like it. Because the song has become more
20 fluent, you've found yourself enjoying it more.

In a follow-up study, Leavitt and Christenfeld tested this fluency explanation by repeating their experiment on a different group of 240 undergraduate students. This time, the researchers
25 used stories written for junior or high school students that use common tropes and plot devices. They reasoned that, for these simple and fairly predictable stories, fluency should already be high, and spoilers would have no effect on enjoyment
30 if fluency was truly at work. As predicted, they found that students rated these stories equally enjoyable with or without spoilers.

The passage most strongly implies that

A) people rarely enjoy new styles of music the first time they encounter them.

B) avoiding spoilers makes people too anxious to relax and enjoy a story.

C) predictable stories are typically more enjoyable than surprising stories.

D) listening to music and reading stories are similar in some respects.

Question 6

This passage is adapted from "Have scientists really found something harder than diamond?" by Paul Coxon. ©2016 by Paul Coxon.

Hardness is an important property of materials and often determines what they can be used for, but it is also quite difficult to define. For minerals,
Line scratch hardness is a measure of how resistant it is
5 to being scratched by another mineral.

There are several ways of measuring hardness but typically an instrument is used to make a dent in the material's surface. The ratio between the surface area of the indentation and the force
10 used to make it produces a hardness value. The harder the material, the larger the value. The Vickers hardness test uses a square-based pyramid diamond tip to make the indent.

Mild steel has a Vickers hardness value of
15 around 9 GPa while diamond has a Vickers hardness value of around 70–100 GPa. Diamond's resistance against wear is legendary and today 70% of the world's natural diamonds are found in wear-resistant coatings for tools used in cutting,
20 drilling and grinding, or as additives to abrasives.

The problem with diamond is that, while it may be very hard, it is also surprisingly unstable. When diamond is heated above 800°C in air its chemical properties change, affecting its strength
25 and enabling it to react with iron, which makes it unsuitable for machining steel.

The passage most strongly suggests that which of the following is necessary for machining steel?

A) A mineral that is not too hard

B) A mineral that is not too soft

C) A mineral that reacts with iron

D) A mineral that does not react with iron

Question 7

This passage is adapted from "The Country of the Blind and Other Stories" by H. G. Wells. First published in 1911.

As I sit writing in my study, I can hear our Jane bumping her way downstairs with a brush and dust-pan. She used in the old days to sing hymn
Line tunes, or the British national song for the time
5 being, to these instruments, but lately she has been silent and even careful over her work. Time was when I prayed with fervour for such silence, and my wife with sighs for such care, but now they have come we are not so glad as we might have
10 anticipated we should be. Indeed, I would rejoice secretly, though it may be unmanly weakness to admit it, even to hear Jane sing "Daisy," or, by the fracture of any plate but one of Euphemia's best green ones, to learn that the period of brooding
15 has come to an end.

Yet how we longed to hear the last of Jane's young man before we heard the last of him! Jane was always very free with her conversation to my wife, and discoursed admirably in the
20 kitchen on a variety of topics—so well, indeed, that I sometimes left my study door open—our house is a small one—to partake of it. But after William came, it was always William, nothing but William; William this and William that; and
25 when we thought William was worked out and exhausted altogether, then William all over again. The engagement lasted altogether three years; yet how she got introduced to William, and so became thus saturated with him, was always a secret. For
30 my part, I believe it was at the street corner where the Rev. Barnabas Baux used to hold an open-air service after evensong on Sundays. Young Cupids were wont to flit like moths around the paraffin

flare of that centre of High Church hymn-singing.
35 I fancy she stood singing hymns there, out of
memory and her imagination, instead of coming
home to get supper, and William came up beside
her and said, "Hello!" "Hello yourself!" she said;
and etiquette being satisfied, they proceeded to
40 talk together.

7

It is reasonable to conclude that Jane is

A) upset because of the end of a romantic
relationship.

B) too clumsy to be very good at her job.

C) more passionate about singing than she is
about work.

D) habitually shy and aloof around her employers.

Question 8

This passage is adapted from "Why can't we remember
our early childhood?" by Jeanne Shinskey. ©2016 by
Jeanne Shinskey.

It is true to some extent that a child's ability
to verbalize about an event at the time that it
happened predicts how well they remember it
Line months or years later. One lab group conducted
5 this work by interviewing toddlers brought to
accident and emergency departments for common
childhood injuries. Toddlers over 26 months,
who could verbalize about the event at the time,
recalled it up to five years later, whereas those
10 under 26 months, who could not talk about it,
recalled little or nothing. This suggests that
preverbal memories are lost if they are not
translated into language.
However, most research on the role of
15 language focuses on a particular form of
expression called narrative, and its social
function. When parents reminisce with very
young children about past events, they implicitly
teach them narrative skills—what kinds of events
20 are important to remember and how to structure

talking about them in a way that others can
understand.
Unlike simply recounting information for
factual purposes, reminiscing revolves around
25 the social function of sharing experiences with
others. In this way, family stories maintain the
memory's accessibility over time, and also
increase the coherence of the narrative, including
the chronology of events, their theme, and
30 their degree of emotion. More coherent stories
are remembered better. Maori adults have the
earliest childhood memories (age 2.5) of any
society studied so far, thanks to Maori parents'
highly elaborative style of telling family stories.
35 Reminiscing has different social functions in
different cultures, which contribute to cultural
variations in the quantity, quality, and timing of
early autobiographical memories.

 8

The passage most strongly implies that differences
in the retention of early childhood memories

A) are difficult to predict based on specific
factors.

B) usually disappear by the time people reach
adulthood.

C) cannot be explained by individual development
alone.

D) exist between individuals but not between
particular groups.

Question 9

This passage is adapted from "How digital technology
spawned retro's revival" by Steven Wilf and Peter Siegelman. ©2016 by Steven Wilf and Peter Siegelman.

Most people probably think of digital
technology as a radically transformative
phenomenon that has swept away the past, in the
Line same way the automobile destroyed the buggy-
5 whip industry, or the printing press superseded
the illuminated manuscript. But the "enabling"

aspects of digital technologies are equally worth celebrating.

To be sure, computers and the rise of the
10 Internet have decimated many old products and ways of doing business. At the same time, they've facilitated the quirky and old-fashioned, allowing for the development of niche markets in specialized products. As in the
15 world of architecture, a layered landscape with the new rubbing shoulders with the old is far more appealing than one where innovation has wiped away any semblance of the past. And it's comforting to know that while your new board
20 game will ultimately wear out, it won't monitor your pulse, track your whereabouts, or take your phone calls.

 9

The passage most strongly suggests that old-fashioned technologies have which of the following advantages over digital technologies?

A) Old-fashioned technologies are more durable than digital technologies.

B) Old-fashioned technologies cannot collect personal information from their users.

C) Old-fashioned technologies "enable" the production of digital technologies.

D) Old-fashioned technologies tend to be easier to use than digital technologies.

Question 10

This passage is adapted from "Explainer: microRNA, the puppet master of the genome" by Pamela Ajuyah and Nham Tran. ©2015 by Pamela Ajuyah and Nham Tran.

Up until about two decades ago, one type of RNA, called microRNA, or just miRNA—by virtue of them being very short, only 18-25 letters
Line long—were thought to be the junk mail of the
5 genome, with no biological function. But today we know that these miRNA are actually not junk but play a very important role in regulating the activity of other parts of your DNA.

The discovery of the structure of DNA led to

10 the "central dogma" that our genetic information is stored as a DNA code, which is then converted into an RNA message (mRNA). The tiny protein factories, ribosomes, then read the mRNA. These decode the messages and create proteins, which
15 are the workhorses of biology. All of this activity is constantly taking place within our cells and it all starts from the genome.

Your genome contains all the instructions a cell needs to function in the form of our 20,000-odd
20 genes. But, surprisingly, these genes only make up around 2% of our entire genome. So the question is: what does the remaining 98% of our DNA actually do?

For biologists, those important emails that
25 slipped into the junk mail folder and were disregarded were miRNAs. That was until the first functional miRNA, lin-4, was officially discovered in 1993. Scientists were looking at the development of the nematode worm,
30 Caenorhabditis elegans, and found that lin-4 inhibited protein synthesis of the lin-14 gene.

They subsequently found that miRNA can physically bind to mRNA and stop it from creating proteins. Thus it effectively suppresses
35 the activity of a gene. This discovery was the first evidence of miRNA negatively regulating RNA coding for proteins. So, it turns out that the 98% of our genome that was regarded as "junk" might have a function after all.

 10

The passage most strongly implies that scientists initially missed the importance of miRNA because

A) they had not identified a specific function that miRNA serves.

B) they did not fully understand the structure of DNA.

C) they did not have microscopes powerful enough to view miRNA.

D) they were too focused on other features of the genetic code.

Question 11

This passage is adapted from The Woman With One Hand by Richard Marsh. First published in 1899.

One day, I saw in the paper: "If James Southam, at one time of Dulborough, will apply to the undersigned, he will hear of something
Line to his advantage--Messrs. Cleaver and Caxton,
5 Solicitors, Thirteen, Bacup Street, London, S.E."
I clipped that advertisement out of the paper under the waiter's nose, and put it in my waistcoat pocket.

On referring to a directory in a convenient
10 post-office, I found that Bacup Street was in the neighborhood of the Old Kent Road. That did not seem to be a promising address, and Number Thirteen seemed to be the shabbiest house which it contained. An untidy youth received me. After
15 keeping me waiting for a quarter of an hour, he ushered me into a room beyond. In this inner room there were two men. One was seated at a table, the other was standing with his hat at the back of his head in front of the empty fireplace.
20 They looked at me, then they looked at each other; and, unless I am mistaken, they exchanged a glance of surprise. The man at the table addressed me, without evincing any desire to rise.

11

The passage most nearly implies that the two men were surprised as a result of

A) having a visitor so early in the morning.

B) a servant leading James inside after explicit directions not to.

C) the shabby clothes and looks of the narrator when he arrived at their house.

D) the appearance of James Southam, which was different than expected.

Question 12

This passage is adapted from Lay Down Your Arms! by Bertha von Suttner. First published in 1889.

Several days passed without my seeing Tilling again. Every evening I went to the theatre, expecting and hoping to meet him, but in vain.
Line My reception day brought me many visitors,
5 but, of course, not him. It was not like him after his decisive "You really must not expect from me, countess," to present himself at my house on a day of the kind. I was all on fire to see him again, to make amends for my rudeness on the former
10 occasion, and get another hour of a talk—an hour's talk the delight of which would now be increased a hundredfold by the consciousness, which had now become plain to me, of my love.

The following Saturday brought me Tilling's
15 cousin, the lady at whose ball I had made his acquaintance. On her entrance my heart began to beat.

12

Why did the entrance of Tilling's cousin cause the narrator's heart to beat?

A) The narrator was eager to hear from the woman about Tilling.

B) The narrator was intimidated by the woman's beauty.

C) The narrator was nervous to see the woman's reaction to her prior rudeness.

D) The narrator was trying to hide her feelings from the woman.

Question 13

This passage is adapted from "What is brain plasticity and why is it so important?" by Duncan Banks. ©2016 by Duncan Banks.

Part of the body's ability to recover following damage to the brain can be explained by the damaged area of the brain getting better, but most is the result of neuroplasticity—forming new neural connections. In a study of Caenorhabditis elegans, a type of nematode used as a model organism in research, it was found that losing the sense of touch enhanced the sense of smell. This suggests that losing one sense rewires others. It is well known that, in humans, losing one's sight early in life can heighten other senses, especially hearing.

13

The passage most strongly suggests that improved sense of smell is a result of

A) a species-specific brain function present in the Caenorhabditis elegans.

B) the unpredictable restoration of senses during neuroplasticity.

C) the formation of new neural connections in the brain.

D) an improvement of all senses during recovery from damage to the brain.

Question 14

This passage is adapted from "Finding a fix for Newfoundland's troubled drinking water" by Steven Liss. ©2018 by Steven Liss.

Chlorine has been used to disinfect drinking water and prevent waterborne disease since the early 1900s. It has been a great success, preventing millions of deaths and making potable water widely available at a low cost.

Many water utilities add chlorine twice during treatment. Primary disinfection kills the pathogens found in untreated, raw water drawn from rivers, lakes and other sources. Secondary disinfection maintains drinking water quality within the distribution system.

However, when disinfectants such as chlorine come into contact with naturally occurring organic matter, including algae, bacteria, soil, decomposed plant material or animal feces, they form compounds called disinfection byproducts, including trihalomethanes (THMs) and halogenic acetic acids (HAAs).

Long-term exposure to disinfection byproducts is associated with an increased risk of bladder cancer. Asthma and other breathing issues have also been linked to exposure to disinfection byproducts in swimming pools.

Many of the communities in Newfoundland and Labrador are remote, and their drinking water is often sourced from ponds and rivers with high levels of natural organic matter and delivered over long distances. Newfoundland surface water is also heavily influenced by extreme and variable weather, creating optimal conditions for the formation of disinfection byproducts.

14

It is reasonable to assume that Newfoundland and Labrador's drinking water is prone to the formation of "disinfection byproducts" because of its

A) inadequate treatment with disinfectants.

B) high levels of natural organic matter.

C) contamination by water from ponds and rivers.

D) surplus of THMs and HAAs.

1. (B) is the correct answer. The passage explains changes in the writing process that were brought on by the use of computers, which includes one author's claim that "plots have become very interesting to [him]" since he began using a computer. The passage then distinguishes those changes, including plotting, from "style," emphasizing the distinction by saying that these other changes are "a far cry from" style and defining this separate concept of style. Altogether, this implies a strong distinction between style and plot. (A) is incorrect because the passage argues that computers have indeed had an influence on the writing process, just not on the writing style. (C) is incorrect because the author does not imply that one tool is better for writing than the other. (D) is incorrect because the author does not dwell on the similarities between typewriters and computers.

2. (A) is the correct answer. The passage states that too much energy can break chemical bonds and damage samples, meaning they can only be viewed a few times under an electron microscope; it also states that helium atoms have less beam energy, which suggests that a helium-based microscope would address the problem described above, and would allow for more views of each sample. (B) is incorrect because the passage does not mention relative cost. (C) is incorrect because the passage does not compare the level of magnification between the two types of microscopes. (D) is incorrect because the passage discusses the energy produced by the microscopes' beams, not the energy they require to run.

3. (C) is the correct answer. The phrase "she had never even heard of Morton Elder" implies that Morton Elder is quite well known among local residents. The "town scapegoat," refers back to this familiar person; a scapegoat is someone who gets blamed for bad things, so the negative connotation of the word "notorious" matches this description. (A) is incorrect because the women are surprised that the minister's wife does not know him, implying he is well known and thus not a newcomer to the town. (B) is incorrect because nothing in the passage suggests Morton Elder is ignorant of village customs. (D) is incorrect because the minister's wife had never heard of Morton Elder and therefore could not already respect him.

4. (D) is the correct answer. The passage explicitly contrasts the finality of a period with the way that an ellipsis "can invite the recipient to continue the conversation." The passage states that periods can appear standoffish or unfriendly, so contrastively, ellipses do not appear unfriendly. (A) is incorrect because the passage does not mention how any punctuation may or may not be unprofessional. (B) is incorrect because the passage states that punctuation generally does affect how text messages are received. (C) is incorrect because the passage states that the use of ellipses is on the rise.

5. (D) is the correct answer. The passage uses music as a way to explain a psychological concept (fluency) that may also apply to stories; this implies that they have enough similarity to share this concept. (A) is incorrect because although the passage does suggest that people tend to like songs as they become familiar to them, it would be too strong to say that people rarely enjoy a song or new style of music on their first exposure. (B) is incorrect because the passage does not suggest that avoiding spoilers makes people anxious. (C) is incorrect because although the passage discusses an experiment focusing on predictable stories, it does not compare how enjoyable they are to surprising stories.

6. (D) is the correct answer. The passage states that high temperatures "enabling [the diamond] to react with iron" is what "makes it unsuitable for machining steel"; therefore, one can conclude that machining steel would require the opposite. (A) and (B) are incorrect because neither the hardness nor the softness of a diamond are mentioned as problems specifically with machining steel. (C) is incorrect because the passage suggests the opposite, as explained above.

7. (A) is the correct answer. In the first paragraph, the passage states that Jane has stopped singing since she began a "period of brooding," suggesting something has damaged her mood. In the second paragraph, the passage says that the narrator and his wife have "heard the last of" Jane's "young man," to whom she was engaged for three years. The fact that Jane and William were engaged makes it clear their relationship was romantic, and that her brooding happened at the same time as Jane stops mentioning William suggests that the engagement's break has caused Jane's period of brooding. (B) is incorrect because although the passage describes Jane as "bumping her way downstairs," it does not imply she is bumping into anything. It also does not suggest at any point that Jane is bad at her job. (C) is incorrect because Jane's singing is presented as a habit, not a passion. (D) is incorrect because the passage presents Jane as usually friendly and talkative with her employers, as she used to be "always very free with her conversation to my wife," which is quite oppositional to shy and aloof.

8. (C) is the correct answer. The passage points out that adults in certain cultures tend to retain more early childhood memories than adults in other cultures; if trends in retention of early childhood memories are influenced by cultural factors, they cannot be solely based on individual development. (A) is incorrect because the passage does identify specific factors that can assist in predicting the retention of early childhood memories. (B) is incorrect because the passage explicitly identifies differences in the retention of early childhood memories between adults. (D) is incorrect because the passage does identify some differences between groups, specifically based on different group cultures.

9. (B) is the correct answer. The passage states that it is "comforting" that a board game, an example of an old-fashioned, non-digital technology, cannot collect information about personal matters such as the user's pulse, location, or phone calls. (A) is incorrect because the passage does not imply that old-fashioned technologies are more durable than digital technologies; in fact, when it uses the example of the board game, the passage points out that it "will ultimately wear out." (C) is incorrect because the passage actually highlights the ways that digital technologies enable the production of old-fashioned technologies, not the other way around. (D) is incorrect because the passage does not compare how easy it is to use old-fashioned versus digital technologies.

10. (A) is the correct answer. The passage states that scientists stopped disregarding miRNA when they identified the first functional miRNA, and goes on to describe what specific function that miRNA serves. This suggests that the main reason scientists had previously disregarded miRNA was because they had not yet found a specific function it served; they recognized its importance once they did find such a function. (B) is incorrect because the passage does not suggest that scientists did not understand the structure of DNA. (C) is incorrect because the passage does not say anything about needing more powerful microscopes to view miRNA. (D) is incorrect because the passage never claims that scientists were too preoccupied with "other features of the genetic code" to see the use of miRNA, only that they could not find any use for miRNA until recently.

11. (D) is the correct answer. The two men presumably placed the advertisement in the paper, since they are the ones James is brought to upon his arrival at the residence in the ad he answers, and "looked at me, then they looked at each other; and [...] exchanged a glance of surprise." This implies they are surprised at his appearance, as this is the only thing they could judge during these initial moments of their first interaction, without words. Therefore, (D) is most plausible. (A) is incorrect as the time of day is not mentioned in the passage. (B) is incorrect because there is no indication the servant was disobeying orders. (C) is incorrect because the house is described as shabby, not the narrator.

12. (A) is the correct answer. The passage is almost exclusively about the narrator's relentless yearning to meet Tilling again, and since his cousin is the only connection to him that the narrator mentions, she is most likely anxious to satisfy this yearning (as well as she can while being ignored by Tilling) by talking to Tilling's cousin. (B) is incorrect because the passage does not indicate details about the woman's beauty. (C) is incorrect because the passage does not indicate that the woman had any knowledge of the rudeness. (D) is incorrect because there is no evidence that the narrator was attempting to hide her feelings.

13. (C) is the correct answer. The passage indicates that during recovery from brain damage, new neural connections are formed. It also indicates that losing one sense rewires another, therefore, the improved sense of smell is a result of new neural connections. (A) is incorrect because the passage does not suggest that improved smell is a brain function, nor does it indicate that the phenomenon is species-specific. (B) is incorrect because the passage gives no indication of unpredictability of the restoration of senses. (D) is incorrect because the passage makes no mention of an improvement of all senses during recovery. Rather, it suggests improvement in one after losing another.

14. (B) is the correct answer. The passage states that Newfoundland and Labrador's drinking water is "sourced from ponds and rivers with high levels of natural organic matter," and that when disinfectants come into contact with this organic matter (which the post implies will happen to the drinking water of Newfoundland and Labrador), disinfection byproducts are formed. (A) is incorrect because the passage states that it is the water's treatment with disinfectants that causes the formation of "disinfection byproducts," not a lack of treatment. (C) is incorrect because the passage says that Newfoundland and Labrador water mostly comes from ponds and rivers, not that it is contaminated by ponds and rivers. (D) is incorrect because the passage states that THMs and HAAs are examples of, not reasons for the formation of disinfection byproducts.

Similar Situation
Part 3

Similar Situation questions require you to demonstrate your understanding of situations and relationships described in the passage by selecting a description of an analogous situation or relationship, often between objects unlike those described in the passage.

They may require you to differentiate between analogous choices and those that offer similar objects in different situations or relationships, choices that draw an analogy with a relationship in the passage other than the one being asked about, or choices that match the passage in tone but not situation.

DIRECTIONS

Every passage or paired set of passages is accompanied by a number of questions. Read the passage or paired set of passages, then use what is said or implied in what you read and in any given graphics to choose the best answer to each question.

Question 1

This passage is adapted from "Showbiz politics: through campaign songs, candidates become stars" by Kathryn Cramer Brownell. ©2015 by Kathryn Cramer Brownell.

Campaign music has a deep and rich history in American elections. As the party system expanded and formalized during the 19th century, so too did
Line the place of music in campaigns. Back then, state
5 party leaders would adjust lyrics and melodies in an attempt to appeal to regional musical tastes. Songs were a way for local party workers to communicate and promote the party's platform and its candidates.

1

Which of the following situations is most analogous to the place of campaign music in elections?

(A) A traveling bakery adjusts its selection of goods to match each region's specific tastes.

B) A speaker travels all around the United States during election period talking about campaign issues.

C) A singer gives performances all across the country of her top five most popular songs.

D) A local leader decides to bring up his town's major issues to a visiting national politician.

Question 2

This passage is adapted from "Did snakes evolve from ancient sea serpents?" by Mike Lee and Alessandro Paici. ©2016 by Mike Lee and Alessandro Paici.

One of the enduring controversies in evolution is why snakes evolved their long, limbless bodies. The prevailing theory is that they evolved from
Line lizards and are really just an extreme type of
5 legless lizard. And as many long-bodied lizards are burrowers, there is a widespread view that snakes developed their serpentine bodies underground.

But a study of a primordial four-legged
10 fossil snake published this week suggests it was aquatic. This suggests snakes lost their legs and elongated their bodies underwater, for eel-like swimming, before crawling ashore eons later. The fossil in question is one of the most exquisite and
15 controversial fossils of modern times. Dubbed Tetrapodophis (meaning "four-legged snake"), it lived alongside the dinosaurs in what is now Brazil, about 120 million years ago. Amazingly, almost every single bone is preserved in this
20 tiny worm-sized fossil, including four small but perfectly-formed legs.

2

Which hypothetical situation involves the same reversal discussed by the author?

A) A popular theory about the origins of the universe gained new support based on recent scientific observations from a space probe.

B) The mainstream philosophy about the benefits of education was debated at a national conference that presented controversial new ideas.

C) Reigning ideas about the inspiration behind Shakespeare's works were replaced with new ideas based on additional information gathered.

D) Major beliefs about the evolution of reptiles were publicized in a recent science article that disseminated those ideas to the public.

Question 3

This passage is adapted from "First Radio Address," a speech given by King George VI on September 3, 1939, over the radio. King George VI is addressing the British people on the cusp of World War II.

In this grave hour, perhaps the most fateful in our history, I send to every household of my peoples, both at home and overseas, this message,
Line spoken with the same depth of feeling for each
5 one of you as if I were able to cross your threshold and speak to you myself.

For the second time in the lives of most of us we are at war. Over and over again we have tried to find a peaceful way out of the differences
10 between ourselves and those who are now our enemies. But it has been in vain. We have been forced into a conflict. For we are called, with our allies, to meet the challenge of a principle which, if it were to prevail, would be fatal to any
15 civilized order in the world. It is the principle which permits a state, in the selfish pursuit of power, to disregard its treaties and its solemn pledges; which sanctions the use of force, or threat of force, against the sovereignty and independence
20 of other states. Such a principle, stripped of all disguise, is surely the mere primitive doctrine that "might is right"; and if this principle were established throughout the world, the freedom of our own country and of the whole of the British
25 Commonwealth of Nations would be in danger. For the sake of all that we ourselves hold dear, and of the world order and peace, it is unthinkable that we should refuse to meet the challenge.

The principle illustrated in lines 12 - 25 ("For we ... danger") is best conveyed by which additional example?

A) A country makes a treaty with terms heavily favoring its own interests.

B) Two countries go to war with one another over a disputed border.

C) A colony declares war in order to achieve its independence.

D) A nation uses its military power to threaten another country into granting it special privileges.

Question 4

This passage is adapted from *The Story of Tim*, translated by George Borrow. First published in 1913.

In a certain village there lived an old man
who had lost almost the whole of his hair, partly
from age, and partly from the friction of his fur
Line cap, which he never laid aside, either by day or
5 night. He had a son named Timoney, who was a
sharp lad enough, but who had learned nothing
but to play on the fife. The old man thinking that
music, however sweet, would never fill the belly,
and that it was quite impossible to live on an
10 empty stomach, determined to have the boy taught
some trade, and he deemed it expedient to consult
his old woman on the subject. Accordingly, he
requested her opinion, adding that he would wish
to see the boy either a blacksmith, or a tailor.
15 "No!" cried the old woman. "I'll have him
neither the one nor the other. The blacksmith by
always going amidst fire and soot is so begrimed
that he looks rather like a devil than a man.
Would you make a monster of him? As for a
20 tailor—I don't deny that tailoring is a rare art,
but sitting doubled up, in a little time brings on a
consumption."
"Then what would you make of him?" cried
the old man.
25 "Make of him?" said she, ; "why a goldsmith
or a painter, or something similar."
"And do you know," said the old man, "how

much money one must lay down to have him
bound either to a goldsmith or a painter? Why, he
30 would swallow up all we have, or more."

Which of the following is most analogous to the situation presented in the passage?

A) Two sisters debate on where it would be best for their brother to live.

B) Two people debate about the merits of their respective jobs.

C) A man and a woman argue about where to go on vacation.

D) A father and a son discuss the pros and cons of modern art.

Question 5

This passage is adapted from "Imagine if technology could read and react to our emotions" by David Tuffley. ©2015 by David Tuffley.

Computers have always been good at doing
fast calculations, but adapting to the emotional
state of the person using the computer presents
Line a grand challenge. The field is called affective
5 computing, and soon it will be an important factor
in the way people and computers communicate
with each other. The computer will interpret your
body language to determine how you are feeling
and then tailor its response intuitively, just as we
10 do with each other. What's more, we will like it,
because it is far more intuitive than the keyboard,
mouse, and touch screen as an input method.

Which situation is most similar to the one described in the passage?

A) A dog learns new commands in increasing complexity from its owner.

B) A new study app provides individualized content after learning students' strengths and weaknesses.

C) A computer runs an antivirus program in order to perform at the most efficient speed.

D) A child develops a higher emotional intelligence after heavy socialization in a critical time period.

Question 6

This passage is adapted from "Can technology help fashion clean up its act?" by Suzanne Mancini. ©2016 by Suzanne Mancini.

Chemical waste, mass production, and consumerism are all byproducts of an industrialized global economy. The fashion industry is no different. Technology has
5 helped the industry meet growing demand by making production more efficient. But vast overproduction—propelled by fast fashion's demands for new styles—has led to a host of additional problems: increased chemical waste
10 during production, along with thousands of tons of waste from worn, discarded, or donated clothes.

Which of the following examples is most analogous to waste in the fashion industry?

A) A toy company produces more products than it sends to market in order to keep up with current trends.

B) A chemical company dumps thousands of pollutants each year into a nearby river.

C) A clothing company is expanding its lines to include both bathing suits and children's wear.

D) A newspaper constantly needs new content in order to produce a fresh set of articles each day.

Question 7

This passage is adapted from "Safe passage: we can help save koalas through urban design" by Darryl Jones. ©2016 by Darryl Jones.

Australian cities are remarkable in the sheer diversity of wildlife that somehow manages to live among us, from flocks of raucous cockatoos or noisy lorikeets to the huge numbers of flying
5 -foxes. But such displays of nature in exuberant abundance can be tragically misleading. For the overwhelming majority of wildlife species, relentless urbanization has been catastrophic. Most animals simply die following the arrival of
10 the bulldozers.

Obviously, some species are able to cope better than others. So-called urban exploiters tend to share a number of characteristics such as rapid habituation to the presence of people, a
15 generalist diet, and an ability to be innovative. When it comes to behavioral creativity, though, Australia's marsupials don't seem to score very well. For example, Iit was thought that koalas, in particular, were not good candidates for
20 innovationparticularly innovative.

Which of the following situations is most similar to the situation of urban exploiters mentioned in the passage?

A) A band of settlers moves from their current location to the wild frontier.

B) A pack of wild wolves is domesticated by humans and begins to herd farm animals and protect its owners.

C) A restaurant is able to weather numerous changes in its town by adapting to the growing, changing clientele.

D) A new city has a major impact on the environment that is only mitigated by the innovation of a few pioneers.

Question 8

This passage is adapted from "Citizenship in a Republic," a speech given by Teddy Roosevelt at Le Sorbonne, the University of Paris, on April 23, 1910. Here, Roosevelt discusses the ancient university and its history.

Strange and impressive associations rise in the mind of a man from the New World who speaks before this august body in this ancient institution
Line of learning. Before his eyes pass the shadows of
5 mighty kings and war-like nobles, of great masters of law and theology; through the shining dust of the dead centuries he sees crowded figures that tell of the power and learning and splendor of times gone by; and he sees also the innumerable
10 host of humble students to whom clerkship meant emancipation, to whom it was well-nigh the only outlet from the dark thraldom of the Middle Ages.

This was the most famous university of medieval Europe at a time when no one dreamed
15 that there was a New World to discover. Its services to the cause of human knowledge already stretched far back into the remote past at a time when my forefathers, three centuries ago, were among the sparse bands of traders, ploughmen,
20 wood-choppers, and fisherfolk who , in hard struggle with the iron unfriendliness of the Indian-haunted land, were laying the foundations of what has now become the giant republic of the West.

Which of the following scenarios is most analogous to the contributions of the university to human knowledge?

A) A long-running organization for scientists provides support for members' research.

B) An ancient book was recently discovered to be a forgery.

C) A scientist discovers a new theory that sheds light on an old mystery.

D) A new institution is opened to help fund research on cancer.

Question 9

This passage is adapted from The Black Star by Johnston McCulley. First published in 1921.

Winds whistled up the river, and winds whistled down from the hills, and they met to swirl and gather fury and rattle the city's millions
Line of windowpanes. They poured through the
5 man-made canyons; they dashed out the broad boulevards—and so they came to the attention of Mr. Roger Verbeck, at about the hour of midnight, as he turned over in his warm bed and debated whether to rise and lower the window or take a
10 chance with the rapidly lowering temperature.

"Beastly night!" Verbeck confided to himself, and put his head beneath the covers.

He slept—and suddenly he awakened. A moment before he had been in the midst of a
15 pleasant dream; now every sense was alert, and his right hand, creeping softly under the cover, reached the side of the bed and grasped an automatic pistol that hung in a rack there.

From the adjoining room—his library—there
20 came no flash of an electric torch, no footfall, no sound foreign to the apartment, nothing to indicate the presence of an intruder. Yet Verbeck sensed that an intruder was there.

The situation detailed in the third and fourth paragraphs is most analogous to which of the following?

A) A thief breaks into a house at night and steals the family's expensive jewelry.

B) An antelope at a watering hole suddenly tenses, fearing a nearby predator.

C) A man goes to sleep and has a nightmare about an enemy attacking him.

D) An anxious woman is unable to relax the night before she gives a public speech.

Question 10

This passage is adapted from "Streaming may suffocate the music industry—or save it" by Mike Richards. ©2014 by Mike Richards.

For decades the music industry has warned that illegal copying of music threatens the industry's future, or even the existence of music itself.
Line Broadband internet led to a worldwide blossoming
5 of countless perfect digital copies. Copyright infringement, which the industry likes to call piracy, has soared—and profits have fallen. The music industry attempted to crush piracy using a combination of strong-arm legal tactics and
10 technological fixes including copy protection and digital rights management on CDs and digital files like MP3s. Both have failed, and increasingly users downloading content perceive piracy as a victimless crime.

Which example is most analogous to the rise of piracy in the music industry?

A) The rise of crime in populated urban areas

B) The rise of theft of credit card numbers

C) The rise of reading in the digital age

D) The rise of plagiarism in online news reporting

1. (A) is the correct answer. The passage states that campaign music is adjusted "to appeal to regional musical tastes." This would be similar to a bakery adjusting its selection depending on the specific region it is traveling in. (B) and (C) are incorrect because they contain no connotations of change based on region. (D) is incorrect because the local leader is not traveling to different regions, nor are his ideas, which is an essential component of campaign music mentioned in the passage.

2. (C) is the correct answer. The passage discusses how an initial theory about snakes posited that "they evolved from lizards and are really just an extreme type of legless lizard." It goes on to discuss a recent study discovery that suggests, by contrast, that snakes originally were aquatic. (C) mirrors this, with a prevailing theory being refuted by new evidence. (A) is incorrect as it involves support for an existing theory. (B) is incorrect as it does not include any sense of resolution or change in direction. (D) is incorrect because it involves the publicity of existing ideas, not the discovery of new ones.

3. (D) is the correct answer. The most important aspect of this principle mentioned in the passage is that a state is using force ("might is right") in order to bully other countries, best represented by (D). (A) would still fall within the realm of legality, and includes no aspect of threats. (B) is incorrect because both countries go to war; the passage discusses just one country threatening or using force against another. (C) is incorrect as it does not involve a greater power threatening a lesser, but a colony seeking independence from its mother country.

4. (A) is the correct answer. This example also shows two people debating the best course of action for a third. (B) and (C) are incorrect because the people involved in the discussion are talking about items related to themselves, not a third party. (D) is incorrect because the example involves two people discussing a concept, not a course of action.

5. (B) is the correct answer. The passage describes a technology that adapts based on feedback, so (B) is most similar. (A) and (C) both miss this important aspect of adapting to given feedback based on a relationship between two different entities. (D) also misses this aspect, and discusses a person rather than a machine.

6. (A) is the correct answer. The passage highlights overproduction and changing styles as responsible for waste in the fashion industry, which is most similar to the situation presented in (A). (B) includes mention of waste, but this is not waste due to overproduction of goods, but waste as a byproduct of processes. (C) is incorrect because it talks about expansion, not waste. (D) is incorrect because the reason the newspaper constantly demands new content is a function of its industry (daily news) rather than a function of changing styles and subsequent waste.

7. (C) is the correct answer. Urban exploiters are animals that, despite changes in the environment around them, are able to adapt and thrive. (C) is most analogous to this situation, as a restaurant—while remaining in the same location—is able to adapt to changes going on around it. (A) is incorrect as it includes movement of the group in question, which does not occur with urban exploiters. (B) is incorrect as it involves a change in a group of animals, but due to domestication rather than environmental changes. (D) is incorrect because it does not focus on the effects of environmental change on a specific group at all, and only talks broadly about the environment.

8. (A) is the correct answer. The passage explains that the university "was the most famous university of medieval Europe" and that "its services to the cause of human knowledge already stretched far back into the remote past" even three centuries ago. Thus, the university has contributed to human knowledge for centuries, making (A) the most analogous scenario. (B) is incorrect because it implies the negation of old knowledge, which is not connected to the university or its role. (C) is incorrect because it misses the historical aspect of the university's contributions. (D) is incorrect for the same reason.

9. (B) is the correct answer. The third and fourth paragraphs detail a situation where a man previously resting and at ease is thrown into high alert based on a new stimulus, so (B) is most analogous. (A) is incorrect because in this scenario, the person mentioned (a thief) is not the potential victim but the attacker. (C) is incorrect because the man's fear is in his nightmare, not in reality. (D) is incorrect because the woman is not initially in a relaxed state, as in the original example.

10. (D) is the correct answer. In the passage, the rise of piracy is attributed to the ease of creating "countless perfect digital copies" of music, where users see piracy as "a victimless crime." This aspect of both technology and perceived lack of victims is best mirrored in (D). (A) is incorrect because it misses both of these qualities. (B) is incorrect because, unlike digital piracy, it does involve obvious victims. (C) is incorrect because it includes no aspect of a crime at all.

Finding Evidence
Part 4

$\dfrac{+15}{15}$

Finding Evidence questions require you to review selected lines in a passage and determine which one provides the best evidence for the correct answer to the preceding question, or the best evidence for a claim specified in the question. They will typically require you to review one sentence per answer choice. When you see a Finding Evidence question, keep in mind that it might point you towards evidence that will help you answer the preceding question.

Finding Evidence questions contribute to the Command of Evidence subscore.

DIRECTIONS

Every passage or paired set of passages is accompanied by a number of questions. Read the passage or paired set of passages, then use what is said or implied in what you read and in any given graphics to choose the best answer to each question.

Question 1 & 2

This passage is adapted from "Explainer: what is fan fiction?" by Rukmini Pande. ©2015 by Rukmini Pande.

At its most basic, fan fiction is a genre of amateur fiction writing that takes as its basis a "canon" of "original" material. This original
Line material is most often popular books, television
5 shows, and movies, but can expand to almost anything, from the lives of celebrities to the travels of inanimate objects like the Mars rover. Fanworks, including fan fiction and fan art, are created by fans who are invested in the source
10 material. They seek to expand the narrative universe and share their personal creations with other fans for free.

The main impulse behind fan fiction has always been a playful desire to engage with
15 original works. Yet authors are still subject to modern copyright laws. In Australia, the US, and the EU, copyright exists for the lifetime of the author plus seventy years. Many early Disney film adaptations were derivative works based on out-
20 of-copyright novels—think Alice in Wonderland (1951) and The Jungle Book (1967). In a way, this could be considered a form of fan fiction.

 1

Which of the following is a motivation the passage gives for the development of fan fiction?

A) The desire to earn a profit

B) The need to avoid copyright issues

C) The hope to connect with other writers

D) The chance to engage with valued works

 2

Which choice provides the best evidence for the answer to the previous question?

A) Lines 1 - 3 ("At its … material")

B) Lines 3 - 8 ("This original … rover")

C) Lines 13 - 15 ("The main … works")

D) Lines 21 - 22 ("In a … fiction")

Question 3

This passage is adapted from "How to save inbred, short-faced dogs such as pugs and bulldogs from poor health" by David Sargan. ©2016 by David Sargan.

Short-faced dogs such as pugs, bulldogs (known as English bulldogs in the US) and French bulldogs are among the cutest pets out there, looking very different to the wolves they
[Line 5] descended from. Over the last few years these breeds have become increasingly common, partly thanks to advertising and their popularity among celebrities. In fact, all three breeds are now in Britain's top ten favorite dogs.
[10] But these dogs are the result of an amazing transformation in appearance and temperament caused by selective breeding, which has come at quite a cost to the dogs' health. Around half of them have breathing problems that sometimes lead
[15] to overheating, exercise intolerance, and sleep apnea. Their large heads and narrow pelvises also cause problems in giving birth (forcing Caesarean sections for many if not most) and their skin folds can become infected. Their exposed eyes are also
[20] vulnerable to damage, with about 15% suffering prolapsed third eyelids and many having other types of eye damage. Quite a number of dogs in several of the breeds also succumb to back or hip problems.

3

Which choice best supports the author's claim that short-faced dogs suffer from health problems?

A) Lines 1 - 6 ("Short-faced … from")

B) Lines 5 - 8 ("Over the … celebrities")

C) Lines 8 - 9 ("In fact … dogs")

D) Lines 13 - 16 ("Around half … apnea")

Question 4 & 5

This passage is adapted from "Senate Floor Speech on Cyber Security" by Sheldon Whitehouse. ©2010 by Sheldon Whitehouse.

In the course of my work on the Intelligence and Judiciary Committees, it has become all too clear that our laws have not kept pace with the amazing
[Line 5] technological developments we have seen over the past 15 or 20 years. One of the principal findings of our cyber task force was that most cyber threats— literally the vast majority of cyber threats—can be countered readily if Americans simply allowed automatic updates to their computer software,
[10] ran up-to-date antivirus programs, and exercised reasonable vigilance when surfing the Web and opening e-mails. So we need far more reporting from the government and the private sector to let Americans know what is happening out there on
[15] the wild Web. Disclosures can be anonymized, where necessary, to safeguard national security or protect competitive business interests.

4

The author notes that most security threats can be prevented if

A) users allowed automatic updates to software and ran antivirus programs.

B) the government performs periodic checks on cyber security.

C) more money is allocated to fighting cybercrimes.

D) citizens are educated about the dangers of cyber viruses.

Which choice provides the best evidence for the answer to the previous question?

A) Lines 1 - 5 ("In the ... years")

B) Lines 5 - 12 ("One of ... e-mails")

C) Lines 12 - 15 ("So we ... Web")

D) Lines 15 - 17 ("Disclosures can ... interests")

Question 6

This passage is adapted from The Story of Bessie Costrell by Mrs. Humphry Ward. First published in 1895.

An elderly laborer was walking along the
road which led to the village. To his right lay
the allotment gardens just beginning to be alive
Line with figures, and the voices of men and children.
5 Beyond them, far ahead, rose the square tower of
the church; to his left was the hill, and straight in
front of him the village, with its veils of smoke
lightly brushed over the trees, and its lines of
cottages climbing the chalk steeps behind it.
10 His eye as he walked took in a number of
such facts as life had trained it to notice. Once he
stopped to bend over a fence, to pluck a stalk or
two of oats; he examined them carefully, then he
threw back his head and sniffed the air, looking
15 all round the sky meanwhile. Yes, the season had
been late and harsh, but the fine weather was
coming at last. Two or three days' warmth now
would ripen even the oats, let alone the wheat.
Well, he was glad. He wanted the harvest over.
20 It would, perhaps, be his last harvest at Clinton
Magna, where he had worked, man and boy, for
fifty-six years come Michaelmas. His last harvest!
A curious pleasure stirred the man's veins as
he thought of it, a pleasure in expected change,
25 which seemed to bring back the pulse of youth, to
loosen a little the yoke of those iron years that had
perforce aged and bent him; though, for sixty-two,
he was still hale and strong.

6

Which choice provides the best evidence that the protagonist is excited at the prospect of his final harvest?

A) Lines 1 - 2 ("An elderly ... village")

B) Lines 10 - 11 ("His eye ... notice")

C) Lines 17 - 18 ("Two or three ... wheat")

D) Lines 23 - 27 ("A curious ... him")

Question 7 & 8

This passage is adapted from "Inventing life: patent law and synthetic biology" by Alison McLennan and Matthew Rimmer. ©2012 by Alison McLennan and Matthew Rimmer.

With promises of improved medical
treatments, greener energy, and even artificial
life, the field of synthetic biology has captured
Line the public imagination and attracted significant
5 government and commercial investment. This
excitement reached a crescendo on May 21, 2010,
when scientists at the J. Craig Venter Institute
in the United States announced that they had
made a "self-replicating synthetic bacterial cell."
10 This was the first living cell to have an entirely
human-made genome, which means that all of the
cell's characteristics were controlled by a DNA
sequence designed by scientists. This achievement
in biological engineering was made possible
15 by combining molecular biotechnology, gene
synthesis technology, and information technology.

Which of the following is NOT listed in the passage as a potential application of synthetic biology?

A) Energy

B) Medicine

C) Nutrition

D) Artificial life

Which choice provides the best evidence for the answer to the previous question?

A) Lines 1 - 5 ("With promises … investment")

B) Lines 5 - 9 ("This excitement … cell")

C) Lines 10 - 13 ("This was … scientists")

D) Lines 13 - 16 ("This achievement … technology")

Question 9

This passage is adapted from "Great books, nationhood, and teaching English literature" by Michelle Smith. ©2014 by Michelle Smith.

Britain has recently revised the GCSE (General Certificate in Secondary Education) syllabus for English literature. The category of "prose from
Line different cultures" has been replaced by "modern
5 works from Britain." The change means that classic American novels and plays, such as John Steinbeck's Of Mice and Men, Harper Lee's To Kill a Mockingbird, and Arthur Miller's The Crucible, will no longer be among the choices for
10 required texts.

Students must study at least one Shakespeare play, a 19th-century novel (selected from works by Charles Dickens, Jane Austen, Charlotte Brontë, and Robert Louis Stevenson), a variety
15 of poetry since 1789 (with a focus on the Romantics), and British fiction or drama published from 1914 to the present.

One of the goals of the GCSE in literature is for students to "appreciate the depth and power
20 of the English literary heritage". Of course, when Chaucer, Shakespeare, Milton, Austen, Wordsworth, Dickens, the Brontës, George Eliot, and Woolf are on your team, there's no difficulty in filling a course with British prose and poetry. But
25 shouldn't we aim to read literature across cultures?

9

Which choice best supports the author's concern about the focus on British works reducing variety in the curriculum?

A) Lines 1 - 3 ("Britain has … literature")

B) Lines 11 - 17 ("Students must … present")

C) Lines 18 - 20 ("One of … heritage")

D) Lines 24 - 25 ("But shouldn't … cultures")

Question 10 & 11

This passage is adapted from "Reducing water pollution with microbes and wood chips" by Laura Christianson. ©2016 by Laura Christianson.

Beneath fields of corn and soybeans across the U.S. Midwest lies an unseen network of underground pipes. These systems, which are
Line known as tile drainage networks, channel excess
5 water out of soil and carry it to lakes, streams, and rivers. There are over 38 million acres of tile drainage in the Corn Belt states.

These networks play a vital role in farm production. They allow farmers to drive tractors
10 into fields that would otherwise be too wet and make it possible to plant early in spring. And they boost crop growth and yield by preventing fields from becoming waterlogged.

But drainage systems are also major
15 contributors to water pollution. The water they remove from fields contains nitrogen, which comes both from organic matter in rich Midwestern soil and from fertilizer. This nitrogen over-fertilizes downstream water bodies, causing blooms of algae.
20 When the algae die, bacteria decompose them, using oxygen in the water as fuel.

The result is hypoxic zones, also known as dead zones, where nothing can live. Some of these zones, such as the one that forms in the Gulf
25 of Mexico every year fed by Midwestern farm drainage water, cover thousands of miles.

10

According to the passage, how do tile drainage networks contribute to water pollution?

A) They feed algae into major rivers, which then leads to a proliferation of bacteria.

B) They remove nitrogen from the water, which leads to the death of algae.

C) The water they funnel into lakes, streams, and rivers contains too much nitrogen.

D) They pump oxygen into lakes and rivers, which creates dangerous hypoxic zones.

11

Which choice provides the best evidence for the answer to the previous question?

A) Lines 11 - 13 ("And they … waterlogged")

B) Lines 14 - 15 ("But drainage … pollution")

C) Lines 15 - 18 ("The water … fertilizer")

D) Lines 23 - 26 ("Some of … miles")

Question 12

This passage is adapted from the "Address of the Honorable S.F. Austin," a speech given by S.F. Austin. This speech was delivered in Louisville, Kentucky, on March 7, 1836.

The public has been informed, through the medium of the newspapers, that war exists between the people of Texas and the present
Line government of Mexico. There are, however, many
5 circumstances connected with this contest, its origin, its principles and objects which, perhaps, are not so generally known, and are indispensable to a full and proper elucidation of this subject.
A few years back Texas was the home of the
10 Comanche and other tribes of Indians, who waged a constant warfare against the Spanish settlements.

These settlements at that time were limited to the small towns of Bexar and Goliad, situated on the western limits.
15   In order to bring these tribes into subjection, the government opened Texas for settlement. Foreign emigrants were invited and called to that country. American enterprise accepted the invitation and promptly responded to the call.
20 The first colony of Americans or foreigners ever settled in Texas was by myself. It was commenced in 1821, under a permission to my father, Moses Austin, from the Spanish government previous to the Independence of Mexico.

12

Which choice best supports the conclusion that the government encouraged settlers to go to Texas specifically to help subdue Indian tribes?

A) Lines 1 - 4 ("The public … Mexico")

B) Lines 9 - 11 ("A few … settlements")

C) Lines 15 - 16 ("In order … settlement")

D) Lines 20 - 21 ("The first … myself")

Question 13 & 14

This passage is adapted from Revelations of a Wife: The Story of a Honeymoon by Adele Garrison. First published in 1915.

Our taxi drew into the long line of motor cars before the theatre and slowly crept up to the door. Dicky jumped out, raised his umbrella, and guided
Line me into the lobby. It was filled with men and
5 women, some in elaborate evening dress, others in street garb. Some were going in to their seats, others were gossiping with each other, still others appeared to be waiting for friends.
The most conspicuous of all the women leaned
10 against the wall and gazed at others through a lorgnette which she handled as if she had not long before been accustomed to its use. Her gown was of scarlet chiffon over silk, her brocaded cape was half-slipping from her shoulder, and she rouged
15 outrageously.
I gazed at her fascinated. She typified to me

everything that was disagreeable. What was my horror, then, to see her deliberately smiling at me, then coming toward us with hand outstretched.

20 I realized the truth even before she spoke. It was not I at whom she was smiling, but Dicky. She was Dicky's friend!

13

The passage indicates that the conspicuous woman was

A) a stranger to the narrator and Dicky.

B) an old friend of the narrator's.

C) unknown to the narrator but known to Dicky.

D) a trusted confidante of Dicky's.

14

Which choice provides the best evidence for the answer to the previous question?

A) Lines 1 - 2 ("Our taxi … door")

B) Lines 3 - 4 ("Dicky jumped … lobby")

C) Lines 9 - 12 ("The most … use")

D) Lines 20 - 21 ("It was … Dicky")

Question 15

This passage is adapted from "So who does own the copyright on a monkey selfie?" by Andrew Charlesworth. ©2014 by Andrew Charlesworth.

While visiting a national park in North Sulawesi, wildlife photographer David Slater had his camera stolen—not by a thief, but by an

inquisitive crested black macaque. The resulting
5 selfies are causing controversy and raising questions about the ownership of images on the web. So just who does own the copyright when a monkey gets trigger-happy on your device?

Slater was photographing the endangered
10 monkeys when he left his camera unattended. One of the monkeys began playing with the camera and, fascinated by its reflection and the noise produced when it accidentally took a photo, it snapped hundreds of images of itself. Most were
15 blurred and out of focus, but several of the photos produced unique up-close and personal self-portraits of the rare creature.

But Slater now finds himself in a dispute with Wikimedia, the organization behind the Wikipedia
20 online encyclopedia. Wikimedia has made the images available online in its collection of royalty-free images without Slater's permission. It argues that Slater does not own the copyright to the images as he did not take the photos. Their
25 position is that copyright either belongs to the monkey or to no one.

15

At a picnic, a camera drops from a table and takes a clear picture of a rare bird. Someone claims that the copyright does not belong to the camera's owner. Which of the following statements in the passage supports this claim?

A) Lines 1 - 4 ("While visiting … macaque")

B) Lines 7- 8 ("So just … device")

C) Lines 14 - 17 ("Most were … creature")

D) Lines 23 - 24 ("It argues … photos")

1. (D) is the correct answer. The passage states that highly invested fans develop fan fiction to expand the narrative of popular, existing material such as books, television shows, and movies. (A) is incorrect because the passage indicates that these writers seek to share their work for free. (B) is incorrect because the need to avoid copyright issues is not a motivation, but rather a potential obstacle. (C) is incorrect because the passage nowhere indicates the desire to connect with other writers.

2. (C) is the correct answer. The given lines provide support for the previous answer that the chance to engage with original, valued works is one motivation behind fan fiction. (A) is incorrect because it is a definition of fan fiction, not a motivation for creating it. (B) is incorrect because these lines are further enumerating what fan fiction is instead of listing motivations for its creation. (D) is incorrect because it is talking about a specific set of works instead of a motivation that went into making fan fiction.

3. (D) is the correct answer. Of the choices, only these lines discuss the specific health problems short-faced dogs may have. (A), (B), and (C) all give background on the breeds without going into their various health problems, and are thus incorrect.

4. (A) is the correct answer. The passage indicates that most threats can be countered if users allowed automatic updates, ran antivirus programs, and exercised vigilance when surfing the Web. (B) is incorrect because the passage does not discuss periodic checks by the government. (C) is incorrect because the passage does not discuss money. (D) is incorrect because the passage suggests citizens should be generally notified about what is happening on the Web, and not about cyber viruses in particular.

5. (B) is the correct answer. These lines note that Americans could prevent most cyber threats if they "allowed automatic updates to their computer software, ran up-to-date antivirus programs, and exercised reasonable vigilance when surfing the Web and opening e-mails." (A), (C), and (D) all do not discuss how Americans could counter cyber threats, let alone touch on the specific answer of automatic updates and antivirus programs, and thus are all incorrect.

6. (D) is the correct answer. Only these lines express the man's pleasure at the thought of his final harvest. They discuss a "pleasure" as the man thinks of "it," the it being "his last harvest at Clinton Magna," which is stated right before these lines. (A) opens the story with general background, while (B) and (C) are sentences describing the man's journey through the land, none of which touch on the man's views towards his final harvest, and are thus all incorrect.

7. (C) is the correct answer. Nutrition was not listed as a potential application of synthetic biology. The applications indicated in (A), (B), and (D) were listed as potential uses and are therefore incorrect.

8. (A) is the correct answer. The passage lists the different potential applications of synthetic biology in this line; nutrition is not among them. (B), (C), and (D) are all incorrect as they all focus more specifically on a recent breakthrough, and not the broader applications of synthetic biology.

9. (D) is the correct answer. These lines are the closest the author comes to exhibiting concern over the change in curriculum requirements, as the author highlights the lack of cross-cultural reading in the new curriculum. (A), (B), and (C) are all portions of the passage that simply offer facts to describe the change without offering any insight into the author's opinion.

10. (C) is the correct answer. The passage indicates that the water from these tile drainage networks contains too much nitrogen, which over-fertilizes downstream water bodies. (A) is incorrect because the drainage networks do not feed algae into rivers. Rather, the nitrogen they contain causes blooms of algae. (B) is incorrect because they add, rather than remove, nitrogen to water. (D) is incorrect because the passage nowhere states that the systems pump oxygen into lakes and rivers.

11. (C) is the correct answer. These lines highlight that water funneled by drainage networks contains nitrogen, which leads to a host of other issues. (A) is incorrect because it is a benefit of drainage networks. (B) is incorrect because it notes that these networks contribute to water pollution, but does not state how. (D) is incorrect because it describes hypoxic zones but not how they are created by tile drainage networks.

12. (C) is the correct answer. These lines specifically note the reason why the government opened Texas for settlement, "in order to bring these tribes into subjection." (A) is incorrect as it deals with the war between Texas and Mexico. (B) is incorrect because it is general background on Texas, before the government encouraged settlers to go to Texas. (D) is incorrect because it is a personal fact given by the author about his own role in the settlement of Texas.

13. (C) is the correct answer. The narrator only describes what the woman looks like in the first paragraph, not letting on whether or not she knows her. The narrator then admits that she only realizes why the conspicuous woman approaches them when she greets Dicky, which would not make sense if the narrator knew this woman. The passage concludes that this conspicuous woman "was Dicky's friend!" (A) is incorrect because the passage states that the conspicuous woman is "Dicky's friend!" (B) is incorrect because the narrator never states that the woman is a friend of hers and instead only describes what she looks like and then the woman walking toward and greeting her and Dicky, which does not necessarily convey friendship. (D) is incorrect because it wrongly assumes more information than is indicated in the passage—the woman is only described as "Dicky's friend!" which doesn't necessarily mean Dicky trusts her.

14. (D) is the correct answer. These lines include the narrator's revelation that the conspicuous woman, though a stranger to herself, is known to Dicky. (A), (B), and (C) all do not touch on how the conspicuous woman relates to either the narrator or to Dicky and are therefore all incorrect.

15. (D) is the correct answer. These lines give Wikimedia's reasoning that since Slater did not take the pictures, he does not own the copyright. Since the owner of the camera in this question's example also did not take the photo, they cannot own copyright according to Wikimedia's reasoning. (A) and (C) are incorrect because they do not touch on specific issues of copyright. (B) is only a general question about copyright, not reasoning behind who might own copyright in a given situation.

+10
10

Main Ideas
Part 5

Main Ideas questions require you to identify the main idea of a passage. You may only need to identify a paraphrase of a thesis statement in the passage, or you may need to infer a thesis that is not clearly stated in the passage by considering the thrust of the evidence, arguments, and rhetoric that the author uses.

DIRECTIONS

Every passage or paired set of passages is accompanied by a number of questions. Read the passage or paired set of passages, then use what is said or implied in what you read and in any given graphics to choose the best answer to each question.

Question 1

This passage is adapted from "How studying the old drawings and writings of kids can change our view of history" by Karen Sánchez-Eppler. ©2016 by Karen Sánchez-Eppler.

According to one view, the way children speak, think and observe is not as relevant as adult perceptions of the world. Each life is a
Line progress narrative, and as we mature, it's best
5 to put away "childish things." My research as a cultural historian asks what we might learn if we didn't think about childhood this way. Instead, what if we recognized children as having ways of speaking, thinking, and interpreting that may
10 possess valuable knowledge and insight? How might it change the way we think of historical events and cultural trends, from the Civil War to the publication of Robinson Crusoe?
   Only recently have historians begun studying
15 the history of childhood. It's part of an important strand of historical scholarship that, since the middle of the 20th century, has attempted to look at history "from the bottom up." This sort of approach studies history not only through the lens
20 of the rich and powerful, but also through the lens of everyday life, which includes the perspectives of people excluded from power, like women, slaves, immigrants, and children.

 1

One of the main points that the author seeks to make in the passage is that children

A) have been afforded too much attention in most historical accounts, despite their unreliability.

B) do not have the same mature, relevant perspective on events that adults do.

C) have unique and valuable perspectives on events going on in the world around them.

D) are a marginalized historical group that has suffered from oppression.

Question 2

This passage is adapted from "Some mushrooms glow in the dark—here's why" by Mike Hale. ©2015 by Mike Hale.

Glowing fungi with an on-off system synchronized to their daily rhythms? It sounds implausible, but it's true. Some mushrooms
Line evolved the ability to glow in the dark in order to
5 attract insects to spread their spores, according to new research.

Mushrooms, or fungal fruit bodies—the bit you see above ground—may be familiar to us all as food, but in the real world mushroom-forming
10 fungi only produce these fruit bodies under special conditions. Fruit bodies are produced to disperse their progeny as spores. Many fungi shoot spores into the air from the underside of the mushrooms, relying on moving air currents to passively
15 distribute the spores over a wide area.

So if air movement isn't effective how can spores be dispersed far and wide? One way may be light. Light is attractive to many insects, and indeed, a number of fungi bioluminesce,
20 emitting a pale green light. Insects eat parts of the mushrooms and then unwittingly spread the spores elsewhere. For fungi, there is a selective advantage to glowing in the dark.

2

The passage is primarily concerned with establishing

A) the reproductive cycle of mushrooms.

B) the different uses of glowing fungi.

C) a growing problem for wild fungi.

D) an unusual reproductive adaptation of fungi.

Question 3

This passage is adapted from The Mysterious Affair at Styles by Agatha Christie. First published in 1920.

I retraced my steps to Styles in some annoyance. With Poirot away, I was uncertain how to act. Had he foreseen this arrest? Had
Line he not, in all probability, been the cause of it?
5 Those questions I could not resolve. But in the meantime what was I to do? Should I announce the arrest openly at Styles, or not? Though I did not acknowledge it to myself, the thought of Mary Cavendish was weighing on me. Would it not be a
10 terrible shock to her? For the moment, I set aside utterly any suspicions of her. She could not be implicated—otherwise I should have heard some hint of it.

Of course, there was no possibility of being
15 able permanently to conceal Dr. Bauerstein's arrest from her. It would be announced in every newspaper on the morrow. Still, I shrank from blurting it out. If only Poirot had been accessible, I could have asked his advice. What
20 possessed him to go posting off to London in this unaccountable way?

In spite of myself, my opinion of his sagacity was immeasurably heightened. I would never have dreamt of suspecting the doctor, had not Poirot put
25 it into my head. Yes, decidedly, the little man was clever.

After some reflecting, I decided to take John into my confidence, and leave him to make the matter public or not, as he thought fit.
30 He gave vent to a prodigious whistle, as I imparted the news.

John reflected.

"Never mind," he said at last, "we won't say anything at present. There is no need. As you say,
35 it will be known soon enough."

3

In the passage, the narrator is primarily concerned with

A) contemplating whether to disclose an arrest.

B) speculating about potential suspects of a crime.

C) investigating the whereabouts of Poirot.

D) seeking out John to request his advice.

Question 4

This passage is adapted from "How brain implants can let paralyzed people move again" by Dimitra Blana and Andrew Jackson. ©2016 by Dimitra Blana and Andrew Jackson.

Something as simple as picking up a cup of tea requires an awful lot of action from your body. Your arm muscles fire to move your arm
Line towards the cup. Your finger muscles fire to open
5 your hand and then bend your fingers around the handle. Your shoulder muscles keep your arm from popping out of your shoulder and your core muscles make sure you don't tip over because of the extra weight of the cup. All these muscles
10 have to fire in a precise and coordinated manner, and yet your only conscious effort is the thought: "I know: tea!"

This is why enabling a paralyzed limb to move again is so difficult. Most paralyzed muscles
15 can still work, but their communication with the brain has been lost, so they are not receiving instructions to fire. We can't yet repair damage to the spinal cord, so one solution is to bypass it and provide the instructions to the muscles artificially.
20 Thanks to the development of technology for reading and interpreting brain activity, these instructions could one day come direct from a patient's mind.

We can make paralyzed muscles fire by
25 stimulating them with electrodes placed inside the muscles or around the nerves that supply them, a technique known as functional electrical stimulation (FES). As well as helping paralyzed people move, it is also used to restore bladder
30 function, produce effective coughing, and provide pain relief. It is a fascinating technology that can make a big difference in the lives of people with spinal cord injuries.

 4

The passage devotes the LEAST attention to which of the following topics?

A) The challenges of paralyzed muscles

B) The types of spinal cord injuries

C) Functional electrical stimulation

D) Communication between the brain and muscles

Question 5

This passage is adapted from "Kenneth Clark—the last art historian in pursuit of beauty" by Jonathan Conlin. ©2014 by Jonathan Conlin.

There is currently something of a Kenneth Clark renaissance, with an exhibition devoted to him that just opened at Tate Britain. If there is
Line anything to be gained from going back to Clark's
5 vision of how art patronage should work, it is surely his stress on the societal value of art.

In 1939, Clark wrote: No new style will grow out of a preoccupation with art for its own sake. It can only arise from a new interest in
10 subject matter. We need a new myth in which the symbols are inherently pictorial. However, he was characteristically pessimistic about whether this was possible. In the Renaissance great artists had had great patrons to supply them with "subject
15 matter." Art was a joint venture of artist and society. But the would-be princes at the time of writing were incapable of providing this, while corporate sponsorship had yet to find its feet.

It wasn't just society that had failed. The
20 18th-century Romantic rebellion had seen artists declare independence of society. Their pursuit of art for art's sake had reached a dead end in abstraction, an abstraction that could only ever appeal to a self-regarding clique.

The central idea proposed by Kenneth Clark is that

A) society must patronize the arts if it ever hopes to see any progress.

B) subject matter in art should be focused on people rather than landscapes.

C) art must draw inspiration from society and not just art alone.

D) artists must be independent of society to offer a true perspective.

Question 6

This passage is adapted from "Traveling to Mars with immortal plasma rockets" by Gary Li. ©2016 by Gary Li.

How can we send a settlement to Mars, which is more than 100 times farther away than the moon? The Saturn-Apollo combination could
Line deliver only the mass equivalent of one railroad
5 boxcar to the moon; it would take dozens of those rockets just to build a small house on Mars. Sadly, there are no alternatives for the "chemical" launch rocket; only powerful chemical explosions can provide enough force to overcome Earth's
10 gravity. But once in space, a new fuel-efficient rocket technology can take over: plasma rockets.
Plasma rockets are a modern technology that transform fuel into a hot soup of electrically charged particles, known as plasma, and eject
15 it to push a spacecraft. Using plasma rockets instead of the traditional chemical rockets can reduce total in-space fuel usage by 90 percent. That means we could deliver 10 times the amount of cargo using the same fuel mass. NASA
20 mission planners are already looking into using plasma rocket transport vehicles for ferrying cargo between Earth and Mars.

The passage primarily focuses on which of the following characteristics of plasma rockets?

A) Their lower price in comparison to traditional rockets

B) Their increased efficiency in comparison to traditional rockets

C) The qualities they share with chemical rockets

D) The coordination of space trips with plasma and chemical rockets

Question 7

This passage is adapted from Rob Harlow's Adventures by George Manville Fenn. First published in 1907.

"You should wait till they've sucked 'emselves full and then hit 'em; they're lazy then. Too quick for you now."
Line "The wretches! I shall be spotted all over, like
5 a currant dumpling. I say, Shaddy, do they always bite like this?"
"Well, yes, sir," said the man addressed, about as ugly a specimen of humanity as could be met in a day's march, for he had only one eye, and
10 beneath that a peculiar, puckered scar extending down to the corner of his mouth. Add also that he was about five feet, nine, very broad-shouldered and muscular, and you have Shadrach Naylor, about the last person any one would select for a
15 companion on a trip up one of the grandest rivers of South America.
But there he was that hot, sunny day, standing up in the stern of the broad, lightly built boat which swung by a long rope some fifty feet behind
20 a large schooner. It was hot, blistering hot, and all was very still save for the rippling murmur of the flowing river and the faint buzz of the insect plagues which had come hunting from the western shore, a couple of hundred yards away, while the
25 eastern was fully two miles off, and the voices of the man and the boy he addressed sounded strange in the vast solitudes through which the mighty river ran.

Which choice best describes what happens in the passage?

A) A man and boy on a small vessel are bitten by bugs on a river.

B) A pirate kidnaps a young boy in sweltering heat.

C) A fisherman and his son try unsuccessfully to bring in their catch.

D) Two men stalk a much larger ship, hoping to steal from it.

Question 8

This passage is adapted from "American Medical Association warns of health and safety problems from 'white' LED streetlights" by Richard G. Stevens. ©2016 by Richard G. Stevens.

The American Medical Association (AMA) has just adopted an official policy statement about street lighting: cool it and dim it. The statement
Line comes in response to the rise of new LED street
5 lighting sweeping the country. An AMA committee issued guidelines on how communities can choose LED streetlights to "minimize potential harmful human health and environmental effects."

The AMA's statement recommends that
10 outdoor lighting at night, particularly street lighting, should have a color temperature of no greater than 3000 Kelvin (K). Color temperature (CT) is a measure of the spectral content of light from a source; how much blue, green, yellow and
15 red there is in it. A higher CT rating generally means greater blue content, and a whiter light.

A number of cities have recently retrofitted their street lighting. But in the wake of these installations, residents have complained about the
20 harshness of these lights. An extreme example is the city of Davis, California, where the residents demanded a complete replacement of these high color temperature LED street lights.

What is the author's main point about the installation of new LED street lights?

A) They actually do not save as much energy as once believed.

B) They produce high amounts of heat that could lead to a fire.

C) Their brightness may actually have negative effects on human health.

D) Their blue content helps cool the harshness of the original installed lights.

Question 9

This passage is adapted from "Final frontier films: the movies that astronauts watch in space" by Suman Ghosh. ©2016 by Suman Ghosh.

Which films would you watch in space? Well, in December last year, just days after British astronaut Tim Peake rocketed to the International
Line Space Station (ISS) in a Russian Soyuz spacecraft,
5 Star Wars: The Force Awakens appeared on multiplex screens around the world. As the first release of the space opera for more than a decade, this was an eagerly anticipated affair. And Peake and his fellow astronauts were not denied the
10 excitement, watching the film on an HD projector and screen while orbiting 250 miles above the Earth. "What a place to watch it!" Peake tweeted merrily from his perch in the heavens.

The film was a special addition to more than
15 500 film and television programs available to the astronauts on the ISS. A freedom of information request recently led to the release of NASA's complete list. Whether Russian cosmonauts aboard the ISS have a similar arrangement is yet
20 unknown, but it's likely they all share nicely.

Science fiction films, especially space-related ones, are an important part of the audiovisual spread served up by NASA. This includes 2001: A Space Odyssey, Alien, and its sequels, superhero
25 space operas such as Guardians of the Galaxy and, of course, the complete Star Trek movie series.

The central claim of the passage is that

A) astronauts watch many films in space, including space-related science fiction dramas.

B) most countries seek to provide astronauts different forms of entertainment to ease their isolation.

C) space crews appreciate science fiction dramas more than any other type of film.

D) technological innovations in streaming and internet use allow astronauts to watch films.

The central problem that the author describes in the passage is discovering how

A) tuberculosis spreads through the population.

B) latently infected people develop active TB.

C) proteins produce lung inflammation.

D) different drugs help prevent TB.

Question 10

This passage is adapted from "Inflammatory proteins offer insights into how TB spreads in the lungs" by Mohlopheni Marakalala. ©2016 by Mohlopheni Marakalala.

Tuberculosis—the bacterial lung disease—remains a leading global health problem more than a century after it was first discovered. It is
Line still responsible for about 1.5 million deaths every
5 year. According to the World Health Organization, one-third of the world's population is latently infected with the bacteria that cause TB. Only between 5% and 10% of these people develop the active TB disease in their lifetime.
10 The rest of the latently infected population will never develop the active disease. This is because they're protected by a strong immune system that helps the body to defend itself against the infection. Scientists still do not fully understand
15 why people with latent TB develop active TB. Ongoing research has centered on understanding the state of the immune system and what goes wrong that results in the TB worsening.
Our research looked at one component of the
20 immune system and found that there were proteins in the body that promote lung inflammation, which helps the bacteria that causes TB to spread throughout the lung. Now that we have identified these proteins that are associated with disease
25 progression, the next step is to find the drugs that will inhibit these proteins and limit lung inflammation. Although most TB drugs have been focused on tackling the bacteria, these new drugs are likely to help shorten the treatment course.

1. (C) is the correct answer. The passage asks, "what if we recognized children as having ways of speaking, thinking, and interpreting that may possess valuable knowledge and insight?" The author is a "cultural historian" that questions traditional views of childhood, instead proposing the usefulness of children's perspectives when studying history. (C) is therefore correct. (A) is incorrect because the author is arguing the opposite, that children have historically not received enough attention. (B) is incorrect because the author's perspective is that children do have valuable input. (D) is incorrect because, while the author may agree that children are a marginalized historical group, this is only mentioned briefly, and the author does not imply such children have suffered from oppression.

2. (D) is the correct answer. The majority of the passage talks about how "glowing fungi" have "evolved the ability to glow in the dark in order to attract insects to spread their spores." (A) is incorrect because the reproductive cycle is touched on only in relation to the purpose of the fungi's unusual glowing property—it is not the main point of the passage. (B) is incorrect because the passage only talks about why fungi glow, not other uses for this bioluminescence. (C) is incorrect because the passage is not discussing any growing problem; it is concerned with discussing adaptations and reproductive strategies.

3. (A) is the correct answer. The narrator repeatedly refers to an arrest throughout the passage, and the majority of these references center around the decision of whether or not to disclose this arrest. (B) is incorrect because although the narrator mentions "suspicions," this is only in the context of setting these aside, not speculating about them. (C) is incorrect because the narrator is not investigating the whereabouts of Poirot. In fact, the narrator indicates that Poirot had gone to London. (D) is incorrect because although the narrator does consult John, this only happens at the end of the passage and is only briefly touched on.

4. (B) is the correct answer. The passage does not discuss the different types of spinal cord injuries, beyond mentioning that spinal cord injuries are related to muscle paralysis and can be improved through FES. (A) is incorrect because the passage discusses the challenges of paralyzed muscles in the second paragraph, devoting time to explaining difficulties in repairing such injuries. (C) is incorrect because the entire third paragraph focuses on FES, which is also one of the main points of the passage. (D) is incorrect because the first paragraph is devoted to explaining this communication, which forms the basis for later discussions in the passage.

5. (C) is the correct answer. The passage explains Clark's perspective that new styles of art must "arise from a new interest in subject matter" and not "with art for its own sake." (A) is incorrect because while the passage touches on patronization of the arts, Clark's specific quote and perspectives do not. (B) is incorrect because the passage offers no opinion on whether people or landscapes should be featured in art. (D) is incorrect because the passage discusses society in relation to subject matter; the final reference to artists declaring independence of society is meant as an example of the "pursuit of art for art's sake," something Clark argued against.

6. (B) is the correct answer. The passage notes that plasma rockets "reduce total in-space fuel usage by 90 percent" in comparison to traditional chemical rockets, meaning they are more efficient. Since this efficiency is why the author brings up plasma rockets, (B) is correct. (A) is incorrect because the passage talks about the efficiency, not the price, of the two different rockets. (C) is incorrect because the passage focuses on the differences, not similarities, of plasma and chemical rockets. (D) is incorrect because the passage talks about replacing traditional chemical rockets with plasma rockets, not using them together.

7. (A) is the correct answer. The opening dialogue ("do they always bite like this?") is in reference to insects surrounding the boat, as evidenced in the final passage when the narrator mentions "the faint buzz of the insect plagues which had come hunting from the western shore." The passage also notes the two companions are a man and boy, and that they are in a "lightly built boat" connected to a larger schooner. (B) is incorrect because there is no evidence the elder man is a pirate, even though he is missing an eye. (C) is incorrect because the passage does not indicate either the man or boy is a fisherman. (D) is incorrect because the man and boy are tied to the larger schooner; they are not stealthily stalking it.

8. (C) is the correct answer. The passage notes that the AMA has "issued guidelines" on how communities with LED streetlights can "minimize potential harmful human health and environmental effects." The rest of the passage explains LED lights' increased brightness and urges municipalities to consider human health effects of high color temperature. (A) is incorrect because the passage does not dispute any energy-saving qualities of LED lights. (B) is incorrect because, while the brightness of lights is described on the Kelvin scale, this does not reference physical heat. The passage nowhere discusses heat effects or fire hazards. (D) is incorrect because greater blue content creates more white, or harsh, light.

9. (A) is the correct answer. The passage focuses almost exclusively on the different types of films that astronauts enjoy in space, especially science fiction dramas that take place in space, such as Star Trek and Alien. (B) is too general to be correct; the passage is focused on film, not different forms of entertainment. (C) is incorrect because, though the passage notes that many science fiction films make their way to space, it does not state whether crews have a particular preference in genres. (D) is incorrect because the passage does not focus on how such films are procured, nor is technological innovation the focus of the passage.

10. (B) is the correct answer. The author begins by setting up the problem that only about 5% to 10% of those with latent TB develop active TB, noting that "ongoing research has centered on understanding the state of the immune system and what goes wrong." One potential issue noted is the presence of proteins that promote lung inflammation, helping spread TB. (A) is incorrect because the author does not discuss the spread of TB through different populations. (C) is incorrect because the author is not concerned with how proteins produce lung inflammation. (D) is incorrect because the central problem the author discusses in the passage focuses on the development of TB, not on different drug treatments for the disease.

Summarizing

Part 6

Summarizing questions require you to identify a summary of key details in a part of the passage or the passage as a whole. They may require you to distinguish between significant and irrelevant details, recognize correct sequences of details, or resist answer choices that extend beyond the section in question or fail to summarize the entire area in question.

DIRECTIONS

Every passage or paired set of passages is accompanied by a number of questions. Read the passage or paired set of passages, then use what is said or implied in what you read and in any given graphics to choose the best answer to each question.

Question 1

This passage is adapted from *The Secret Agent: A Simple Tale* by Joseph Conrad. First published in 1907.

Mr. Verloc made his way westward at the hour of half-past ten in the morning. It was unusually early for him; his whole person exhaled the
Line charm of almost dewy freshness. He paused,
5 and through the park railings he beheld men and women riding in the Row, couples cantering past harmoniously, others advancing sedately at a walk, loitering groups of three or four, solitary horsemen looking unsociable, and solitary women
10 followed at a long distance by a groom with a cockade to his hat and a leather belt over his tight-fitting coat. Carriages went bowling by, mostly two-horse broughams, with here and there a victoria with the skin of some wild beast inside
15 and a woman's face and hat emerging above the folded hood.

Mr. Verloc surveyed through the park railings the evidences of the town's opulence and luxury with an approving eye. All these people had to
20 be protected. Protection is the first necessity of opulence and luxury. They had to be protected; and their horses, carriages, houses, servants had to be protected; and the source of their wealth had to be protected in the heart of the city and the heart
25 of the country.

1

Which best summarizes lines 1 - 16?

A) Mr. Verloc stops one morning to observe the town's inhabitants.

B) Mr. Verloc is impressed by the luxury and opulence in the town.

C) Mr. Verloc rushes across a very busy town when he is late to work.

D) Mr. Verloc goes for his daily stroll and greets inhabitants of the town.

Question 2

This passage is adapted from "Found: the missing part of brain's 'internal compass'" by Theresa Burt de Perera and Tim Guilford. ©2015 by Theresa Burt de Perera and Tim Guilford.

If you have taken a walk and would like to return home, you need to have an idea of where you are in relation to your destination. To do this,
Line you need to know which way you are facing and
5 also in which direction home lies. This all seems fairly instinctive to humans and other animals, so how do we manage it?

Our understanding of this surprisingly difficult question has just taken a step forward in a new
10 paper written by Martin Chadwick and colleagues, which pinpoints where in the brain our instinctive sense of the direction towards our destination lies.

One way to successfully navigate from any point to a destination is to learn and remember information about your surroundings and use this information to orient yourself. But the process of learning this spatial information suggests there must be some sort of representation of that information stored somewhere in the brain. This could be thought of as a sort of neuronal map—a way of encoding space that maps information about your surroundings onto your brain cells.

Such a map would allow you to find your way around—a vital ability for any animal's survival. Working out how the brain stores information about space and how this enables us to find our way around efficiently has been the focus of a concerted effort over the past few decades.

2

Which choice best summarizes the third paragraph of the passage (lines 13 - 22)?

A) Brain cells grow and develop over time, shaped by the needs of each individual brain.

B) Most brains are skilled at developing 3-D maps through a series of neurons that fire in response to spatial formations.

C) The brain stores information about your location in a "neuronal map" that translates spatial information to your brain cells.

D) The human brain can engage in different kinds of thinking, including spatial thinking and awareness.

Question 3

This passage is adapted from "First sentences establish a contract with the reader about what is to come" by Camilla Nelson. ©2016 by Camilla Nelson.

First sentences do a special kind of work. They have, as critic Stanley Fish once said, an "angle of lean." They establish a contract with the reader about what is to come; they may sketch in a character, establish a mood, foreshadow a plot, or set out an argument. They seem to set the direction for every other sentence. The first words

are also, in this sense, the last words.

Take, for example, Tolstoy's famous opening from Anna Karenina (1873-77): "All happy families are alike; each unhappy family is unhappy in its own way." The sentence not only sets up one of Tolstoy's key themes—the struggle between happiness and freedom, or, more broadly, between living for oneself and living for others. But it also throws up a series of questions or contradictions that will rule the lives of his characters until the very last page.

3

Which choice best summarizes the passage?

A) Anna Karenina has one of the most evocative first lines in literature.

B) It is possible to judge an author's skill based on the effectiveness of the first line.

C) Good writing requires the careful selection of the correct words to accomplish the author's purpose.

D) First sentences help establish the theme and direction of a literary work.

Question 4

This passage is adapted from "Will the Arctic shift from a carbon sink to a carbon source?" by Michael Rawlins. ©2015 by Michael Rawlins.

Studies show that the warming of the climate system is altering the movement and storage of carbon in the far north of the Earth. And these changes carry global implications. Among the many questions that scientists such as myself are investigating is whether the Arctic will continue being a net absorber of carbon, or shift to become a net emitter.

The Earth's carbon cycle—the movement and storage of carbon between the land, atmosphere and oceans—is a fundamental element of the climate system. Oceans are currently the Earth's greatest carbon sink, meaning they absorb more carbon than they emit.

However, there is a seasonal rise and fall of

emission rates which is largely attributed to the summer "green up" of northern ecosystems from vegetation growth during the short warm season, and CO2 emitted by plant respiration for growth
20 and soil carbon decomposition. Anthropogenic emissions from, for example, people burning fossil fuels add to the land-to-atmosphere transfer.

4

Which of the following statements best summarizes the author's thoughts about the Earth's carbon cycle (lines 9 - 14)?

A) It is a natural and essential process.

B) It is fueled mainly by the Earth's oceans.

C) It is in grave danger of growing out of control.

D) It is a product of human interference.

Question 5

This passage is adapted from *The Fatal Glove* by Clara Augusta Jones Trask. First published in 1892.

Arch's way led past a horticultural store, and his eye wandered longingly over the display of flowers in the window. He must have just one
Line wee white rose, because, only the Sabbath before,
5 while he sat at his mother's feet, she had wept in telling him about the sweet roses that used to grow under the window of the little country cottage where her happy youth had been spent.

The white rose would be like bringing back to
10 her ever so little a bit of the happy past. It could not cost much, and Arch felt wealthy as a prince. He stepped into the store and asked the price of a white rose. The clerk answered him roughly:

"Get out of the store, you young rascal! You
15 want to steal something!"

"I am not a thief, sir," said the boy, proudly, his sallow cheeks crimsoning hotly. "I want a rose for my mother. I guess I can pay for it!"

"It's half a dollar, if you want it," said the man,
20 sneeringly. "Show your money, or take yourself off this minute!"

Archie's countenance fell. He had not half a dollar in all. He turned sadly away, his head drooping, his lip quivering. Oh, how very hard it
25 was to be poor, he thought, looking enviously at the costly carriage, with a pair of splendid grays, standing before the door.

5

Which of the following statements best summarizes the comments in the passage from the clerk?

A) The clerk, nervously and impatiently, tries to sell the young boy a white rose for his mother.

B) The clerk, suspiciously and condescendingly, denies the boy wants to buy the flower honestly.

C) The clerk, indifferently and lazily, scoffs that the boy does not have the means to be in his shop.

D) The clerk, merrily and encouragingly, guides the boy to select a flower for his sweetheart.

Question 6

This passage is adapted from "How TV dating shows helped change love and marriage in China forever" by Pan Wang. ©2016 by Pan Wang.

By the early 1990s, Chinese TV networks found themselves in fierce competition with one another. Economic liberalization had loosened
Line restrictions for what could appear on the airwaves,
5 but there was now the added pressure of turning a profit. More than ever before, networks needed to produce entertaining shows that attracted audiences.

It was during this period that dating shows
10 started to transform, depicting live, on-air matchmaking and dates between single males and females. For example, Human Satellite TV's "Red Rose Date" featured 12 single males and females who interacted with one another by performing,
15 playing games, and having roundtable chats. Audiences could also tune into shows imported from overseas, such as "Love Game," a popular Taiwanese show that matched singles through three rounds of speed dating.

20 These new shows were ways for singles to get

to know each other in a fun, flirty environment. And for those who had little dating experience, it was a model for courtship; soon, the viewing public was able to reconceptualize ideas of love, 25 relationships and marriage.

6

Considering the information given in the first two paragraphs (lines 1 - 19), which of the following is the most accurate description of the development of Chinese TV dating shows?

A) Chinese networks added dating shows to their roster to compete with Taiwanese networks.

B) Chinese TV dating shows had their heyday in the early 90s before petering out.

C) The participants in Chinese dating shows helped shape the content by making it more interactive and modern.

D) Chinese TV dating shows competed for audiences by featuring lighthearted matchmaking.

Question 7

This passage is adapted from "What made Muhammad Ali 'The Greatest' in the ring?" by Allan Hahn. ©2016 by Allan Hahn.

Various boxing authorities have ranked Ali as the best heavyweight boxer in history. He and the legendary Sugar Ray Robinson have
Line been bracketed as the top two across all weight
5 divisions. Ali won a gold medal (as a light heavyweight) at the 1960 Rome Olympics as the culmination of an amateur boxing career in which he won 100 of 105 bouts.
　As a professional, Ali won the world
10 heavyweight championship on three separate occasions over 14 years. He was victorious in 56 of 61 professional bouts, with three of the losses coming late in his career when his athleticism had faded. Sports Illustrated named him as its
15 Sportsman of the 20th Century.
　What made Ali such an outstanding exponent of his sport? It certainly wasn't sheer strength and power. He was never considered to be

among boxing's hardest punchers and more than
20 one-third of his professional contests lasted their full scheduled duration. Nor was he remarkable in terms of height or weight. Rather, Ali's speed, agility, footwork, and general athleticism were among the attributes that most distinguished
25 him from other competitors. It was said he was a heavyweight who moved like a lightweight.

7

As described in the passage, the unique skill Muhammad Ali brought to the sport can best be summarized by which of the following statements?

A) Muhammad Ali was the largest and most powerful heavyweight fighter.

B) Muhammad Ali had the force of a heavyweight fighter, even though he competed as a lightweight athlete.

C) Muhammad Ali was able to end matches quickly and definitively.

D) Muhammad Ali excelled in skill and speed rather than just power.

Question 8

This passage is adapted from "Behavioral study shows that rats know how to repay a favor" by Gilbert Roberts. ©2015 by Gilbert Roberts.

Behavioral scientists have questioned the extent to which non-human animals have the capacity to engage in reciprocity without being
Line exploited by "cheats" who take advantage of
5 their kindness. It seems that this is cognitively demanding, in terms of bringing together the memories of who did what and judging how to respond.
　Researchers Dolivo and Taborsky's latest
10 results show that rats can recall the quality of help provided and by which rat, and adjust their subsequent behavior so as to invest more time and energy in helping those that helped them. Taken together with the Taborsky group's prior findings
15 that rats are more likely to help a partner that had helped them before than one that had not helped

them at all, these results provide interesting insight into how animals are able to manage the challenges of conditional cooperation.

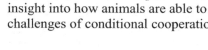

8

According to the passage, rats can engage in reciprocity by

A) performing altruistic acts in order to secure cooperation of other rats.

B) working together to achieve goals that benefit both of them.

C) altering their helping behavior based on past help from other rats.

D) cooperating conditionally so long as neither rat betrays the other.

Question 9

This passage is adapted from *Gladiator* by Philip Wylie. First published in 1930.

Once upon a time in Colorado lived a man named Abednego Danner and his wife, Matilda. Abednego Danner was a professor of biology
Line in a small college in the town of Indian Creek.
5 He was a spindling wisp of a man, with a nature drawn well into itself by the assaults of the world and particularly of the grim Mrs. Danner, who understood nothing and undertook all. Nevertheless these two lived modestly in a frame house on the
10 hem of Indian Creek and they appeared to be a settled and peaceful couple.

The chief obstacle to Mrs. Danner's placid dominion of her hearth was Professor Danner's laboratory, which occupied a room on the first floor
15 of the house. It was the one impregnable redoubt in her domestic stronghold. Neither threat nor entreaty would drive him and what she termed his "stinking, unchristian, unhealthy dinguses" from that room. After he had lectured vaguely to his classes on the
20 structure of the Paramecium caudatum and the law discovered by Mendel, he would shut the door behind himself, and all the fury of the stalwart, black-haired woman could not drive him out until his own obscure ends were served.

9

Which best summarizes Mrs. Danner's view towards Professor Danner's laboratory?

A) She wishes her husband would agree to get rid of the professor renting the room.

B) She worries that the fumes he creates will affect the health of her children.

C) She feels it is a despicable intrusion on her house that she wishes to get rid of.

D) She is frightened of the mysterious experiments that occur behind closed doors.

Question 10

This passage is adapted from "How blockchain could help musicians make a living from music" by Marcus O'Dair. ©2016 by Marcus O'Dair.

In the past few decades, it has grown harder for musicians to make a living, at least from recorded music. Falling CD sales, illegal downloads,
Line the low payments from legal music streaming
5 platforms, and a shift towards buying single tracks rather than whole albums all play their part.

Recently, a number of music industry projects have turned to a particular technology as a possible solution to these problems: blockchain.
10 Blockchain is the software that underpins bitcoin and other cryptocurrencies. Comprised of blocks of data cryptographically chained together in chronological order, it has two key features. It is immutable: data cannot be modified. And it is
15 distributed rather than centralized: many exact copies are maintained independently of each other.

Blockchain technology has been touted as the answer to problems facing industries as diverse as banking, the diamond trade, online gambling and
20 fashion—and now music.

10

Which of the following summarizes the technology of blockchain?

A) Blockchain is an important, novel way to store and transmit data.

B) Blockchain is a sophisticated security technology that prevents illegal downloading.

C) Blockchain is a currency that ensures musicians will get paid.

D) Blockchain is an encrypted software that helps stream music.

1. (A) is the correct answer. The passage notes how Mr. Verloc "made his way westward" at 10:30 in the morning, and then "through the park railings" observes the different actions of various men and women in the town after he pauses. (B) is incorrect because the opulence and luxury of the town is discussed in the next paragraph. (C) is incorrect because the passage gives no indication Mr. Verloc is late for work; indeed, the passage notes he was up at an "unusually early" time for him. (D) is incorrect because the given lines do not describe Mr. Verloc greeting anyone in town.

2. (C) is the correct answer. The third paragraph discusses how the brain encodes special information into "a sort of neuronal map" that functions as "a way of encoding space that maps information about your surroundings onto your brain cells." (A) is incorrect because the paragraph is not focused on brain cells, but how spatial information is recorded in them. (B) is incorrect because the paragraph says nothing about 3-D maps or firing neurons. (D) is incorrect because it is too general; the paragraph is focused on neuronal maps as a part of spatial thinking, not on different types of thinking in general.

3. (D) is the correct answer. The passage explains how first sentences "establish a contract with the reader about what is to come," citing Anna Karenina as one particular example. (A) is incorrect because the passage is focused on the effects of first lines in general; Anna Karenina is only given as one example. (B) is a possible inference of the passage, but it is not a summary of the passage's points, which discuss the function of first lines. (C) is incorrect because it is too general. The passage focuses on first lines, not writing in general.

4. (A) is the correct answer. The given lines note that the Earth's carbon cycle "is a fundamental element of the climate system," and offer the ocean as one example of a "carbon sink." (B) is incorrect because oceans are mentioned as an example, not the cause of the carbon cycle. (C) is incorrect because these lines do not suggest the carbon cycle is out of control (D) is incorrect because the given lines do not mention human interference.

5. (B) is the correct answer. First, the clerk calls the boy a thief, and then refuses to believe he has the money necessary to pay for the white rose the boy wants. He both sneers at the boy and implies he is a liar, so (B) is the best answer. (A) is incorrect as the clerk is not interested in selling to the boy, and wants him gone from his store. (C) is incorrect as the clerk is not indifferent or lazy, but rather actively mocks the boy. (D) is incorrect as the boy is buying the flower for his mother, and the clerk is suspicious and aggressive, the opposite of merry and encouraging.

6. (D) is the correct answer. The first paragraph notes that "Chinese TV networks found themselves in fierce competition with one another." The second paragraph goes on to say that, during this period, "dating shows started to transform," featuring matchmaking and dates that included games, roundtable chats, and more. Thus, a good summary would be (D). (A) is incorrect because the two paragraphs nowhere suggest that Chinese and Taiwanese networks were competing; a Taiwanese show is only brought up in the second paragraph as something from overseas that audiences watched. (B) is incorrect because the paragraphs describe the rise, not fall, of TV dating shows in China. (C) is incorrect because the two paragraphs give no indication that participants on the shows shaped the direction of the content.

7. (D) is the correct answer. The third paragraph states that "Ali's speed, agility, footwork, and general athleticism were among the attributes that most distinguished him from other competitors." (A) is incorrect because the third paragraph notes that Ali "was never considered to be among boxing's hardest punchers." (B) is incorrect because it reverses a statement in the third paragraph that notes some said Ali "was a heavyweight who moved like a lightweight." (C) is incorrect because the third paragraph notes that "more than one-third of his professional contests lasted their full scheduled duration," indicating that he did not always end contests quickly.

8. (C) is the correct answer. The passage indicates that rats can "adjust their subsequent behavior so as to invest more time and energy in helping those that helped them." (A) is incorrect as the passage discusses reciprocal behavior from rats who have already received favors from other rats; it does not suggest rats perform altruistic acts in order to receive such favors. (B) is incorrect because the passage focuses on rats helping partners who had helped them before, not rats working together to achieve common goals. (D) is incorrect because, although it uses language from the passage, nowhere does the passage mention one rat betraying another.

9. (C) is the correct answer. The second paragraph notes that Mrs. Danner feels Professor Danner's laboratory is "the one impregnable redoubt in her domestic stronghold," and that it is "chief obstacle to Mrs. Danner's placid dominion of her hearth," implying it is something she wants to be rid of. (B) is incorrect because no part of the passage suggests that Mrs. Danner has children, let alone that she is worried about their health. (A) is incorrect because the professor is Mrs. Danner's husband; the first paragraph notes he is a professor of biology in Indian Creek. (D) is incorrect because Mrs. Danner is never described as fearful, only disgusted by the laboratory.

10. (A) is the correct answer. The passage notes that blockchain is a "software" that is "comprised of blocks of data cryptographically chained together" with two key features: data cannot be changed, and data is distributed rather than centralized. This is consistent with (A). (B) is incorrect because blockchain is not a security technology. (C) is incorrect because blockchain is not a currency. (D) is incorrect because blockchain has much wider applications than just music; the passage also does not suggest that blockchain software helps "stream" music.

Describing Relationships
Part 7

Describing Relationships questions require you to evaluate relationships between people, events, and ideas. They may require you to make inferences about the nature of the relationship between characters based on their interactions. They may also require you to recognize cause-and-effect, sequence, or other relationships between events. Finally, they may require you to recognize specific logical relationships, comparing and contrasting ideas to determine whether they contradict, support, or add to one another or relate in other ways.

DIRECTIONS

Every passage or paired set of passages is accompanied by a number of questions. Read the passage or paired set of passages, then use what is said or implied in what you read and in any given graphics to choose the best answer to each question.

Question 1

This passage is adapted from "Outsider art can refashion how we think about mental illness" by Victoria Tischler. ©2015 by Victoria Tischler.

There exists a natural space for the mentally ill in the fashion and art worlds. Both of these worlds nurture and even celebrate eccentricity, flamboyance, and unfettered vision. Artists and designers are celebrated style-setters. Fashion and art in society represents the "cool", the "edgy" and the desirable. High fashion is fuelled on fantasy, innovation and experimentation.

Line 5

1

According to the passage, which of the following worlds are the most similar?

(A) Fashion and art

B) Mentally ill and fashion

C) Mentally ill and art

D) Mentally ill and experimentation

Question 2

This passage is adapted from "Earth's magnetic heartbeat, a thinner past and new alien worlds" by Alan Duffy. ©2016 by Alan Duffy.

A key model of Earth's history is that billions of years ago we must have had a thicker atmosphere than now. This thick atmosphere was assumed because the younger Sun was dimmer than it is now, meaning Earth would have frozen without the added greenhouse effect of extra air. Not the conditions one needs for life to arise, nor indeed were hints of any glaciers in ancient rocks of the time.

Line 5

2

The author indicates that, in comparison to Earth's atmosphere billions of years ago, today's atmosphere is

A) thicker.   *Trick*

(B)) thinner.

C) colder.

D) rockier.

Question 3

This passage is adapted from When the King Loses His Head and Other Stories by Leonid Andreyev. Translated by Archibald J. Wolfe. First published in 1919.

There stood once in a public place a black tower with massive fortress-like walls and a few grim bastioned windows. It had been built by robber
Line barons, but time swept them into the beyond, and
5 the tower became partly a prison for dangerous criminals and grave offenders, and partly a residence. In the course of centuries new structures were added to it, and were buttressed against the massive walls of the tower and against one another;
10 little by little it assumed the dimensions of a fair sized town set on a rock, with a broken skyline of chimneys, turrets and pointed roofs.

3

Compared to the earlier tower, the tower a few centuries after

A) was inhabited by robber barons.

B) had additional structures added onto it.

C) grew increasingly deserted.

D) became infamous for its ghosts.

Question 4

This passage is adapted from "What it is like to be a bee: insects can teach us about the origins of consciousness" by Colin Klein and Andrew Barron. ©2016 by Colin Klein and Andrew Barron.

Are insects merely tiny robots? Or, in the phrase popularized by the philosopher Thomas Nagel, is there something it is like to be a bee?
Line Until recently, most scientists and philosophers
5 would have laughed at the question. But now, research is challenging that dismissive attitude towards invertebrate consciousness.

We want to know whether insects can feel and sense the environment from a first-person
10 perspective. In philosophical jargon, this is sometimes called "phenomenal consciousness". Rocks, plants, and robots don't have this. Metaphorically speaking, they are dark inside. Conversely, most of us think that a dog running
15 for its dinner isn't just a little guided missile. It smells its food, wants to eat and sees the world around it as it runs.

4

According to the second paragraph, compared to animals that feel and sense their environment, plants

A) have dark interior thoughts.

B) act mechanically and robotically.

C) lack phenomenal consciousness.

D) sense the environment from a first-person perspective.

Question 5

This passage is adapted from "Ali Smith wins Baileys Prize—historical fiction is on the up" by Sally O'Reilly. ©2015 by Sally O'Reilly.

Conventional historical novels are fundamentally anachronistic. Planting a modern sensibility in the past should stretch credulity
Line beyond its limit, yet it's one of the tropes of
5 realist historical fiction that readers accept almost without question. The past is malleable and mysterious. Historical fiction also falls within the Venn diagram of literary fiction. (Historical novels have been awarded the Man Booker prize
10 for the past three years.) It's also fertile ground for experimentation – as demonstrated by the Goldsmiths prize for experimental fiction.

5

According to the passage, the relationship between historical fiction and literary fiction can be described by which of the following statements?

A) Historical fiction is a competitor to literary fiction.

B) Historical fiction is the precursor to literary fiction.

C) Historical fiction is more respected than literary fiction.

D) Historical fiction is one potential type of literary fiction.

Question 6

This passage is adapted from "Explainer: What do we know about why whales strand themselves?" by Mark Hindell. ©2011 by Mark Hindell.

There is a clear 10–12 year cycle in the number of whales stranding themselves on the beach. This is related to a climate feature known
Line as the zonal (westerly) and meridional (southerly)
5 winds. Persistent zonal and meridional winds result in colder, nutrient-rich waters being driven from the sub-Antarctic to southern Australia, resulting in increased biological activity in the water column during the spring months. This has
10 the effect of attracting whales closer to shore than in other years, making them more vulnerable (but obviously not causing them) to strand.

6

According to the passage, like persistent zonal winds, which of the following can contribute to increased cases of whales stranding themselves?

A) Westerly winds

B) Meridional winds

C) Nutrient-poor waters

D) Water columns

Question 7

This passage is adapted from Pixy's Holiday Journey by George Lang. First published in 1906.

There were three boys in the same class in the polytechnic school in the mountainous Odenwald country, in Hesse Darmstadt, who were such great
Line friends and inseparable companions that the other
5 pupils named them "the three-leaved clover." They were near of an age—about eleven—and near of a size; and their names were Fritz, Paul, and Franz. Fritz was an active, energetic boy, had coal black hair and bright, black eyes which looked out upon
10 the world with the alert glance of a squirrel in a cage. Paul had brown hair, brown eyes and brown complexion, was of reflective manner, and willing to follow where Fritz led. Franz was a robust boy with blonde hair, blue eyes, fair complexion, and
15 cheeks like cherries which had ripened in the sun. They had been firm friends ever since the day that Fritz had had a combat with a larger boy, and Franz and Paul ran to his assistance.

7

The three boys mentioned in the passage differed in

A) size.

B) age.

C) eye color.

D) height.

Question 8

This passage is adapted from "Behind Barbie's success—the cautious evolution of an iconic doll" by Isabelle Szmigin. ©2016 by Isabelle Szmigin.

Love her or hate her, Barbie is a cultural artifact, if not an icon. But other toy manufacturers were not going to stand still, and in
Line the last few years, Barbie has faced competition
5 from a whole host of new dolls vying for girls' and their parents' favor. In 2001 toy maker MGA Entertainment introduced the Bratz dolls, highly stylized made-up dolls that some suggest make Barbie look positively wholesome. In contrast,
10 the Lottie Doll made by British company Arklu is unmistakably a little girl with accessories built around decidedly middle class activities such as pony riding and ballet dancing.

8

According to the passage, which of the following correctly states the relationship of Bratz dolls to the Lottie Doll?

A) Both were developed by the British company Arklu.

B) Both were competitors to the Barbie doll.

C) Bratz dolls were more wholesome than the Lottie Doll.

D) The Lottie Doll was more popular than the Bratz dolls.

Question 9

This passage is adapted from "Nest: the art of birds" by Janine Burke. ©2012 by Janine Burke.

In terms of technique and virtuosity, birds are second to none. They've had millions of years to perfect their talents, much longer than homo
Line sapiens. Michelangelo may have painted the
5 Sistine Ceiling, but he didn't do it with a brush in his mouth and no other form of assistance. Birds are inventive, a need driven by evolution's struggle for survival. Art is sometimes regarded as a leisure activity: if people have the time (and
10 sufficient food and shelter), they can develop the ability to create pleasing and well-made objects.

9

The passage establishes that birds and Michelangelo differ in all of the following ways EXCEPT

A) birds have had longer to perfect their craft.

B) birds do their work with their tools in their mouths.

C) birds complete their masterpieces without help.

D) birds create their artwork over years instead of months.

Question 10

This passage is adapted from "Explainer: what is the molecular clock?" by Al Tanner. ©2015 by Al Tanner.

Sometimes known as the "evolutionary clock" or "gene clock," the molecular clock has foundations in the biological concept of
Line heredity: all life inherits information in the form
5 of genetic molecules (usually DNA) from the previous generation. Since this material gradually changes over time, it can be used to measure how long ago evolutionary events took place. On the largest scale, the molecular clock has enabled
10 paleontologists to unveil the story of evolution over millions of years. And on the smallest scale, epidemiologists are able to trace the spread of disease over mere decades.

10

The passage implies that paleontologists differ from epidemiologists in that they

A) study the molecular clock.

B) focus on how DNA affects heredity.

C) study much broader timescales.

D) are biologists and not chemists.

Question 11

This passage is adapted from "Online ads know who you are, but can they change you too?" by Rebecca Walker Reczek, Christopher A. Summers, and Robert W. Smith. ©2016 by Rebecca Walker Reczek, Christopher A. Summers, and Robert W. Smith.

Behavioral targeting uses information about nearly everything you do online—clicks, searches, social media, what you've bought and browsed—
Line to select ads that marketers think will appeal to
5   you based on your unique online behavior. Our recent research shows, however, that these ads do more than reflect your past or future preferences. They can change how you see yourself in fundamental ways.

11

Based on the passage, which choice best describes the relationship between online ads and self-perception?

A) Self-perception influences the selection of online ads.

B) Online ads can influence self-perception.

C) Self-perception is one important part of online ads.

D) Online ads use behavioral targeting like self-perception.

1. (A) is the correct answer. The passage states that "There exists a natural space for the mentally ill in the fashion and art worlds. Both of these worlds nurture and even celebrate eccentricity, flamboyance, and unfettered vision." Here, "these worlds" refers to the fashion and art worlds, which the passage says are working in the same way, so (A) is correct. The passage mentions there is a space for the mentally ill in these two worlds, but does not compare the mentally ill to these worlds, so (B), (C), and (D) can be eliminated.

2. (B) is the correct answer. The passage states that "billions of years ago we must have had a thicker atmosphere than now," meaning today's atmosphere is thinner. (A) is incorrect because the passage states the atmosphere is thinner, not thicker than it used to be. (C) is incorrect because the passage mentions the Sun was dimmer and the atmosphere was colder in the past, not today. (D) is incorrect because the author never states that the atmosphere is rocky.

3. (B) is the correct answer. The passage notes that "in the course of centuries new structures were added" to the fortress. (A) is incorrect because the passage indicates the tower "had been built by robber barons" which doesn't necessarily mean they also inhabited it. (C) is incorrect because the passage states that the tower becomes more crowded, not less. (D) is incorrect because the passage does not mention ghosts.

4. (C) is the correct answer. The passage defines "phenomenal consciousness" as the ability to "feel and sense the environment from a first-person perspective." Rocks, plants, and robots are offered as counterexamples to insects that definitively lack this trait. (A) is too literal; the passage states that plants may be "dark inside," meaning they lack consciousness, which is mentioned multiple times throughout the passage. (B) is incorrect because the passage asks earlier if insects act robotically, but does not connect this to plants. (D) is incorrect because the passage says that plants, as opposed to (potentially) insects, lack a first-person perspective, along with rocks and robots.

5. (D) is the correct answer. The passage says that "historical fiction also falls within the Venn diagram of literary fiction," meaning it is a subset. Historical fiction is not mentioned as a competitor (A) or precursor (C), so both options are incorrect. (D) is incorrect because the passage does not compare the respect levels of the two types of literature.

6. (B) is the correct answer. The passage notes that "persistent zonal and meridional winds" create "increased biological activity in the water column," which in turn leads whales closer to shore and being stranded. (A) is incorrect because westerly winds are associated with zonal winds, not separate from them. (C) is incorrect because it is nutrient-rich waters that help contribute to whales stranding themselves. (D) is incorrect because the water column is a location, not a factor in whether or not whales strand themselves.

7. (C) is the correct answer. The passage mentions that Fritz has black eyes, Paul has brown eyes, and Fritz has blues. The boys "were near of an age" and "near of a size," so (A), (B), and (D) can be eliminated.

8. (B) is the correct answer. The passage mentions that "other toy manufacturers were not going to stand still" as Barbie gained in popularity, and mentions two examples, Bratz dolls and the Lottie Doll, who competed for market share. (A) is incorrect because Arklu developed the Lottie Doll, but not the Bratz dolls. (C) is incorrect because the Lottie Doll was more wholesome; the passage states that the Bratz dolls made "Barbie look positively wholesome" in contrast, while the Lottie Doll featured a little girl participating in middle-class activities. (D) is incorrect because the passage does not touch on the relative popularity of these dolls.

9. (D) is the correct answer. The passage does not compare the length of time it takes birds to create their nests to the length of time it takes Michelangelo to complete his creations. (A) is incorrect because the passage does note that birds have "had millions of years to perfect their talents," while Michelangelo has not. (B) and (C) are incorrect because the passage states that "Michelangelo may have painted the Sistine Ceiling, but he didn't do it with a brush in his mouth and no other form of assistance."

10. (C) is the correct answer. The passage notes that the molecular clock helps "paleontologists to unveil the story of evolution over millions of years," while "epidemiologists are able to trace the spread of disease over mere decades." (A) is incorrect because both use the molecular clock in their work. (B) is incorrect because neither focuses on how DNA affects heredity. (D) is incorrect because the passage is not concerned with classifying either profession under the fields of biology or chemistry.

11. (B) is the correct answer. The passage states that online ads "can change how you see yourself in fundamental ways," which is another way to say self-perception. (A) is incorrect because it reverses the correct relationship. (C) is incorrect because self-perception is never indicated as a part of online ads. (D) is incorrect because the passage does not state that self-perception is a type of behavioral targeting.

Vocabulary in Context
Part 8

Vocabulary in Context questions require you to identify a word or phrase that means the same thing as another word or phrase as it is used in the passage. They will typically focus on words or phrases that have many possible meanings, and therefore require you to evaluate context rather than relying merely on memorized vocabulary. You may need to avoid choices that have a generally appropriate sense or tone but are too imprecise, have at least one dictionary definition that is very close to the sense being used but carry tone or connotations that do not match the context, or very closely match some dictionary definition of the word or phrase being asked about that is not the sense being used in the passage.

DIRECTIONS

Every passage or paired set of passages is accompanied by a number of questions. Read the passage or paired set of passages, then use what is said or implied in what you read and in any given graphics to choose the best answer to each question.

Question 1

This passage is adapted from "Explainer: surrealism" by Natalya Lusty. ©2016 by Natalya Lusty.

As the longest-running avant-garde movement of the 20th century, Surrealism's scope and richness is perhaps unparalleled in its influence of modern
Line art and culture. Largely an aesthetic movement—
5 embracing painting, sculpture, photography, film, poetry, novels, fashion, and advertising—its engagement with psychoanalysis, Marxism, and philosophy helped shape its distinctive intellectual, political, and creative endeavors.

 1

As used in line 3, "unparalleled" most nearly means

A) linear.

B) circular.

C) unmatched.

D) unprecedented.

Question 2

This passage is adapted from "Underwater microscope provides new views of ocean-floor sea creatures in their natural setting" by Jules Jaffe, Andrew Mullen, and Tali Treibitz. ©2016 by Jules Jaffe, Andrew Mullen, and Tali Treibitz.

When researchers bring marine samples back to the lab, it's impossible to exactly mimic the environment they came from—what we observe
Line might not perfectly reflect creatures' real lives.
5 Better, then, to bring the lab to the ocean.

 2

The authors use the phrase "exactly mimic" (line 2) most nearly to mean:

A) accurately mock.

B) faithfully impersonate.

C) precisely replicate.

D) correctly parody.

Question 3

This passage is adapted from The Old Stone House by Anne March. First published in 1884.

Aunt Faith sat alone on the piazza, and sad thoughts crowded into her heart. It was her birthday,—the first day of June,—and she could
Line look back over more than half a century, with that
5 mournful retrospect which birthdays are apt to bring.

The phrase "crowded into" (line 2) most likely means

(A) filled

B) congested

C) grew

D) destroyed

Question 4

This passage is adapted from "As more vulnerabilities are discovered, is it time to uninstall antivirus software?" by David Glance. ©2016 by David Glance.

For years everyone has been told that they should run antivirus software on their computers for the best possible protection against the ever-
Line growing tide of viruses, Trojans, and general
5 malware on the Internet.

As used in lines 3 - 4, "ever-growing tide" is closest in meaning to

A) timeless problem.

B) enlarging danger.

(C) always expanding number.

D) heavily impactful wave.

Question 5

This passage is adapted from "Grey dawn or the twilight years? Let's talk about growing old" by Kate Burridge and Réka Benczes. ©2016 by Kate Burridge and Réka Benczes.

Ageism appeared in the early colonial period, and was fueled by Australia's perception of itself as a "young society."

As used in line 2, "fueled" most nearly means

A) inspired.

B) gassed.

(C) driven.

D) maintained.

Question 6

This passage is adapted from "Cunning drongo cries wolf in the 'language' of other species" by Christopher N. Templeton. ©2014 by Christopher N. Templeton.

A new study published in the journal Science has shown how a species of African birds called fork-tailed drongos will cry wolf in a bid to steal
Line a free lunch from those they alarm. They wait for
5 an unsuspecting pied babbler or meerkat to find an especially tasty morsel such as a lizard or cricket. Then the drongo screams blue murder and, as the terrified animal runs for cover, swoops in and nabs the abandoned meal.

As it is used in line 3, the word "bid" can reasonably be said to mean all of the following EXCEPT:

A) attempt.

B) endeavor.

C) effort.

(D) offer.

Question 7

This passage is adapted from The Bee Hunters by Gustave Aimard. First published in 1865.

On the 27th July, 1858, a cavalier, mounted on a magnificent mustang, was carelessly following the banks of the Rio Bermejo. This cavalier, clad
Line in the leather dress worn by Mexican hunters, was,
5 as far as one could judge a man not more than thirty years of age.

7

As used in line 5, the word "judge" most nearly means

A) ascertain.

B) critique.

C) arbitrate.

D) mediate.

Question 8

This passage is adapted from "Antimatter changed physics, and the discovery of antimemories could revolutionize neuroscience" by Harriet Dempsey-Jones. ©2016 by Harriet Dempsey-Jones.

A new theory, backed by animal research and mathematical models, suggests that at the same time that a memory is created, an "antimemory"
Line is also spawned—that is, connections between
5 neurons are made that provide the exact opposite pattern of electrical activity to those forming the original memory.

8

As it is used in line 4, the word "spawned" most precisely refers to

A) the death of an antimemory.

B) the creation of an antimemory.

C) the destruction of a memory.

D) the connection of two neurons.

Question 9

This passage is adapted from "Computing changed the 'flow' of watching television" by Bjorn Nansen. ©2016 by Bjorn Nansen.

Historically, we used to think of television as part of the mass media, along with radio, newspapers, and so on. But with the turn to
Line computational media, sometimes known as "new
5 media", we began redefining established questions around audiences and ownership of media. This computational shift is particularly evident if we contrast the experience of television from an early broadcast in 1956 with today.

9

As it is used in line 7, the word "evident" most nearly means

A) verified.

B) clear.

C) distinct.

D) uncertain.

Question 10

This passage is adapted from "Number-crunching Higgs boson: meet the world's largest distributed computer grid" by Tom Whyntie. ©2015 by Tom Whyntie.

The world's largest science experiment, the Large Hadron Collider, has potentially delivered one of physics' "Holy Grails" in the form of the
Line subatomic particle known as the Higgs boson.
5 A huge amount of data has allowed scientists to study properties of the Higgs boson in great detail.

10

The word "delivered" in line 2 refers to how scientists at the Large Hadron Collider

A) were able to transport the Higgs boson to a new experimental site.

B) published a groundbreaking paper on one of the fundamental particles.

C) consulted with scientists outside of their country about data on the Higgs boson.

D) revealed evidence of an important subatomic particle through its collected data.

1. (C) is the correct answer. "Unparalleled" means having no equal or match in skill, as unmatched also means. (A) and (B) can be eliminated because "unparalleled" does not refer to any literal geometric shape, which are not discussed at all in this passage. (D) is incorrect because "unprecedented" implies something that has not happened before, where the use of "unparalleled" only means "unsurpassed" or "unmatched."

2. (C) is the correct answer. The authors use "exactly mimic" to describe how researchers are trying to duplicate, or replicate, the exact environment that marine samples came from. (A) is incorrect because "mock," like "mimic" means to act like, however "mock" means to act like in order to make fun of, while the passage is merely talking about replicating something to study, not make fun of, something. (B) and (D) are incorrect because the researchers are trying to make a copy of an environment in their labs, not pretend to be one or copy it for the purpose of making fun of it, as " impersonate" and "parody" mean, respectfully.

3. (A) is the correct answer. "Crowded into" means to fill something, in this case Aunt Faith's heart with sad thoughts. (B) is incorrect because to "congest" something means to fill it up but specifically to the point of clogging it, whereas "crowded into" only matches the filling up part of "congest"'s meaning. (C) is incorrect because "crowded into" means Aunt Faith's sad thoughts entered her heart at such a rate as to almost fill it, whereas "grew" implies they were born there. (D) is incorrect because it is not a synonym of "crowded."

4. (C) is the correct answer. "Ever-growing tide" is meant to express the continued growth in numbers of viruses and other malware. (A) is incorrect because viruses and other computer bugs are not timeless or eternal. (B) is incorrect because "ever-growing tide" is only "of viruses, Trojans, and general malware," not necessarily the danger they pose. (D) is incorrect because the "tide" is "of viruses, Trojans, and general malware," not a literal wave.

5. (C) is the correct answer. "Fueled" means to power or feed something, which makes sense contextually, since the passage states that Australia saw itself as a "young society," an idea that could logically lead to developing prejudices based on the age of a non-majority group of people. (A) and (D) are incorrect because "fueled" means to feed or power something, not "inspire" or necessarily "maintain." (B) is incorrect because "gassed" as a verb means to fill something with gas, which is not possible when speaking about ageism and perception, both of which are intangible and thus impossible to physically fill with gas, as this word implies.

6. (D) is the correct answer. "Bid" is used when describing the action of attempting to steal a free lunch, so (A), (B), and (C) can all be eliminated, given that they are synonyms. This only leaves (D), which means to give instead of take something, and thus is the correct choice.

7. (A) is the correct answer. "Judge" here means "tell," which is synonymous with "ascertain." (B) is incorrect because the sense of "judge" here is more evaluation than critique. (C) is incorrect because this word means to resolve a conflict, which "judge" is not synonymous with. (D) is incorrect because this word means to balance two opposing sides to come to an agreement, which "judge" does not mean.

8. (B) is the correct answer. "Spawned" means to be born or created, which this answer option states. (A) is incorrect as it states the opposite meaning of "spawned." (C) is incorrect because the passage does not imply a memory is destroyed in this process, only that an "antimemory" is created. (D) is incorrect because "spawned" is referring to antimemory, not to connections between neurons.

9. (B) is the correct answer. The word "evident" means obvious, or clear, the latter of which this answer option states. (A) is incorrect because "evident" is used to refer to the apparent obviousness of the computational shift, not any verification or corroboration of the shift. (C) is incorrect because the sentence is not implying the computational shift is "distinct" or different from anything. (D) is incorrect because it is not a synonym of "evident."

10. (D) is the correct answer. The passage discusses how a large amount of data collected by scientists at the Large Hadron Collider has allowed them to study the Higgs boson. Thus, it is most likely that "delivered" here refers to this accumulation of data that provides additional insights into this particle. (A) is incorrect because it is too literal. There is no evidence that the scientists were physically transporting the particle. (B) is incorrect because there is no mention of any papers, groundbreaking or otherwise in this passage. (C) is incorrect because "delivered" contains no connotations of consultation, nor does the passage mention this kind of cooperation between scientists.

Ivy Global

Section 2
Rhetoric

Questions in the Rhetoric domain test your ability to analyze the arguments in a passage, the structure of the passage, the purpose behind specific rhetorical choices, and the points of view of characters or authors.

There are 8 specific question types in this domain:

Development			
RW	Word Choice	RP	Purpose
RO	Overall Structure	RC	Finding Arguments
RPW	Internal Structure	RR	Author's Reasoning
RV	Point of View	RE	Author's Evidence

Word Choice
Part 1

Word Choice questions require you to interpret the effects of word choices in the passage. They may ask about individual words or short phrases. They may ask you to determine how the word choice influences the tone or emphasis of the passage, satisfies a certain rhetorical goal, or shapes the overall meaning, but they do not require you merely to interpret the meaning or tone of the word or phrase being asked about.

DIRECTIONS

Every passage or paired set of passages is accompanied by a number of questions. Read the passage or paired set of passages, then use what is said or implied in what you read and in any given graphics to choose the best answer to each question.

Question 1

This passage is adapted from Two Prisoners by Thomas Nelson Page. First published in 1898.

One day, a fat, fawn-colored puppy came waddling up to Mildred on the street. Mildred begged her father to let her keep the dog. He said
Line she might, until they could find the owner, but
5 that it was a beautiful puppy and the owner would probably want him. Mildred took him to her veranda and played with him, and that night she actually smuggled him into her bed.

1

The author uses the term "smuggled" (line 8) to indicate that Mildred

A) stole the puppy from its owner.

B) ran away from her home with the puppy.

C) cuddled with the puppy in her bed.

D) covertly took the puppy with her to sleep.

Question 2

This passage is adapted from "Rhythm on the brain, and why we can't stop dancing" by Peter Keller. ©2016 by Peter Keller.

Music and dance are far from idle pastimes. They are universal forms of expression and deeply rewarding activities that fulfill diverse social
Line functions. Both feature in all the world's cultures
5 and throughout history.

2

In line 1, the phrase "idle pastimes" is intended as

A) a contrast to the activities of music and dance.

B) the category that includes both music and dance.

C) an example of some forms of music and dance.

D) the definition of art forms like music and dance.

Question 3

This passage is adapted from "Using computers to better understand art" by Ricky J. Sethi. ©2016 by Ricky J. Sethi.

Computer analysis of even previously well-studied images can yield new relationships that aren't necessarily apparent to people. In fact, these techniques could actually help us discover how
Line humans perceive artworks. Art scholars believe
5 that a strong indicator of an artist's style is the use of color and how it varies across the different parts of a painting. Digital tools can aid this analysis.

3

When the author asserts that computer analysis can "yield new relationships" (line 2), he most likely means that computer analysis can

A) help bring together scientists and artists.

B) educate students on different artistic techniques.

C) illuminate connections between art and perception.

D) aid scholars in analyzing which colors are most popular.

Question 4

This passage is adapted from "From perspiration to world domination—the extraordinary science of sweat" by Vybarr Cregan-Reid. ©2016 by Vybarr Cregan-Reid.

There are distinct thermoregulatory advantages to being a two-legged human. Being merely upright, for example, means that less of the sun
Line hits you when it's at its hottest. The bipedal
5 human exposes only about 7% of their surface area to sunlight; it is triple this for a quadruped. This fact alone means that being on two legs enables you to move with greater heat efficiency.

4

Use of the phrase "greater heat efficiency" (line 8) to describe one of the benefits of being two-legged is meant to refer to

A) internal temperature regulation.

B) changes in weather patterns.

C) experimental lab conditions.

D) intensity of the sun's rays.

Question 5

This passage is adapted from The Girl on the Boat by P.G. Wodehouse. First published in 1920.

Through the curtained windows of the furnished flat which Mrs. Horace Hignett had rented for her stay in New York, rays of golden
Line sunlight peeped in like the foremost spies of some
5 advancing army. It was a fine summer morning. The hands of the Dutch clock in the hall pointed to thirteen minutes past nine; those of the ormolu clock in the sitting-room to eleven minutes past ten; those of the carriage clock on the bookshelf
10 to fourteen minutes to six. In other words, it was exactly eight; and Mrs. Hignett acknowledged the fact by moving her head on the pillow, opening her eyes, and sitting up in bed. She always woke at eight precisely.

5

In the passage, the phrase "acknowledged the fact" (lines 11 - 12) likely indicates that Mrs. Hignett

A) was skeptical of the varying times on the clocks.

B) checked the time on her watch before moving.

C) was aware of the time and responded to it.

D) resented the need to wake up so early.

Question 6

This passage is adapted from "In loud rooms our brains 'hear' in a different way—new findings" by Joachim Gross and Hyojin Park. ©2016 by Joachim Gross and Hyojin Park.

When we talk face-to-face, we exchange many more signals than just words. We communicate using our body posture, facial

Line expressions, and head and eye movements; but
5 also through the rhythms that are produced when someone is speaking.

6

When the author says that "we exchange many more signals" (lines 1 - 2), she most likely means that we

A) use encoded words to express meaning.

B) make heavy use of nonverbal communication.

C) can never know how many nonverbal signals humans use.

D) utilize body posture to convey subtle messages.

Question 7

This passage is adapted from "Probing Cervantes's pages offers more than his bones ever will" by Tyler Fisher. ©2014 by Tyler Fisher.

After years spent securing funds and permissions, a team of forensic scientists and historians have launched an intensive search

Line for the remains of Miguel de Cervantes, author
5 of Don Quixote. Using the latest techniques of infrared imaging and ground-penetrating radar, the Spanish researchers are scanning the floors and walls of the Trinitarian Convent Church in Madrid, where Cervantes is most likely entombed.
10 The full investigation may last as long as a year. The first few weeks will involve meticulously mapping voids in the floors and niches in the walls to determine the most promising burial sites, while ensuring minimal disturbance to the cloistered
15 nuns who still reside in the convent.

7

When the author states that researchers are trying to find "the most promising burial sites" (line 13), he most likely means that the researchers are

A) searching for the proper site to bury deceased nuns residing in the convent.

B) seeking out the most likely places where the remains of Cervantes can be found.

C) trying to locate the place where Don Quixote was buried.

D) looking for other holy sites in the Trinitarian Convent Church.

Question 8

This passage is adapted from "Food allergies linked to overactive immune system at birth" by Leonard C. Harrison, Peter Vuillermin, and Yuxia Zhang. ©2016 by Leonard C. Harrison, Peter Vuillermin, and Yuxia Zhang.

New research has found children who are born with overly active immune cells are more likely to develop allergies to milk, eggs, peanuts, wheat,

Line and other common foods. This finding could
5 lead to future treatments for babies to prevent childhood food allergies. We discovered changes in immune cells at birth that were associated with an increased risk of babies developing food allergies in the first year of age. In essence, these
10 babies have immune systems that are "primed" for allergic disease by the time they are born.

8

The passage's use of the phrase "common foods" (line 4) most likely refers to

A) the most dangerous foods for children.

B) the major food groups.

C) children's favorite foods.

D) foods that are regularly consumed.

Question 9

This passage is adapted from The Wall Street Girl by Frederick Orin Bartlett. First published in 1915.

Before beginning to read the interesting document in front of him, Jonas Barton, senior member of Barton & Saltonstall, paused to clean
Line his glasses rather carefully, in order to gain
5 sufficient time to study for a moment the tall, good-looking young man who waited indifferently on the other side of the desk. He had not seen his late client's son since the latter had entered college—a black-haired, black-eyed lad of seventeen,
10 impulsive in manner and speech. The intervening four years had tempered him a good deal.

9

In saying "tempered him a good deal," (line 11), the narrator implies that the young man

A) is no longer as impulsive as he was when he was younger.

B) has an even more volatile temper than in his youth.

C) is both bigger and stronger than when Jonas last saw him.

D) grew into a savvy negotiator and businessman.

Question 10

This passage is adapted from "How cute things hijack our brains and drive behavior" by Morten L. Kringelbach, Alan Stein, and Eloise Stark. ©2016 by Morten L. Kringelbach, Alan Stein, and Eloise Stark.

Together with our colleagues Marc Bornstein from the National Institute of Child Health and Human Development and Catherine Alexander
Line from the University of Oxford, we have reviewed
5 the existing research on the topic and discovered that cuteness is more than something purely visual. It works by involving all the senses and strongly attracting our attention by sparking rapid brain activity. In fact, cuteness may be one of
10 the strongest forces that shape our behavior—potentially making us more compassionate.

10

The phrase "more than something purely visual" mentioned in lines 6 - 7 most directly refers to the fact that cuteness

A) works primarily by sound rather than sight.

B) appeals to not just one sense, but many.

C) often takes unexpected visual forms.

D) makes us more compassionate.

Question 11

This passage is adapted The System of Doctor Tarr and Professor Fether" by Edgar Allan Poe. First published in 1845.

As we rode up to the gateway, I perceived it slightly open, and the visage of a man peering through. In an instant afterward, this man came
Line forth, accosted my companion by name, shook him
5 cordially by the hand, and begged him to alight. It was Monsieur Maillard himself. He was a portly, fine-looking gentleman of the old school, with a polished manner, and a certain air of gravity, dignity, and authority which was very impressive.
10 My friend, having presented me, mentioned

my desire to inspect the establishment, and received Monsieur Maillard's assurance that he would show me all attention, now took leave, and I saw him no more.

11

In the context of the passage, the author's use of the phrase "begged him to alight" (line 5) is primarily meant to convey the idea that Monsieur Maillard

A) wishes for the narrator's companion to descend and enter the establishment.

B) is in desperate need for funds to keep his establishment running.

C) needs the narrator to enter the building quickly in case of any onlookers.

D) appears to be a friendly but insecure host.

Question 12

This passage is adapted from "Why there's fresh hope for stroke patients who are struggling to communicate" by Marian Brady. ©2016 by Marian Brady.

Language is complicated. To read and understand the written word, for instance, you need visual skills to see the words, sustained attention to read to the end of each sentence, and
Line a memory of the meaning of earlier sentences.
5 Meanwhile, spoken communication can be undermined by stroke-related impairments to the muscles required to produce speech (dysarthria), by stroke-related impairments to hearing ability, and by other effects such as depression or fatigue.
10

12

When the author states that "spoken communication can be undermined by stroke-related impairments" (lines 5 - 6), she most likely means that

A) stroke patients can write better than they can speak.

B) speech impairments can lead to strokes.

C) strokes can cause speech-related damages.

D) conversation is more difficult with stroke patients.

Question 13

This passage is adapted from "Accounting for power: the history of an industry that shaped the world" by Christina Ionela Neokleous. ©2016 by Christina Ionela Neokleous.

In ancient Mesopotamia, Babylonia, Egypt, Rome, and Greece, the world saw the first flowering of an industry that would document and
Line shape its progress. Wealthy landowners, emperors,
5 princes and kings would keep track of their gold and grain using papyrus, stones or wooden tablets to keep records after purchases and sales. This was how the art of accountancy was born.

13

When the author says that "the world saw the first flowering of an industry" (lines 2 - 3), she most likely means that

A) ancient rulers witnessed the first blooming of the industrial age.

B) accounting had a number of eyewitnesses in its early years.

C) workers in Mesopotamia, Babylonia, Egypt, Rome, and Greece were admired throughout the world.

D) certain ancient regions observed the early development of a new business.

Question 14

This passage is adapted from "Particle physics discovery raises hope for a theory of everything" by Vakhtang Kartvelishvill. ©2015 by Vakhtang Kartvelishvill.

The standard model of particle physics, which describes every particle we know of and how they interact, was given much credence when *Line* the Higgs boson was discovered in 2012. Now,
5 measurements of a rare particle-physics decay at the Large Hadron Collider offer further support for the model—but also hints at ways to find out what lies beyond it.

The standard model is cherished by physicists
10 because it can explain most of the fundamental phenomena in nature by referencing just a handful of elementary particles. These particles include quarks (one of the components of an atom) and electron-like particles called leptons—along with
15 their so-called antiparticles which are identical but have opposite charge.

14

What does the author suggest in line 9 when he states that "the standard model is cherished by physicists"?

A) Physicists are attached to the reigning model of particle physics.

B) Physicists are grateful for new developments in the field of particle physics.

C) Physicists greatly prefer the older models of particle physics.

D) Physicists feel nostalgia toward earlier models of particle physics.

Question 15

This passage is adapted from The Halo by Bettina von Hutten. First published in 1907.

A straight stretch of dusty Norman road dappled with grotesque shadows of the ancient apple-trees that, bent as if in patient endurance of *Line* the weight of their thick-set scarlet fruit, edged it
5 on both sides.

Under one of the trees, his back against its gnarled trunk, sat an old man playing a cracked fiddle. He played horribly, wrenching discords from the poor instrument, grinning with a kind of
10 vacant malice as it shrieked aloud in agony.

15

In the second paragraph, the phrase "shrieked aloud in agony" (line 10) is meant to express how

A) the man's singing voice was frightening and loud.

B) the instrument the man was playing sounded.

C) the audience responded to the old man's performance.

D) the wind sounded ripping through the apple-trees.

Question 16

This passage is adapted from "Diamond geysers: rule-breaking Iceland completes its miracle economic escape" by Alan Shipman. ©2016 by Alan Shipman.

Disgruntled Icelanders recently forced their prime minister to quit, and are threatening to hand power to self-styled pirates at an early election. *Line* But whereas other European voters are culling
5 traditional parties out of weakness, Iceland's are rebelling out of strength. In contrast to eurozone countries that remain deeply constrained by excessive external debt, Iceland has just paid down its foreign obligations by a cool US$61
10 billion, returning them to the safe 2006 level.

16

In the context of the passage, the statement in lines 4 - 6 most nearly means that

A) Europe is suffering from a number of contentious revolutions.

B) Icelanders are making political changes out of a position of power.

C) Iceland has overthrown its government and handed power to pirates.

D) Iceland plans to take over the rest of Europe in the next elections.

Question 17

This passage is adapted from "Despite some progress, the Olympics is still an uneven playing field" by Leigh Robinson. ©2016 by Leigh Robinson.

The argument that taking part in the Olympic Games raises the international profile of a country just doesn't stack up. How many people
Line can remember the 205 nations that took part in
5 London? Probably the same amount that will remember all the countries that take part in Rio in 2016. Because it is sad but true that a significant number of nations will appear at the opening ceremony on August 5 and then simply fade into
10 obscurity until the games in Tokyo in 2020.

17

When the author says that many nations will "fade into obscurity until the games in Tokyo in 2020" (line 10), she most likely means that these nations will

A) disappear from the world map unless they appear at the next Olympics.

B) lose political power in the gap between the Olympic games.

C) struggle to achieve athlete recognition outside of the Olympic games.

D) not be remembered by the international community until the next Olympics.

Question 18

This passage is adapted from "Animals in research: C. elegans (roundworm)" by Hannah Nicholas. ©2013 by Hannah Nicholas.

One species of worm—Caenorhabditis elegans—has contributed more to medical science in the past few decades than you might think
Line possible. Some 50 years ago, South African
5 biologist Sydney Brenner identified development and the nervous system as the next big challenge of biology. Brenner went in search of a model organism that would be suitable for studies of development and the nervous system. A small
10 animal that could be easily cultivated and that had a short life cycle would be required. Ultimately, Brenner alighted on a nematode (roundworm) called Caenorhabditis elegans.

18

In the context of the passage as a whole, it is most reasonable to infer that the phrase "has contributed more to medical science in the past few decades than you might think possible" (lines 2 - 4) means that

A) the Caenorhabditis elegans has been instrumental in conducting and publishing biological research.

B) the nematode has certain developmental problems that have yielded important insights for scientists.

C) the Caenorhabditis elegans has been used successfully by researchers to advance knowledge of development and the nervous system.

D) the roundworm has helped scientists solve an important neurological development disorder.

Question 19

This passage is adapted from The Blockade Runners" by Jules Verne. First published in 1865.

The Clyde was the first river whose waters were lashed into foam by a steam-boat. It was in 1812 when the steamer called the Comet ran
Line between Glasgow and Greenock, at the speed of
5 six miles an hour. Since that time more than a million of steamers or packet-boats have plied this Scotch river, and the inhabitants of Glasgow must be as familiar as any people with the wonders of steam navigation.

19

In the context of the passage, what do the lines 1 - 2 mean?

A) The Clyde was the first steamboat on the Scotch river.

B) The first river that a steamboat traveled on was The Clyde.

C) The Clyde was the first site polluted substantially by steamboats.

D) Eventually, steamboats could no longer travel on the shallow Clyde.

Question 20

This passage is adapted from "Kennewick Man will be reburied, but quandaries around human remains won't" by Samuel Redman. ©2016 by Samuel Redman.

A mysterious set of 9,000-year-old bones, unearthed nearly 20 years ago in Washington, is finally going home. Following bitter disputes, five
Line Native American groups in the Pacific Northwest
5 have come together to facilitate the reburial of an individual they know as "Ancient One." One of the most complete prehistoric human skeletons discovered in North America, "Kennewick Man" also became the most controversial.

20

In the context of the passage, the author's statement in lines 1 - 3 most nearly means that

A) the spirit of the Kennewick Man can finally rest upon his reburial.

B) an ancient artifact is being returned to a Native American museum.

C) the Kennewick Man's remains are going to be reburied.

D) a set of ancient remains are being returned to the deceased man's family.

1. (D) is the correct answer. "Smuggled" here is used to indicate that Mildred snuck the puppy into her bed that night to sleep with her. (A) is incorrect, as Mildred found, not stole, the puppy. (B) is incorrect because Mildred did not run away from home. (C) is incorrect because "smuggled" does not have an alternate meaning of "cuddled," even though it is possible that Mildred did cuddle with the puppy.

2. (A) is the correct answer. The passage states that music and dance are "far from idle pastimes," indicating that music and dance do not fall into this category and are, in fact, opposite to it. (B), (C), and (D) can all be eliminated because they lose this meaning of contrast.

3. (C) is the correct answer. The passage states that new techniques of computer analysis "could actually help us discover how humans perceive artworks," giving the potential example of art scholars analyzing color using digital tools. (A) is incorrect because the passage does not mention bringing artists together with scientists, only bringing a new tool to art scholars. (B) is incorrect because the passage doesn't touch on student education. (D) is incorrect because the popularity of colors are never mentioned in the passage.

4. (A) is the correct answer. The passage is focused on the benefits of being bipedal (versus being a quadruped), noting that less of the body is exposed to the sun. As the earlier part of the passage references "thermoregulatory advantages," it can be inferred that "greater heat efficiency" here refers to this internal temperature regulation. (B), (C), and (D) are all incorrect because "greater heat efficiency" is meant to describe something that is an advantage of "being on two legs," an advantage which the passage never mentions as having the power to control weather patterns, lab conditions, or the sun's rays.

5. (C) is the correct answer. "Acknowledged the fact" here is used as an expression simply to mean that Mrs. Hignett responded to the time, 8:00, by opening her eyes and sitting up. It is reasonable to infer that she was aware of the time and responded to it in this way, as "she always woke at eight precisely." (A) is incorrect because the passage does not indicate Mrs. Hignett is skeptical of the other clocks. (B) is incorrect because Mrs. Hignett does not check the time on her watch in the passage. (D) is incorrect because the passage gives no indication Mrs. Hignett is resentful.

6. (B) is the correct answer. The passage explains that we "communicate using our body posture, facial expressions, and head and eye movements," all forms of nonverbal communication. Since "many more signals" is followed by "than just words," it can be inferred that the author is talking specifically about nonverbal communication. (A) is incorrect because the author is talking about nonverbal communication, not encoded words. (C) is incorrect because the author is merely comparing the number of verbal to nonverbal communicative signals humans exchange when speaking face-to-face, not talking about nonverbal signals only. (D) is incorrect because it is too specific; body posture is only mentioned as just one example of nonverbal communication.

7. (B) is the correct answer. The researchers are already searching for the remains of Cervantes in the passage; this phrase is used to indicate that they are trying to determine the most likely places where they may find the author, before they start digging. (A) is incorrect because the researchers are not looking for locations to bury the nuns. (C) is incorrect because the researchers are searching for where Cervantes is buried, not his fictional character Don Quixote. (D) is incorrect because the researchers are looking for Cervantes, not holy sites.

8. (D) is the correct answer. The passage gives examples like milk, eggs, peanuts, and wheat. It can be inferred that "common foods" refers to foods that regularly show up in children's diets. (A) is incorrect because the phrase "common foods" does not indicate danger. (B) is incorrect because, while these foods may be prevalent, the passage does not suggest they cover the major food groups. (C) is incorrect because the passage doesn't comment on children's preference for such foods.

9. (A) is the correct answer. The narrator states that the last time James Barton saw the young man was before he entered college, and characterizes him then as "impulsive in manner and speech," before stating that "the intervening four years had tempered him a good deal." "Tempered" refers to the adjustment of one's disposition, and the term "intervening" indicates that there was a change that took place in this area, and since the force behind this effect, "four years" can be assumed as college, it can be implied that the young man is no longer "impulsive in manner." (B) is incorrect because it lacks this contrast, taking it in the opposite direction. (C) is incorrect because the passage only comments on the hair and eye colour of the young man, not his physical size or capabilities. (D) is incorrect because "good deal" means "a lot" here, and does not refer to a business agreement.

10. (B) is the correct answer. The authors explain that cuteness is not "purely visual" and "works by involving all the senses." (A) is incorrect because the authors are talking about multiple senses, not just sound, and doesn't imply another sense is superior to the visual one. (C) is incorrect because, while it is plausible, the authors here never mention the visual forms cuteness takes. (D) is incorrect because while this is a later conclusion of the authors, the fact that cuteness is apparent to more than one sense is only offered as a precursor to the fact that cuteness involves all our senses.

11. (A) is the correct answer. Monsieur Maillard greets the narrator's companion by shaking his hand and begging him to "alight," a word meaning to descend from a mode of transportation. Since Maillard is described as having "a polished manner" and "a certain air of [...] dignity, and authority" it make sense to infer that, in this context, "begging" does not mean pleading, but rather amiably expressing hospitality. (B) is incorrect because the passage does not indicate Monsieur Maillard is in desperate need of anything; he is only greeting his guest. (C) is incorrect because Monsieur Maillard does not rush his guests into his establishment. (D) is incorrect because Monsieur Maillard's greeting is characterized as quite different from insecure, as he is described as shaking the narrator's friend's hand "cordially" and has a "polished manner and a certain air of [...] dignity, and authority which was very impressive," meaning Maillard is polite and confident.

12. (C) is the correct answer. Here, the author notes that spoken communication is sometimes "undermined" by stroke-related impairments, or damages. The cause is stroke-related impairments, and the effect is more difficult spoken communication. (A) is incorrect because the given lines are not comparing stroke patients' speaking versus writing ability. (B) is incorrect because it swaps the cause-effect relationship. (D) is incorrect because it is too broad; the author makes no sweeping claim that conversations are more difficult with stroke patients, and is talking in the given lines about a much more specific effect strokes can have on patients.

13. (D) is the correct answer. The lines indicate that the regions mentioned right before (Mesopotamia, Babylonia, Egypt, Rome, and Greece) were the first to see the development of the new business of accounting. The following lines document how this "flowering of an industry" occurred: landowners, princes, and emperors would use papyrus, stone, or wooden tablets to keep records. (A) is incorrect because the passage nowhere discusses the industrial age; the industry referenced in the given lines refers to accounting, not the industrial age. (B) is incorrect because it is too literal; "saw" here is used in a more metaphorical sense, not to suggest that the development of accounting had eyewitnesses. (C) is incorrect because the lines are not focused on workers or laborers in the regions mentioned.

14. (A) is the correct answer. The passage here notes that physicists "cherish" the standard model "because it can explain most of the fundamental phenomena in nature by referencing just a handful of elementary particles." Thus, physicists are fond of the standard model, the meaning expressed in these lines. The earlier paragraph notes some new additions to the standard model, so it can be inferred that the "standard model" is the reigning model that is being expanded upon. (B) is incorrect because "cherished" means to value something, whereas "gratitude" implies feelings of thankfulness, which are not synonymous. (C) is incorrect because the author in the given lines is not comparing the standard model to other models, only mentioning scientists' attachment to it. (D) is incorrect because physicists are not looking back on a previous model, but rather appreciating a current popular model.

15. (B) is the correct answer. The sentence is describing how the man "played horribly," with the "it" right before the given phrase referencing the man's cracked fiddle. "Shrieked aloud in agony" is thus referencing the sound of the fiddle; the author is using personification to indicate how the fiddle sounded. (A) is incorrect because "it" refers to the fiddle, not the man's singing voice. (C) is incorrect because the passage gives no indication of an audience, nor does the phrase reference an audience's reaction. (D) is incorrect because the apple-trees are mentioned in the first paragraph, and not referenced here.

16. (B) is the correct answer. The lines indicated mention how European voters are "culling," or getting rid of, traditional parties "out of weakness," while Iceland's voters are "rebelling out of strength." The lines surrounding this give clues as to the context: while other eurozone countries are "deeply constrained by external debt," Iceland has paid down its foreign obligations, so it can be inferred that the position of strength noted here is meant to indicate Iceland's relative position of power. The lines are concerned with changes to traditional parties, and the sentence before mentions the prime minister, power, and elections, so it can be inferred that these are political parties. Thus, it is reasonable to conclude the given lines mean Iceland is making political changes out of a position of power, in contrast to other Europeans. (A) is incorrect because it is too general and misses the contrast set up in the given lines between European voters and Icelandic voters. (C) is incorrect because it is too extreme; the previous sentence mentions threats to hand power to "self-styled pirates," but the passage does not indicate Iceland has handed over power to pirates. (D) is incorrect because the contrast set up here is meant to compare Iceland with other European countries, and there is no indication that Iceland plans to take control of these other European countries.

17. (D) is the correct answer. The author is stating here that many nations who participate in the Olympics hoping to raise their international profile will only "fade into obscurity" in the interim period between Olympics; in other words, their international profile will not be highlighted in any significant, lasting way. (A) is incorrect because it is too extreme—the passage discusses how a country's profile might be showcased by the Olympics, and there is no indication that the Olympics are the deciding factor of whether or not countries appear on actual world maps. (B) is incorrect because the lines are concerned with a country's profile, not political power. (C) is incorrect because the lines are not discussing athlete recognition, but a country's international profile.

18. (C) is the correct answer. In the context of the passage, it can be inferred that the Caenorhabditis elegans has contributed to medical science based on its use in "studies of development and the nervous system." In other words, researchers have used this worm in research that has led to important biological insights. (A) is incorrect because it is not the worm itself that is conducting research. (B) is incorrect because the passage nowhere indicates the nematode has developmental problems; instead, its usefulness in research is connected to its popularity among research scientists. (D) is incorrect because it is unsupported by the passage, which mentions no specific breakthroughs.

19. (B) is the correct answer. The phrase "whose waters were lashed into foam" is a fancy way of saying that the Clyde was the first river that a steamboat traveled upon. The rest of the passage discusses the expansion of steamboats, so it is clear that the lines here are indicating the initial run of a steamboat on a river. (A) is incorrect because The Clyde is a river, not a steamboat. (C) is incorrect because the passage never mentions pollution. (D) is incorrect because the passage does not suggest that steamboats could not travel on the Clyde; the phrase "lashed into foam" describes how water would turn into foam from the steamboats travelling on it and moving it around quickly, or "lashing" it.

20. (C) is the correct answer. The sentence directly after the lines in question state that there is a reburial being facilitated, the word "reburial" suggesting the bones of "Kennewick Man" are returning to a place they were before, buried. (A) is incorrect because the lines referenced only indicate the movement of the man's bones, not anything about his spirit. (B) is incorrect because the bones are not being returned to a Native American museum; they are being reburied. (D) is incorrect because the 9,000-year-old bones are being returned to tribes, not to family members.

Overall Structure
Part 2

Overall Structure questions require you to analyze the overall structure of the passage. They may require you to understand and select a choice that describes the overall narrative arc of a story, the organization of an argument, or the order and pattern in which information is provided in expository writing.

These questions do not necessarily require you to understand or identify the main idea or central purpose of the passage, but rather to identify how pieces of the passage fit together.

DIRECTIONS

Every passage or paired set of passages is accompanied by a number of questions. Read the passage or paired set of passages, then use what is said or implied in what you read and in any given graphics to choose the best answer to each question.

Question 1

This passage is adapted from The Adventures of Bobby Orde by Stewart Edward White. First published in 1908.

At nine o'clock one morning Bobby Orde, following an agreement with his father, walked sedately to the Proper Place, where he kept his cap and coat and other belongings. The Proper Place
5 was a small, dark closet under the angle of the stairs.

Bobby knew the way perfectly. You went to the fire-engine house; and then to the left after the court-house was Mr. Proctor's; and then, all at
10 once, the town. Father's office was in the nearest square brick block.

He turned in to the straight, broad stairway that led to the offices above. The stairway, and the hall to which it mounted were dark and smelled of old
15 coco-matting and stale tobacco. He marched down the hall to the door of his father's offices.

Within were several long, narrow desks burdened with large ledgers and flanked by high stools. On each stool sat a clerk—five of them.
20 An iron "base burner" stove occupied the middle of the room. Its pipe ran in suspension here and there through the upper air until it plunged unexpectedly into the wall. A capacious wood-box flanked it. Bobby was glad he did not have to fill
25 that wood-box at a cent a time.

Against the walls at either end of the room and next to the windows were two roll-top desks at which sat Mr. Orde and his partner. Two or three pivoted chairs completed the furnishings.
30 "Hullo, Bobby," called Mr. Orde, who was talking earnestly to a man; "I'll be ready in a few minutes."

1

The passage as a whole can primarily be characterized as the narrator's description of

A) the fulfillment of a promise Bobby Orde made to his father.

B) Mr. Orde's leisurely stroll through the city before work.

C) a typical day at the accounting office Bobby works at.

D) Bobby's first visit to his father's workplace.

Question 2

This passage is adapted from "Highway to hearing hell: musicians and the danger of deafness" by Trevor Cox. ©2016 by Trevor Cox.

Deafness isn't only a concern for rock musicians, or drum and bass DJs—from classical violinists to pop singers, in recent years it's become
Line clear that anyone around music a lot has reason to
5 be equally worried.

The largest study into noise-induced hearing loss in musicians was published in 2014. Three million Germans were examined, including 2,227 professional musicians. They found that the
10 musicians were about four times as likely to report a new noise-induced hearing loss compared to the general population.

Many studies into classical musicians have also found evidence of problems. One study from
15 the 1990s found that violinists and violists have more hearing loss in their left ear compared to their right ear. This loss of hearing is caused by the musician's own instruments, as the violin is placed under the chin with the left ear almost touching the
20 instrument. Five studies have found that between 37% and 58% of classical musicians experience hearing loss. For rock and pop the numbers are similar, with studies finding that just under half of musicians suffering from a hearing loss.

2

Which of the following best describes the structure of the passage as a whole?

A) An anecdote about a classical musician that lost her hearing

B) A warning about the dangers of listening to loud music

C) A discussion of a widespread problem for musicians

D) A summary of a landmark study in 2014 on hearing loss

Question 3

This passage is adapted from "For female architects, the loss of Zaha Hadid is personal" by Despina Stratigakos. ©2016 by Despina Stratigakos.

As a luminary in the world of architecture, Zaha Hadid, who died on March 31, was a celebrity whose name, face, and buildings are known by
Line millions. But the grief felt by women architects
5 is on a different, intimate scale. With Hadid's passing, we have lost a role model in a field that has few others. That is not to say that there are not a great many accomplished and inspiring women in architecture. But none have achieved Hadid's
10 prominence—as, indeed, have few male architects. Against all odds, and a great deal of prejudice, she broke one glass ceiling after another, no mean feat when that glass was as hard and thick as concrete.

Her buildings redefined our ideas of what was
15 possible, from the bursting energy of the Vitra Fire Station in Weil am Rhein, Germany, to the undulating angles of the Guangzhou Opera House in China. Hadid, in 2014, became the first woman to win the Pritzker Architecture Prize. Two years
20 later, she became the first woman awarded the Royal Institute of British Architects Royal Gold Medal in her own right.

As I explore in my new book Where Are the Women Architects?, role models are deeply
25 important. Having a personal relationship with a role model is not necessary; an effective role model may be a prominent figure in the profession or even a historical one. Role models boost self-esteem by countering negative stereotypes that cast
30 doubt on a person's abilities to perform well in the profession. They increase motivation for career advancement and success. And they foster a sense of identification with a field, combating alienation.

Which choice best describes the developmental pattern of the passage?

A) It describes a general phenomenon and then a specific example of that phenomenon.

B) It focuses on the early years of an important figure and then describes the figure's legacy.

C) It opens with a history of a profession and goes on to discuss a pivotal woman in that profession.

D) It describes the impact of a specific woman and then defines a general term.

Question 4

This passage is adapted from "There's still much to learn by visiting the giant planet Jupiter" by Lucyna Kedziora-Chudczer. ©2016 by Lucyna Kedziora-Chudczer.

After a five-year journey, NASA's Juno spacecraft this week reached Jupiter and was successfully inserted into its orbit. This is only
Line the second spacecraft after the Galileo mission
5 in 1995 to enter into orbit around the planet, the largest in our solar system.

Over the next eight years, Galileo gave us an unprecedented view of the turbulent and stormy Jovian atmosphere. It detected intense
10 lightning activity over regions much larger than typical storms on Earth. Observations with its Near Infrared Mapping Spectrometer (NIMS) and imaging camera revealed the movement of clouds that resembled streaming jets along the
15 banded structure of the planet. It found billowing updrafts and downdrafts and led to the discovery of ammonia clouds forming in the lower layers of the thick atmosphere of the planet.

One of the highlights of the Galileo mission
20 was a release of a probe that descended into the swirling abyss of clouds. It was able to map the vertical profile of atmospheric pressure, temperature, and composition until it melted and vaporized under the crushing pressure of the
25 planetary interior.

Over the course of the passage, the focus shifts from

A) the description of a new spacecraft to a discussion of the success of the previous mission.

B) the announcement of the arrival of the Juno spacecraft to a description of the key breakthroughs that occurred as a result.

C) the analysis of important new data to an explanation of how scientists were able to collect that data.

D) the overview of the history of spacecraft to the look at the most recent spacecraft mission.

Question 5

This passage is adapted from A Fourth Form Friendship by Angela Brazil. First published in 1911.

"Two pencils, an india-rubber, a penknife, camp stool, easel, paint-box, a tube of Chinese white, a piece of sponge, paint rag, and water tin,"
Line said Aldred Laurence, checking each item off on
5 her fingers. "Can I possibly want anything else? My block, of course! How could I be so stupid as to forget it? It's no good taking pencils and paints if I've nothing to draw upon!"

"Hello, Aldred! What a spread!" exclaimed
10 Keith, rousing himself from the luxuries of a comfortable chair and an absorbing book to notice that his sister had put on her hat, that her gloves lay on a chair, and that she was already beginning to pack some of the articles in question inside
15 a home-made portfolio of dark-green American cloth. "The table looks like an art repository!" he continued. "Have you suddenly turned into a Rubens, or a Raphael? Where are you going with all those traps?"

20 "I want to make a sketch of old Mrs. Barker's cottage," she replied. "The clematis is out over the porch, and it looks lovely. I heard Mr. Bowden say yesterday that it was a splendid subject. Don't you remember, he made a picture of it last year?"

25 "So he did, and a jolly good one too. Yours won't be anything like up to that, Sis!"

"I dare say not, but you needn't discourage me from trying, at any rate."

"Oh, I'm not discouraging you. Go by all
30 means, and good luck to your efforts! You can show me the masterpiece when you come back;" and the boy, flinging his legs over one arm of the chair, settled himself in an even more inelegant and reposeful attitude than before, and plunged
35 again into the fascinating adventures of Captain Kettle.

5

Which of the following is NOT an accurate description of the passage?

A) A conversation between a brother and sister

B) A description of a girl preparing to go make a sketch

C) An account of someone on her way to start a project

D) A depiction of an argument between Mr. and Mrs. Barker

Question 6

This passage is adapted from "The global impact of air conditioning: big and getting bigger" by Lucas Davis. ©2016 by Lucas Davis.

With a heat wave pushing the heat index well above 100 degrees Fahrenheit through much of the U.S., most of us are happy to stay indoors
Line and crank the air conditioning. And if you think
5 it's hot here, try 124°F in India. Globally, 2016 is poised to be another record-breaking year for average temperatures. This means more air conditioning. Much more.

In a paper published in the Proceedings of
10 the National Academy of Science (PNAS), Paul Gertler and I examine the enormous global potential for air conditioning. As incomes rise around the world and global temperatures go up, people are buying air conditioners at
15 alarming rates. In China, for example, sales of air conditioners have nearly doubled over the last five years. Each year now more than 60 million

air conditioners are sold in China, more than eight times as many as are sold annually in the United
20 States.

This is mostly great news. People are getting richer, and air conditioning brings great relief on hot and humid days. However, air conditioning also uses vast amounts of electricity. A typical
25 room air conditioner, for example, uses 10–20 times as much electricity as a ceiling fan.

Meeting this increased demand for electricity will require billions of dollars of infrastructure investments and result in billions of tons of
30 increased carbon dioxide emissions. A new study by Lawrence Berkeley Lab also points out that more ACs means more refrigerants that are potent greenhouse gases.

6

The passage can best be described as:

A) a call for consumers to boycott a dangerous industry.

B) an overview of recent rise in temperatures globally.

C) a caution about the increased use of a newly popular appliance.

D) a reflection on the waste in modern appliances.

Question 7

This passage is adapted from "Truth-seeking heroes to low-brow diggers: a history of press reporters told through fiction" by Sarah Lonsdale. ©2016 by Sarah Lonsdale.

Fictions about journalists from the past often reveal deeper truths about the inner workings of the journalism industry than standard histories of
Line the press do. Many of them are told by journalists
5 with newsroom experience, or freelance contributors to the press and provide granular, day-by-day commentary on the evolution of the news media. And there are dozens of these forgotten fictions, now gathering mildew on
10 secondhand booksellers' shelves, with enigmatic titles such as Mightier Than the Sword, The Paper Palace, and Paperchase End. Written by reporters

of past decades, together they construct a vibrant, alternative history of the newspaper press, told by its foot soldiers.

Journalists are compulsive storytellers and cannot resist chronicling their own lives and aspects of their trade. As one of the latest in a long line of journalists to turn their newspaper experience into fiction, Annalena McAfee (The Spoiler, 2011) said: "I've only ever met one journalist who didn't want to write a book."

However, today it is fashionable among contemporary writers to stereotype journalists in fiction, from the mendacious Rita Skeeter in the Harry Potter novels to the murderous Vernon Halliday in Ian McEwan's Amsterdam (1998). Guardian journalist-turned-novelist James Meek acknowledges the difficulty of writing a "good" journalist in post-Leveson Britain. Not only would he or she appear preachy, dull, and pompous, but no reader would believe in them, he says. The trouble is, most journalists have never rifled through celebrity bins or hacked phones, and most still want to inform, clarify, and enlighten. In today's world, we need journalist-heroes more than ever.

7

The last paragraph differs from the first paragraph in that in the last paragraph the author:

A) hints that journalists are not able to craft fiction as well as nonfiction.

B) discusses one of the difficulties of writing fictional accounts of journalists.

C) touches on journalists' interest in experimenting with fiction.

D) explains why most journalists do not read fiction today.

Question 8

This passage is adapted from "A measles mystery: how could the vaccine prevent deaths from other diseases too?" by Michael Mina. ©2015 by Michael Mina.

Before vaccination, measles was responsible for millions of childhood deaths. Today it remains a cause of great illness and death in low-resource countries, killing over 140,000 children worldwide every year.

Where measles vaccines have been introduced, childhood deaths often plummet by as much as 50%. Measles is deadly, but before the vaccines were introduced in 1963, the virus did not directly cause half of all childhood disease deaths. In other words, where measles vaccines have been introduced, they were associated with reductions in more childhood disease deaths than were actually caused by the measles.

The reason for these major drops in mortality has been a central mystery surrounding the vaccine for decades. Many researchers figure that there are two ways that the measles vaccine could prevent more deaths than are strictly due to measles virus. First, the vaccine itself could have long-lasting non-specific immune-boosting properties that protect the recipient from other diseases. Second, the measles infection could have long-lasting effects that predispose someone to other diseases.

The first hypothesis has been investigated, but as the World Health Organization (WHO) recently reported, there is insufficient evidence to explain a purely immune-boosting effect from the vaccine. On the other hand, recent strong evidence was shown to suggest the latter—that measles infections may induce long-term negative effects on the immune system by deleting immune memory cells, and that these effects may be prevented through vaccination.

8

Which of the following best describes the structure of the passage?

A) An overview of the history of measles from the early twentieth century to today

B) A warning about potential side effects of the measles vaccine

C) A presentation of an interesting fact and a description of potential explanations for that fact

D) A discussion of the various risks and benefits of common vaccines like measles

Question 9

This passage is adapted from Rosemary by C.N. and A.M. Williamson. First published in 1906.

There was a young man in Monte Carlo. He had come in a motor car, and he had come a long way, but he hardly knew why he had come.

Line
5   It would be Christmas soon, and he thought that he would rather get it over with on the Riviera than anywhere else, because the blue and gold weather would not remind him of other Christmases which were gone—pure, white, cold Christmases, musical with joy-bells and sweet

10   with aromatic pine, the scent of trees born to be Christmas trees.

There had been a time when he had fancied it would be a wonderful thing to see the Riviera. He had thought what it would be like to be a rich

15   man, and bring a certain girl here for a moon of honey and roses.

She was the most beautiful girl in the world, or he believed her so, which is exactly the same thing; and he had imagined the joy of walking

20   with her on just such a terrace as this Casino terrace where he was walking now, alone. She would be in white, with one of those long ermine things that women call stoles; an ermine muff (the big, "granny" kind that swallows girlish arms up

25   to the dimples in their elbows) and a hat which they would have bought together in Paris.

They would have walked together, they two, and he would have been so proud of her, that

every time a passer-by cast a glance of admiration
30   at her face, he would feel that he could hardly keep in a laugh of joy, or a shout, "She is mine— she is mine."

But he had been poor in the old days, when from far away he had thought of this terrace, and

35   the moon of honey and roses, and love. It had all been a dream, then, as it was now; too sweet ever to come true.

9

Over the course of the passage, the main focus of the narrative shifts from

A) the man's arrival at a new place to his fantasies about how he hoped his life would have gone.

B) the description of the journey to the Riviera to a description of the various sights at the Riviera.

C) the travels of a man and his wife at a certain resort town to the disappearance of the man's wife.

D) the account of a man and woman secretly meeting to the revelation that the two must never see each other again.

Question 10

This passage is adapted from "Health Check: can people actually multitask?" by Craig Speelman. ©2016 by Craig Speelman.

Young people often claim they are experts at multitasking. That they can monitor several electronic devices at once makes it seem to be the

Line
case. But research regularly demonstrates when
5   they try to do two things at once, they tend to do both tasks poorly. Either they make more errors, or they take longer than they would if they did one thing at a time.

In one study, university students' laptops were

10   monitored by a spyware program during lectures. It found students attempted to multitask by checking course material and taking lecture notes as well as looking at emails, engaging in social media, surfing the web, and playing games. The study found the

15 more often students engaged with non-course-
related material during the lecture, the worse their
academic performance was in the course.

So, can we do two things at once? Additional
research shows that it depends on the nature of
20 the tasks we want to perform simultaneously, how
aroused we are, the extent of our experience with
each of the tasks, and how much we care about the
quality of our performance.

10

Overall, the passage can best be described as

A) the description of research on a common
activity.

B) a comparison of the multitasking abilities of
the young and old.

C) the story of one university's attempt to increase
student engagement.

D) a look at different ways to increase efficiency
in school.

Question 11

This passage is adapted from "The extraordinary life of
Whistler's mother" by Daniel E. Sutherland. ©2015 by
Daniel E. Sutherland.

Anna Matilda (McNeill) Whistler (1804–1881)
may have been a quiet, diminutive woman, but
she was a mighty force in the lives of those
Line around her. She completed the bulk of her formal
5 education in Brooklyn and became more firmly
grounded in the teaching of the Episcopal Church.
Her city-hopping continued at 17 when, following
the death of her father, Anna and her mother
lived variously in New York, Baltimore, and
10 Georgetown. In her mid-20s, she spent more than
a year in Great Britain, where she had two half-
sisters. It was the first of 11 Atlantic crossings she
made during her life.

By the time she married George Washington
15 Whistler in 1831, her travels and several
residences had not only exposed Anna to a
variety of social and cultural environments, but
they had also taught her perseverance, patience,

and independence—qualities she would come to
20 depend on.

11

According to the narrator, what did Anna Whistler
do prior to spending a year in Great Britain?

A) Bore a son

B) Married George Whistler

C) Crossed the Atlantic 11 times

D) Lived in Georgetown

Question 12

This passage is adapted from "If the world's soils keep
drying out, that's bad news for microbes (and people)" by
Brajesh Singh, Fernando T. Maestre, and Manuel Delgado
Baquerizo. ©2016 by Brajesh Singh, Fernando T. Maestre,
and Manuel Delgado Baquerizo.

In two related studies, our research team
looked at the impact of the drying trend on soil
microbial diversity, and at whether these soils are
Line likely to become less fertile and productive as a
5 consequence. In the first study, we looked at 80
dryland sites, on all continents except Antarctica,
to see how the composition, abundance, and
diversity of soil bacteria and fungi change in
response to drying soils. We found that soil
10 bacterial and fungal diversity and abundance
reduced as these drylands get drier. This is largely
because when soils dry out, plant cover and soil
organic carbon content both decline, which in turn
affects the bacteria and fungi living in the soil.
15 In the second study, we investigated the
relationship between microbial diversity and a
range of functions such as soil fertility and plant
productivity. We looked at drylands all over the
world, and compared them with a wide variety
20 of temperate ecosystems in Scotland including
grasslands, forests, croplands and bogs.

12

Which of the following does the passage indicate occurred first chronologically?

A) The researchers compared drylands with temperate ecosystems in Scotland.

B) The researchers looked at dryland sites in Antarctica.

C) The researchers examined changes in soil in response to drying.

D) The researchers investigated the relationship between microbial diversity and different soil functions.

Question 13

This passage is adapted from "The Bishop" by Anton Chekhov. First published in 1902.

The evening service was being celebrated on the eve of Palm Sunday in the Old Petrovsky Convent. When they began distributing the palm
Line it was close upon ten o'clock, the candles were
5 burning dimly, the wicks wanted snuffing; it was all in a sort of mist. In the twilight of the church the crowd seemed heaving like the sea, and to Bishop Pyotr, who had been unwell for the last three days, it seemed that all the faces—old and young, men's
10 and women's—were alike, that everyone who came up for the palm had the same expression in his eyes. In the mist he could not see the doors; the crowd kept moving and looked as though there were no end to it. The female choir was singing, a
15 nun was reading the prayers for the day.

13

At the time of the events of the story, Bishop Pyotr is

A) at a service the evening before Palm Sunday.

B) about to come down with a terrible cold.

C) collecting palms after the evening service.

D) leading a service on Palm Sunday.

Question 14

This passage is adapted from "Can reading fiction literally change your mind?" by Gregory Currie. ©2016 by Gregory Currie.

It has long been held—from the high-minded humanism that Dr. Samuel Johnson espoused in the 18th century to the likes of the fiercely serious
Line literary critic FR Leavis in the 20th century—that
5 literature is good for you. But while once the only evidence considered necessary was that of the critic's judgment and sensitivity, Oatley and other psychologists today are to be thanked for demanding rather more concrete evidence.

14

The author states that literature has been considered beneficial over a period of several

A) months.

B) years.

C) decades.

D) centuries.

Question 15

This passage is adapted from "The rise and fall of the Knoedler, New York's most notorious art gallery" by Jeff Taylor. ©2016 by Jeff Taylor.

After suddenly closing in 2011 in the wake
of massive lawsuits, Knoedler Gallery and its
former director, Ann Freedman, are finally having
Line their day in court: they're currently faced with a
5   civil lawsuit leveled by collector (and chairman
of Sotheby's) Domenico de Sole, who thought he
had bought an US$8.3 million Rothko from the
gallery. It was actually painted by Pei-Shen Qian,
a Chinese immigrant living in Queens.
10   But the collapse of the Knoedler, New York's
oldest art gallery, was much more protracted
and complex than the forgery trial taking place.
The gallery's fall has much to do with profound
changes in the gallery business over the last
15   century and the increasing scarcity of profitable
secondary market material.

15

Which of the following occurred first
chronologically in the passage?

A) Lawsuits against Knoedler

B) Knoedler Gallery closing

C) Civil court case against Knoedler

D) Ann Freedman serving time

Question 16

This passage is adapted from "How proteins unwind RNA" by Daniel Oppenheimer. ©2012 by Daniel Oppenheimer.

Biologists have discovered the mechanism by
which a group of proteins, known as DEAD-Box
proteins, unravel RNA (ribonucleic acid).
Line Double-stranded RNA, which translates genetic
5   information to synthesize proteins, is remodeled
for different processes within the cell. But until
now, no one knew how this occurred.
Biologists found that one part of the
DEAD-box protein locks onto the RNA molecule
10   as another part bonds to the chemical energy

ATP. This configuration causes a third bit of the
protein to come down between the two strands
of RNA, grab one strand and twist it away. This
process appears to be universal across the family
15   of DEAD-box proteins, therefore across all types
of life, and it is an important mechanism for cell
division. DEAD-box proteins have been linked to
diseases such as cancer, where the over-expression
of these proteins lead to uncontrolled cell division.

16

In the passage, the author claims that part of the
DEAD-Box protein bonds to ATP

A) before the DEAD-box protein locks onto RNA.

B) as the DEAD-box protein locks onto RNA.

C) after the DEAD-box protein moves between
two strands of RNA.

D) in between cycles of RNA replication.

Question 17

This passage is adapted from White Jacket by Herman Melville. First published in 1892.

The way I came by it was this.
When our frigate lay in Callao, on the coast of
Peru—her last harbor in the Pacific—I found myself
Line without a grego, or sailor's surtout; and as, toward
5   the end of a three years' cruise, no pea-jackets
could be had from the purser's steward: and being
bound for Cape Horn, some sort of a substitute was
indispensable; I employed myself, for several days,
in manufacturing an outlandish garment of my own
10   devising, to shelter me from the boisterous weather
we were so soon to encounter.

17

The narrator indicates that which of the following happened after his frigate stationed itself on the coast of Peru?

A) The frigate returned to the Pacific.

B) The narrator purchased a pea-jacket.

C) The narrator created his own coat.

D) A storm hit the docked boat.

Question 18

This passage is adapted from "A dark night is good for your health" by Richard G. "Bugs" Stevens. ©2015 by Richard G. "Bugs" Stevens.

During the night, in the dark, body temperature drops, metabolism slows, and the hormone melatonin rises dramatically. When the Sun
Line comes up in the morning, melatonin has already
5 started falling, and you wake up. This natural physiological transition into and out of night is of ancient origin, and melatonin is crucial for the process to proceed as it should.

18

Based on the passage, which of the following occurs prior to the Sun coming up in the morning?

A) Melatonin levels have started falling.

B) Melatonin levels have started rising.

C) The body wakes itself up.

D) The body's metabolism speeds up.

Question 19

This passage is adapted from "Has the library outlived its usefulness in the age of Internet? You'd be surprised" by Donald A. Barclay. ©2016 by Donald A. Barclay.

In the last two decades, the total number of U.S. public libraries slightly increased—inching up from 8,921 in 1994 to 9,082 in 2012 (a gain of
Line 2.14 percent). Over the same period, the data also
5 show that use of public libraries in the U.S. went up as well.

Here's what data on circulation (books and other items checked out to library users) and annual visits to public libraries reveal. The
10 number of books and other items borrowed from U.S. public libraries increased from 6.5 items per capita in 1993 to 8.0 items per capita in 2012 (up 23 percent). Over the same time span, the number of visits to U.S. public libraries rose 22.5 percent.

19

Which of the following represents the correct order of events mentioned in the passage?

A) The number of U.S. public libraries increased, and then the use of U.S. public libraries increased.

B) The use of U.S. public libraries increased, and then the number of U.S. public libraries increased.

C) The number and use of U.S. public libraries increased during the same period.

D) The number and use of U.S. public libraries decreased during the same period.

Question 20

This passage is adapted from "Which Came First: The Feathers or the Flight?" by Matthew J. Greenwold and Roger H. Sawyer. ©2012 by Matthew J. Greenwold and Roger H. Sawyer.

Bird feathers may have evolved more recently than previously thought, and the development of powered flight may have been the key that
Line sparked their evolution, researchers have found.
5   By studying the molecular history of the beta-keratin proteins that make up feathers, claws, and scales, researchers at the University of South Carolina were able to chart the genomic history of several modern birds including the zebra finch
10 and the chicken. They were surprised to discover that the first feathers evolved from scale and claw proteins, and were incapable of flight. Distinct feather beta-keratins only evolved around 125 million years ago—perhaps as a response to the
15 development of powered flight.

20

According to the passage, what happened before the development of distinct feather beta-keratins?

A) The first birds flew using feather and scale wings.

B) The first feathers evolved from scale and claw proteins.

C) Researchers discovered powered flight led to the development of feathers.

D) The zebra finch and chicken diverged in evolutionary history.

1. (A) is the correct answer. The beginning of the passage notes that Bobby Orde left his house "following an agreement with his father." Thus, it can be inferred that Bobby's journey to his father is in fulfillment of a promise, and the passage describes the process of that fulfillment. (B) is incorrect because Bobby, not Mr. Orde, is walking in the passage. (C) is incorrect because there is no evidence Bobby works at an accounting office, and the passage does not describe a typical day at one. (D) is incorrect because there is no evidence in the passage to support the idea that this was Bobby's first time there.

2. (C) is the correct answer. The passage discusses the dangers of hearing loss as a result of prolonged exposure to loud music for musicians, citing studies and data to provide evidence about this problem. (A) is incorrect because it is too narrow. The passage does not just focus on just one story. (B) is incorrect because, while the passage can serve as a warning, its overall structure is geared towards describing a widespread issue, not on issuing a caution to readers. (D) is incorrect because it is too specific. The passage mentions many studies, and does not just focus on the 2014 study mentioned in the second paragraph.

3. (D) is the correct answer. The passage opens with the life and legacy of Zaha Hadid and then goes on to define "role models." (A) is incorrect because the passage starts with a discussion of a specific figure, Hadid, and not a description of a general phenomenon. (B) is incorrect because the passage does not move from a discussion of Hadid's early years to her legacy; it begins by describing her legacy and moves on to define "role models." (C) is incorrect because the passage does not begin with a broad discussion of the history of architecture.

4. (A) is the correct answer. The passage opens with a discussion of a new spacecraft, Juno, reaching Jupiter's orbit. It then goes on to discuss the Galileo mission, which occurred earlier in 1995. (B) is incorrect because the important results discussed in the latter part of the passage relate to the Galileo spacecraft, not the Juno. (C) is incorrect because the passage does not get into much detail about how data was collected. (D) is incorrect because the passage does not examine the history of spacecraft.

5. (D) is the correct answer. The passage does not depict an argument between Mr. and Mrs. Barker; siblings Aldred and Keith exchange some words, but they are siblings, with the last name of Laurence. (A) is incorrect because it could describe the passage, as siblings Aldred and Keith are interacting here. (B) is incorrect because it could describe the passage as well, since Aldred is preparing to go make a sketch of Mrs. Barker's cottage. (C) is incorrect because the passage does depict Aldred on her way to start a project, her sketch.

6. (C) is the correct answer. The passage discusses the recent rise in use of air conditioning, and potential repercussions of this trend. (A) is incorrect because the author does not call for readers to boycott air conditioning. (B) is incorrect because the passage is primarily focused on air conditioning, not just the global rise in temperatures. (D) is incorrect because the passage focuses on air conditioning specifically, not "modern appliances" as a whole.

7. (B) is the correct answer. The last paragraph focuses on how difficult it is to write a "good" journalist in fiction, given the tendency for many "contemporary writers to stereotype journalists in fiction," an idea which is not discussed in the first paragraph. (A) is incorrect because the author nowhere implies that journalists' fiction craft is inferior. (C) is incorrect because the passage discusses journalists dabbling in fiction throughout. (D) is incorrect because the last paragraph does not imply that, even with these less-than-flattering accounts, journalists do not read fiction at all.

8. (C) is the correct answer. The passage presents an interesting fact—that the measles vaccine provides more protection than just against measles—and a description of different hypotheses that would explain this. (A) is incorrect because the passage is not a history of measles, but focuses on interesting properties of the measles vaccine. (B) is incorrect because the author presents the measles vaccine positively by claiming that this vaccine marked an end to the mass childhood death the disease once caused, and further explains that this vaccine is "associated with reductions in more childhood disease deaths than were actually caused by the measles." (D) is incorrect because the passage does not touch on any risks of the measles vaccine, only describing its benefits.

9. (A) is the correct answer. The man arrives at Monte Carlo, and proceeds to think about how he hoped his life would have gone: arriving rich to the Riviera, along with a beautiful woman. (B) is incorrect because the passage does not focus on the man's journey or the Riviera's sights. (C) and (D) are incorrect because the woman is only in the man's head; the passage is filled with phrases such as "would have" and "would be," suggesting these are fantasies of the man, and the narrator states that these fantasies "had all been a dream [...] too sweet to ever come true."

10. (A) is the correct answer. The passage focuses on research on multitasking, looking at one study on university students' laptops and more broadly discussing "additional research" that monitored young people attempting to multitask. It concludes with some general insights on this research. (B) is incorrect because the passage does not compare young people to old people. (C) is incorrect because it is too narrow; the passage is not focused on one university, and only mentions a university in connection to a supporting study. (D) is incorrect because the passage focuses on multitasking, not efficiency in school.

11. (D) is the correct answer. The passage mentions that Anna "spent more than a year in Great Britain" in her mid-20s. This is after she lived in Georgetown at around age 17 with her mother. The passage does not mention a son, so (A) is incorrect. (B) and (C) are incorrect because Anna Whistler married George Whistler and crossed the Atlantic 11 times only after her year in Great Britain.

12. (C) is the correct answer. In the first study, researchers "looked at 80 dryland sites…to see how the composition, abundance, and diversity of soil bacteria and fungi change in response to drying soils." (A) is incorrect because the researchers compared drylands to temperate ecosystems in the second study. (B) is incorrect because the passage notes that researchers specifically did not look at drylands in Antarctica. (D) is incorrect because the researchers investigated this relationship in the second study, which logically occured after the first study.

13. (A) is the correct answer. The first line in the passage notes that "the evening service was being celebrated on the eve of Palm Sunday in the Old Petrovsky Convent," which is when the story takes place. The bishop is observing the faces of those who came up for the palms. (B) is incorrect because the bishop has just been sick for three days, and is not at the beginning of his illness. (C) is incorrect because palms are just being distributed at the time of the story, not collected. (D) is incorrect because the passage does not indicate the bishop is leading a service, and the time of the story is the eve of Palm Sunday, not Palm Sunday itself.

14. (D) is the correct answer. The author notes that "it has long been held—from the high-minded humanism that Dr. Samuel Johnson espoused in the 18th century to the likes of the fiercely serious literary critic FR Leavis in the 20th century—that literature is good for you." The 18th to 20th centuries represent a period of a couple of centuries, so (D) is correct. (A), (B), and (C) are all periods that are too short, and are therefore incorrect.

15. (A) is the correct answer. The passage notes that Knoedler suddenly closed in 2011 "in the wake of massive lawsuits," meaning after these lawsuits, which the other answer options state as first chronologically. (B) and (C) are incorrect because the gallery closing and the civil court case followed option (A), the lawsuits, so they did not occur first chronologically in the passage compared to the other answer options that were mentioned in the passage. (D) is incorrect because the passage does not mention Ann Freedman serving time.

16. (B) is the correct answer. The author notes that "biologists found that one part of the DEAD-box protein locks onto the RNA molecule as another part bonds to the chemical energy ATP." After this, a third part of the protein comes between the two strands of RNA. Thus, the first two steps happen simultaneously. (A) is incorrect because it implies the protein locks onto RNA first, not simultaneously as the passage states. (C) is incorrect because part of the DEAD-Box protein bonds to ATP before it moves between two strands of RNA, not after. (D) is incorrect because the passage is not concerned with what happens in between cycles of RNA replication.

17. (C) is the correct answer. The narrator notes that after the frigate "lay in Callao, on the coast of Peru," he found himself without a "grego, or sailor's surtout." Based on the reference to pea-jackets, it can be inferred this is some type of coat, which the narrator employs himself in manufacturing over the next few days. (A) is incorrect because Callao is noted as "the last harbor in the Pacific," so the ship does not return there immediately after. (B) is incorrect, as the narrator never states they bought a pea coat, but instead states that he had to make one himself. (D) is incorrect, as the narrator is wary of a storm, but does not indicate one hit.

18. (A) is the correct answer. The passage states that "when the Sun comes up in the morning, melatonin has already started falling," so falling melatonin levels occur prior to the Sun rising. (B) is incorrect because the passage states that melatonin levels fall before the Sun rises, which is the opposite of what this option states. (C) is incorrect because the body wakes up after or during the sunrise, based on the passage. (D) is incorrect because the passage only mentions the body's metabolism slowing down as night falls.

19. (C) is the correct answer. The first paragraph notes that "in the last two decades," the number of U.S. public libraries slightly increased, and that "over the same period," the use of public libraries went up as well. Thus, the increases occurred simultaneously. (A) and (B) are incorrect because they imply one happened after the other, while the passage states they happened simultaneously. (D) is incorrect because the number and use of U.S. public libraries is said to have increased, not decreased.

20. (B) is the correct answer. The passage notes that "the first feathers evolved from scale and claw proteins," and were incapable of flight, but feather beta-keratins evolved "as a response to the development of powered flight," implying birds initially had feathers evolved from scale and claw proteins but could not fly, and developed beta-keratins later on, once they began to evolve to be able to fly. (A) is incorrect because the passage does not state that feathered birds were flying before the development of feathers. (C) is incorrect because researchers conducted their studies in the modern period, long after these developments. (D) is incorrect because the passage offers no evidence about when the zebra finch and chicken diverged.

Internal Structure

Internal Structure questions require you to identify the role that one part of a passage plays in its overall structure. They may require you to identify the role of sentences or paragraphs in introducing main or supporting ideas, providing transitions between ideas, summarizing ideas and their relationships, describing conclusions, or accomplishing other rhetorical goals.

DIRECTIONS

Every passage or paired set of passages is accompanied by a number of questions. Read the passage or paired set of passages, then use what is said or implied in what you read and in any given graphics to choose the best answer to each question.

Question 1

This passage is adapted from "The late Gordon Darling and the gentle art of philanthropy" by Sasha Grishin. ©2015 by Sasha Grishin.

The death of Gordon Darling AC, CMG, on August 31, 2015, at the age of 94, reminded many in the arts community of the key role
Line that he played in fostering the visual arts in
5 Australia. Darling was dubbed "the patron saint of Australian printmaking" for the very generous support he gave to the print collection of the National Gallery of Australia, while the support and vision provided by him and his wife, Marilyn
10 Darling, led to the establishment of the National Portrait Gallery.
       Through the Gordon Darling Foundation, which they established in 1991, they undertook a vast range of activities, including acquiring
15 and commissioning artwork for national, state, and regional public art galleries, support for the publication of many hundreds of scholarly art books and exhibition catalogues, training programs for curators, and a broad range of
20 innovative and scholarly research art projects.
       Outside the visual arts community, has anyone heard of Gordon Darling? Gordon Darling's death was noted in passing in federal parliament, and the general media ran a number of short news stories
25 and tributes, but at some distance from the headlines.

1

Which of the following statements best describes the way the first paragraph functions in the passage as a whole?

A) It provides background on why the figure of Gordon Darling was so influential in Australia.

B) It shows why Gordon Darling's legacy was mixed despite his many accomplishments.

C) It examines the role of printmaking in modern Australian art.

D) It explains the origins of the National Portrait Gallery in Australia.

Question 2

This passage is adapted from "Gemini Planet Imager—a new eye to scan the sky for exoplanets" by Peter Tuthill. ©2014 by Peter Tuthill.

There is excitement in astronomy and planetary science departments worldwide as the new Gemini Planet Imager, housed in the Gemini
Line South Telescope in the Chilean Andes, turns its
5 razor-sharp gaze to the skies. This device, known as GPI for short, is the first of a small handful of sophisticated instruments to attempt a task that until recently was considered all but impossible: to image the faint mote of light betraying
10 the presence of a planet nestled against the overwhelming glare of its host star.

Planets in orbit around distant stars— exoplanets—are now known to adorn more than 1,000 star systems. There is possibly five times
15 that number under strong suspicion awaiting only final confirmatory data to join the club.

You could be forgiven for thinking this avalanche of discovery—all coming in the past 20 years—has settled most of the important questions
20 in exoplanetary science. The reality, though, is it hasn't. The sample of exoplanets we now have tells us far more about the limitations of the techniques we use to find them than it does about the exoplanets themselves. We have only seen the
25 tip of the iceberg.

2

Without the last paragraph, the passage would contain no hints that

A) some researchers have discovered proof of life on exoplanets.

B) recently developed technologies like GPI have their limitations.

C) the media has deliberately misrepresented technology like GPI.

D) technologies in exoplanetary science are highly unreliable.

Question 3

This passage is adapted from Across the Cameroons by Charles Gilson. First published in 1916.

Late on a September afternoon, in the year 1913, two boys returned to Friar's Court by way of the woods. A well-bred Irish water-spaniel
Line followed close upon their heels.
5 The one, Henry Urquhart, home for his holidays from Eton, was the nephew of Mr. Langton, the retired West African judge, who owned Friar's Court. The other was Jim Braid, the son of Mr. Langton's head-gamekeeper, who had
10 already donned the corduroys and the moleskin waistcoat of his father's trade. A friendship had already sprung up between these two which was destined to ripen as the years went on, carrying both to the uttermost parts of the world,
15 through the forests of the Cameroons, across the inhospitable hills west of the Cameroon Peak, even to the great plains of the Sahara.

Henry was a boy of the open air. He was never happier than when on horseback. As for Jim,
20 he was no rider, but there were few boys of his age who could hit a bolting rabbit or a rocketing pheasant with such surety of aim.

The path they followed led them past the bungalow. As they drew near they saw there was a
25 light in the window, and within was Mr. Langton, a tall, grey-haired man, who sat at his writing-desk, poring over his books and papers.

3

The main purpose of the information in the third paragraph is to

A) indicate that Henry was the superior rider to Jim.

B) demonstrate the stark contrast between the personalities of the boys.

C) foreshadow a rift in the friendship between Henry and Jim.

D) give additional insights into the characters of Henry and Jim.

Question 4

This passage is adapted from "Is online therapy as good as talking face-to-face with a clinician?" by Jo Abbott. ©2016 by Jo Abbott.

Smartphones, tablets and computers are increasingly expanding the availability of health services. This means we can access help
Line anonymously at a time and place that suits us.
5 Currently, only about one-third of people with mental health difficulties obtain help. While there are various reasons for this, practical factors such as availability of health professionals and travel, time, and financial restrictions may limit access to
10 mental health care. People may also be reluctant to seek help, either because of concerns about the stigma attached to mental illness or because of a preference to self-manage symptoms. While technology is not always a replacement for face-
15 to-face treatment for mental health difficulties, it can offer increased choice and flexibility. It may also motivate some people to take that first step in seeking help.
Digital mental health treatment often involves
20 working your way through a structured, online program based on standard, evidence-based psychological treatment methods. Many are based on cognitive behavioral therapy (CBT), whereby you learn to identify and change unhelpful
25 thoughts and behaviors that contribute to your symptoms. Digital mental health services offer more choices and greater flexibility in how we get help.

4

The language of the third paragraph is most likely intended to convey a sense of

A) scientific reliability.

B) clinical fear.

C) general ambivalence.

D) widespread confusion.

Question 5

This passage is adapted from "Historians and novelists fight turf wars" by Christopher Kremmer. ©2015 by Christopher Kremmer.

We all love history. It helps us get our bearings and comforts us with the knowledge that we are part of the larger human narrative. But our love of
Line history is often a jealous one that seeks to control
5 the story and license those permitted to write it.
In 2006, at the height of the mudslinging that began when Kate Grenville allegedly claimed her novel The Secret River (2005) was a new form of historiography, historian Inga Clendinnen
10 countered that the novelist's only "binding contract" with their readers was "not to instruct or to reform, but to delight." The message was clear: if it's reliable history you're after, trust the experts (historians), not liberty-taking literary artists.
15 But is the line between truth and fiction really so clear when it comes to history? And if not, is there scope for historians and novelists to re-engage, with a view to learning from—rather than bludgeoning—each other?

5

Which of the following best describes the way the first paragraph functions in the passage?

A) It provides a summary of the major points of the passage.

B) It introduces the topic of the passage by moving from a general statement to a specific claim.

C) It offers a specific anecdote about literature drawn from the author's own experiences.

D) It presents a unique problem and lays out how the author plans to solve it.

Question 6

This passage is adapted from "What a Moroccan crater reveals about a rare double whammy from the skies" by David Baratoux and Hasnaa Chennaoui Aoudjehane. ©2016 by David Baratoux and Hasnaa Chennaoui Aoudjehane.

Morocco, and particularly its southern desert, is scattered with treasure that came from the skies: meteorites. These extraterrestrial rocks are up to
Line 4.5 billion years old, approximately the age of our
5 solar system, and offer vital clues about Earth's origins.

Large meteorite falls can be catastrophic. In contrast with small meteoritic fragments, larger objects are not decelerated by the atmosphere
10 and hit the ground at a tremendous velocity. The collision forms what's called an impact structure. Scientists have identified about 189 impact structures around the world, such as Mexico's Chicxulub crater. This particular event
15 is associated with the mass extinction of many species, including dinosaurs. There are generally no remnant pieces of the large meteorite that causes such a structure: it is entirely molten or vaporized immediately after collision. Meteorites,
20 then, are not usually found close to impact structures.

Africa is home to one of the world's most recently discovered impact structures, up in the High Atlas Mountains of Morocco. Iron
25 meteorites were also found right at the impact's location. This is unusual—everyone initially assumed that the meteorites' fall had created the impact structure. But our research reveals a different story: the impact structure was already
30 there when the meteorites fell. It means that two meteorites struck at the same place, possibly with an interval of millions of years.

6

The main function of the third paragraph in relation to the passage as a whole is to

A) give a specific example of something defined in the previous paragraph.

B) summarize the main points of the passage and form a conclusion.

C) offer a counterexample that disproves a claim in the first paragraph.

D) explain how meteorites can offer insights into Earth's origins.

Question 7

This passage is adapted from Gunpowder Treason and Plot by Harold Avery, Fred Whishaw, and R.B. Townshend. First published in 1901.

Old Dan Mudge, fisherman, of Brixham, Devon, saw a curious sight one afternoon as he walked along the shore between his own village
Line and another of the name of Churston, in order to
5 see whether the gale of the preceding night had disturbed his lobster-pots.

A curiously shaped object floated and bobbed in the still lively sea, fifty yards from shore, and from the midst of the object there seemed to
10 rise—yes, he was sure of it—a child's cry.

"I must wade in and see to that matter," thought old Dan. "It isn't deep where she's floating now."

"She" consisted, as he plainly saw when he had
15 approached a little nearer, of a most elaborately made floating nest. Two lifebuoys, held apart by thick wire zigzags, floated one above the other; and slung upon the uppermost, hanging between it and the other, was a basket. In the basket, lying
20 securely fastened among cushions and blankets, were two splendid little boys, one of whom slept soundly; the other yelled loudly. From their likeness to each other, it was plain that they were brothers.
25 Old Dan Mudge was astonished beyond words—so astonished that he omitted to save the lifebuoys with their ingenious appendage, but

simply took the two children out and carried them ashore, leaving their peculiar raft to itself and to
30 the mercy of the waves.

7

The main purpose of the first, second, and third paragraphs is to show

A) how Old Dan Mudge ran his lobster business.

B) that Old Dan Mudge was an immoral character.

C) where Old Dan Mudge was traveling on vacation.

D) why Old Dan Mudge treaded into the water.

Question 8

This passage is adapted from "Older people may be better learners than we think" by Nicki Russell and Reema Rattan. ©2014 by Nicki Russell and Reema Rattan.

Older people may be able to learn more from visual information than their younger counterparts, according to a study published today
Line in the journal Current Biology. "The take-home
5 message the study authors gave was that healthy older people are good at learning," said Professor Henry Brodaty, co-director of the Center for Healthy Brain Aging. "They have the same plasticity, but they're not as good at filtering out
10 other information."
The brain needs to be able to easily learn new information (plasticity), and filter out irrelevant information (stability). The experiment was designed to test whether ageing affects the brain's
15 plasticity, stability, or both. The researchers had ten 67 to 79-year-olds and ten 19 to 30-year-olds view screens displaying six letters interspersed with two numbers. Each screen also had moving dots in the background, and the participants were
20 asked to report just the numbers.
They found younger people had strong plasticity and stability, meaning only important information—the numbers—was learned. The older participants, on the other hand, learned the
25 numbers but also picked up on the movement of the background dots.

8

The main function of the third paragraph is to

A) summarize the conclusions described in the passage.

B) give an example of additional research supporting the passage's main point.

C) describe the results of the study the passage focuses on.

D) define key terms that were used throughout the passage.

Question 9

This passage is adapted from "The return of the breeze block" by Naomi Stead. ©2016 by Naomi Stead.

Breezeblocks are having a moment in the sun. Having been painfully hip in the architecture of the 1950s and 60s, they were used so extensively,
Line in both houses and commercial buildings, that
5 they became ubiquitous anywhere in the world where it was hot—including throughout Australia.
While particularly associated with a beachy, holiday feeling—Gold Coast motels, houses in Palm Springs—they were so widely used that
10 they can still be found everywhere. But after that postwar high point, they fell drastically out of favor, and languished for the next fifty years, built into the walls and gardens of our youths, widely loathed and reviled for being ugly and out of date.
15 Now their fortunes have turned again and architects, for the moment at least, can't get enough of them: at the 2016 Houses Awards, announced two weeks ago, the "Best house under 200 meters squared" went to the Naranga Avenue
20 House, by James Russell Architect—a lovely minimal house with a tight, rigorous plan, which undoubtedly won the award because of its "skin of delicate breezeblocks," described by the awards jury as having "a sublime, ephemeral quality."

9

One of the main purposes of the last paragraph is to show that

A) breezeblocks are once again in style.

B) architects are experimenting more than ever.

C) architectural competitions favor breezeblocks.

D) breezeblocks are a protected national art form.

Question 10

This passage is adapted from "Scientists are using drones to help predict coastal erosion" by John Barlow. ©2016 by John Barlow.

A large chunk of chalk recently collapsed into the sea from the Seven Sisters cliffs, a world-renowned beauty spot located on England's
Line East Sussex coastline. To many, they are a
5 quintessentially English landmark—and the British press was quick to show concern. The usual questions that follow these types of events involve the rate at which the coastline is eroding and potential risks to the public.
10 Answering these questions is difficult from a scientific perspective—sets of data regarding rock fall are often not available and those that are available are often incomplete. Approximately 53% of England and Wales' coastline exhibit cliffs
15 and shore platforms. These cliffs retreat through episodic rock falls that can range in size from small pebbles to hundreds of thousands of cubic meters. Analysis of historical aerial photographs can go some way to establishing the rate of retreat
20 over decades. However, this approach does not provide information on individual rock fall events.
Since the turn of the millennium, the evolution of sea cliffs has received greater attention from earth scientists. The interaction of the local
25 climate, waves and tidal range with cliff materials makes changes in these land forms difficult to predict over large areas.
In order to develop an understanding of the relative frequency of rock fall events of differing
30 magnitudes, an inventory of events through time is required. This can then be used to both predict future change as well as establish the potential

risk posed by rock falls to both the public and to infrastructure. The way forward therefore seems
35 to involve mapping technology that is capable of capturing both large and small rock falls as they occur along a section of coast.

10

One main purpose of the last paragraph is to suggest

A) why most rock fall events occur on the British coast.

B) what experiments have received the most attention from the media.

C) how future studies of rock fall events should best be conducted.

D) which zones are the most dangerous for the public.

Question 11

This passage is adapted from The Viking Blood by Frederick William Wallace. First published in 1920.

Janet made Alec McKenzie a good wife. She supplied the ambition and aggressiveness which her husband lacked. No one could say he lowered
Line himself by marrying Janet McKinnon, for she
5 was quick to realize her husband's assets in the way of family connections and genuine ability, and she carried herself as if she were the accepted niece, by marriage, of the Laird of Dunsany. Other mates' wives called on her, more out of curiosity
10 than kindness, but she would have none of them and treated them coldly.

11

The statement "She supplied the ambition and aggressiveness which her husband lacked" (lines 1 - 3) functions in the passage to

A) show that Janet felt trapped within her marriage.

B) describe Janet's many ambitions and her plans to execute them.

C) support the narrator's view that Janet was a valuable spouse to Alec.

D) explain why other wives did not take to Janet and treated her coldly.

Question 12

This passage is adapted from "Taking the ouch out of vaccines: the future of needle-free vaccination" by C. Raina MacIntyre, Daniel Salmon, and Elizabeth Kpoze-houen. ©2016 by C. Raina MacIntyre, Daniel Salmon, and Elizabeth Kpozehouen.

English physician Edward Jenner developed the first vaccine more than 200 years ago to protect against smallpox. It was needle-free,
Line involving arm-to-arm inoculation with the
5 vaccinia virus. Vaccinology as a discipline and a public health intervention developed exponentially in the mid-20th century. Vaccines against diphtheria, tetanus, whooping cough, and polio were the first to have a major impact on
10 disease burden globally.

But as more vaccines are developed, the challenge of delivering them with minimal pain, anxiety, and number of visits to the doctor has increased. New, needle-free technologies offer an
15 additional solution.

12

The authors use the example of Edward Jenner in order to

A) explain the history of the use of needles in medicine.

B) situate historically the development of vaccines.

C) give an example of a doctor who campaigns against needles.

D) emphasize the unreliability of early vaccines.

Question 13

This passage is adapted from "Bad news: why TV is going the same way as print journalism" by Richard Sambrook and Rasmus Kleis Nielsen. ©2016 by Richard Sambrook and Rasmus Kleis Nielsen.

Television news has been—and currently remains—the most powerful platform in the world for news and information. For more than
Line 50 years, it enjoyed a privileged position in a
5 low-choice environment with large audiences and high levels of trust. But of course the internet has changed that. We now live in a high-choice environment with rapid changes in technology and consumption to which TV news is having to
10 adapt. Viewing in countries such as the US and the UK has declined by 3%-4% per year on average since 2012.

13

In the context of the passage, what do the authors mean when they state that television enjoyed a "privileged position" (line 4)?

A) Television news jobs were open only to elites at the time.

B) Television was the dominant source of news for those 50 years.

C) Television was the main entertainment for generations of Americans.

D) Television was loved by many people before the internet.

Question 14

This passage is adapted from "The spectacular peacock spider dance and its strange evolutionary roots" by Michael Kasumovic, Damian Ellas, and Madeline Girard. ©2015 by Michael Kasumovic, Damian Ellas, and Madeline Girard.

Peacock spiders (Maratus volans) are a group that is unique to Australia. So to explore peacock spider courtship, we collected 128 male and
Line female spiders from around Sydney and brought
5 them back into the lab. Males use vibrations early on to gain a female's attention. When they are sure she's watching, they begin to escalate courtship by waving their front legs and showing off their fan. If the female begins ignoring the male, they
10 change their strategy and begin vibrating more.

We found that there was a very low success rate: only 16 of the 64 males were successful! And it was visual signaling effort that best predicted success—so the tux was more effective than the
15 serenade.

The phrase "the tux was more effective than the serenade" (lines 14 - 15) is most likely meant to

A) imply that female peacock spiders exclusively consider physical appearance when selecting a mate.

B) provide a relatable analogy to peacock spiders' fans and vibrations.

C) suggest that other species might benefit from adopting the visual signaling strategies of peacock spiders

D) explain that a fan display is more effective than vibrations at initially attracting female spiders' attention

Question 15

This passage is adapted from The Dark Forest by Hugh Walpole. First published in 1916.

His was the first figure to catch my eye that evening in Petrograd; he stood under the dusky lamp in the vast gloomy Warsaw station, with
Line exactly the expression that I was afterwards to
5 know so well. His face, with its mild blue eyes, straggly fair moustache, expressed anxiety and pride, timidity and happiness, apprehension, and confidence.

He was exactly what I had expected. He was
10 not, however, alone, and that surprised me. By his side stood a girl, obviously Russian, wearing her Sister's uniform with excitement and eager anticipation, her eyes turning restlessly from one part of the platform to another, listening with an
15 impatient smile to the remarks of her companion.

In the context of the passage, the narrator's use of the phrase "exactly the expression that I was afterwards to know so well" (lines 4 - 5) is primarily meant to convey the idea that the narrator

A) had trouble reading the young man's shifting moods at first.

B) believes the young man to be moody and excitable.

C) would soon come to have some sort of relationship with the man.

D) foresees an impending conflict with the young man and wishes to avoid it.

Question 16

This passage is adapted from "This is what happens to footballers' brains when they miss penalties" by Recep Gorgulu and Tim Woodman. ©2016 by Recep Gorgulu and Tim Woodman.

Our research has consistently shown an interesting thing about the way players miss vital penalties—they often make the exact error they *Line* are trying to avoid. A player places the ball on the
5   penalty spot in a tournament and tells himself, "aim left; just don't hit the left post." During training or a less-important match, they would find the back of the net with ease every time.

But this is a high-pressure match—a stadium
10   full of screaming fans and hundreds of millions of viewers around the world watching him take those steps back. And more often than not, the player who misses won't have kicked the ball wide of the post or over the crossbar. He'll have kicked it
15   precisely at the left post. Since this is the thing he set out to not do, we call it the "ironic error."

In the context of the passage, the author's statement in lines 6 - 8 most nearly means that footballers

A) have an easier time scoring in low-pressure situations.

B) are more relaxed shooting penalties when they are able to practice often.

C) require extensive training in order to hit penalties correctly.

D) make more errors when they have an audience of any kind.

Question 17

This passage is adapted from "Life lessons from the editing suite of Paul Cox" by Jonathan auf der Heide. ©2016 by Jonathan auf der Heide.

I was introduced to Paul Cox at his home office in Albert Park in 2006. As I walked into his office, led by our mutual friend, the actor and editor Aden *Line* Young, Paul got up from his desk and shook my
5   hand with both of his, repeating my name as if it was some kind of relief to finally have met me. As though these two paths were destined to cross.

Our conversation centered around films, love, art, and our mutual hatred for the Grand Prix,
10   held annually in Albert Park. It was a profound experience that I have witnessed with others many times since. Paul had the ability to make whomever he was meeting feel like the most important person in the world—two lost kindred spirits finding
15   common ground in a mad, mad world.

In the context of the passage, the primary function of lines 12 - 15 is to

A) suggest that Paul was a brilliant artist and filmmaker.

B) cast doubt on the authenticity of Paul during the narrator and Paul's meeting.

C) reveal the narrator's conflicted feelings toward his host.

D) shed light on the narrator's feelings toward Paul during their meeting.

Question 18

This passage is adapted from "Dolly's 'sisters' show cloned animals don't grow old before their time" by Kevin Sinclair. ©2016 by Kevin Sinclair.

It's now 20 years since the birth of Dolly the sheep, the first mammal to be cloned. This groundbreaking scientific achievement was
Line accompanied by warnings that Dolly might age
5 prematurely because she had been cloned from adult sheep cells, whose "biological clock" had not been reset. Fears were heightened in 2001 when Dolly was diagnosed with osteoarthritis at five years of age (she died two years later). This
10 was heralded as evidence of premature ageing, although the condition is actually very poorly described in sheep.
　　We wanted to better understand how the cloning process affected the health of the animals
15 produced and so we've been studying a group of cloned sheep, including four of Dolly's "identical sisters". We found that most of the animals are actually in good health for their age. There was little sign of blood glucose problems, high blood
20 pressure or osteoarthritis, all of which were highlighted as potential problems. This suggests that the cloning technique can, after all, produce perfectly normal and viable offspring that don't grow old before their time.

18

The author uses the description of Dolly's illness and premature death (lines 7 - 12) to suggest that

A) scientists did not know how to properly care for cloned sheep.

B) cloned sheep are rarely as healthy as natural-born sheep.

C) sheep that develop osteoarthritis die more quickly than others.

D) the public took Dolly's death to mean confirmation of an existing fear.

Question 19

This passage is adapted from Penelope and the Others by Amy Walton. First published in 1892.

Penelope Hawthorne sat in the school-room window-seat at Easney Vicarage, one afternoon, looking very gravely out at the garden.
Line She had sat there for some time, with her
5 hands in her lap and a little troubled frown on her forehead, and anyone who knew her well would have guessed at once that she was thinking over a "plan."
　　Penelope was just thirteen years old, the
10 eldest of the Hawthorne children, and as she was a thoughtful girl and fond of reading, she often made very good plans for her brothers and sisters' amusement, partly out of her own head, and partly out of books. But this particular plan quite puzzled
15 her, for it had nothing to do with amusement, and she did not at all see how it was to be carried out. Yet it was much too good to be given up.
　　The plan was this. To buy a new Chinese mandarin for Miss Unity Cheffins.

19

The sentence in lines 14 - 16 serves to

E) show why Penelope's new plan was different from ones that came before.

F) explain why Penelope is so morose that afternoon.

A) hint that Penelope was scheming with her brothers and sisters to make a plan.

B) express that Penelope was no longer as fond of coming up with plans as before.

Question 20

This passage is adapted from "What does it mean to think and could a machine ever do it?" by Peter Ellerton. ©2016 by Peter Ellerton.

The idea of a thinking machine is an amazing one. It would be like humans creating artificial life, only more impressive because we would be creating consciousness. Or would we?
It's tempting to think that a machine that could think would think like us. But a bit of reflection shows that's not an inevitable conclusion. Just because a computer acts like it has a mind, it doesn't mean it must have one. It might be all show and no substance, an instance of a philosophical zombie.

20

The author uses the phrase "Or would we?" in line 4 to make the point that

A) scientists have not yet developed a way to create artificial life.

B) creating consciousness is more complicated than creating artificial life.

C) the public is wary of the creation of any "thinking machines."

D) machines have already had consciousness programmed into them.

1. (A) is the correct answer. The first paragraph explains that Darling was named "the patron saint of Australian printmaking" and states that he played a large role in fostering visual arts in Australia. This sets the stage for the rest of the passage, which goes on to describe additional achievements and then questions why Darling's death was not a leading headline in the media. (B) is incorrect because the passage presents Darling positively. (C) is too general; the paragraph and passage are focused on Gordon Darling. (D) is too specific, as the National Portrait Gallery is mentioned only in reference to Gordon Darling.

2. (B) is the correct answer. The last paragraph takes a different turn in the passage, noting that GPI and other relevant technologies have not settled all important exoplanetary science questions, and that there are many limitations to such techniques. (A) is incorrect because the passage does not indicate researchers have found proof of the existence of life on other planets. (C) is incorrect because the passage does not mention the media, let alone indicate the media willfully misrepresented technology. (D) is incorrect because it is too extreme; the last paragraph hints at the limitations, but not unreliability, of such technology.

3. (D) is the correct answer. The third paragraph mentions a few additional details about Henry and Jim that provide more insight into these characters. (A) is incorrect because, though the information is true, this is too specific, as this is touched on just as much as the fact that Jim is a superior hunter. (B) is incorrect because the details given don't indicate any drastic difference between the boys. (C) is incorrect because the paragraph is not foreshadowing a rift; in fact, an earlier paragraph states that the boys' friendship "was destined to ripen as the years went on," indicating the opposite.

4. (A) is the correct answer. The third paragraph uses words like "structured, online program" and "standard, evidence-based psychological treatment methods," and follows with the example of cognitive behavioral therapy. The result is language that is scientific and structured, lending a sense of credibility and reliability to the topics discussed. (B) is incorrect because the third paragraph merely describes how digital mental health services work and claims these "offer more choices and greater flexibility in how we get help," implying a positive opinion that wouldn't logically induce fearful reactions. (C) is incorrect because the third paragraph only characterizes digital mental health services as a positive thing, which "ambivalent" contradicts. (D) is incorrect because the paragraph describes digital mental health treatment in a straightforward manner, which would most likely not cause confusion.

5. (B) is the correct answer. The first paragraph starts with the general claim that "We all love history" and transitions to the rest of the passage with the specific claim that our love of history "seeks to control the story." (A) is incorrect because the first paragraph does not summarize the major points of the passage. (C) is incorrect because the first paragraph does not contain a specific anecdote. (D) is incorrect because the first paragraph does not offer any solutions.

6. (A) is the correct answer. The previous paragraph defines and describes "impact structures," while the third paragraph gives the specific example of an impact structure in the High Atlas Mountains in Morocco. (B) is incorrect because the third paragraph offers an example and does not summarize the passage's points. (C) is incorrect because the paragraph describes a surprising finding about the location of the meteorite, which isn't a counterexample for the first paragraph, which only claims meteorites contain clues about Earth's origins. (D) is incorrect because the the third paragraph offers an explanation only for when a certain impact structure appeared on Morocco in relevance to two meteorites, and never mentions how this might offer insight into the entire planet Earth's origins.

7. (D) is the correct answer. The first three paragraphs explain why Old Dan Mudge was out, and then why he waded into the water: because he heard a child's cry. (A) is incorrect because only the first paragraph touches on Dan's business, and this is not the main purpose of this or any other paragraph. (B) is incorrect because Old Dan Mudge is portrayed positively, as rescuing the two babies, and not as a man without morals. (C) is incorrect because the passage does not indicate Old Dan Mudge is on vacation, nor are his travels the focus of the first three paragraphs.

8. (C) is the correct answer. In the passage, the first paragraph offers a summary and overview, the second describes the experimental setup, and the third discusses the experiment's results. (A) is incorrect because the third paragraph is a summary of results of an experiment, not a conclusion. (B) is incorrect because the study discussed is the one the entire passage focuses on. (D) is incorrect because the third paragraph does not give definitions of key terms.

9. (A) is the correct answer. The paragraph states that "fortunes have turned again" and that at least for the moment, architects "can't get enough" of breezeblocks, giving as one example the 2016 House Awards. (B) is incorrect because the paragraph does not focus on architectural experimentation. (C) is too broad a conclusion to draw; only one competition is said to have been won by a property "because of its 'skin of delicate breezeblocks,'" which isn't enough evidence to believe all architectural competitions favor that architectural style. (D) is incorrect because the passage does not describe breezeblocks as an art form, let alone suggest they are protected.

10. (C) is the correct answer. The final paragraph notes that, in order to understand rock fall events, scientists should create "an inventory of events through time," going on to add that "the way forward therefore seems to involve mapping technology." The author here is offering solutions and suggestions on studying rock fall events. (A) is incorrect because this is not a claim made in the passage or paragraph. (B) is incorrect because the paragraph is discussing potential future areas for research, not discussing experiments that had already been conducted. (D) is incorrect because the paragraph does not compare the danger in various zones of Britain or elsewhere.

11. (C) is the correct answer. This sentence comes right after the statement that "Janet made Alec McKenzie a good wife," and details how Janet does this to provide support in defense of this statement. (A) is incorrect because this line only indicates that Janet provides emotions which her husband does not, and while "ambition" and "aggressiveness" are feelings that could be indicative of feelings of entrapment within a marriage, there is no indication in the passage that Janet feels this way, nor do either of these terms necessarily betray feelings of entrapment. (B) is incorrect because there is no mention that Janet feels trapped, and claiming a character has ambition and aggressiveness does not on its own betray feelings of being in a restrictive situation. (D) is incorrect as it references a later, unrelated part of the passage, where it is actually Janet who treats the wives coldly, and not vice versa.

12. (B) is the correct answer. Edward Jenner is mentioned as the man who "developed the first vaccine more than 200 years ago." The passage moves from this example into a brief history of vaccinology before moving on to the discussion of new, needle-free technologies. (A) is incorrect because Edward Jenner did not use needles to vaccinate. (C) is incorrect because, though Jenner did not use needles, there is no evidence he campaigned against them. (D) is incorrect because the passage does not imply that Jenner's vaccines were unreliable.

13. (B) is the correct answer. Using the term "privileged," meaning of an advantaged position, the authors explain that television had an advantage as a news source because of it "low-choice environment" and "large audiences and high levels of trust." (A) is incorrect because the passage does not discuss television jobs. (C) is incorrect because the passage is focused on news, not entertainment. (D) is incorrect because the passage does not compare people's love for the internet to their love for television.

14. (B) is the correct answer. The 'tux' is analogous to the spider's fan and the 'serenade' is analogous to the spider's vibrations, and since this phrase says that the tux was "more effective" than the serenade, this mirrors the results that "it was visual signalling effort that best predicted success." Both a 'tux' and a 'serenade' are things that are familiar to humans, making this passage about spiders relatable to human readers. (A) is incorrect because the phrase merely communicates that one mating tactic is more effective than another, which in no way implies that only one mating tactic is considered. (C) is incorrect because this entire passage concentrates solely on peacock spiders and never mentions other species, and this phrase uses 'tux' and 'serenade,' both of which are specific of peacock spiders' appearance and mating habits.

15. (C) is the correct answer. Here, it is plausible that the narrator's reference to an expression that she or he would soon know well implies some continued engagement with the man, without which the expression could not exist. (A) is incorrect because the narrator only states the feelings they believe the man to have, never a sense of confusion as a result of interpreting these feelings. (B) is incorrect because the given lines do not mention the young man's mood, only his facial expression. (D) is incorrect because the narrator gives no indication here that she or he predicts a conflict with the young man.

16. (A) is the correct answer. The given lines indicate that players have an easier time finding the back of the net, or scoring, in low-pressure situations such as training or less-important matches. (B) is incorrect because the lines are not talking about the frequency of practice and its effect on players. (C) is incorrect because the lines do not discuss the need for extensive training. (D) is incorrect because the author indicates that players make much fewer errors there.

17. (D) is the correct answer. The given lines show that the narrator felt that, when speaking to Paul, he was "the most important person in the world," something he hypothesizes that Paul is able to do with all visitors. (A) is incorrect because the given lines are not concerned with addressing Paul's talents as an artist or filmmaker. (B) and (C) are incorrect because the lines describe Paul positively, not negatively.

18. (D) is the correct answer. The given lines are preceded by "Fears were heightened in 2001 when," which indicates there was already dread present towards Dolly's mortality, which the passage then says were "heralded as evidence of" premature aging, something the passage indicates earlier on as something the public was worried about. (A) is incorrect because the passage doesn't mention scientists' lack of care as a cause of Dolly's death. (B) is incorrect because, though some interpreted Dolly's death this way, the rest of the passage features examples of healthy cloned goats, making it clear that they disagree with this stance. Thus, the author was not using Dolly's death as a cautionary tale. (C) is incorrect because the author never states this as a belief of theirs, but instead mentions only Dolly's osteoarthritis, prefacing it with "Fears were heightened in 2001 when," using it as a reason for why people were worried about the wellbeing of sheep.

19. (A) is the correct answer. Penelope's new plan is said to have "had nothing to do with amusement," unlike many of her plans before, which are said to be "for her brothers and sisters' amusement". This sentence clearly lays out this difference. (B) is incorrect because, while Penelope is troubled and thoughtful, these adjectives are not nearly as intense as "morose" or "very sad." (C) is incorrect because the passage only describes Penelope as thinking to herself about a plan, not scheming with her brothers and sisters. (D) is incorrect because the passage does not indicate Penelope is now less fond of coming up with plans.

20. (B) is the correct answer. The author notes that even though "the idea of a thinking machine is an amazing one," and that "it would be like humans creating artificial life, only more impressive because we would be creating consciousness," this possibility is actually not as simple as it sounds. The next paragraph goes on to state that "just because a computer acts like it has a mind, doesn't mean it must have one." The phrase "Or would we?" serves as the transition point, whereby the author expresses such doubts. (A) is incorrect because it is consciousness, not artificial life, that the phrase is referring to. (C) is incorrect because the passage does not touch on the public's opinion of thinking machines. (D) is incorrect because the passage concentrates on what the potential of machine consciousness is, which cannot implies it has already been achieved.

Point of View

Part 4

Point of View questions require you to draw inferences about authors' and characters' perspectives. You may need to identify fairly direct paraphrases of thesis statements or draw browd inferences from the tone of a passage and the general thrust of an author's argument. You may need to draw inferences about an author's unstated beliefs and attitudes or about their relationship to the subject matter. You may need to compare the points of view of two or more characters, and, on paired passages, you may need to compare the points of view of two authors.

DIRECTIONS

Every passage or paired set of passages is accompanied by a number of questions. Read the passage or paired set of passages, then use what is said or implied in what you read and in any given graphics to choose the best answer to each question.

Question 1

This passage is adapted from *A Dark Night's Work* by Elizabeth Gaskell. First published in 1863.

In the county town of a certain shire there lived (about forty years ago) one Mr. Wilkins, a conveyancing attorney of considerable standing.
Line
5 The certain shire was but a small county, and the principal town in it contained only about four thousand inhabitants; so in saying that Mr. Wilkins was the principal lawyer in Hamley, I say very little, unless I add that he transacted all the legal business of the gentry for twenty miles round. His
10 grandfather had established the connection; his father had consolidated and strengthened it, and, indeed, by his wise and upright conduct, as well as by his professional skill, had obtained for himself the position of confidential friend to many of the
15 surrounding families of distinction.

1

It can reasonably be inferred that the narrator views Hamley as

A) a relatively small place.

B) an exceptional lawyer.

C) an upstanding businessman.

D) a prosperous shire.

Question 2

This passage is adapted from "The future of genetic enhancement is not in the West" by G. Owen Schaefer. ©2016 by G. Owen Schaefer.

Would you want to alter your future children's genes to make them smarter, stronger, or better-looking? As the state of the science
Line brings prospects like these closer to reality,
5 an international debate has been raging over the ethics of enhancing human capacities with biotechnologies such as so-called smart pills, brain implants, and gene editing. This discussion has only intensified in the past year with the
10 advent of the CRISPR-cas9 gene editing tool, which raises the specter of tinkering with our DNA to improve traits like intelligence,

athleticism and even moral reasoning.

So are we on the brink of a brave new world
15 of genetically enhanced humanity? Perhaps. And
there's an interesting wrinkle: It's reasonable
to believe that any seismic shift toward genetic
enhancement will not be centered in Western
countries like the U.S. or the U.K., where many
20 modern technologies are pioneered. Instead,
genetic enhancement is more likely to emerge out
of China.

2

It can reasonably be inferred from the passage that
the author views genetic enhancement of humans as

A) repugnant.

B) unsettling.

C) noteworthy.

D) laudable.

Question 3

This passage is adapted from "Elizabeth I, the Spanish Armada and the art of painting politics" by Gabriele Neher.
©2016 by Gabriele Neher.

Few images are as well-known as the Armada
painting, which shows Queen Elizabeth I basking
in the aftermath of the greatest military success
Line of her long reign, the defeat of a Spanish Armada.
5 The value of the Armada painting lies in its
masterful storytelling, beautifully executed by the
unknown painter who committed the narrative
to canvas sometime after the actual events of
the feared and foiled invasion. Elizabeth, in a
10 splendid and jeweled gown, occupies the center of
the painting, flanked by two images. Both scenes
show a fleet. On the left, the English fleet rides
high on tranquil and becalmed waters, basking
in sunshine, whilst on the right, the Spanish fleet
15 is battered by ferocious high waves. Elizabeth's
presence has becalmed the waves for her own
navy, resulting in the destruction of enemy ships.

3

The point of view from which the passage is told is
best described as that of

A) an admirer of the Armada painting of Queen
Elizabeth I.

B) a historian of Elizabethan England.

C) an enthusiast of navy-based art such as the
Armada painting.

D) an artist concerned with the reception of the
portrait of Queen Elizabeth I.

Question 4

This passage is adapted from "Musa genome mapped:
that's bananas!" by Harjeet Khanna. ©2012 by Harjeet
Khanna.

The current edition of Nature carries a paper
that marks a major milestone for both bananas
and plant biotechnology. Some 18 research
Line groups—ten from France, three from USA, one
5 from Switzerland, one from Czech Republic,
one from UK, one from Australia, and one
from Netherlands—have published the first
draft sequence of the 523-megabase genome of
DH-Pahang, a doubled-haploid genotype of the
10 subspecies malaccensis, that contributed one of
the three acuminate genomes of the common
dessert banana, Cavendish.

This is the first completed sequence of the
11 chromosomes of banana, and it provides
15 the first detailed genetic blueprint of the most
important fruit crop in the world and one of the
most important food crops after staple cereals and
cassava. This publicly available finished sequence
is anchored to the genetic map, providing both
20 the linear order of the 36,542 genes and their
positions on the 11 banana chromosomes.

4

Details in the passage suggest that the author views the publication of the genome of the Cavendish banana as

A) inevitable.

B) groundbreaking.

C) irrelevant.

D) controversial.

Question 5

This passage is adapted from A Princess of Mars by Edgar Rice Burroughs. First published in 1917.

I am a very old man; how old I do not know. Possibly I am a hundred, possibly more; but I cannot tell because I have never aged as other
Line men, nor do I remember any childhood. So far as
5 I can recollect I have always been a man, a man of about thirty. I appear today as I did forty years and more ago, and yet I feel that I cannot go on living forever; that some day I shall die the real death from which there is no resurrection. I do not
10 know why I should fear death, I who have died twice and am still alive; but yet I have the same horror of it as you who have never died, and it is because of this terror of death, I believe, that I am so convinced of my mortality.

5

The passage is written from the perspective of someone who is

A) convinced he will live forever.

B) afraid of dying.

C) suffering from a long illness.

D) young but prepared for death.

Question 6

This passage is adapted from "Learning music increases blood flow to the brain" by the University of Liverpool. ©2014 by the University of Liverpool.

Brief musical training appears to increase blood flow to the left side of the brain. In two studies, researchers analyzed the brain activity of
Line musicians and non-musicians while they took part
5 in music and word tasks.
Similar brain areas were activated for musicians, while non-musicians' brains showed different activity. But after 30 minutes of musical training, the non-musicians' brain areas showed
10 similar activity to the musicians. Researcher Amy Spray said the research suggests areas of the brain that process music and language are shared, and musical training may lead to an increased use of the brain's left hemisphere.

6

The tone of the passage can best be described as

A) informative.

B) skeptical.

C) confused.

D) excited.

Question 7

This passage is adapted from "How photography evolved from science to art" by Nancy Locke. ©2015 by Nancy Locke.

In its first incarnation, photography seemed to be more of a scientific tool than a form of artistic expression. Many of the earliest photographers
Line didn't even call themselves artists: they were
5 scientists and engineers—chemists, astronomers, botanists, and inventors. While the new form attracted individuals with a background in painting or drawing, even early practitioners like Louis Daguerre or Nadar could be seen more as
10 entrepreneurial inventors than as traditional artists.
One reason early photographs were not considered works of art because, quite simply,

they didn't look like art: no other form possessed
the level of detail that they rendered. When the
American inventor Samuel F. B. Morse saw
the daguerreotype shortly after its first public
demonstration in Paris in 1839, he wrote, "The
exquisite minuteness of the delineation cannot
be conceived. No painting or engraving ever
approached it."

7

Which choice best describes Samuel F. B. Morse's
view of the daguerreotype?

A) He felt it to be a superior form of art to
painting and engraving.

B) He saw it as a brilliant scientific instrument for
observation.

C) He was impressed by the intense level of detail
it captured.

D) He viewed it as a rough precursor to the
modern photograph.

Question 8

This passage is adapted from "Deadly medical errors are
less common than headlines suggest" by Richard Gunderman. ©2016 by Richard Gunderman.

A report published in May from researchers at
Johns Hopkins claims that medical errors are the
third leading cause of death in the U.S., behind
only heart disease and cancer. According to the
researchers, medical errors account for 251,454
U.S. deaths each year—and they regard this figure
as an underestimate.

That's the sort of finding that makes headlines.
Indeed, you might have read about this report
in the newspaper or even seen it reported on the
evening news. But the methods the researchers
used to draw this conclusion are flawed, and
that means that the conclusion that medical
error is the third leading cause of death is highly
questionable. When a report like this gets broad
media coverage, it can foster unwarranted mistrust
of medicine, which could prevent people from
seeking needed care—a concern to everyone who
takes care of patients.

8

The passage indicates that the author views data
mentioned in the first paragraph with

A) confusion.

B) acceptance.

C) skepticism.

D) delight.

Question 9

This passage is adapted from Leslie's Loyalty by Charles
Garvice. First published in 1905.

While Leslie was painting in her sitting-room,
the door opened, and a tall, thin man entered.

This was Francis Lisle, her father. He was a
man this side of fifty and carried a portable easel
in one hand, and held a canvas under his arm.

He set the easel up in a corner, placed the
canvas on it upside down, and crossing his hands
behind his back, stood with bent head gazing at it
for some moments in silence. Then he said, in a
voice which matched the dreamy face:

"Leslie, come here."

Leslie glided to him.

"Now, Leslie, look at that sky. There is a
wealth of form and color in that right hand corner,
and I—yes, I think it is the best, by far the best
and truest thing I have as yet done."

Leslie leaned forward, and softly, swiftly,
placed the picture right side up.

It had not very much improved by the
transposition. It was—well, to put it bluntly, a
daub of the most awful description.

Leslie looked at it with a sad little expression
in her eyes, the pitying look one sees in the face
of a woman whose life is spent in humoring the
weakness of a beloved one; then she said, gently:

"It is very striking, papa."

"Striking!" repeated Francis Lisle. "Striking! I
like that word. Tell me, now, Leslie, what it is in it
that catches your fancy most."

Leslie looked at it carefully.

"I—I think that heap of sea-weed nicely
painted, papa," she said, putting her arm round his
neck.

"Heap of sea-weed?" his brows knitted. "Heap

35 of sea-weed? I don't see anything of the kind."

"There, papa," she said, pointing.

"My dear Leslie, I have always suspected that your sight was not perfect, that there was some defect in its range power; that is not a heap of
40 sea-weed, but a fisherwoman mending her nets!"

9

Over the course of the passage, it becomes clear that Leslie views her father's painting

A) with admiration and respect.

B) as inferior to her own.

C) with astonishment and shock.

D) as unskilled and amateurish.

Question 10

This passage is adapted from "There must be smarter security than a ban on 'dumb' passwords" by Mike Johnstone. ©2016 by Mike Johnstone.

Microsoft now says it wants to compile a list of what it calls dumb passwords that will not be allowed on its system. That dumb passwords are
Line a problem is undeniable, as the online security
5 company SplashData gleefully publishes its annual list of the most common passwords, where "password" and "123456" are, ahem, quite high in the list. This shows people choose convenience over security when it comes to setting a password
10 (but they still want privacy).

The systematic response is that users are constantly being asked to set more complex passwords with upper, lower case, numbers, symbols etc., to the point we get password
15 fatigue. Asking us to keep changing passwords just encourages minor or incremental changes to the same supposedly unguessable passwords, something even Britain's intelligence agency GCHQ recognizes is a problem.
20 This mode of thinking works well for some problems, but the whole idea is rendered moot when anyone can easily download a lists of millions of the most common passwords.

10

The author's attitude toward "dumb passwords" is best described as

A) approving.

B) hopeful.

C) indifferent.

D) skeptical.

1. (A) is the correct answer. Hamley is the location in which Mr. Wilkins practices, containing "only about four thousand inhabitants." Since the narrator says that "in saying that Mr. Wilkins was the principal lawyer in Hamley, I say very little," it can be inferred that the narrator views Hamley as small. (B) and (C) can be eliminated because Hamley is a place, not a person. (D) is incorrect because the narrator does not imply that the town itself is prosperous.

2. (C) is the correct answer. The passage is almost completely made up of facts instead of opinions or positive or negative adjectives, but the author does characterize genetic enhancement as a "seismic shift," which indicates they believe this topic to be of great importance. The author does not state negative opinions toward the technology, so (A) and (B) can be eliminated. The author does not praise the technology, so (D) is also incorrect.

3. (A) is the correct answer. The author praises the Armada painting and its "masterful storytelling." (B) is incorrect because the passage does not offer enough clues to conclude that the author is a historian of this era, only that he/she is an admirer of the painting he describes. (C) is too broad; the author expresses pleasure with the Armada painting, but not navy-based art as a whole. (D) is incorrect because the passage offers no evidence that the author is an artist, or that he/she is concerned about the portrait.

4. (B) is the correct answer. The author calls the publication of the paper "a major milestone for both bananas and plant biotechnology." (A) is incorrect because the author does not suggest the discovery was inevitably going to occur. (C) is incorrect because the author emphasizes the importance of the paper. (D) is incorrect because the passage nowhere indicates controversy or disputes surrounding the publication of the paper.

5. (B) is the correct answer. The narrator notes that it is because of his "terror of death" that he is "so convinced of my mortality," showing that he fears death. (A) is incorrect because the narrator states he believes himself to be mortal. (C) is incorrect because the passage offers no evidence the narrator is suffering from a long illness. (D) is incorrect because the narrator says he is "a very old man."

6. (A) is the correct answer. The author of this passage only describes their main topic by offering detailed information about a study and then a researcher's summary of what this study suggests, all of which convey the idea that the passage is informing its readers about the topic, instead of, for example, giving opinions or catering to emotions. (B) and (C) are incorrect because the author gives no negative opinions or information about musical training, thus keeping the tone from being negative. (D) is incorrect because it is too strong; the passage only gives facts about a kind of research and its results, and never mentions something in the future the author is looking forward to eagerly.

7. (C) is the correct answer. The passage notes that Morse wrote that "the exquisite minuteness of the delineation cannot be conceived. No painting or engraving ever approached it." Therefore, it can be inferred he is impressed by its detail, which surpassed that of paintings or engravings. (A) is incorrect because Morse does not regard the daguerreotype as an art form when he compares it to paintings and engravings. (B) is incorrect because while Morse might have felt the daguerrotype was a great scientific tool because of its high level of detail, the passage does not state that this is why he praised its detail, only that he praised it.(D) is incorrect because there is no evidence that, at the time, photographs were even available, so Morse would not be able to comment on the daguerreotype's relationship to them.

8. (C) is the correct answer. The author notes in the second paragraph that "the methods the researchers used to draw this conclusion are flawed," referencing the data about medical errors mentioned in the first paragraph. The author goes on to state that such data "can foster unwarranted mistrust of medicine," suggesting skepticism with such figures. The author does not indicate confusion, so (A) is incorrect. (B) is incorrect because the author is concerned about the presentation of the data, and does not accept it. (D) is incorrect because the author views the data negatively, not with delight.

9. (D) is the correct answer. In the passage, Leslie humors her father by praising his painting, even though he originally sets it wrong-side-up. She later mistakes what he meant to be a fisherwoman for a "heap of sea-weed." Even though she praises his work, it is clear that she views it as amateurish and unskilled, and is only humoring him. (A) is incorrect as Leslie does not view the painting as good. (B) is incorrect because there is no evidence Leslie compares her father's paintings to her own. (C) is incorrect because Leslie nowhere expresses astonishment or shock.

10. (D) is the correct answer. The author notes that the response to ask users to set more complex passwords "just encourages minor or incremental changes," and will not ultimately lead to a solution or increased security. (A) and (B) are incorrect because they are too positive, as the author states "That dumb passwords are a problem is undeniable". (C) is incorrect because the author does take a stance towards dumb passwords when they say the problem with them is "undeniable," which "indifferent" contradicts.

Purpose
Part 5

Purpose questions ask you to identify an author's rhetorical goals in terms of the purpose of portions of the passage. They may ask about anything from a specific word or phrase choice to the overall structure the author uses to express an argument. They are distinct from questions about effect, organization, and point of view in that they require you to make inferences about the author's perspective and then combine those inferences with observations about the effects of certain choices to draw conclusions about the purpose served by those choices.

DIRECTIONS

Every passage or paired set of passages is accompanied by a number of questions. Read the passage or paired set of passages, then use what is said or implied in what you read and in any given graphics to choose the best answer to each question.

Question 1

This passage is adapted from "Since ancient Greece, the Olympics and bribery have gone hand in hand" by Nigel Crowther. ©2016 by Nigel Crowther.

Even in a founding myth of the ancient Olympics, bribery played a central role. According to the poet Pindar, the king of Pisa bribed Hermes'
Line son Myrtilus to tamper with his opponent's chariot
5 wheels.
During the ancient Olympics, athletes, their fathers and trainers made oaths not to "sin against the games." But some didn't take this oath as seriously as others. For example, the travel writer
10 Pausanias wrote about how, in 388 B.C., the boxer Eupolus bribed his three opponents at Olympia. The officials punished all four contestants. Sixty-six years later, a pentathlete named Callippus offered his competitors money to throw the contest
15 in his favor. And, according to the philosopher Philostratus, trainers often lent money to athletes at high rates of interest for the sole purpose of bribery.
Meanwhile, some Olympic contestants competed for city-states other than their own as
20 a result of bribery, or assumed bribery. After his Olympic victory, the runner Sotades of Crete was bribed to compete for the rival city of Ephesus. In response, his home city expelled him. In the fifth century B.C., wealthy residents of Syracuse enticed
25 Astylus of Croton to compete for their city and, a century later, the runner Dicon of Caulonia. In the former case, the citizens of Croton turned Astylus' house into a prison and destroyed his statue.

1

In the context of the passage, the primary function of lines 9 - 28 is to:

A) show the origins of different myths of corruption in the Olympics.

B) demonstrate the history of bribery in Greece.

C) provide examples of bribery in the early Olympic games.

D) condemn ancient Olympic athletes for their widespread corruption.

Question 2

This passage is adapted from "Male-only gene trick could leave invasive fish species floundering" by Ron Thresher. ©2014 by Ron Thresher.

A genetic modification that creates male-only populations could give us a new weapon against invasive fish such as carp that plague our
Line waterways. "Daughterless technology," which
5 works by removing females so a population can no longer breed, has previously been used to tackle mosquitos. But new CSIRO research shows that it also works on fish. The technology is safe and could be used to greatest effect with other
10 forms of pest control. It might also be used to control other vertebrate pests such as cane toads.

2

The most likely purpose of the passage is to

A) warn against the dangers of a risky new technology.

B) detail how a group of scientists controlled the overpopulation of carp.

C) suggest that CSIRO research needs more funding to continue its work.

D) explain how an existing technology could be applied to a new problem.

Question 3

This passage is adapted from The Christmas Story from David Harum. First published in 1898.

Considering John's employment by David Harum, it was natural that he should wish to think as well of him as possible, and he had
Line not (or thought he had not) allowed his mind to
5 be influenced by the disparaging remarks and insinuations which had been made to him, or in his presence, concerning his employer. He had made up his mind to form his opinion upon his own experience with the man, and so far it had
10 not only been pleasant but favorable, and far from justifying the half-jeering, half-malicious talk that had come to his ears. It had been made manifest to him, it was true, that David was capable of a sharp bargain in certain lines, but it seemed to him that
15 it was more for the pleasure of matching his wits against another's than for any gain involved.

3

The passage serves primarily to

A) show John's enthusiasm for his new position.

B) illustrate David Harum's esteem of John despite local gossip.

C) describe John's knowledge of and attitude towards his employer.

D) establish the competitive setting in which the story takes place.

Question 4

This passage is adapted from "Accurate science or accessible science in the media—why not both?" by Joshua Conrad Jackson, Ian Mahar, Jaan Altosaar, and Michael Gaultois. ©2016 by Joshua Conrad Jackson, Ian Mahar, Jaan Altosaar, and Michael Gaultois.

Every day, millions of people take to search engines with common concerns, such as "How can I lose weight?" or "How can I be productive?"
Line In return, they find articles that offer simple
5 advice and quick solutions, supposedly based on what "studies have shown." A closer look at these articles, however, reveals a troubling absence of scientific rigor. Few bother to cite research or discuss studies' methodologies or limitations. The
10 authors seldom have scientific training.

As young scientists from four diverse fields (psychology, chemistry, physics, and neuroscience), we've noticed that much writing about science, particularly on topics most relevant
15 to the daily lives of readers, is currently failing to resolve the trade-off between accessibility and accountability. Rigorous findings shared by researchers in specialist journals are obscured behind jargon and paywalls, while accessible
20 science shared on the internet is untrustworthy, unregulated, and often click-bait.

If this communication crisis is due to a lack

of scientifically literate voices, the solution
may be for more scientists to enter the fray.
25 Scientists have the expertise to publicly correct
misinterpretations of their and others' data. By
developing new ways to disseminate science
knowledge, they can help prevent inaccurate and
overhyped stories from gaining traction. We argue
30 that scientists bear a responsibility to reform the
way their work is ultimately communicated.

4

The authors' purpose in writing this passage is most
likely to

A) lament the current state of science journalism.

B) offer a solution to an observed problem.

C) argue that scientists should become journalists.

D) suggest that more science articles should be
open-access.

Question 5

This passage is adapted from "Before you judge personality tests, consider what they don't judge" by Nick
Haslam. ©2014 by Nick Haslam.

Many job seekers are wary of personality
testing. They will accept prying interviews and
secretive reference checks, but baulk at having
Line their personalities assessed. A review of studies
5 conducted in 17 countries found personality tests
were judged less favorably than most selection
tools, disliked almost as much as handwriting
analysis.
Personality testing and handwriting analysis
10 have their unpopularity in common, but they differ
in an important way. Personality tests are valid
predictors of performance on the job. A vast body
of research shows test scores help to identify who
is suited to particular kinds of work and who will
15 do them well.
This conclusion should not be surprising.
Personality traits influence all aspects of our lives,
and the workplace is no exception. Personality
characteristics predict happiness, social attitudes,
20 susceptibility to disease, economic behavior,
relationship breakdown, and even longevity.

Success at work is not simply a matter of being
able to perform particular tasks. It also depends
on motivation and the capacity to handle stress,
25 complexity, and the social context within an
organization. Personality traits are especially
relevant to this broader context of work. They tell
us how people are likely to behave rather than
merely what narrow skills they possess.

5

It can reasonably be inferred that one of the
functions of the passage is to

A) detail the utility of personality tests in the
workplace.

B) suggest that some employers violate
employees' rights during interviews.

C) argue that personality tests are poor indicators
of job performance.

D) offer evidence of the usefulness of personality
tests like handwriting analysis.

Question 6

This passage is adapted from "Explainer: how viruses can
fool the immune system" by Kim Jacobson. ©2015 by
Kim Jacobson.

The immune system protects us from the
constant onslaught of viruses, bacteria, and other
types of pathogens we encounter throughout life. It
Line also remembers past infections so it can fight them
5 off more easily the next time we encounter them.
But the immune system can sometimes misbehave.
It can start attacking its own proteins, rather than
the infection, causing autoimmunity. Or, it can
effectively respond to one variant of a virus, but
10 then is unable to stop another variant of the virus.
This is termed the original antigenic sin (OAS).
OAS occurs when the initial successful
immune response blocks an effective response
when the person is next exposed to the virus. This
15 can have potentially devastating consequences
for illnesses such as the mosquito-borne dengue.
There are around 400 million dengue infections
worldwide each year and no vaccine is available.

Reinfection of someone who has been exposed to
20 dengue previously can result in life-threatening
hemorrhagic fever. OAS is also thought to limit our
immune responses to the highly variable influenza
virus, increasing the chance of pandemics.

6

The primary purpose of the passage is to

A) suggest that OAS infections inhibit the
immune system.

B) explain the dangers of illnesses such as dengue
infections.

C) show one particular limitation of the immune
system.

D) document the rise of common pandemics such
as influenza.

Question 7

This passage is adapted from Saved at Sea by Mrs. O.F.
Walton. First published 1887.

It was a strange day, the day that I was born.
The waves were beating against the lighthouse,
and the wind was roaring and raging against
Line everything. Had not the lighthouse been built very
5 firmly into the strong solid rock, it, and all within
it, must have been swept into the deep wild sea.
It was a terrible storm. My grandfather said he
had never known such a storm since he came to
live on the island, more than forty years before.
10 Many ships went down in the storm that day,
and many lives were lost. But in the very midst of
it, when the wind was highest, and the waves were
strongest, and when the foam and the spray had
completely covered the lighthouse windows, I,
15 Alick Fergusson, was born.

7

The details in lines 1 - 11 primarily serve to
suggest the

A) dangerous conditions under which the
narrator's grandfather had to travel.

B) difficulty of the narrator's birth on an isolated
coast.

C) severity of the weather on the day of the
narrator's birth.

D) bad weather patterns that frequented the island.

Question 8

This passage is adapted from "What the expansion of
the Suez Canal shows about shifts in global shipping" by
Satya Savitzky. ©2015 by Satya Savitzky.

Egypt has opened a second lane to the Suez
Canal amid much fanfare. The $8 billion dollar
expansion adds 35 kilometers of new channels
Line to the existing canal and another 35 kilometers
5 where existing bodies of water were dredged to
make way for larger ships. This will supposedly
increase capacity from 50 transits a day to 97
and cut waiting times from 18 to 11 hours, which
the Suez Canal Authority claims will more than
10 double annual revenue to $13.2 billion by 2023.
In the 21st century, driven largely by growth
in China's manufacturing exports, there are now
many more ships plying the sea lanes. And these
ships are increasing in size. The world's largest
15 is the size of four football fields and can carry
19,000 20-foot cargo containers. As a result, the
narrow passages that provide economical links
between centers of production and consumption—
like Panama, Suez, and Malacca—are as much
20 obstacles to global trade as facilitators of it. The
expansion of Suez is therefore part of a much
larger picture of global growth in shipping.

The statistics cited by the author throughout the passage are used to illustrate that

A) growth in global shipping has necessitated expansion of trade passages like the Suez Canal.

B) recent changes to the Suez Canal cannot compete with other channels like Panama and Malacca.

C) China's manufacturing exports are growing faster than shipping companies can keep up with.

D) shipping companies are having trouble increasing profits in the face of new competition.

Question 9

This passage is adapted from "Academic print books are dying. What's the future?" by Donald A. Barclay. ©2015 by Donald A. Barclay.

The print-format scholarly book, a bulwark of academia's publish-or-perish culture, is an endangered species. The market that has
Line sustained it over the years is collapsing. Sales of
5 scholarly books in print format have hit record lows. Per-copy prices are at record highs. In purely economic terms, the current situation is unsustainable.

Bleak as it may seem, the good news is
10 that this need not mean the end of long-form scholarship. Facing a dismal market, a number of leading scholarly publishers are taking steps to change the economic model of the scholarly book. This change involves moving from a foundation
15 in print to a foundation in digital, and from a focus on sales to libraries to a focus on open access.

Besides rescuing the scholarly book from oblivion, open-access digital books offer many advantages over their print forbearers: The
20 number of potential readers dwarfs what is possible for a run of a few hundred printed copies. Open-access scholarly books can be used, wholly or in part, as course texts at no costs to students.

The main purpose of the passage is to

A) champion the value of print books.

B) suggest that the market for academic work is collapsing.

C) argue that scholars are making major changes in their writing.

D) detail a major change in scholarly publications.

Question 10

This passage is adapted from "Parakeets are the new pigeons—and they're on course for global domination" by Hazel Jackson. ©2016 by Hazel Jackson.

Parakeets are Britain's fastest growing bird population and are on a trajectory to global domination. Outside of their native southern Asia
Line and sub-Saharan Africa, breeding populations
5 are now established in at least 65 cities around Europe, and more than 30 countries across five continents.

Such non-native, or "invasive" species are one of the biggest causes of biodiversity loss in
10 the world today, and can cause severe economic damage. Understanding these species is incredibly useful for any attempt to design environment policy and prevent further invasions. Populations of invasive ring-necked parakeets (Psittacula
15 krameri) provide an excellent case study, owing to their patterns of rapid growth and spread.

It can reasonably be inferred from the passage that the information about invasive species is meant to

A) detail one potential threat to the parakeet population in Britain.

B) provide context for the role of parakeets in Britain's environment.

C) set out the main thesis that the author argues in the passage.

D) show why British researchers are attempting to expel parakeets in the nation.

Question 11

This passage is adapted from "How the painting got its name" by Ruth Yeazell. ©2015 by Ruth Yeazell.

The history of the picture title is a history of the last 300 years: when images begin to widely circulate, the arts market grew, and public viewing
Line spaces, like the 18th-century Salon or the modern
5 museum, were established. At the same time, new technological developments, from popular prints to computer images, allowed for inexpensive reproductions to reach a wider audience.

In earlier periods, when works of art were
10 produced for a small elite, there wasn't much need for titles: the patron and artist typically negotiated a picture's subject, and the eventual owners more or less knew what they'd be seeing. (Even today, few pictures that hang in private homes are
15 accompanied by titles.)

But all this changed once paintings began to circulate and people began to encounter images at a significant remove—both physical and temporal—from their creation. Titles, ultimately,
20 are a function of the democratization of viewing; the more heterogeneous the viewing public, the greater the need for titles.

11

In the third paragraph, the discussion of the change in titling pictures mainly serves to

A) emphasize that titles were part of the democratization of viewing.

B) show that artists titled paintings as they gained more individual fame.

C) demonstrate that patrons in later years began to demand titles.

D) illustrate how art went from a medium of the masses to a medium for the elite.

1. (C) is the correct answer. The passage as a whole is focused on describing how Olympic athletes and trainers didn't take the oath to not "sin against the games" seriously. The given lines provide specific examples of athletes and contestants accepting bribery in the Olympic games, supporting the author's point. (A) is incorrect because the given lines are specific examples, not origins of myths. (B) is incorrect because it is too broad; the corruption is related to the Olympics, and does not reflect the history of all corruption in Greece. (D) is incorrect because the author is merely chronicling the corruption without offering any personal feelings towards the events he is chronicling.

2. (D) is the correct answer. The passage describes how "daughterless technology," already successfully used against mosquitos, could be used to control the population of invasive fish like carp. (A) is incorrect because the passage describes the technology as "safe." (B) is incorrect because the passage is talking about a possible solution to the problem of overpopulation of carp; it does not imply the problem has been taken care of already. (C) is incorrect because the passage nowhere discusses funding.

3. (C) is the correct answer. The passage focuses on John's feelings toward David Harum, his employer, with additional details of what John has heard regarding this man. (A) is incorrect because the passage does not describe John's enthusiasm for his work, or offer any details of that work; it is primarily focused on his employer. (B) is incorrect because the passage does not discuss David's feelings towards John, and the local gossip mentioned has to do with David, not John. (D) is incorrect because the passage does not focus on setting primarily, and instead on the two characters of John and David.

4. (B) is the correct answer. The scientists suggest that, to combat the lack of rigor in current journalism, more scientists should "enter the fray" and help determine how their work is communicated to the public. (A) is incorrect because the authors do not just cite problems with the state of science-based journalism, but offer a solution. (C) is incorrect because the author indicates scientists should become more involved in the communication of their work, but does not imply that they should switch fields entirely. (D) is incorrect because the authors focus on the communication of scientific ideas to the public, and not accessibility of research articles, even though this is a supporting detail mentioned in the second paragraph.

5. (A) is the correct answer. The passage focuses on how personality tests can be "valid predictors of performance on the job" since "personality traits influence all aspects of our lives," including the workplace. (B) is incorrect because the passage does not suggest such tests violate employees' rights. (C) is incorrect because the passage suggests just the opposite, that personality tests are good indicators of workplace performance. (D) is incorrect because handwriting is not described as an example or subset of personality tests.

6. (C) is the correct answer. The passage focuses on the original antigenic sin (OAS), which is when the immune system "can effectively respond to one variant of a virus, but then is unable to stop another variant of the virus." The immune system is then ineffective in combatting a virus. (A) is incorrect because OAS is not an infection. (B) is incorrect because the passage spends little time focused on the danger of illnesses like dengue, but discusses the immune system's responses to various dangers throughout. (D) is incorrect because the passage only mentions influenza once, near the end, and does not document the rise of pandemics.

7. (C) is the correct answer. The information about the roaring wind, beating waves, and ships lost in the storm all serve to describe the storm as severe on the day the narrator was born. (A) is incorrect because the passage gives no indication the narrator's grandfather was traveling that day. (B) is incorrect because the narrator talks about the weather, but does not indicate the birth itself was difficult, nor is there evidence in the passage that the place is an "isolated coast" (in fact, it is described as an "island" in the second paragraph). (D) is incorrect because the narrator's grandfather states that the weather is unusual, and that he "had never known such a storm since he came to live on the island, more than forty years before."

8. (A) is the correct answer. The statistics cited in the passage show that ships are "increasing in size" and number, and that changes to the Suez Canal aim to add "35 kilometers of new channels" in order to help facilitate trade in the face of such changes. (B) is incorrect because the statistics do not compare the Suez, Panama, and Malacca channels. (C) is incorrect because it is too specific; the statistics cited have to do with trade through channels in general, not specifically trade of Chinese exports. (D) is incorrect because the statistics mentioned in the passage are not related to shipping companies' profits.

9. (D) is the correct answer. The passage discusses the death of "the print-format scholarly book" and the potential rise of the open-access digital book in its place. (A) is incorrect because the author details a change in the dissemination of scholarly work, without lamenting the loss of print books or arguing for their value. (B) is incorrect because the author only suggests the print market is collapsing, not the market for academic work in general. (C) is incorrect because the passage does not imply scholars are changing their work, and in fact, the author notes that changes to the market "need not mean the end of long-form scholarship."

10. (B) is the correct answer. The information given by the author about invasive species help provide some clues about how parakeets might influence Britain's environment, since the passage notes that parakeets are one relevant case study of invasive species. (A) is incorrect because parakeets are an invasive species, not threatened by one. (C) is incorrect because the information about invasive species provides background, but does not lay out an argument. (D) is incorrect because the passage nowhere says that British researchers are trying to expel parakeets.

11. (A) is the correct answer. The author's discussion of changes in the titling of paintings shows how titles became more central as paintings "began to circulate and people began to encounter images at a significant remove," all of which were part of the "democratization of viewing." (B) is incorrect because according to the passage, there is no evidence that the titling of paintings had to do with the fame of the artists. (C) is incorrect because patrons did not demand titles. (D) is incorrect because the passage discusses how art started as a medium for the elite and then spread to the masses, not the other way around.

Finding Arguments
Part 6

These questions ask you to identify claims or counterclaims made in the passage. The claims might be paraphrased in questions so that you need to parse complex sentences and challenging vocabulary in order to locate a claim in the passage. In passages with more than one speaker or in paired passages, you may need to distinguish between claims made by different speakers in order to tell who is making which argument.

DIRECTIONS

Every passage or paired set of passages is accompanied by a number of questions. Read the passage or paired set of passages, then use what is said or implied in what you read and in any given graphics to choose the best answer to each question.

Question 1

This passage is adapted from Jessie Carlton by Francis Forrester. First published in 1861.

On a bright afternoon of a warm day in October, Jessie Carlton sat in the parlor of Glen Morris Cottage. Her elbows rested on the table, her face
Line was held between her two plump little hands,
5 and her eyes were feasting on some charming pictures which were spread out before her. A pretty little work-basket stood on a chair at her side. It contained several yards of rumpled patchwork, two pieces of broadcloth with figures partially
10 worked on them as if they were intended for a pair of slippers, a watch-pocket half finished, and a small piece of silk composed of very little squares. On the table close to her left elbow was a cambric handkerchief with some embroidery just begun in
15 one of its corners. A needle carelessly stuck into it showed that Jessie had been working on it when her eyes were attracted by the pictures she was now studying with such close attention.

1

In the passage, the narrator claims that Jessie switched activities because she

A) became captivated by the beautiful pictures nearby.

B) grew bored of sewing and wanted to stretch her legs.

C) had a great deal of embroidery that she still had to do.

D) needed to clean up the table in front of her before dinner.

Question 2

This passage is adapted from "How we got to now: why the US and Europe went different ways on GMOs" by Paul B. Thompson. ©2015 by Paul B. Thompson.

There is a myth that circulates on both sides of the Atlantic: Americans accepted genetically modified organisms (GMOs) in their food supply
Line without question, while the more precautionary
5 Europeans rejected them. But GMOs went through a period of significant controversy in the US during the early years starting in the 1980s.

A boomerang effect is only now being felt in the US, as the last half-decade has seen a rise
10 in consumer concern, state-based initiatives for labeling and the emergence of "GMO-free" claims on a growing number of products marketed in the US. In Europe, meanwhile, the controversy seems to have never subsided. Earlier this month, half of
15 the European Union's 28 countries indicated they intend to opt out of a new GM crop plan, apparently over concerns over food safety, in a blow to the biotech industry.

2

One of the main arguments the author is trying to make in the passage is that

A) Europeans have stricter safety standards than the US.

B) GMOs are nowhere near as risky as many nations have made them out to be.

C) controversies surrounding GMOs have been significant in the US and not just Europe.

D) new food safety laws have improved trade between the US and Europe.

Question 3

This passage is adapted from "How reading fiction can help students understand the real world" by Melissa Tandiwe Myambo. ©2016 by Melissa Tandiwe Myambo.

The real world is often overwhelmingly complicated. Literature can help. This is true at universities too: courses in comparative literature
Line offer students new insights into their chosen
5 disciplines by unlocking new, varied perspectives.

How can those studying political science truly grasp the terror of living under a dictator? Perhaps by reading Mario Vargas Llosa's The Feast of the Goat, a magnificent historical novel about the tyrannical
10 Trujillo regime in the Dominican Republic. Students who read it are unlikely to forget the dizzying Cold War political intrigues that led the US to first support Trujillo and then implement sanctions against him. In area studies, students must learn about the politics
15 of postcolonial government. Chinua Achebe's 1966 novel, A Man of the People, explores how rapidly post-independence revolutionary zeal can turn venal as the corrupt, greedy postcolonial elite seizes the reins of power from the colonizer only to further
20 strangle the majority.

3

The passage portrays literature most nearly as:

A) an underappreciated but essential college discipline

B) a useful tool to help students understand other viewpoints.

C) a controversial means by which politicians make their stories known.

D) a way for universities to supplement tricky political science syllabi.

Question 4

This passage is adapted from "How science can genetically strengthen endangered plants and agriculture" by Muhammad Nakhooda. ©2016 by Muhammad Nakhooda.

As the human population swells—and in the face of a changing and unpredictable climate—the demand for natural resources increases. This leads
Line to distressing rates of deforestation to prepare land
5 for agriculture, medicinal, and forestry products. Related to this is an alarming reduction in species worldwide. This can only be ameliorated through urgent, intensive, and sustainable agroforestry and conservation initiatives. This involves
10 the conservation of natural forests as well as renewable plantation efforts. But to date only a scattering of such projects are in place worldwide.

4

The passage best supports which of the following conclusions about deforestation?

A) It is driven primarily by the desire for medicinal products.

B) Misguided conservationism hinders efforts to halt deforestation.

C) The increase in human population contributes to it.

D) Renewable plantation efforts are another facet of it.

Question 5

This passage is adapted from Rick and Ruddy by Howard R. Garis. First published in 1920.

Rick Dalton sat on the sandy beach tossing white stones and bits of shell into the little waves that broke almost at his feet. The tide was just
Line on the turn; soon it would come in, and the big,
5 booming rollers would drive Rick farther up toward the dunes, where the wind was making a queer, whistling sound as it bent the long spears of saw-edged grass, whipping off venturesome, gray hoppers, that had boldly crawled up, perhaps to
10 get a better view of the heaving ocean.

"I don't care!" murmured Rick.

Just why he said that Rick didn't know, for he did care very much about something—and that was to have a dog. He dug his fingers deep in the
15 sand, scooped up a wet mass of it in his palm, and tossed it high into the air. It fell about him in a little shower, and then, as Rick was about to repeat this, a wave, larger than any of the others, rolled up and nearly wet his feet.

5

The passage identifies Rick as being both

A) upset and in self-denial.

B) angry and remorseful.

C) conflicted and in tears.

D) calm and confused.

Question 6

This passage is adapted from "The future of personal satellite technology is here—are we ready for it?" by Elizabeth Garbee and Andrew Maynard. ©2016 by Elizabeth Garbee and Andrew Maynard.

Satellites used to be the exclusive playthings of rich governments and wealthy corporations. But increasingly, as space becomes more democratized,
Line these sophisticated technologies are coming
5 within reach of ordinary people. Just like drones before them, miniature satellites are beginning to fundamentally transform our conceptions of who gets to do what up above our heads.

As a recent report from the National Academy
10 of Sciences highlights, these satellites hold tremendous potential for making satellite-based science more accessible than ever before. However, as the cost of getting your own satellite in orbit plummets, the risks of irresponsible use grow.

6

The passage characterizes the increased democratization of space as

A) transformative.

B) dangerous.

C) unprecedented.

D) irresponsible.

Question 7

This passage is adapted from "Detroit, 1932: when Diego Rivera and Frida Kahlo came to town" by Henry Adams. ©2015 by Henry Adams.

The Detroit of 1932 had many parallels to the Detroit of today. The city was teetering toward bankruptcy. People were out of work.
Line The city was so pressed for funds that it seriously
5 considered closing its art museum and selling off its collection—just as it did when Detroit filed for bankruptcy in 2013. And social unrest was in the air. On March 7, 1932, the Ford Hunger March took place, during which laid-off factory workers
10 clashed with anti-union enforcers hired by Henry Ford. Four marchers were killed, while 60,000 people took part in the funeral procession.

It was in this atmosphere of financial depression and social unrest that the burly
15 Mexican muralist Diego Rivera—an avowed communist, fresh off a visit to the Soviet Union— came to Detroit to execute a massive mural for the Detroit Institute of Arts (DIA). With him, he brought his petite new bride, Frida Kahlo.

7

The passage indicates that Detroit

A) declared bankruptcy in 1932.

B) was a hostile environment for many artists.

C) favored factory workers over factory owners in its laws.

D) has suffered more than one period of hardship.

Question 8

This passage is adapted from "Pesticides are not the only way to deal with our biggest food competitor: insects" by Pia Addison, Antoinette Malan, Ken Pringle, and Matthew Addison. ©2015 by Pia Addison, Antoinette Malan, Ken Pringle, and Matthew Addison.

With the early beginnings of formalized agriculture some 11,000 years ago, a major socioeconomic change occurred that resulted in
Line human population growth and development. But
5 insects are equally if not more adaptable than humans. They too began to benefit from large homogenous plantings of food crops. We have been competing with them for food ever since.

At the end of the 19th century—when
10 agriculture largely shifted from subsistence to commercial—pest problems began to threaten farmers' livelihoods. This resulted in ever-decreasing tolerance for pests and led to the pesticide era, initially with the use of products
15 such as Paris Green and later to lead arsenate, DDT, and the new age pesticide products we use today.

But there are alternative control methods. A number are being developed and applied in fruit
20 crops in South Africa. These methods have no detrimental effects on the environment. They leave no harmful residues on fruit. They promote sustainable fruit production. They are effective and target pests specifically. These methods are
25 not new, and were already documented as early as 1500 BC.

8

The author asserts that alternative control methods

A) are not new technology but old strategies.

B) have severe effects on the environment.

C) leave harmful residues on crop products.

D) are not as effective in targeting pests as pesticides.

Question 9

This passage is adapted from A Spoil of Office by Hamlin Garland. First published in 1897.

Early in the cool hush of a June morning in the seventies, a curious vehicle left Farmer Councill's door, loaded with a merry group of young people.
Line It was a huge omnibus, constructed out of a heavy
5 farm wagon and a hay rack, and was drawn by six horses. The driver was Councill's hired man, Bradley Talcott. Councill himself held between his vast knees the staff of a mighty flag in which they all took immense pride. The girls of the grange
10 had made it for the day.
Laughter and scraps of song and rude witticisms made the huge wagon a bouquet of smiling faces. Everybody laughed, except Bradley, who sat with intent eyes and steady lips, his
15 sinewy brown hand holding the excited horses in place. This intentness and self-mastery lent a sort of majesty to his rough-hewn face.

9

The author most strongly implies that Bradley Talcott views his role with

A) amusement and enjoyment.

B) fear and loathing.

C) intensity and repugnance.

D) seriousness and respect.

Question 10

This passage is adapted from "Global agriculture study finds developing countries most threatened by invasive pest species" by Dean Paini. ©2016 by Dean Paini.

As the world becomes more connected, invasive species are spreading further. While these species pose threats to our ecosystems,
Line they arguably pose an even greater threat to our
5 agriculture and food security. Insect pests such as silverleaf whitefly, Asian gypsy moth, and Khapra beetle, are all ranked as major threats and can have significant and far-reaching impacts on agriculture and forest industries around the world.

10

According to the passage, what does the author believe to be the major danger of insect pests?

A) Damage to agricultural crops

B) Spread of diseases

C) Damage to ecosystems

D) Spread of invasive species

Question 11

This passage is adapted from "Why Prince's music will become more accessible after his death" by Peter K. Yu. ©2016 by Peter K. Yu.

Estates and their lawyers have been widely criticized for being greedy and for taking aggressive legal actions to limit public access
Line to the works of the deceased. While property
5 owners have unrestricted rights to dispose of their property—including inheritance—copyrights have become particularly problematic considering that they last for 70 years after an author's death.
Nevertheless, some estates have managed to
10 make the works of the deceased more widely available. A leading example concerns Franz Kafka. Before he died at the young age of 41, he left specific instructions to his friend and executor, Max Brod: My last request: Everything I leave
15 behind me … in the way of diaries, manuscripts, letters (my own and others'), sketches and so on,

to be burned unread.

Having already verbally declined his friend's request in person, Brod refused to burn the manuscripts after the writer's death. Had he followed Kafka's instructions, we would never have read some of Kafka's masterpieces, such as "The Trial" and "The Castle." We might never even have known Kafka's talents, as he published less than 450 pages in his lifetime.

11

An unstated assumption made by the author is that some authors

A) do not always act in the best interest of their own estates.

B) are temperamental geniuses that need literary managers.

C) assume their friends will keep their legacy alive.

D) write their best work in the last few years of their lives.

Question 12

This passage is adapted from "Restoring the Everglades will benefit both humans and nature" by Peter Frederick. ©2016 by Peter Frederick.

Everglades National Park (ENP) is our only national wetland park, and one of the largest aquascapes in the world. Perhaps more than any other U.S. national park, ENP's treasures are hard to defend. Lying at the southern end of an immense watershed the size of New Jersey, ENP is caught between the largest man-made water project in the world upstream and a rapidly rising ocean downstream.

The park and the wider Everglades ecosystem have suffered immense ecological damage from years of overdrainage to prevent flooding and promote development. In 2000 Congress approved the largest ecological restoration project in the world—the Comprehensive Everglades Restoration Plan, which is expected to take more than 35 years to complete and cost at least $10.5 billion. In addition to repairing some of the

damage to this unique ecosystem, the restoration is designed to ensure reliable clean drinking water supplies for South Florida cities and protect developed areas from flooding. The plan is making progress—but the closer it gets to its goal, the more the details matter, and some of those details have become roadblocks.

12

In the passage, the author claims that the Comprehensive Everglades Restoration Plan

A) has been a large waste of government money.

B) is slowly achieving its goals despite some obstacles.

C) still is not achieving its major goals.

D) finished its work after 35 difficult years.

Question 13

This passage is adapted from "Ten facts you need to know about the chicken and eggs on your table" by Sonia Yun Liu. ©2016 by Sonia Yun Liu.

No chickens or eggs produced in Australia contain added hormones, and they have not been given hormones for decades. Independent tests by the Department of Agriculture, Fisheries and Forestry confirm that Australian chicken meat is free of added hormones.

Not that it would be easy to give them hormones anyway. Growth hormones are proteins similar to insulin used to treat diabetes. Like insulin, they can only be injected into the body because they are broken down in the digestive tract. Therefore, it is pointless to provide chickens growth hormones in their food because they would be rendered ineffective. And given a typical commercial shed may accommodate 40,000 to 60,000 birds per shed, it is simply logistically impossible to inject hormones into each chicken.

13

Which of the following does the author argue about injecting hormones into chickens?

A) It is an unsafe process that damages human health.

B) It is nowhere near as dangerous as once believed.

C) It is a practice that some farmers are reconsidering.

D) It would be operationally unfeasible in most farms.

Question 14

This passage is adapted from We Girls by Mrs. A.D.T. Whitney. First published in 1870.

We were very much astonished when Grandfather Holabird came in and told us, one morning, of his having bought the empty Beaman
Line house, that nobody had lived in for five years.
5   We were a great deal more astonished when he came in again, another day, and proposed that we should go and live in it.
     We were all a good deal afraid of Grandfather Holabird. He had very strict ideas of what people
10 ought to do about money. Or rather of what they ought to do without it, when they didn't happen to have any.
     Mrs. Stephen pulled down the green blinds when she saw him coming that day, him and his
15 cane. She said she didn't exactly know which it was she dreaded; she thought she could bear the cane without him, or even him without the cane; but both together were "scare-mendous."

14

The narrator mentions the incident of Mrs. Stephen pulling down the green blinds primarily to support the idea that

A) the family was afraid of Grandfather Holabird.

B) the family hated the new Beaman house.

C) Grandfather Holabird was a nuisance to the neighborhood.

D) Grandfather Holabird was unaware of Mrs. Stephen's presence.

Question 15

This passage is adapted from "When it comes to recognizing family, you can't make a monkey out of a macaque" by Anwesha Ghosh. ©2014 by Anwesha Ghosh.

Female macaques invest a lot in their babies, starting from pregnancy through to bringing up their young ones. They want to prevent inbreeding
Line and so they prefer to find unrelated males as
5   mates. This should mean that they would evolve the ability to differentiate between related and unrelated males.
     However, researcher Dana Pfefferle found, in a study on rhesus macaques, that females spend
10 the same amount of time looking at photos of both related and unrelated males. This might be because macaque society has a gender bias. Males are ranked higher and could be a threat to them. So when shown pictures of a male, a
15 female could be conflicted between choosing new mates by differentiating between unrelated and related males and keeping an eye out for males just looking for trouble. This causes them to spend equal time staring at images of related and
20 unrelated males.

The passage makes the claim that female macaques' attention to pictures of males is heavily influenced by gender bias because these females

A) are the ones that choose their mates, and they must be careful in their selection.

B) are much more likely to spend time looking at pictures of male rather than female macaques.

C) must not only choose between mates, but be wary of male threats to them or their offspring.

D) are submissive to male macaques and so cannot maintain eye contact with any male for too long.

1. (A) is the correct answer. The passage states that Jessie was staring at "some charming pictures which were spread out before her" and that a needle stuck into some embroidery "showed that Jessie had been working on it when her eyes were attracted by the pictures she was now studying with such close attention." (B) is incorrect because Jessie does not leave the table. (C) is incorrect because Jessie stopped embroidery and started looking at pictures, not the other way around. (D) is incorrect because the passage gives no indication Jessie is cleaning up the table.

2. (C) is the correct answer. The author argues that GMOs in the US "went through a period of significant controversy" in the 1980s, and that such controversies are now resurfacing. This, as the passage states, runs contrary to the myth that GMO controversies have primarily occurred in Europe. (A) is incorrect because it is too broad; the passage is focused on attitudes towards GMOs only in the US and Europe, not "many nations." (B) is incorrect because the author of the passage does not comment on the safety of GMOs, only different regions' responses to them. (D) is incorrect because the passage does not discuss trade laws between the US and Europe.

3. (B) is the correct answer. The passage notes that literature can unlock "new, varied perspectives," and gives examples of novels that help students understand the perspectives of historical groups. (A) is incorrect because the author does not imply literature is underappreciated. (C) is incorrect because the passage does not suggest politicians use literature in this way. (D) is incorrect because while political science and area studies courses may utilize literature, the passage does not suggest that this is one of the main roles of literature, nor does it imply that such syllabi are "tricky."

4. (C) is the correct answer. The passage states that as the human population swells, "the demand for natural resources increases," which in turn leads to more deforestation to make room for agriculture and other industries. (A) is incorrect because the passage states a few different reasons for deforestation, with medicinal needs only one among many. (B) is incorrect because the passage is advocating for conservation initiatives, not suggesting they hinder preservation efforts. (D) is incorrect because renewable plantation efforts are one attempt to ameliorate deforestation, not a facet of deforestation.

5. (A) is the correct answer. Rick is upset in the passage that he does not have a dog, but he denies this emotion even to himself, exclaiming, "I don't care!" The passage does not identify Rick as being sorry about wrongdoings he committed in the past, as "remorseful" indicates, so (B) is incorrect. (C) is incorrect because the passage does not indicate Rick is in tears. (D) is incorrect as Rick tosses clumps of wet sand into the air after we are told that he is upset about not having a dog, making it reasonable to assume this action was done in frustration, which "calm" is not synonymous with.

6. (A) is the correct answer. The passage states that "miniature satellites are beginning to fundamentally transform our conceptions of who gets to do what up above our heads." Since this type of technology is part of what the author calls the democratization of space, (A) is the correct answer. (B) is incorrect because the author does not imply these changes will be dangerous. (C) is incorrect because the passage notes a previous example, drones, that mirrors the current one. (D) is incorrect because, though the passage notes that "the risks of irresponsible use grow" with wider access to technology, it does not state that the democratization of space itself is an irresponsible act.

7. (D) is the correct answer. The passage notes that 1932 Detroit had many similarities to the Detroit of today, citing its early economic problems and social unrest. Since it compares this time to modern Detroit, it can be inferred that the passage is claiming Detroit suffered more than one period of hardship. (A) is incorrect because the passage says Detroit teetered near bankruptcy, but does not say it declared it. (B) is incorrect as the passage states that Detroit was an inhospitable environment for art itself, as it depicts the city considering selling parts of its collection to help dig itself out of debt, which does not necessarily mean people in Detroit were hostile against the artists themselves. (C) is incorrect because there are no laws mentioned in this passage.

8. (A) is the correct answer. The passage states that alternative control methods "are not new, and were already documented as early as 1500 BC," implying they are an older strategy. (B) is incorrect because the passage says "these methods have no detrimental effects on the environment." (C) is incorrect because the passage says the opposite, that "they leave no harmful residues on fruit." (D) is incorrect because the passage also states that such methods "are effective and target pests specifically."

9. (D) is the correct answer. Unlike the laughing group of companions that Bradley Talcott is driving around, Talcott himself is serious and quiet, "with intent eyes and steady lips, his sinewy brown hand holding the excited horses in place." This "intentness and self-mastery" indicates that Talcott takes his job seriously, and respects the position and skill required. (A) is incorrect because it is the party that is amused and merry, not Talcott. (B) is incorrect because the passage does not indicate Talcott dislikes or fears his job. (C) is incorrect because there is no evidence Talcott feels his job is repugnant, or revolting.

10. (A) is the correct answer. The passage notes that invasive species are spreading further, with the greatest threat posed to "agriculture and food security." (B) is incorrect because the spread of diseases is not mentioned in the passage. (C) is incorrect because the passage ranks damage to "agriculture and food security" as an "even greater threat" than damage to ecosystems. (D) is incorrect because this is a symptom, not result, of the issue the author is talking about.

11. (A) is the correct answer. The author notes that Max Brod, Kafka's friend and executor of his will, did not burn Kafka's works. Had he not, "we might never even have known Kafka's talents." Implicit in this is the passage's author's belief that authors like Kafka do not always act in the best interest of their estates. (B) is incorrect as it is too specific to be supported by the passage; the author only speaks about the temperment of one author, and never hints about the temperment, genius, or need for a manager for any other author. (C) is incorrect because even though Kafka's friend helped keep his legacy alive by publishing his stories posthumously, however Kafka, nor any other authors mentioned by the author, assumed this would happen. (D) is incorrect as the passage does not indicate when Kafka wrote his masterpieces, and cannot assume they were in the latter portion of his life.

12. (B) is the correct answer. The author notes that this plan "is making progress" but that some details "have become roadblocks" or obstacles. (A) is incorrect as the author does not suggest the plan was a waste of money. (C) is incorrect because the author notes that the plan is making progress. (D) is incorrect because 35 years represents the anticipated time frame, not the number of years already worked on the project.

13. (D) is the correct answer. The author writes that "it is simply logistically impossible to inject hormones into each chicken," given the number of chickens in a typical commercial shed. (A) and (B) are incorrect because the passage does not focus on the effects of hormones on human health. (C) is incorrect because the passage indicates the practice has been discontinued for decades, not that some farmers are only now reconsidering it.

14. (A) is the correct answer. The passage notes that "we were all a good deal afraid of Grandfather Holabird," with Mrs. Stephen later pulling down the blinds because she "dreaded" him and found him "scare-mendous." (B) is incorrect because Mrs. Stephen's drawing of the blinds had nothing to do with the new house. (C) is incorrect because Mrs. Stephen is never said to feel annoyed, but instead to draw the blinds right before her feelings of dread and fear are expressed, establishing a cause and effect relationship. (D) is incorrect because there is no evidence in the passage to support the conclusion that Grandfather Holabird was unaware of Mrs. Stephen's presence.

15. (C) is the correct answer. The passage notes that "females spend the same amount of time looking at photos of both related and unrelated males" and that "this might be because macaque society has a gender bias." The author goes on to explain that a female may spend this time looking at photos because they are determining which is the better mate, and "keeping an eye out for males just looking for trouble.

(A) is incorrect because "gender bias" refers to females being ranked lower than males, not the fact that females are the ones who select mates. (B) is incorrect because the study mentioned does not compare the time female macaques spend looking at male vs. female pictures. (D) is incorrect because eye contact is never mentioned in this passage.

Author's Reasoning

Part 7

Author's Reasoning questions require you to follow the reasoning used by the author or speaker and identify the role of specific claims in the structure of an argument. They will not generally ask you to determine whether an author is using valid reasoning, but may require you to notice the importance of a statement in terms of its role in a valid argument. For example, you may need to infer that an author offers a specific definition of an important term in order to avoid an objection based on a different possible sense of that term than the one being used in the passage.

DIRECTIONS

Every passage or paired set of passages is accompanied by a number of questions. Read the passage or paired set of passages, then use what is said or implied in what you read and in any given graphics to choose the best answer to each question.

Question 1

This passage is adapted from "This is War," a speech given by Woodrow Wilson on April 2, 1917. In it, Wilson is addressing the United States Congress.

On the third of February last I officially laid
before you the extraordinary announcement of the
Imperial German Government that on and after
the first day of February it was its purpose to put
5 aside all restraints of law or of humanity and use
its submarines to sink every vessel that sought
to approach either the ports of Great Britain and
Ireland or the western coasts of Europe.
    That had seemed to be the object of the
10 German submarine warfare earlier in the war, but
since April of last year the Imperial Government
had somewhat restrained the commanders of its
undersea craft in conformity with its promise then
given to us that passenger boats should not be
15 sunk and that due warning would be given to all
other vessels which its submarines might seek to
destroy, when no resistance was offered or escape
attempted, and care taken that their crews were
given at least a fair chance to save their lives in
20 their open boats.
    The precautions taken were meager and
haphazard enough, as was proved in distressing
instance after instance in the progress of the
cruel and unmanly business, but a certain degree

25 of restraint was observed. The new policy has
swept every restriction aside. Vessels of every
kind, whatever their flag, their character, their
cargo, their destination, their errand, have been
ruthlessly sent to the bottom without warning
30 and without thought of help or mercy for those
on board, the vessels of friendly neutrals along
with those of belligerents. Even hospital ships and
ships carrying relief to the sorely bereaved and
stricken people of Belgium, though the latter were
35 provided with safe conduct through the proscribed
areas by the German Government itself and were
distinguished by unmistakable marks of identity,
have been sunk with the same reckless lack of
compassion or of principle.

Before the author makes his case about the ruthlessness of German submarine warfare, he

A) notes that other European countries have been just as vicious in their submarine attacks.

B) concedes that initially, the German government exercised some restraint in attacking vessels.

C) admits that some of the German response has been provoked by American vessels.

D) calls for an international peace treaty that will end submarine warfare.

Question 2

This passage is adapted from "Explainer: what is a gene drive and how could it wipe out malaria?" by Michael Bonsall. ©2015 by Michael Bonsall.

Our understanding of the natural world is now so great we can manipulate the DNA blueprints for any living thing on Earth. We can replace
Line genes for traits we don't like with others we prefer
5 and even add genes that don't occur naturally in an organism. Over the last few years, scientists have developed several methods for editing genes in this way.

We have also developed a way to introduce
10 these gene changes to an entire population of a species. This "gene drive" process has most recently been used to alter the DNA of small groups of mosquitoes so that they no longer carry the malaria parasite, raising the possibility of
15 eliminating the disease altogether. But meddling with nature in this way carries huge implications that need careful consideration.

A guide molecule makes sure the DNA sequence is cut in exactly the right place. Getting
20 this wrong will probably cause damage to non-target genes that could harm the organism. And just because we can edit the DNA within a species doesn't mean we should. We need strong leadership at all levels—ethical, scientific,
25 political—and appropriate regulations to ensure these new technologies can prosper without unintended consequences.

The passage suggests that the "gene drive" process could lead to unintended damage because

A) it will lead to an increase in communicable diseases like malaria.

B) cutting the DNA sequence improperly could damage genes and harm the organism.

C) scientists will allocate funding away from the treatment of genetic diseases.

D) the process may lead to unintended mutations in the target genes.

Question 3

This passage is adapted from "After 450 years, we still don't know the true value of Shakespeare" by Kate Mc-Luskie. ©2014 by Kate McLuskie.

The extent of Shakespeare's legacy 450 years on from his birth is incalculable. But this, of course, does not stop some from trying. To many
Line the crown of Britain's cultural output, Shakespeare
5 is integral to our very language, widely celebrated, studied, acted, seen. So sourcing hard evidence on the cultural value of Shakespeare is a fool's game, if a fun one.

To start with, both the words in the concept
10 of "cultural value" are so overloaded, so controversial, that real figures for either of them are impossible to find. Are we talking about the anthropological or the aesthetic version of culture? Are we in the realm of economic use, exchange,
15 symbolic or discursive value? And Shakespeare? Are we referencing the texts, the editions, the amateur and professional productions, or the stories, the adaptations, the movies?

The only evidence we have is about the life,
20 writing, and social relationships of the writer. And this cannot hope to explain the crazy variety of ideas and objects that shelter under the most famous name in history.

The range of questions in lines 12 - 18 mainly serves to support the author's point that

A) Shakespeare's legacy is much broader than once believed.

B) pinning down the definition of cultural value is a complicated prospect.

C) more cultural historians are required to make sense of Shakespeare's legacy.

D) culture is predominantly determined by literature rather than visual art.

Question 4

This passage is adapted from "Whether stored electronically or written on calf skin, knowledge has never been more threatened" by Richard Ovenden. ©2016 by Richard Ovenden.

Information is constantly under attack. The current debate around the longstanding use of vellum (a parchment made using calf skin) for
Line printing key legislative documents highlights the
5 continued concern over this. Some are advocating a switch from vellum to archive paper, which costs much less and can last up to 500 years.

Recorded information is certainly vulnerable: paper and parchment, and the inks and pigments
10 that are written, drawn or painted on their surfaces, can decay and disappear if not stored in controlled environmental conditions. And digital information is even more susceptible to degradation than that recorded on vellum.
15 Operating systems and information environments change and develop rapidly, and as a result information created and stored on older systems easily can become unusable. It's by no means certain that the digital information created by our
20 parliament today will still be secure and reliably accessible in 200 years.

Which of the following statements from the passage is an acknowledgement by the author that digital storage of information is not necessarily more permanent?

A) "Information is constantly under attack."

B) "Some are advocating a switch from vellum to archive paper, which costs much less and can last up to 500 years."

C) "Recorded information is certainly vulnerable: paper and parchment, and the inks and pigments that are written, drawn or painted on their surfaces, can decay and disappear if not stored in controlled environmental conditions."

D) "Operating systems and information environments change and develop rapidly, and as a result information created and stored on older systems easily can become unusable."

1. (B) is the correct answer. In the second paragraph, the author notes that "since April of last year the Imperial Government had somewhat restrained the commanders of its undersea craft in conformity with its promise," before detailing how recently, such restraint has been abandoned. (A) is incorrect because the author focuses only on German submarine attacks. (C) is incorrect because the author nowhere justifies German attacks by suggesting they have been provoked. (D) is incorrect because an international peace treaty is not mentioned in the passage.

2. (B) is the correct answer. The passage notes that if a guide molecule does not cut the DNA sequence in the right place, damage could occur "to non-target genes that could harm the organism." (A) is incorrect because malaria is an illness that could be combatted with the gene drive process, not a potential consequence of it. (C) is incorrect because there is no mention of funding in this passage. (D) is incorrect because the passage offers no support that the process will cause mutations.

3. (B) is the correct answer. The given questions serve to emphasize how difficult it is to define cultural value, as it can have many different meanings. (A) is incorrect because the given questions ask about culture in general, not Shakespeare in particular. (C) and (D) are incorrect because they are not points made or hinted at by the author.

4. (D) is the correct answer. The sentence about operating systems and information environments shows that digital information is not necessarily more stable and permanent than written paper, since the technology can change so rapidly. (A) is incorrect because it is not (on its own) specifically about digital storage of information. (B) and (C) are incorrect because they refer to physical paper, not the digital storage of information.

Author's Evidence

Part 8

Author's Evidence questions require you to identify claims or arguments that serve as supporting evidence for a larger argument. They may require you to correctly select paraphrases of simple logical arguments, factual claims, or statistics. They may also require you to draw some conclusions from simple quantitative comparisons using general number sense. For example, you may need to notice that one quantity is much larger than another even when they're expressed in slightly different terms. They will not actually require you to perform calculations, however. They may also require you to select choices that paraphrase information in terms of its role in the author's argument.

DIRECTIONS

Every passage or paired set of passages is accompanied by a number of questions. Read the passage or paired set of passages, then use what is said or implied in what you read and in any given graphics to choose the best answer to each question.

Question 1

This passage is adapted from "The calamity of the disappearing school libraries" by Debra Kachel. ©2015 by Debra Kachel.

Look at my state of Pennsylvania, where schools are not required to have libraries. Prisons must have them. Barber and cosmetology schools
Line must have them. They are compulsory in nursing
5 programs. But in public schools they are optional.
Or consider the city of Houston, Texas, where decisions on school staffing for certain positions, including certified librarians, are left to the discretion of school principals. It is not alone
10 in that.
Also at work in the minds of budget cutters may be the hoary falsehood that the internet has made the need for libraries obsolete.
But those who think that the internet replaces
15 a library must think it is okay to use WebMD instead of going to a doctor.
Librarians teach information literacy – how to separate the useful from the less useful, the credible from the inaccurate, and how to navigate
20 the internet safely.

1

Which of the following points from the passage does the author use to support the opinion that library services are not obsolete?

A) Libraries in Pennsylvania schools are not mandatory.

B) WebMD is not a replacement for a visit to the doctor's.

C) Houston school principals are in charge of school staffing.

D) It is false that the internet has made libraries obsolete.

Question 2

This passage is adapted from "Vanadium: the 'beautiful metal' that stores energy" by Helena I. Gomes and Helen Abigail Baxter. ©2016 by Helena I. Gomes and Helen Abigail Baxter.

An unheralded metal could become a crucial part of the renewables revolution. Vanadium is used in new batteries that can store large amounts
Line of energy almost indefinitely, perfect for remote
5 wind or solar farms.

Vanadium is not only beautiful, but strong. Adding small percentages of it creates exceptionally light, tough, and more resilient steel alloys. Henry Ford was the first to use it
10 on an industrial scale, in the 1908 Model T car chassis, and today the vast majority of vanadium is used in structural steel, mainly to build bridges and buildings.

2

The author includes information about Henry Ford in order to

A) detail an untested application of vanadium.

B) show the history of the use of vanadium.

C) suggest vanadium has become obsolete.

D) introduce a counterargument about vanadium use.

Question 3

This passage is adapted from "Readjustment," a speech given by Warren G. Harding on May 24, 1920.

My countrymen, there isn't anything the matter with the world's civilization, except that humanity is viewing it through a vision impaired
Line in a cataclysmal war. Poise has been disturbed, and
5 nerves have been racked, and fever has rendered men irrational. Sometimes there have been draughts upon the dangerous cup of barbarity. Men have wandered far from safe paths, but the human procession still marches in the right direction.
10 America's present need is not heroics, but healing; not nostrums, but normalcy; not revolution, but restoration; not agitation, but adjustment; not surgery, but serenity; not the dramatic, but the dispassionate; not experiment,
15 but equipoise; not submergence in internationality but sustainment in triumphant nationality. It's one thing to battle successfully against the world's domination by a military autocracy because the infinite God never intended such a program; but
20 it's quite another thing to revise human nature and suspend the fundamental laws of life and all of life's requirements.

3

The authors most likely include the list in lines 10 - 16 ("America's … nationality") to

A) detail America's involvement in the current war.

B) emphasize the potential risks of entering the war.

C) highlight America's current needs through a series of contrasts.

D) suggest that peacetime in America will be even more difficult than war.

Question 4

This passage is adapted from "Publishing should be more about culture than book sales" by Dallas J. Baker. ©2016 by Dallas J. Baker.

It seems too obvious to point out that publishing is a cultural activity, not just a process for corporations to make money. That being said, we rarely talk or write about publishing without talking about money, about book sales. That's because, even though contemporary publishing has seen the emergence of diverse independent publishers and the self-publishing boom, it is still dominated by multinational corporations. And corporations are all about the numbers.

Most books are produced by one of the "big five" publishing multinationals (Penguin Random House, Macmillan, HarperCollins, Hachette, or Simon & Schuster). In fact, for some of those multinational corporations, books and writing aren't even the largest part of their business. HarperCollins and Hachette are both subsidiaries of media companies (News Corp and Lagardère respectively). Commercial or "traditional" publishing is not so much aimed at telling a story and hopefully making a profit but at making a profit by telling a story.

In this publishing climate, culture is always subsumed to business. The book and its story or narrative are merely a vehicle to generate sales and as such are understood as a unit of exchange rather than as an artifact of expression and meaning.

4

When arguing that publishing is still "dominated by multinational corporations," the author

A) names specific companies that have prioritized business over culture.

B) notes that some large publishers are part of much larger corporate businesses.

C) cites statistics that show business in publishing has grown in recent years.

D) gives examples of various books that are geared more towards profit than culture.

Question 5

This passage is adapted from "The age of solastalgia" by Glenn Albrecht. ©2012 by Glenn Albrecht.

The built and natural environments are now changing so rapidly that our language and conceptual frameworks have to work overtime just to keep up. Under the intertwined impacts of global development, rising population, and global warming, with their accompanying changes in climate and ecosystems, there is now a mismatch between our lived experience of the world, and our ability to conceptualize and comprehend it.

Solastalgia has its origins in the concepts of "solace" and "desolation." Solace has meanings connected to the alleviation of distress or to the provision of comfort or consolation in the face of distressing events. Desolation has meanings connected to abandonment and loneliness. The suffix -algia has connotations of pain or suffering. Hence, solastalgia is a form of "homesickness" like that experienced with traditionally defined nostalgia, except that the victim has not left their home or home environment. Solastalgia, simply put, is "the homesickness you have when you are still at home." The concept of solastalgia has had considerable international impact since its creation and has helped revive interest in the relationships between humans and place at all scales.

5

In the passage, the author uses which of the following to advance his points about solastalgia?

A) A dictionary definition of the word "solastalgia"

B) A discussion of the origin and meaning of solastalgia

C) A personal example of experienced solastalgia

D) A quote from an expert about solastalgia

Question 6

This passage is adapted from "What can fish mouths teach us about engineering clog-free filters?" by S. Laurie Sanderson. ©2016 by S. Laurie Sanderson.

Until 15 years ago, we thought that most filter-feeding fish used oral structures called gill rakers in the same way that we use coffee filters or spaghetti
Line strainers. These so-called dead-end sieves force
5 water to pass straight through the pores of the mesh. But dead-end sieves always clog as particles accumulate over time to cover the filter surface.

The water flows right through a colander and leaves the spaghetti trapped on the mesh, but a fish
10 needs to move the food from the gill raker filter to the back of its mouth for swallowing. Dead-end sieves would cause problems for fish, since their gill rakers would clog and fish don't have a tongue to move food particles off the gill rakers. So, we
15 knew they must be using some other filtering technique.

By putting a biomedical endoscope inside the mouths of feeding fish, colleagues and I discovered in 2001 that several common fish species use
20 crossflow filtration instead of trapping particles directly on a dead-end sieve. During crossflow filtration, small secondary streams of fluid pass through each filter pore—perpendicular to the filter surface, like in dead-end filtration. But the main
25 stream of fluid—the "crossflow"—is directed to travel across (parallel to) the filter surface, lifting particles off the filter and preventing the pores from clogging with particles.

6

Which of the following, if true, would contradict the author's argument about dead-end sieves?

A) Fish all have a special appendage that functions like a tongue.

B) Fish are extremely efficient at filtering water.

C) Fish do not have gill rakers that clog easily.

D) Fish consume a diet mostly of small particles.

Question 7

This passage is adapted from "It takes a lot of water to feed us, but recycled water could help" by Rachel Carey, Jennifer Sheridan, and Seona Candy. ©2016 by Rachel Carey, Jennifer Sheridan, and Seona Candy.

Australians eat a lot of water—the water that is used to produce our food. New findings estimate that more than 475 liters of water are
Line used to grow each person's food every day. This
5 is just the irrigation water used to grow our food. We consume much more than 475 L if you include rainwater or water used in processing and manufacturing.

To put this in context, the amount of water
10 used to grow food for the city of Melbourne each year (758 GL) is around double the amount of water used in people's homes (376 GL). The amount of water needed to feed a country like Australia will increase as the population grows,
15 but the availability of water for food production is likely to decrease, due to the impacts of climate change and greater competition.

7

The authors mention figures about water consumption in the first paragraph (line 49) primarily to support their claim that

A) Australians consume vast amounts of water.

B) Australians are set to encounter another drought.

C) people need to monitor the amount of water they consume.

D) people are unaware of the waste that goes into food production.

Question 8

This passage is adapted from "Academics do want to engage with business, but need more support" by Drew Evans and Carolin Plewa. ©2016 by Drew Evans and Carolin Plewa.

Publications are, and will continue to be, critical for the advancement of knowledge and for the reputation of academics and universities alike.
Line But does that mean academics aren't interested in
5 working with business? We don't think so.

Recently researchers undertook a benchmarking survey to test this assumption. The academic engagement with end users survey was designed to capture the perceptions and attitudes
10 of academics when it comes to engaging with business, government, or non-profit organizations. The survey sampled 20% of the total academic employees across three universities. The findings were that the most academics (nine out of ten)
15 were motivated to engage with business to help translate their research into practice. 86% were motivated to engage in order to have an impact on society.

8

In lines 6 - 18, the authors make use of which of the following to support their argument?

A) The results of a recent study

B) Their own personal experience

C) Statistics from their own research

D) The statements of experts

Question 9

This passage is adapted from "Explainer: what it will take to make computer science education available in all schools" by Marie desJardins. ©2015 by Marie desJardins.

The start of the new millennium saw many ups and downs in the area of computer science. Enrollment in computer science and computer
Line engineering degrees peaked in 2000, at the height
5 of the "dot-com bubble."

But soon after the "dot-com bust" in 2000, the number of new majors dropped rapidly. By 2007, the Taulbee survey reported only 46,226 undergraduates in doctoral-granting institutions.
10 Despite the short-term tech downturn following the "bust," the computing industry grew rapidly throughout the 2000s. So, by 2007, the computing industry was sounding the alarm about the dire shortage of trained computing professionals.
15 Indeed, that very same year, the Bureau of Labor Statistics predicted that computing would be the fastest-growing professional sector, with a projected 10-year growth rate of 24.8%.

Starting in 2007, those of us in academia
20 started to notice a few more students in our classes, and then a lot more. In spring 2009, when I was the undergraduate program director for UMBC's CS program, we held an emergency meeting to decide how to handle the fact that all
25 of the sections of our required discrete math class had a waiting list. Within a year or two, every computer science professor in the country knew it was not just a blip. As we scrambled to hire more faculty, increase class sizes, and try to find ways
30 to accommodate our increasingly long waiting lists, the students just kept coming.

9

In lines 12 - 18, the author uses which of the following to support her claim about the decline of computer science and computer engineering majors?

A) Surveys and statistics

B) Research studies and experiments

C) Anecdotes and stories

D) Logic and mathematical formulas

Question 10

This passage is adapted from "Ancient asteroid impacts yield evidence for the nature of the early Earth" by Andrew Glikson. ©2016 by Andrew Glikson.

The nature of the early Earth's crust prior to about 4 billion years ago—about half a billion years following formation of the Earth—is
Line
5   shrouded in mystery. Precious few traces remain today of the ancient crust for geologists to examine, with the oldest crustal rocks dating back to about 4 billion years.

The discovery in the early 2000s of grains of zircons (zirconium silicate) dating back to
10   4.4 billion years, found in sediments in Western Australia, has not yet fully resolved this mystery. This is because zircons are resistant to erosion but other minerals and rock fragments are more easily weathered and eroded. The silica-rich rocks
15   from which the zircons were derived may have come from early granitic crust or they could have crystallized from silica-rich volcanic melts or melt sheets produced by asteroid impacts. So we need more information about what their origin might be.

10

In the second paragraph, the author backs up his claim that the discovery of zircons "has not yet fully resolved this mystery" by

A) detailing the unreliability of zircon-related data.

B) mentioning a relevant property of zircons.

C) citing a major researcher in the field.

D) discussing a study on the history of zircons.

Question 11

This passage is adapted from The Five Knots by Fred M. White. First published in 1908.

Wilfrid Mercer's modest establishment was situated in High Street, Oldborough. A shining brass plate on the front door proclaimed
Line   him physician and surgeon, but as yet he had
5   done little more than publish his name in the town. It had been rather a venture to settle in a conservative old place like Oldborough, where, by dint of struggling and scraping, he had managed to buy a small practice. By the time this was done
10   and his house furnished, he would have been hard put to it to lay his hands on fifty pounds. As so frequently happens, the value of the practice had been exaggerated; the man he had succeeded had not been particularly popular, and some of
15   the older patients took the opportunity of going elsewhere.

It was not a pleasant prospect, as Mercer admitted, as he sat in his consulting-room that wintry afternoon. He began to be sorry that he had
20   given up his occupation of ship's doctor. The work was hard and occasionally dangerous, but the pay had been regular and the chance of seeing the world alluring.

While he sat gazing idly into the growing
25   darkness, watching the thin traffic trickle by, he heard the sound of a motor horn and a moment later a big Mercedes car stopped before his door. There was an imperative ring at the bell, which Wilfrid answered in person.

11

Which of the following details is used in the passage to indicate how Wilfrid was having trouble settling into his new profession?

A) His work as a ship's doctor had been hard and sometimes dangerous.

B) His only client was a man driving a big Mercedes.

C) His establishment was on High Street in the center of town.

D) His purchase of a practice was not as lucrative as promised.

1. (B) is the correct answer. The author uses this example as an analogy to show that, like doctors, librarians are necessary for learning "how to separate the useful from the less useful, the credible from the inaccurate," which sources like WebMD and the internet in general cannot do because of their abundance of information but lack of certified guidance. (A) is incorrect because this is merely a statement about which social institutions are required to have libraries, which doesn't provide any information about how useful libraries may be. (C) is incorrect because facts about who is in charge of staffing schools don't necessarily have anything to do with libraries, just schools in general. (D) is incorrect because this is just a statement about an information source not being able to replace libraries, not information about why this is true, which supportive evidence is.

2. (B) is the correct answer. The author mentions Henry Ford in order to trace the history of vanadium use back to his 1908 Model T car chassis. (A) is incorrect as the information about Henry Ford claims he used it on "an industrial scale," meaning it has been tested on a large scale, not not at all. (C) is incorrect as the author nowhere indicates vanadium is obsolete or out-of-date as a technology. (D) is incorrect as the mention of Henry Ford's successful industrial use of vanadium supports the author's claim that it is "exceptionally light, tough, and more resilient," not counters it.

3. (C) is the correct answer. The list here provides a series of contrasts about America's needs; very similar language is used in the passage when the author writes about "America's present need." The contrasts are meant to highlight what the American people require in contrast to what they may currently be experiencing. (A) is incorrect because the lines are not about American involvement in war specifically, but America generally. (B) is incorrect because the lines do not detail any potential risks that are specific to entering a war. (D) is incorrect because the author is talking generally about needs, and never hints about what will happen to the country during peacetime.

4. (B) is the correct answer. The author notes that some of the "big five" publishers, including HarperCollins and Hachette, are "both subsidiaries of media companies." (A) is incorrect because the author talks generally about businesses prioritizing profit over culture, but names none of the companies specifically to challenge their priorities. (C) is incorrect because the author cites no statistics in the passage. (D) is incorrect because the author does not mention specific books as examples.

5. (B) is the correct answer. The author supports their conclusion that solastalgia is "the homesickness you have when you are still at home" by providing the word's two parts' meanings, which they say are grounded in "the concepts of 'solace' and 'desolation,'" and then explaining how these concepts fuse to create this word. (A) is incorrect because the passage gives no official dictionary definition of "solastalgia." (C) is incorrect because the author does not give a personal example of the concept. (D) is incorrect because no expert is quoted in the passage.

6. (A) is the correct answer. The author notes that "dead-end sieves would cause problems for fish, since their gill rakers would clog and fish don't have a tongue to move food particles off the gill rakers." However, if a fish did have a tongue-like appendage, this argument would no longer be valid. (B), (C), and (D) all would not negate the author's arguments about how dead-end sieves cause issues for fish.

7.   (A) is the correct answer. The figures mentioned are meant to show the large amount of water that Australians consume, which is the content of the first sentence: "Australians eat a lot of water." (B) is incorrect because it is unsupported by the passage; the authors do not touch on the possibility of drought specifically. (C) is incorrect because the authors do not call for people to monitor their water intake. (D) is incorrect because the authors present these figures not to highlight waste, but to highlight water use.

8.   (A) is the correct answer. The authors use a recent survey on academic engagement with end users in order to offer support for their view that academics are interested in working with businesses. (B) is incorrect because the given lines do not represent the personal experience of the authors. (C) is incorrect because the authors did not conduct this survey. (D) is incorrect because the given lines represent the results of a study, and not just the statement of "experts."

9.   (A) is the correct answer. The author claims that "Enrollment in computer science and computer engineering degrees peaked in 2000," before citing the Taulbee survey, which reports the statistic that, in 2007, "only 46,226 undergraduates in doctoral-granting institutions" were reported. The word "only" suggests this is not a large number, and since the "peak" was reported 7 years before this "only 46,226," we can assume these two facts suggest a decline in computer science and computer engineering majors, which is the author's claim that these new majors "dropped rapidly." (B) is incorrect as the author mentions no research studies or experiments, only data from surveys and a government bureau. (C) is incorrect because the author similarly does not reference personal stories. (D) is incorrect because the author relies on concrete figures, not logic or mathematical formulas.

10. (B) is the correct answer. The author notes in the first sentence of the second paragraph that the discovery of zircons has not resolved the mystery of the nature of Earth's early crust, going on to state that this is because "zircons are resistant to erosion but other minerals and rock fragments are more easily weathered and eroded," which in turn has implications when researchers are attempting to determine the origins of silica-rich rocks. (A) is incorrect because the author does not imply that any collected data is unreliable, only that some is difficult to interpret. (C) is incorrect because the author does not cite any researcher in the passage, let alone in support of this point. (D) is incorrect because no specific study is mentioned in this paragraph.

11. (D) is the correct answer. The first paragraph details Wilfrid's struggles with his new practice, where the narrator notes that "the value of the practice had been exaggerated; the man he had succeeded had not been particularly popular, and some of the older patients took the opportunity of going elsewhere." Thus, Wilfrid is not making as much from the practice as he would have hoped and as the seller had promised. (A) is incorrect because this detail is about Wilfrid's work on a ship, not his work in his new practice. (B) is incorrect; someone comes to Wilfrid's door after parking a big Mercedes, but there is no evidence this is his only client. (C) is incorrect because the passage never indicates that this fact about the practice has anything to do with Wilfred's struggles settling into his new profession.

Section 3
Synthesis

Questions in Synthesis domain test your ability to combine information from multiple sources. Some of them require you to answer questions using information from two passages, while others require you to answer questions using information from a passage and a graphic.

There are 2 specific question types in this domain:

Development			
M	Comparing Passages	Q	Graphics

Comparing Passages
Part 1

Comparing Passages questions require you to compare or contrast information from two passages. They may require you to identify similarities or differences in tone, arguments, perspectives, details, or central themes and ideas. They may also require you to draw conclusions about the implications of two pieces of information from different sources. For example, you might need to consider a general rule described in one passage and a detail in a second passage to draw a conclusion that extends beyond the scope of either passage alone.

There is always one pair of passages on the SAT Reading section, and there will always be a few of these questions following each pair.

DIRECTIONS

Every passage or paired set of passages is accompanied by a number of questions. Read the passage or paired set of passages, then use what is said or implied in what you read and in any given graphics to choose the best answer to each question.

Question 1

Passage 1 is adapted from "Here are some more reasons why liberal arts matter" by Cecilia Gaposchkin. ©2015 by Cecilia Gaposchkin. Passage 2 is adapted from "In the push for marketable skills, are we forgetting the beauty and poetry of STEM disciplines?" by Paul Myers. ©2015 by Paul Myers.

Passage 1

Lately, in the heated call for greater STEM (science, technology, engineering, math) education at every level, the traditional liberal arts
Line have been needlessly portrayed as the villain, and
5 STEM fields falsely portrayed as the very opposite of the liberal arts.
　　The detractors of the liberal arts tend to argue that STEM-based education trains for careers, while non-STEM education does not. They deem
10 the content of a liberal arts education irrelevant. The author of a recent article simply titled, "The Liberal Arts are Dead; Long Live STEM" conveyed this sentiment when he said, "Science is better for society than the arts."
15 　　I see this misunderstanding even at my own institution, as a humanist who oversees pre-major advising and thus engages with students from all over the university. The idea that STEM is something separate and different than the liberal
20 arts is damaging to both the sciences and their sister disciplines. Pro-STEM attitudes assume that the liberal arts are quaint, impractical, often elitist, and always self-indulgent, while STEM fields are practical, technical, and represent at once "the
25 future" and "proper earning potential."

Passage 2

Thousands of students are preparing to begin their job searches with newly earned STEM (science, technology, engineering, and mathematics) degrees in hand, eagerly waiting
30 to use the logical, analytical, and practical skills they've acquired.
　　However, as qualified as they might be, they could be missing one critical component of the STEM field—art. I pursued an education and career
35 in computer science and mathematics and know only too well that in the field of computer science, there is often an emphasis on elegance and beauty alongside sheer practicality. Indeed, programming itself is sometimes referred to as an art.

It is the same in related fields. The discipline of mathematics has long championed beauty as an important quality of ideas and proofs. And, of course, many engineers value elegance and beauty as important components in their designs and solutions.

1

The authors of Passage 1 and Passage 2 would likely agree

A) disciplines outside of STEM have value as well.

B) engineering and mathematics are more difficult than humanities.

C) STEM educations provide the best career options.

D) art is an essential component of STEM disciplines.

Question 2

Passage 1 is adapted from "Opposition to genetically modified animals could leave millions hungry" by James D. Murray and Jenny Graves. ©2016 by James D. Murray and Jenny Graves. Passage 2 is adapted from "Because we can, does it mean we should? The ethics of GM foods" by Christopher Mayes. ©2014 by Christopher Mayes.

Passage 1

In a world with a ballooning population and deteriorating environment, we will need to use every trick in the book to stave off mass starvation. According to the Food and Agriculture Organization of the United Nations, there are 795 million people (more than 10% of the world population) who are chronically undernourished. This includes 161 million children, of which 3.1 million die from hunger each year.

We need to double food production, with less land and less water, and prevent further environmental degradation. One of the most promising approaches is genetically modified (GM) animals to produce more food with less, and improve animal health and welfare.

Passage 2

Food is cultural, social, and deeply personal, so it's no surprise that modifications to the way food is produced, distributed, and consumed often lead to ethical debates. Developments in the genetic modification (GM) of foods and crops have resulted in a raft of controversies. Ethics can help here. While science determines whether we can safely modify the genetic makeup of certain organisms, ethics asks whether we should. Ethics tries to move beyond factual statements about what is, to evaluative statements about the way we should act towards ourselves, each other and the environment we inhabit.

2

Passage 2 differs from Passage 1 in that only Passage 2

A) discusses GM products in agriculture.

B) addresses the need to feed a growing population.

C) focuses on the ethical implications of GM foods.

D) uses statistics in support of the author's arguments.

Question 3

Passage 1 is adapted from "Concrete jungle: cities adapt to growing ranks of coyotes, cougars, and other urban wildlife" by Peter Alagona. ©2015 by Peter Alagona. Passage 2 is adapted from "Urbanization brings animals and diseases closer to home" by Kurt Zuelke. ©2014 by Cadhia Firth and Kurt Zuelke.

Passage 1

In recent years, a host of charismatic wild species, the coyote being only the most famous, have returned to American cities in numbers not seen for generations. The time has come for us to accept that these animals are here to stay, and develop a new approach to urban wildlife.

Despite their reputations, large wild animals are just not very dangerous. By far the most dangerous animals in North America, as measured

10 in human fatalities, are bees, wasps, and hornets.
Next are dogs—man's best friend—followed
by spiders, snakes, scorpions, centipedes and
rats. The most dangerous animal, globally and
throughout human history, is undoubtedly the
15 mosquito. Coyotes are nowhere on the list.

Passage 2

Our world is becoming increasingly urbanized.
In 1950, just 30% of the world's population lived
in urban areas. This number is now over 50%
and rising. By 2050, two-thirds of the world's
20 population are expected to be urban dwellers. The
increasing size and density of human populations
are creating challenges for human health. A
new report highlights the biosecurity risk of
urbanization as cities become hotspots for new
25 and emerging infectious diseases.
      The number of emerging infectious diseases
that infect people has more than tripled the
1940s. Around two-thirds of these are zoonotic,
which means that they have spilled over into
30 human populations from animals. The number of
emerging diseases is likely to continue to increase,
driven by the globalization of travel and trade,
climate change and, of course, urbanization.

Question 4

Passage 1 is adapted from "Music training speeds up
brain development in children" by Assal Habibi. ©2016
by Assal Habibi. Passage 2 is adapted from "Could early
music training help babies learn language?" by Christina
Zhao. ©2016 by Christina Zhao.

Passage 1

Over the past two decades, several investigators
have reported differences in the brain and behavior
of musicians compared to non-musicians. Music
Line training has been found to be related to better
5 language and mathematical skills, higher IQ,
and overall greater academic achievement. Also,
differences between musicians and non-musicians
have been found in areas of the brain related to
hearing and movement, among others.

Passage 2

10 Music training early in life (before the age of
seven) can have a wide range of benefits beyond
musical ability. For instance, school-age children
(six to eight years old) who participated in two
years of musical classes showed better brain
15 responses to consonants compared with their peers
who started one year later. This suggests that music
experience helped children hear speech sounds.

3

The main purpose of each passage is to

A) detail the rise in wildlife in American cities.

B) assess a particular risk connected to
    urbanization.

C) discuss the dangers of infectious disease
    transmission.

D) argue that urbanization has led to major health
    risks.

4

Which choice best states the relationship between
the two passages?

A) Both passages discuss how music training can
    affect the brain and cognition.

B) Both passages discuss how listening to music
    can affect childhood development.

C) Both passages focus on music, but only
    Passage 1 connects music to the brain.

D) Both passages focus on language and music,
    but only Passage 2 focuses on mathematical
    skills.

Question 5

Passage 1 is adapted from "Interstellar greenhouse: how a single molecule could be key to growing plants in microgravity" by Rupesh Paudyal. ©2016 by Rupesh Paudyal. Passage 2 is adapted from "Taking plants off planet—how do they grow in zero gravity?" by Anna-Lisa Paul and Robert Feri. ©2015 by Anna-Lisa Paul and Robert Feri.

Passage 1

Plants use the pull of Earth's gravity to know which way is down and grow their root in that direction, while sending their shoot in the opposite direction (an ability known as gravitropism).
Line
5 One way they do this is by using special gravity-sensing cells that contain starch-packed compartments called amyloplasts. Due to the high amount of starch in these amyloplasts, they are heavier than the rest of the cells, so they sink to
10 the bottom.

In the weightlessness of space, the amyloplasts do not sink, so plants lose some of their ability to perceive gravity. However, that's not the only way they work out which way is up or down. Earth
15 experiments have shown that even plants with starchless amyloplasts, which don't allow them to detect gravity, can still display good levels of gravitropism.

Thus, we need to better understand how
20 the lack of gravity affects plant growth. One possibility is that it all comes down to the plant growth hormone known as indole-3-acetic acid or "auxin". This remarkable molecule is about a thousand times smaller than a dust particle but
25 influences almost every stage of a plant's life cycle, from germination to death.

Passage 2

Certain root growth strategies that everyone had assumed need gravity actually don't require it at all. To seek out water and nutrients, plants
30 need their roots to grow away from where they are planted. On Earth, gravity is the most important "cue" for the direction to grow, but plants also use touch to help navigate around obstacles.

In 2010, we saw that the roots of the plants
35 we grew on the International Space Station (ISS) marched across the surface of their Petri plate in a perfect example of root skewing—no gravity

required. So what's really behind root skewing on orbit, since it's obviously not gravity?
40 Plants on the ISS do have a potentially second source of information from which they could get a directional cue: light. We hypothesized that in the absence of gravity, light plays a bigger role in root guidance.

5

Which best describes the overall relationship between Passage 1 and Passage 2?

A) Both passages focus on how gravity helps plants determine where to grow, but they take different sides on whether plants can grow in space.

B) Both passages focus on how plants grow in space without gravitational clues, but touch on different mechanisms through which plants achieve this.

C) Both passages discuss the effects of chemicals on the plant growth processes in space.

D) Both passages discuss the growth cycles of plants, but focus on different types of plants.

Question 6

Passage 1 is adapted from "Are assigned readings from women professors different?" by Jeff Colgan. ©2015 by Jeff Colgan. Passage 2 is adapted from "Should female faculty get bonus points to correct for gender bias in student evaluations?" by Sara B. Pritchard. ©2015 by Sara B. Pritchard.

Passage 1

Do male and female instructors differ in the way they teach international relations (IR)? New evidence suggests that they do. We found that
Line female instructors design courses differently
5 than male instructors. This happened in two ways. First, we found that female scholars tend to assign more readings by female authors than male instructors. In our sample, men were authors of "only" 71.5% of readings in courses taught
10 by female instructors. Male instructors, on the other hand, assigned readings that were 79.1%

by male authors. Statistically, that difference is very unlikely to happen by random chance. Put differently, female instructors assign 36% more
15 readings by women (including coed teams) than male instructors do, or about five readings per course.

Passage 2

Now that most colleges and universities have completed their spring semesters, course instructors
20 are opening up sealed manila envelopes, all over the country, to read their teaching evaluations. And, like each year, what they'll find has been pervasively slanted by gender bias. Often women faculty find comments in their evaluations that
25 are more personal in nature, comments that have nothing to do with their teaching abilities or competencies. For instance, it's common for female faculty to read comments about their appearance and fashion choices. It would be easy to write off
30 such comments as absurd, or simply inappropriate. But the fact is that these comments speak to the ways that female instructors are perceived differently in the classroom, particularly when they teach large courses.

6

Which statement best describes the relationship between the passages?

A) Passage 1 focuses on differences in reading assignments based on professors' gender, while Passage 2 focuses on differences in evaluations based on professors' gender.

B) Passage 1 focuses on the content of specific courses, while Passage 2 focuses on the gender bias within different courses.

C) Passage 1 focuses on differences in college instruction, while Passage 2 focuses on differences in high school instruction.

D) Passage 1 focuses on gender bias in course evaluations, while Passage 2 focuses on gender bias in reading assignments.

Question 7

Passage 1 is adapted from "What does it mean to preserve nature in the Age of Humans?" by Ben A. Minteer and Stephen Pyne. ©2015 by Ben A. Minteer and Stephen Pyne. Passage 2 is adapted from "Does nature have value beyond what it provides humans?" by Michael Paul Nelson, Jeremy T. Bruskotter, and John A. Vucetich. ©2015 by Michael Paul Nelson, Jeremy T. Bruskotter, and John A. Vucetich.

Passage 1

Ecologist Erle Ellis says we've simply "outgrown" nature, and so we have to become more comfortable within the "used and crowded
Line planet" we've made. Andrew Revkin, author of
5 the Dot Earth environmental blog for the New York Times, sounds a similar theme, arguing that the whole idea of "saving" a nature viewed outside the human presence is an anachronism. What we need instead, he suggests, is to focus on
10 restoring a bipartisan politics able to cope with the challenges of living in and managing a human-driven world.

But all this talk of a more human-driven world and a species that is now "too big for nature" is
15 dismissed by wilderness activist Dave Forman, who spies a dark future awaiting us if we continue on the current path. Foreman condemns the vision of the "Anthropoceniacs" who he argues are promoting nothing less than the technological
20 takeover of life on the planet. We need to remind ourselves, he writes, "that we are not gods."

Passage 2

In our research we found that the premise currently underpinning so much conservation effort is wildly mistaken. A survey we conducted
25 with Ohio residents demonstrated that more than 82% of Ohioans acknowledged the intrinsic value of wildlife. A nationally representative survey of adults revealed very similar numbers (81%). Moreover, we see this high level of intrinsic
30 value attribution across demographic groups: whether rural residents or urbanites, rich or poor, male or female, hunters or non-hunters. Interestingly, more than 90% of people who
35 strongly identified as "conservationists" in the Ohio survey acknowledged nature's intrinsic value. This suggests that conservationists who

reject nature's intrinsic value are out of the mainstream of their peers.

7

Which point about conservationism is explicit in Passage 1 and implicit in Passage 2?

A) Ohions on the whole are more interested in conservation than most Americans.

B) Americans have to acknowledge that we have outgrown nature.

C) People in varied demographic groups acknowledge the intrinsic value of nature.

D) Not all conservationists agree on the goals and methods of their movement.

Question 8

Passage 1 is adapted from "From scourge to savior: using viruses to treat serious disease" by Dave Hawkes. ©2014 by Dave Hawkes. Passage 2 is adapted from "Viruses are highly evolved infectious agents—perfect to go after cancer" by Gwennaëlle Monnot. ©2016 by Gwennaëlle Monnot.

Passage 1

Viruses have traditionally been mankind's enemies, causing disease and often mutating out of the reach of our medicines. But now a new
Line technology is conscripting them into doing good.
5 Viral vectors show great promise, so expect to hear a lot more about them in the future.

Viral vectors are basically viruses modified to not cause disease that are then used to introduce genetic material into cells. These genes can alter
10 the behavior of the cells to cure disease or allow scientists to learn about the nature of the cells. Viral vectors are already being used by scientists to understand how our genes influence our bodies—from how we form memories through
15 to why blood pressure increases when we're stressed. The next frontier in their use will be to actually treat diseases in humans.

Passage 2

Infections are a double-edged sword when it comes to cancer. On the one hand, infections
20 are our foes. Several viruses, such as the human papillomavirus, are well known to produce pre-malignant lesions that may lead to the development of tumors. Chronic inflammation, which is sometimes caused by pathogens such
25 as viruses and bacteria, has also been linked to cancer formation.

But there is another side to the relationship between cancer and infections, in which the latter can mediate tumor regression. This potential for
30 pathogens to be our friends in the fight against cancer was again confirmed recently, when the results of a phase III clinical trial showed encouraging results in melanoma patients. In this study, the patients' response to treatment was
35 significantly improved when their tumors were injected with a genetically modified virus. But although it has not been well publicized, the idea of using pathogens as an anti-cancer weapon is not new and actually started more than a century ago.

8

Both Passage 1 and Passage 2 view the use of viruses in medical treatments with

A) optimism.

B) caution.

C) confusion.

D) outrage.

Question 9

Passage 1 is adapted from "How happiness is challenging GDP as the measure of a country's health" by Paul Anand. ©2016 by Paul Anand. Passage 2 is adapted from "Why happiness is not enough to replace GDP" by Annie Austin. ©2014 by Annie Austin.

Passage 1

Denmark reclaimed its place as the happiest country in the world, according to the latest annual World Happiness Report. Switzerland,
Line Iceland, Norway, and Finland followed in quick
5 succession at the top. The nations that top the usual measure of a country's health—its Gross Domestic Product, or GDP, which shows overall economic output—were much lower down. The US came 13th, the UK 23rd and China 83rd.
10 This goes to show that GDP is by no means a conclusive measure of well-being, and the report reflects moves to recognize this.

Countries at both ends of the scale remind us why we need to measure happiness. Income
15 isn't the be all and end all of life quality, and research into human flourishing continues to grow as a result. Partly this reflects the increasing availability of data measuring subjective markers of happiness. But it also shows a dissatisfaction
20 with modern economic ways of thinking, where morality and ethics take a back seat and bureaucratic cost-benefit analysis is the norm.

Passage 2

The idea that data on happiness and well-being can be used to guide government policy
25 has steadily gained popularity over the past decade. But as we seek ways to replace, or at least complement GDP as a measure of national success, we risk falling into old traps. One measure that is gaining popularity all over the
30 world is particularly problematic.

It has long been accepted that GDP is a woefully inadequate measure of national well-being. As Bobby Kennedy put it as far back as 1968, this type of macro-economic indicator
35 "measures everything, in short, excerpt that which makes life worthwhile." Since then, the Beyond GDP movement has gained momentum. The UK, for example, has developed a well-being framework that includes multiple dimensions of

40 life, including health, relationships, work, the natural environment, and political participation.

9

Unlike Passage 1, Passage 2

A) discusses alternate rankings of countries besides GDP.

B) touches on country-specific measurements of well-being.

C) indicates the World Happiness Report is underutilized.

D) views GDP as an inadequate measure of nations' well-being.

Question 10

Passage 1 is adapted from "Libraries aren't 'dead in the water'—even if some have given up" by Briony Birdi. ©2016 by Briony Birdi. Passage 2 is adapted from "Who says libraries are dying? They are evolving into spaces for innovation" by Crystie Martin. ©2015 by Crystie Martin.

Passage 1

Libraries aren't over; they will just look different. Elizabeth Elford of the Society of Chief Librarian observed "there will be fewer
Line public libraries when we come out the other side,
5 but they will be better and more innovative." I sincerely hope that she is right, but I question whether the closure of so many public libraries could be characterized as a positive development.

Passage 2

With the expansion of digital media, the rise
10 of e-books, and massive budget cuts, the end of libraries has been predicted many times over. While it is true that library budgets have been slashed, causing cuts in operating hours and branch closures, libraries are not exactly dying. In
15 fact, libraries are evolving.

10

Which of the following represents the views of each passage on the future of libraries

A) Passage 1 is optimistic, while Passage 2 is pessimistic.

B) Passage 1 is concerned, while Passage 2 is optimistic.

C) Passage 1 is elated, while Passage 2 is concerned.

D) Passage 1 is uncertain, while Passage 2 is elated.

Question 11

Passage 1 is adapted from "How tiny black spots shed light on part of the Homo naledi mystery" by Francis Thackeray. ©2016 by Francis Thackeray. Passage 2 is adapted from "Homo naledi: determining the age of fossils is not an exact science" by John Hawks. ©2015 by John Hawks.

Passage 1

Many questions have been thrown up by the discovery in South Africa of a previously unidentified human relative, Homo naledi. Perhaps the one that's grabbed people's attention the most is
5   how Homo naledi's bones ended up in the Dinaledi Chamber.

To date, no opening has been found within the Dinaledi Chamber apart from the existing entrance. But might there have been an additional entrance
10   at some time in the past? New research I have conducted and published in the South African Journal of Science centered on mysterious black spots found on Homo naledi bones from the cave.

I strongly believe that there was possibly a
15   temporary entrance into the chamber, in addition to the one used by explorers today. This is because those mysterious black spots are manganese dioxide and were probably deposited on the bones by lichen. And lichen need light to grow—so there
20   must have been some light penetrating into the Dinaledi chamber.

Passage 2

We do not know the actual geological age of the Dinaledi fossils, the single largest fossil hominin find in Africa, but the discovery of Homo
25   naledi still provides insight into how our ancestors evolved. The Dinaledi fossil collection is one of the most complete ever discovered, representing nearly the entire anatomy of a previously unknown species. Yet our team made no statement
30   or conclusion about the fossils' geological age. I reviewed with Ed Yong some of the reasons why it is difficult to determine the age of the fossils.

The bottom line is that, for now, we have little idea how old the fossils may be. Most
35   fossil hominins are found in association with extinct animals, which give us at least a general indication of their age. Famous fossil discoveries from more than a century ago, such as the Spy Neanderthal skeletons from Belgium and the first
40   Homo erectus from Java, were found together with long-extinct creatures that indicated they were of great antiquity. This won't work for Homo naledi because we have found no other animals in association with the hominin bones.

11

Based on the information presented in Passage 1, which of the following could be a reason for the claim made in Passage 2 that no other fossils were found with the Homo naledi's remains?

A) No other large creatures lived in the same habitat and region as Homo naledi.

B) The Homo naledi was a fierce type of hominid that was extremely territorial.

C) There was never any opening in the cave through which living creatures could enter.

D) The opening closed before any other creatures were able to make their way inside the caves.

Question 12

Passage 1 is adapted from "Ad skipping and blocking could spur an advertising arms race" by David Waller. ©2016 by David Waller. Passage 2 is adapted from "Tired of pop-up ads? The 'native' alternative could be worse" by David Waller. ©2014 by David Waller.

Passage 1

Much to the disappointment of advertisers and ad agencies, many people do not like advertising. Some will do anything to avoid advertisements,
Line and increasingly they have the tools to do so. Ad-
5 blocking apps have now expanded to podcasting, with apps that enable 15-second skips to avoid spoken ads within podcasts. But while some people may like the idea of being able to avoid all advertising, advertisers are still finding new ways
10 to get brand names seen by the general public.

And not everyone hates advertising enough to actively avoid it. Many opt in to receive targeted marketing from companies they know. An entire industry is developing around data-
15 based marketing—the key is control. Having control gives someone the ability to determine how they interact with the marketing message and to influence the presentation and content. But in some media platforms there is a lack of control,
20 which can be frustrating.

Passage 2

Over the years the online world has become crowded with advertising pop-ups (which can be blocked), banner advertising (which can be annoying) and sponsored ads (which can
25 be ignored). The reducing effectiveness of getting noticed has led to a new form of product placement appearing online with efforts being made for corporations to become part of the news content.
30 This takes the form of "content marketing" where content is produced and used "to build trust and engagement with would-be customers." This type of marketing has attracted a raft of different labels, including branded content marketing,
35 sponsored media content, custom content, corporate journalism, brand journalism, and brand publishing—and increasingly, journalists are helping marketers to do it.

12

A new advertisement for shoes involves paying journalists to write email newsletters that are sent to customers who have opted in. The author of both passages would likely view this advertising as

A) effective, as it gives consumers control and utilizes content marketing.

B) revolutionary, as it bypasses traditional media and reduces paper waste.

C) risky, as it does not allow companies to expand their customer base to new markets.

D) foolish, as it ignores data-based marketing in favor of sponsored advertising.

Question 13

Passage 1 is adapted from "Ghostwriters haunt our illusions about solitary authors" by Camilla Nelson. ©2015 by Camilla Nelson. Passage 2 is adapted from "Whose line is it anyway? The murderer, his mother, and the ghost writers" by Christopher Kremmer. ©2016 by Christopher Kremmer.

Passage 1

Until recently, any conversation about ghostwriting would have quickly wandered into the murky and more disreputable parts of
Line commercial literary production, such as hoaxes
5 and forgeries or, in academic circles, the specter of contract plagiarism. Over the course of the last decade, this has changed. Everybody knows Tom Clancy doesn't write all of his own novels. Neither does Wilbur Smith or James Patterson.
10 Most people would realize that Learning to Fly wasn't written by Victoria Beckham, but by Pepsy Denning. It was Tom Watts who wrote David Beckham's My Side. Other ghosts with books regularly in the international top-ten include
15 Andrew Crofts and Mark McCrum.

Passage 2

The literary intersections of journalism, creative non-fiction, book publishing and "ghost-writing" are crowded, with a variety of

conflicting interests but no single code of ethics.
Is a journalist bound by copyright laws when
someone eager to tell their own story hands them
their unpublished account of a highly newsworthy
subject without conditions attached? Are they
bound by their various journalism codes of ethics
when writing books, rather than news stories?
Journalists remain publishers' first pick for ghostwriting assignments because they write quickly
and colorfully, are not afraid of imposing a given
meaning on a set of available facts, know what
makes headlines, and meet their deadlines.

13

The authors of Passages 1 and 2 both make
reference to

A) the ethical responsibilities of journalists to the
   public and to their sources.

B) the nebulous distinction between accepted and
   frowned upon ghostwriting practices.

C) different fiction writers that have used
   ghostwriters effectively.

D) the difficulty of publishers in finding suitable
   and reputable ghostwriters.

Question 14

Passage 1 is adapted from "Beyond Pluto: New Horizons'
mission is not over yet" by Jonti Horner and Jonathan
P. Marshall. ©2015 by Jonti Horner and Jonathan P.
Marshall. Passage 2 is adapted from "Pluto and its col-
lision-course place in our solar system" by Jonti Horner
and Jonathan P. Marshall. ©2015 by Jonti Horner and
Jonathan P. Marshall.

Passage 1

Despite the difficulties posed by being
more than 4.5 billion kilometers from home,
the spacecraft New Horizons is certain to
revolutionize our understanding of the Pluto
system. The data it obtains will shed new light
on the puzzle of our solar system's formation and
evolution, and provide our first detailed images of
one of the system's most enigmatic objects.

But the story doesn't end there. Once Pluto

recedes into the distance, New Horizons will
continue to do exciting research. The craft has a
limited amount of fuel remaining, nowhere near
enough to turn drastically, but enough to nudge it
towards another one or two conveniently placed
targets.

Passage 2

Soon, the New Horizons Spacecraft will tear
past Pluto, giving us our first close-up view of the
enigmatic dwarf planet. As it flies past, the seven
instruments on board will capture every moment
of their fleeting encounter. Over the months
that follow, that data will trickle back to Earth,
providing vital new clues to help piece together
the story of our solar system's formation and
evolution.

But what do we already know about Pluto
and its place in our solar system? Most science
is generally experimental in nature. If you want
to find out how something works, you can hit it
with a hammer, boil it in a test tube or make it
run through a complicated maze. Astronomy, by
contrast, is an observational science. We can't
really experiment (except through clever use of
computers). Instead, we gather observations and
use them to piece together the story of how, when,
why, and where something happened.

14

Are the statements made about astronomy by the author of Passage 2 consistent with the actions taken in Passage 1?

A) Yes, because Passage 1 describes how observations can aid scientists in understanding our solar system's history.

B) Yes, because Passage 1 describes how experimental data can help scientists determine the age of the planets.

C) No, because Passage 1 describes how observations of Pluto will be conducted by a spacecraft and not in a laboratory.

D) No, because Passage 1 describes how experimental data will likely not be reliable enough to use.

Question 15

Passage 1 is adapted from "Why being able to distinguish between a good and a bad fat matters so much" by Voster Muchenje and Carlos Nantapo. ©2016 by Voster Muchenje and Carlos Nantapo. Passage 2 is adapted from "Health check: are saturated fats good or bad?" by Rosemary Stanton. ©2014 by Rosemary Stanton.

Passage 1

Fatty acids are a component of the fat found in foodstuffs such as meat, eggs, milk, vegetables, snacks, vegetable oils and most spreads. There are
Line both "good" and "bad" fatty acids. On average,
5 fatty acids make up about 45% of people's daily calorie intake. This is much more than the recommended 20% to 35%. The challenge is to improve dietary options so that fatty acid intakes are within the recommendations, which are set to
10 help people reduce their risk of developing diet-related chronic diseases. These have been on the rise, especially in developing nations.

Passage 2

Cholesterol is a waxy substance found only in animal products. It's an essential component of
15 our bodies, easily made within the body. A diet high in particular saturated fatty acids can increase

cholesterol production, assisted by genetic factors, to levels that dramatically increase the risk of heart attacks. The fats in food are categorized
20 on the basis of their chemical structure as saturated, monounsaturated or polyunsaturated. Polyunsaturated fatty acids are further divided into omega 3s and omega 6s. Of the many saturated fatty acids in foods, three (myristic acid, palmitic
25 acid and lauric acid) have the greatest effect in raising blood cholesterol.

15

Based on the information in Passage 2, which of the following might be a result of the increased fatty acid consumption mentioned in Passage 1? People who eat a higher percentage of fatty acids in their diet

A) should see a reduction in heart attack risk.

B) can tolerate higher fatty acid levels.

C) may develop higher cholesterol levels.

D) will have an increased risk of cancer.

Question 16

Passage 1 is adapted from "Explainer: what is modernism?" by Andrew McNamara. ©2014 by Andrew McNamara. Passage 2 is adapted from "Explainer: what is postmodernism?" by Daniel Palmer. ©2014 by Daniel Palmer.

Passage 1

Modernist art consciously engages with everyday life. Particularly after the first world war, one of the main aims was to make the latest
Line aesthetic offerings available to all social classes.
5 Modernism is typified by a general commitment to exploratory experimentation. Yet it also comprises a wider process that elevates challenge, critical autonomy, and creative innovation. Implicit in modernism's challenge is the idea
10 that predetermined rules, cherished precedent, or even shared parameters of understanding need not necessarily govern future cultural expression. This is a new cultural horizon.
The most immediate impact of such

transformed cultural expectations is that
innovative modernist art is not always well
understood or recognized when first produced.
Famous examples include the unfavorable
reaction to Russian composer Stravinsky's
20 ballet score for The Rite of Spring in 1913, now
considered a 20th-century modernist classic.

Passage 2

The difficulty of defining postmodernism as a
concept stems from its wide usage in a range of
cultural and critical movements since the 1970s.
25 Postmodernism describes not only a period but
also a set of ideas, and can only be understood
in relation to another equally complex term:
modernism. Modernism was a diverse art and
cultural movement in the late 19th and early 20th
30 centuries whose common thread was a break with
tradition, epitomized by poet Ezra Pound's 1934
injunction to "make it new!".

The "post" in postmodern suggests "after."
Postmodernism is best understood as a
35 questioning of the ideas and values associated
with a form of modernism that believes in
progress and innovation. Modernism insists on
a clear divide between art and popular culture.
But like modernism, postmodernism does not
40 designate any one style of art or culture. On the
contrary, it is often associated with pluralism
and an abandonment of conventional ideas of
originality and authorship in favor of a pastiche of
"dead" styles.

16

The author of Passage 2 would most likely respond
to the discussion of The Rite of Spring in Passage 1
by noting that

A) the ballet score, like many modernist works,
broke with tradition.

B) Stravinsky's work was pluralistic and rejected
many conventional ideas.

C) The Rite of Spring was actually more a
postmodernist than modernist work.

D) music in general is a divisive modernist
medium.

Question 17

Passage 1 is adapted from "How to stop vampire bats
wreaking havoc (no stakes or garlic required)" by Julio
Benavides and Daniel Streickler. ©2016 by Julio Benavides and Daniel Streicker. Passage 2 is adapted from
"Ebola: bats get a bad rap when it comes to spreading
diseases" by Alexandra Kamins, Marcus Rowcliffe, and
Olivier Restif. ©2014 by Alexandra Kamins, Marcus Rowcliffe, and Olivier Restif.

Passage 1

Vampire bats live between northern Mexico
and northern Chile, and they are a major problem.
They are now the main cause of human deaths
from rabies in the region. Between 2009 and 2013,
5 vampire bats bit 20,000 people in Peru alone,
according to the country's health minister; and in
communities across the Amazon, where bites are
commonplace, the rate of rabies infection could be
almost as high as 1% per year.
10 The virus is also steadily expanding into areas
that were historically free of the disease, as we
discovered through our recent work in Peru. As
many as 12 new governmental districts become
infected per year on average, which has doubled
15 the number of outbreaks at national level. We
found that the virus invades new areas in waves
that advance at between 10km and 20km per year.
The advance is stalled only by tall mountains that
rise above the altitudes where bats thrive.

Passage 2

One of the greatest global health threats lies in emerging diseases, which have never been seen before in humans or—as with Ebola—appear sporadically in new locations. Most emerging diseases are zoonoses, meaning they are caused
25 by pathogens that can jump from animals into people. Out of more than 300 emerging infections identified since 1940, over 60% are zoonotic, and of these, 72% originate in wildlife.

Whereas some zoonotic infections, such as
30 rabies, cannot be transmitted between human patients, others can spread across populations and borders: in 2003, SARS, a coronavirus linked to bats, spread to several continents within a few weeks before it was eliminated. The unpredictable
35 nature and novelty of zoonotic pathogens make them incredibly difficult to defend against and respond to. But that does not mean we are helpless in the face of emerging ones. Because we know that the majority of zoonoses pass from
40 wildlife, we can start to identify high-risk points for transmission by determining which wildlife species may pose the greatest risk.

17

How would the authors of Passage 2 classify the rabies infection described in Passage 1?

A) A coronavirus

B) A transmission

C) An outbreak

D) A zoonose

Question 18

Passage 1 is adapted from "What exercise does to your bones" by Alex Ireland. ©2016 by Alex Ireland. Passage 2 is adapted from "How your resolution to exercise more this year could be a recipe for injury" by Neil Tuttle. ©2013 by Neil Tuttle.

Passage 1

Our bones are a living organ that grows and changes shape throughout our life. Much of this shaping results from forces which press, pull, and
Line twist the skeleton as we move, and the biggest of
5 these forces is caused by our muscles.

Bones experience huge forces during movement. When a triple jumper's heel hits the ground, the force is around 15 times their body weight—or the weight of a small car. As a result,
10 bones also experience huge impact and muscle force during daily tasks, totaling more than five times body weight even during walking. These forces squash, twist and bend bones. The shin bone briefly becomes nearly a millimeter shorter
15 as your foot hits the ground when running. The bone senses these small changes, and can grow dramatically—in the months after starting exercise—in order to reduce the risk of breaking.

Passage 2

There are two peak times for injury when
20 starting exercise—one in the first two weeks and one in the period between eight and 11 weeks. The first peak includes a high incidence of stress fractures. Bones get stronger and re-model in response to increased exercise, but the process
25 takes time. Increased load produces stress on the bone and stimulates remodeling to build up bone strength.

The process of remodeling begins with re-absorption of old bone and results in the
30 temporary weakening of the total bone structure. If the same high level of loading is repeated, then the weakened bone can be stressed and possibly even damaged. And this leads to a downward spiral that can culminate in a stress fracture.
35 Similar processes occur for other systems of the body, where the very loading that stimulates the capacity of a tissue to increase, frequently also results in a transient reduction in tissue strength.

18

How would the author of Passage 2 most likely respond to the author of Passage 1's claim that bones "can grow dramatically—in the months after starting exercise—in order to reduce the risk of breaking?"

A) The author would argue that instead of strengthening bones, exercise can actually weaken them and lead to increased injury.

B) The author would agree that bones increase in strength, but with the caveat that certain windows within this time period offer elevated risks of injury.

C) The author would caution that only some forms of exercise strengthen bones, while others can lead to stress fractures and a loss in tissue strength.

D) The author would counter that most increases in bone strength occur within weeks and not months of starting an exercise regimen.

Question 19

Passage 1 is adapted from "Explainer: what makes a winning swimmer?" by Elaine Tor. ©2016 by Elaine Tor. Passage 2 is adapted from "Take your marks…the science behind the perfect swimming dive" by Elaine Tor. ©2014 by Elaine Tor.

Passage 1

Races at the international level are often decided by as little as 0.01 of a second. When the start signal sounds, swimmers typically enter the water with a dive off their block (or perform an in-water dive for backstroke). The start contributes anywhere between 1% and 26% of total race time. Typically defined as the time from the start signal to when the swimmer's head reaches 15m, an elite swimmer can complete the start of the race in between 5.4 and 8 seconds, depending on stroke. This is the part of the race when the swimmer is traveling fastest. The importance of the start is, of course, greater in shorter races.

Passage 2

It is important to remember the fastest starter is not always the one that enters the water first. The fastest starters are the ones that can maintain the highest velocity for the longest after they enter the water. Prior to hitting the water, a swimmer must learn to maximize their take-off horizontal velocity while also reducing their reaction time, but if a swimmer does not optimize the underwater phase, increasing their take-off horizontal velocity won't be advantageous to start performance.

19

Which choice best describes how Passage 2 interacts with the points raised in Passage 1?

A) Passage 2 builds on the point about starters mentioned in Passage 1 and notes an additional important factor.

B) Passage 2 refutes the major argument of Passage 1 and makes a bold new claim.

C) Passage 2 agrees with the major points of Passage 1 and offers additional evidence in support of those points.

D) Passage 2 discusses how athletes react and respond to the ideas presented in Passage 1.

Question 20

Passage 1 is adapted from "Climate change, fire may wipe out Australia's giant gum trees" by Megan Clement and David Bowman. ©2012 by Megan Clement and David Bowman. Passage 2 is adapted from "Australia's gum trees at risk" by Nathalie Butt. ©2016 by Nathalie Butt.

Passage 1

As Australia gears up for another risky bushfire season this summer, some of its most iconic and valuable forests are at risk. Giant gum trees rely
Line
5 on fire to regenerate, but an increase in major bush fires due to climate change could stunt their growth, a Tasmanian ecologist has warned. Furthermore, the University of Tasmania's Professor David Bowman says giant gum trees— which can act as valuable carbon stores—may
10 become a thing of the past.

Giant gum trees can grow up to 100 meters, and are hundreds of years old. "They are a globally unique rainforest tree that recovers from bushfires with explosive growth to out-compete
15 the other rainforest trees," Bowman said. "With climate change, we see the trend in increasing fire weather, and if the trees get burned in quick succession you can actually lose them because they don't have any seeds." And while the trees
20 may act as valuable carbon sinks now, Bowman says insulating them from fire in the long-term is impossible.

Passage 2

Heat waves, droughts and floods expected under climate change will alter environmental
25 conditions so much that many gum trees will no longer survive in their native ranges. Due to their long regeneration times and the relatively short dispersal distances of their seeds, the trees are highly vulnerable to climate change.
30 Many of Australia's approximately 750 eucalypt species may not be able to keep up with climate change sufficiently to avoid heavy losses—and these will in turn have cascading impacts on local wildlife and other plants.
35 Researchers applied mid-range and extreme climate scenarios to 108 eucalypt species and grouped them by climate region across Australia.

20

How would the author of Passage 2 most likely respond to Bowman's claim in Passage 1 that if gum trees "get burned in quick succession you can actually lose them because they don't have any seeds"? The author of Passage 2 would

A) argue that unless bush fires are contained immediately, gum trees will lose all reproductive ability.

B) claim that gum trees actually multiply after bush fires and so are not threatened by them.

C) posit that gum trees may actually develop seeds in order to cope with this evolutionary pressure.

D) dispute this claim by noting that gum trees have seeds, even though they do not travel far.

1. (A) is the correct answer. Passage 1 highlights the value of a liberal arts education, while Passage 2 discusses the value of art which may be missing in some STEM fields. Thus, both authors would likely agree with (A). (B) is incorrect because there is not enough evidence in the passage to support the idea that both authors believe STEM disciplines are more difficult; they do not directly address difficulty of various fields. (C) is incorrect because Passage 2 especially does not compare career options of those with STEM educations to career options of those with other educations. (D) is incorrect because Passage 1 does not address art, only humanities in general.

2. (C) is the correct answer. The first passage focuses on issues of feeding a burgeoning population, mentioning GM animals as one potential solution. Only Passage 2 discusses ethical implications of GM foods, so (C) is correct. (A) is incorrect because both passages discuss GM agricultural products. (B) is incorrect because it describes the focus of Passage 1, not Passage 2. (D) is incorrect because Passage 1, not Passage 2, uses statistics.

3. (B) is the correct answer. Although the passages focus on different risks (threats posed by wildlife in Passage 1, and infectious diseases transmitted by animals in Passage 2), both are concerned with looking at the dangers of such risks with the rise of urbanization. (A) is incorrect because this is a focus of Passage 1, but not Passage 2. (C) and (D) are incorrect because they are a focus of Passage 2, but not Passage 1.

4. (A) is the correct answer. Both passages focus on how music training can benefit the brain and cognition, especially language skills. (B) is incorrect because only Passage 2 discusses childhood development. (C) is incorrect because both passages connect music with cognition. (D) is incorrect because only Passage 1 touches on mathematical skills.

5. (B) is the correct answer. Both passages focus on how plants can grow in space without gravitational clues, but Passage 1 touches on the hormone "auxin" and Passage 2 touches on light as possible alternative clues that plants use. (A) is incorrect because both passages mention that plants can grow in space; they simply offer different explanations as to how plants accomplish this. (C) is incorrect because, while Passage 1 focuses on the chemical auxin, Passage 2 discusses how "light plays a bigger role in root guidance" than gravity and does not mention chemicals. (D) is incorrect because the passages do not focus on different types of plants, and discuss growth cycles only in relation to their larger points about gravity and growth in space.

6. (A) is the correct answer. Passage 1 focuses on the different types of reading assignments female vs. male professors give students, while Passage 2 focuses on the different types of evaluations that male vs. female professors receive. (B) is incorrect because both passages touch on gender bias. (C) is incorrect because both passages focus on colleges, not high schools. (D) is incorrect because it flips the two passages; Passage 1 is focused on gender bias in assigned readings, while Passage 2 is focused on gender bias in course evaluations.

7. (D) is the correct answer. Passage 1 makes explicit that different conservationists disagree, giving the example of Ellis and Revkin in contrast to men like Forman. Passage 2, while it does not discuss such disagreements as explicitly, does note that most who identify as conservationists agree with the intrinsic value of nature—though the passage implies that others do not, as it mentions "that conservationists who reject nature's intrinsic value are out of the mainstream of their peers." (A) is incorrect because neither passage makes this claim. (B) is incorrect because only Passage 1 addresses this claim. (C) is incorrect because this is an explicit claim in Passage 2.

8. (A) is the correct answer. Both passages discuss the potential use of viruses to treat diseases. Passage 1 talks about how viral vectors may soon be used to treat diseases in humans, noting that they show "great promise." Passage 2 talks about how pathogens can be "our friends in the fight against cancer." (B) is incorrect because neither passage discusses potential caveats or drawbacks to using viruses to treat diseases. (C) is incorrect because both passages present their information in a straight-forward manner as opposed to a scattered, unclear way that would imply confusion, and neither ever characterize this information as confusing. (D) is incorrect because neither passage mentions angry opinions about using viruses in medical treatments. Both passages discuss the many benefits of using viruses in medical treatments, and the first passage characterizes this tactic as "doing good," and the second passage claims that the use of viruses to treat illness in one specific instance shows "encouraging results."

9. (B) is the correct answer. While Passage 1 talks about the World Happiness Report in general, and different countries' rankings, only Passage 2 discusses a country-specific measure of well-being, in the mention of the UK's development of "a well-being framework that includes multiple dimensions of life." (A) is incorrect because Passage 1 does discuss an alternate ranking, the World Happiness Report. (C) is incorrect because the World Happiness Report is mentioned specifically in Passage 1, not Passage 2. (D) is incorrect because both passages agree that GDP is an inadequate measure of nations' levels of well-being.

10. (B) is the correct answer. Passage 1 notes that "libraries aren't over; they will just look different," but then questions "whether the closure of so many public libraries could be characterized as a positive development," thus expressing concern. Passage 2 is optimistic, noting that libraries are not dying, but "evolving." (A) is incorrect because Passage 1 is not optimistic, since it questions "whether the closure of so many public libraries could be characterized as a positive development," while Passage 2 ends with "libraries are not exactly dying. In fact, libraries are evolving" alluding that they see libraries as continuing to exist, which is the opposite of pessimism when talking about whether or not libraries will still exist in years to come. (C) is incorrect as Passage 1 is much more cautious than elated, as it expresses uncertainty with the phrase "I question whether the closure of so many public libraries could be [...] positive [...]" and Passage 2 is focused on the adaptability of libraries, which is cause for celebration when questioning their place in the future, which "concerned" is oppositional to. (D) is incorrect because Passage 2 is positive, but not "elated," which would require more hyperbolic language, which this passage does not.

11. (D) is the correct answer. The author of Passage 1 indicates that "there was possibly a temporary entrance into the chamber," so this could mean other creatures, though they had a window of opportunity, did not make their way inside the caves. (A) and (B) are incorrect because there is no information in either passage to support these views. (C) is incorrect because Passage 1 indicates there might have been a temporary opening.

12. (A) is the correct answer. The first passage discusses how marketing is moving towards systems where customers can "opt in to receive targeted marketing from companies they know," such as an email newsletter. The second passage notes that "content marketing" can be used to build trust with customers by providing them with branded content—such as a journalist writing relevant articles in an email newsletter. Thus, the author would likely view such an advertisement positively, given that it includes two forward-thinking marketing strategies mentioned in the passages. (B) is incorrect because neither passage is concerned with paper waste in advertisements, and "revolutionary" is too strong. (C) and (D) are incorrect because they imply that the author would take a negative, rather than positive view, towards this form of advertisement, which is incorrect.

13. (B) is the correct answer. Passage 1 discusses how, in recent history, ghostwriting was plagued with discussions about hoaxes, forgeries, and plagiarism, while Passage 2 discusses different ethical questions journalists must cope with. Thus, both touch on the ill-defined distinction between acceptable and unacceptable ghostwriting practices. (A) is incorrect because only Passage 2 mentions ethics, asking if journalists are "bound by their various journalism code of ethics when writing books [...]?" (C) is incorrect as only Passage 1 mentions authors who have used ghostwriters, such as Tom Clancy and James Patterson. (D) is incorrect because neither passage talks about the struggle to find reputable ghostwriters.

14. (A) is the correct answer. Passage 2 describes astronomy as "an observational science" and how "we gather observations and use them to piece together the story of how, when, why, and where something happened." Passage 1 backs up these statements because it presents an instance where observations, from the spacecraft New Horizons, can be used in order to make determinations about "the puzzle of our solar system's formation and evolution." (B) and (D) are incorrect because Passage 1 talks about observations, not experimental data. (C) is incorrect because, though true, it does not give a reason why the actions described in Passage 1 are consistent with the views of astronomy given in Passage 2.

15. (C) is the correct answer. Passage 2 notes that "a diet high in particular saturated fatty acids can increase cholesterol production," so those who eat a diet higher in fatty acids may see increased cholesterol levels. (A) is incorrect because Passage 2 indicates the reverse, that such people would be at an increased risk for a heart attack. (B) is incorrect because neither passage talks about "tolerance" of fatty acid levels. (D) is incorrect because Passage 2 does not discuss cancer risk.

16. (A) is the correct answer. Passage 2 discusses modernism as "a diverse art and cultural movement...whose common thread was a break with tradition," and so the author would likely respond to the discussion of a modernist work by noting this distinction. (B) is incorrect as Passage 2 notes that postmodern art, not modern art, is pluralistic and rejects conventional ideas. (C) is incorrect as nothing in Passage 2 indicates that the author believes the qualities of The Right of Spring would fit the category of "postmodernist." (D) is incorrect because the author of Passage 2 does not single out music as a medium or suggest that it is particularly divisive.

17. (D) is the correct answer. Passage 1 describes how rabies is given by vampire bats to humans. Passage 2 defines "zoonoses" as diseases that "are caused by pathogens that can jump from animals to people," and gives rabies as an example of "zoonotic infections." (A) is incorrect because this is the umbrella virus of which SARS is given as one example in Passage 2, not rabies. (B) is incorrect because neither passage mentions an opinion that rabies infection should be considered an "outbreak," or even that it is a sudden, massive problem, as this term implies. (C) incorrect because only Passage 1 mentions outbreaks.

18. (B) is the correct answer. The author of Passage 2 agrees that "bones get stronger and re-model in response to increased exercise," but notes two peak times during which injury is even more likely, "one in the first two weeks and one in the period between eight and 11 weeks." (A) is incorrect because the author of Passage 2 does acknowledge that bones can get stronger as a result of exercise. (C) is incorrect because the author of Passage 2 does not compare different forms of exercise. (D) is incorrect as the author of Passage 2 discusses timeframes in relation to injuries, but not to overall increases in bone strength, so there is no evidence to back up this assertion.

19. (A) is the correct answer. Passage 2, like Passage 1, notes how start times are important, but mentions an additional factor to consider: that "the fastest starter is not always the one that enters the water first," but the one who "can maintain the highest velocity for the longest after [entering] the water." (B) is incorrect because while Passage 1 stresses the importance of a fast start when trying to win races, Passage 2 states that starts are important as well as other factors, therefore not refuting Passage 1 but merely building on its main point. A true refuting would be Passage 2 claiming that fast start times are not important to winning races. (C) is incorrect because, while it does agree with Passage 1's point that a strong start is paramount to winning a race, it offers evidence to support a different point it makes (maintaining speed is also important to winning) instead of offering more evidence to support Passage 1's main claim. (D) is incorrect because Passage 2 does not discuss athlete responses.

20. (D) is the correct answer. Passage 2 notes that "due to their long regeneration times and the relatively short dispersal distances of their seeds, the trees are highly vulnerable to climate change." This contradicts Bowman's statement that gum trees have no seeds. (A) is incorrect because the author of Passage 2 does not imply that gum trees may lose reproductive ability for any reason. (B) is incorrect because both passages note the dangers of changes in climate, and Passage 2 mentions no specific benefits of bush fires. (C) is incorrect because the author of Passage 2 nowhere discusses evolutionary pressures.

Graphics
Part 2

Graphics questions require you to find information in a graphic element that accompanies the passage. They may require you to identify information presented directly by the graphic, draw conclusions on the basis of one or more pieces of information presented in a graphic, or compare the information presented in a graphic with information in the passage or the question stem and draw conclusions.

DIRECTIONS

Every passage or paired set of passages is accompanied by a number of questions. Read the passage or paired set of passages, then use what is said or implied in what you read and in any given graphics to choose the best answer to each question.

Question 1

This passage is adapted from "There's a sunny future ahead for rooftop solar power: here's why" by Bernhard Mitchell. ©2015 by Bernhard Mitchell.

Over the past five years the world has seen a dramatic fall in the cost of solar energy, particularly rooftop solar panels or solar
Line photovoltaic power. It is now a real alternative
5 and considerable player in the power markets. This puts solar power into a very competitive spot within the next five years.

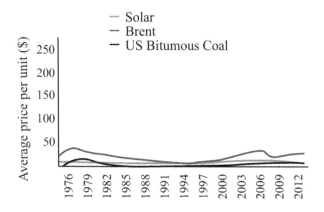

1

It can reasonably be inferred from the passage and graphic that

A) solar power is the cheapest form of energy on the market.

B) while coal has increased in price in the past decade, solar has decreased in price.

C) solar power is the most viable form of energy currently available to consumers.

D) even though solar has decreased in price, it is still behind coal in consumer usage.

Question 2

This passage is adapted from "Every song has a color—and an emotion—attached to it" by Stephen Palmer and Karen B. Schloss. ©2015 by Stephen Palmer and Karen B. Schloss.

There's a small minority of people—maybe one in 3,000—who have extremely strong connections between music and colors. They are
Line called chromesthetes, and they spontaneously
5 "see" colors as they listen to music. But our research team mainly wanted to know how the non-chromesthetes and chromesthetes would compare in terms of emotional

effects. Interestingly, the emotional effects for
chromesthetes were almost as strong as those for
non-chromesthetes on some dimensions (happy/
sad and strong/weak), but weaker on others (calm/
agitated and angry/not-angry).

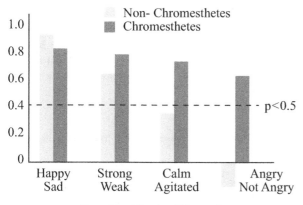

Emotional Rating Dimension

2

Which concept is supported by the passage and by the
information in the graph?

A) Music has less of an emotional effect on
   chromesthetes, on average, than it does on non-
   chromesthetes.

B) Non-chromesthetes have a greater aptitude for
   music than do chromesthetes.

C) Chromesthetes experienced every type of
   emotion when listening to music except for
   anger.

D) Chromesthetes were most often happy while
   listening to music, while non-chromesthetes were
   most often sad.

Question 3

This passage is adapted from "Hunting, fishing, and farming
remain the biggest threats to wildlife" by Sean Maxwell,
James Watson, and Richard Fuller. ©2016 by Sean Maxwell,
James Watson, and Richard Fuller.

Climate change threatens 19% of globally
threatened and near-threatened species—including
the critically endangered mountain pygmy possum
and the southern corroboree frog. It's a serious
conservation issue. Yet our new study shows that
by far the largest current hazards to biodiversity are
overexploitation and agriculture.

Overharvesting

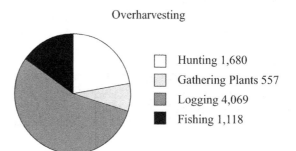

#'s = number of species affected

3

Information from the graph best supports which of the
following statements?

A) Hunting has a greater effect on animal species
   than livestock farming.

B) Aquaculture only has a negligible effect on
   species' survival.

C) Cropping affects more species than timber
   plantations, livestock farming, and aquaculture
   combined.

D) Logging kills more than 4,000 animals each year
   and hunting kills over 1,500 animals each year.

Question 4

This passage is adapted from "Goodbye to the barbershop?" by Kristen Barber. ©2016 by Kristen Barber.

With their red, white and blue striped poles, dark Naugahyde chairs and straight razor shaves, barbershops hold a special place in American
Line culture. As a sociologist, I find barbershops
5 fascinating because they've also traditionally been places where men spend time with other men, forming close relationships with one another in the absence of women. Many patrons will even stop by daily to simply chat with their barbers, discuss the
10 news or play chess. A real community is created in these places, and community is important to health and well-being.

Metropolitan area	Employment	Employment per thousand jobs	Hourly mean wage
White Plains, NY Metropolitan Division	960	0.19	$12.11
Houston, TX	720	0.26	$13.17
Los Angeles, CA Metropolitan Division	710	0.18	$10.06
Wichita Falls, TX	40	0.66	$18.46

4

The table above would support which of the following conclusions?

A) There are more barbers per square foot in New York than in Houston.

B) There are more job opportunities for barbers in Wichita Falls than in New York.

C) A larger percentage of the population holds jobs as barbers in Wichita Falls than in Houston.

D) 18% of the population in Los Angeles is employed as barbers.

Question 5

This passage is adapted from "Museum economics: how the contemporary art boom is hurting the bottom line" by Robert Ekelund. ©2016 by Robert Ekelund.

Art museums, which I would argue make some of the most important contributions to contemporary culture, number about 1,575 and are
Line also very popular. One of the most famous, New
5 York's Metropolitan Museum of Art ("the Met"), for example, saw a record 6.5 million visitors in 2015, making it the world's third most popular museum.

Distribution of Museums by State, FY 2014

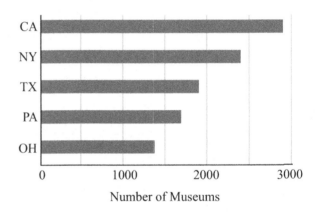

Number of Museums

5

Which claim about museum distribution is supported by the graphic?

A) California has the greatest number of museums per square mile.

B) New York, California, and Texas all have over 2,000 museums.

C) Ohio is the state in the U.S. with the least number of museums.

A) Texas has approximately twice as many museums as Ohio.

Question 6

This passage is adapted from "Forest loss has halved in the past 30 years, latest global update shows" by Rod Keenan. ©2015 by Rod Keenan.

Forest loss has halved over the past 30 years, according to the 2015 Global Forest Resources Assessment. Between 1990 and 2015, global
Line forest area declined by 3%, but the rate of loss has
5 halved between the 1990s and the past five years. Most of this loss occurs in the tropics.

Natural forest area by climatic domain

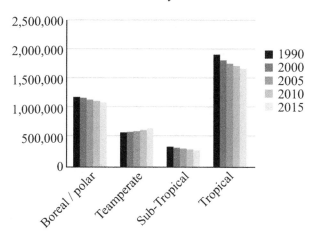

Question 7

This passage is adapted from "The truth behind our 'dangerous' public debt levels" by Philip Soos. ©2013 by Philip Soos.

When discussing public debt, it makes sense to compare it to the size of the economy, or GDP (Gross Domestic Product). Quoting
Line absolute figures is not sufficient to understanding
5 the scale of any debt. GDP represents the size of a country's income, though, of course, governments can only commandeer a portion of that income through taxation.

Federal Government Gross Debt to GDP Ratio 1901 - 2012

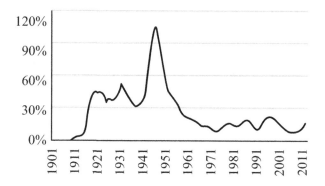

6

Which statement best summarizes the information presented in the graph?

A) Forest area has remained relatively stable in the past few decades in all forests except tropical.

B) Forest loss has decreased most significantly in tropical forests in the past two decades.

C) There are more sub-tropical forests than temperate forests.

D) Only temperate forests have seen an increase in habitat loss in recent years.

7

Based on the table, of the following years, when was the ratio of federal government gross debt to GDP highest?

A) 1911

B) 1931

C) 1971

A) 1991

Question 8

This passage is adapted from "Why London's secondary schools have improved so much" by Merryn Hutchings. ©2014 by Merryn Hutchings.

London's secondary schools have seen rapid improvement in the last decade. Inner London from being the worst-performing region in
Line England in 2003 to having better school results
5 than any region outside London. Furthermore, it has long been known that disadvantaged pupils (those receiving free school meals) in London performed above the national average.

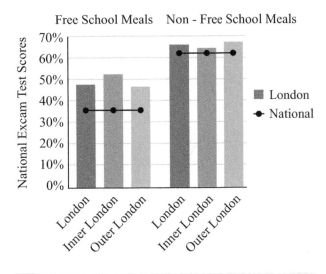

8

What information discussed in the passage is represented by the graph?

A) Test performance of disadvantaged versus non-disadvantaged pupils

B) Number of free school meals offered in various parts of London

C) Where the highest number of free school meals are offered in the U.K.

D) The overall academic success of students who receive free school meals versus those that do not

Question 9

This passage is adapted from "February carbon dioxide levels average 400 ppm for the first time" by Paul Krummel and Paul Fraser. ©2015 by Paul Krummel and Paul Fraser.

CO_2 concentrations have climbed relentlessly over the past 200 years. Air and ice measurements allow us to trace the dramatic rise in carbon
Line dioxide levels from about 280 ppm before the
5 start of the industrial era around the year 1800, to a global average of 397 ppm in 2014. That's an increase of 42%, largely due to human activities.

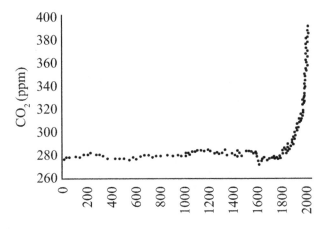

9

What statement is best supported by the data presented in the figure?

A) Carbon levels increased most dramatically between the years 1600 and 1800.

B) Carbon levels remained relatively stable for the past 200 years.

C) Carbon levels were greater in 1200 than in 1600.

D) Human activity dramatically increased carbon levels starting around 1800.

Question 10

This passage is adapted from "Infographic: how much does the world spend on science?" by Andrew Steele. ©2013 by Andrew Steele.

The percentage of GDP invested in research and development varies widely across the world. South Korea is powering ahead at 3.7% of GDP
Line (and its investment is increasing rapidly, up from
5 2.8% in 2005). The UK is below average by most international measures, spending 1.7% of GDP on research.

% GDP invested in scientific research

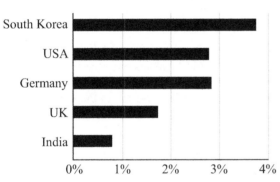

Government and business funding of
scientific research in the G20

10

According to the graph, which statement is true about the percent GDP invested in scientific research?

A) India spends the least amount of its GDP globally on scientific research.

B) The U.S. spends less money than South Korea on scientific research.

C) Germany spends a greater proportion of its GDP on scientific research than the U.K.

D) South Korea spends as much money on scientific research as the U.K. and India combined.

Answers & Explanations

1. **(B) is the correct answer.** This statement reflects information that can be reasonably concluded from the given graph and passage. The passage states that solar power has gone down in price, and the graph backs up this assertion, comparing solar power to two other energy sources, including coal, which has gone up in price in the past decade. (A) is too broad a conclusion to be reached from the passage and graphic alone; another type of power, such as wind, for example, could be even cheaper, but there is not enough information to reach this conclusion. (C) is incorrect because it is too strong; there is not enough evidence in the passage to back up this assertion. Furthermore, "viable" is vague here and not clearly defined. (D) is incorrect because the graphic says nothing about consumer usage of coal.

2. **(A) is the correct answer.** For almost every dimension shown in the graph, chromesthetes showed less of an emotional correlation than did non-chromesthetes. (B) is incorrect because the passage and graphic do not discuss musical aptitude of either group. (C) is incorrect because the graph shows emotional correlation; it does not indicate the experience, or lack thereof, of an emotion. (D) is incorrect because the graphic and passage do not compare the relative frequency of emotions of either group when listening to music.

3. **(C) is the correct answer.** The numbers indicated represent species affected. Cropping affects 4,692 species, while timber plantations, livestock farming, and aquaculture affect 730, 2,267, and 112 species respectively, well below 4,692 species. (A) is incorrect because hunting affects less species than livestock farming (1,680 versus 2,267). (B) is incorrect because aquaculture does affect 112 species; there is not enough information in the graphic to suggest that this is negligible, even though it is less than any other sources listed. (D) is incorrect because the numbers given represent species affected, not number of animals killed.

4. **(C) is the correct answer.** In Wichita Falls, the "employment per thousand jobs" as shown in the table is 0.66, while it is only 0.26 in Houston. Thus, more of the population as a percentage holds a job as a barber in Wichita Falls versus Houston. (A) is incorrect as the table gives no information about number of barbers per square foot. (B) is incorrect as the table likewise does not discuss job opportunities for barbers. (D) is incorrect because the table shows that the employment per thousand jobs is 0.18 in Los Angeles, which is not the same as stating that 18% of the population is employed as barbers.

5. **(B) is the correct answer.** The graph shows that these three states all have over 2,000 museums. (A) is incorrect because the graphic shows number of museums, not museums per square mile. (C) is incorrect because there is not enough information to draw this conclusion; another state, not represented, may have less museums. (D) is incorrect because Texas would need to have around 3,000 museums to have "approximately twice a many museums as Ohio," which has close to 1,500, however Texas only have approximately 2,000.

6. **(A) is the correct answer.** The graph shows that the forest area in boreal/polar, temperate, and sub-tropical forests has remained relatively stable over the past couple of decades, but the area of tropical forests has gone down. (B) is incorrect because the graph shows forest area, not forest loss. (C) is incorrect because the graph shows a greater area for temperate, not sub-tropical, forests. (D) is incorrect because the graph shows area and not habitat loss.

7. **(B) is the correct answer.** Even though this year may not be the highest point on the graph, it represents the highest value of the ratio of federal government gross debt to GDP in comparison to all others. (A), (C), and (D) are all much smaller values and can be eliminated.

8. (A) is the correct answer. The passage discusses how "disadvantaged pupils (those receiving free school meals) in London performed above the national average," the same topic in the graphic. (B) and (C) are incorrect because the graphic depicts exam performance, not number of students receiving free school meals. (D) is incorrect because it is too broad; the graphic shows exam performance, but it would be incorrect to extend this more generally to overall academic success, which the graphic does not depict.

9. (C) is the correct answer. Based on the figure alone, it is possible to conclude that carbon levels were lower in 1600, where they take a small dip, than in 1200. (A) is incorrect as the greatest dramatic increase happens between 1800 and 2000, not 1600 and 1800. (B) is incorrect as carbon levels remained stable for about 1800 years, but have changed dramatically in the past 200, according to the figure. (D) is incorrect because the figure only shows carbon levels; it indicates nothing about human activity, so this statement is not supported solely by the information in the figure, which is what the question asks about.

10. (C) is the correct answer. The graph compares the percentage of GDP each country spends on scientific research, and shows that Germany spends nearly 3% of its GDP on scientific research, which is larger than the UK's less than 2%. (A) is incorrect because the graph does not present every country in the world, so this would be a false assumption; another country may spend less of its GDP on scientific research and just not be pictured here. (B) and (D) are incorrect because the values shown are not absolute, but instead represent amounts countries spend on scientific research, relative to their GDP. A smaller country may spend a greater proportion of its GDP on scientific research while a larger country spends a smaller proportion, but the latter could still be numerically spending more, since its GDP is likely greater to begin with.

Ivy Global

Writing

Chapter 3

Section 1

Development

Questions in the Development domain test your ability to make revisions that improve the overall structure and clarity of a passage. You will need to select choices that clearly express central ideas in the passage, add or remove information based on how well it develops clear ideas, and synthesize information from graphical elements alongside the passage.

Development questions contribute to the "Expression" subscore. They also contribute to the "Command of Evidence" cross-test score.

There are 4 specific question types in this domain:

Development			
DP	Main Idea	DF	Relevant Information
DS	Supporting Evidence	DQ	Graphic Analysis

Main Idea

Part 1

Main Idea questions ask you to add, revise, or delete a main idea statement in the passage. They may ask about an idea that is central to a single paragraph or about an idea that is central to the passage as a whole. To answer them correctly, consider the context and select the choice that best expresses the overall meaning of the rest of the paragraph or passage. Avoid answer choices that focus too much on specific details, introduce irrelevant ideas, or fail to clearly express a central idea.

DIRECTIONS

Every passage comes with a set of questions. Some questions will refer to a portion of the passage that has been underlined. Other questions will refer to a particular location in a passage or ask that you consider the passage in full.

After you read the passage, select the answers to questions that most effectively improve the passage's writing quality or that adjust the passage to follow the conventions of standard written English. Many questions give you the option to select "NO CHANGE." Select that option in cases where you think the relevant part of the passage should remain as it currently is.

Question 1

How Atolls Are Formed

An atoll is a special type of coral reef, distinguished by its striking, ring-like shape. It forms in a complicated way. Have you ever heard of islands being formed by volcanic eruptions? Atolls are also partly formed by volcanoes, but where volcanic islands are high and mountainous, atolls are low. How, exactly, do atolls come to be?

The English scientist Charles Darwin, who travelled in the South Pacific from 1831-1836, developed a theory about atoll formation that is still generally accepted. Darwin suggested that an atoll takes the place of a mountainous volcanic island. When the volcano becomes extinct, it slowly subsides into the sea. At the same time, coral starts to surround the island in a circular reef. In time, the volcanic island disappears, leaving a ring of coral in its place. Pieces of the coral break off over time and collect to form sandbars and, eventually, low ring-shaped islands. This is a slow process, taking up to 30 million years.

[1] Cave features like stalagmites and stalactites can also take millions of years to form, and the processes that form them can easily be disrupted by reckless human explorers. Corals grow at a rate of only 0.3 to 2 centimeters per year, but sea-levels are now rising at a rate of 3.4 centimeters per year. A change of 3.4 centimeters per year might not seem like much, but it's far more rapid than the natural processes involved in

30 atoll formation. As seas rise too rapidly for corals to keep up, the reefs will sink to depths at which they can no longer survive—and the low atoll islands will disappear beneath the waves.

1

Which choice best establishes the main idea of this paragraph?

A) NO CHANGE

B) Ironically, though atolls form as islands subside into the sea, rising seas now threaten their survival.

C) Pollution and other dangers are a constant threat to atolls.

D) Naturally, a feature that was formed by something sinking beneath the sea will be threatened when the sea rises.

Question 2

Rising Temperatures, Spreading Fevers

2 Early symptoms of Chagas disease can include fever, rashes, vomiting; in its second phase, the disease can even cause heart failure. This can

Line have serious consequences for human health,

5 because many tropical diseases are transmitted by insects. There was an outbreak of dengue fever, transmitted by tropical mosquitos, in Florida in 2009. Malaria, another mosquito-borne illness, has been almost totally eradicated in the United States

10 since the 1950s. However, the mosquitoes that can transmit the disease remain common—and the risk of an outbreak increases as mosquito populations increase and spread. Chagas disease, transmitted by kissing bugs, is unfamiliar to many US residents,

15 and those who suffer from it mostly contracted the disease in Latin America. However, recent testing of kissing bugs in Arizona and California showed

that more than half carried the parasite that causes Chagas disease. While there are still only a few

20 reported cases of Chagas disease in the United States, the disease could become endemic as kissing bug populations expand.

2

Which choice best establishes the main idea of this paragraph?

A) NO CHANGE.

B) Kissing bugs are not the only insect known to spread dangerous diseases: malaria, which is spread by mosquitoes, kills over 200,000 people every year worldwide.

C) The range of the tropical insects is expanding as the climate grows warmer, and the populations are increasing in some places where they already exist as year-round conditions become more hospitable

D) Scientists now believe that the Black Death, a pandemic which killed between 75 and 200 million people in the Middle Ages, was spread by fleas.

Question 3

Canal Grass: A Cautionary Tale

However, the canal has brought more than trade to Panama. Maritime traffic also brings in a host of exotic species, which can wreak havoc on the local

Line ecosystem, preying on native species or competing

5 with them for scarce resources or space.

3 14,000 ships pass through the Panama Canal each day, many carrying exotic species. It is believed to have been imported to Panama by Americans hoping to control erosion along the

10 banks of the canal in the 1920s, and it has become so ubiquitous around the canal that it is commonly

called "canal grass." Each year, however, it spreads further beyond the banks where it was first planted, taking over more and more terrain
15 once occupied by dense jungles.

Canal grass has a strange ally in its expansion: fire. The grass easily ignites in the tropical nation's long, hot dry-season. While the stalks of the grass are destroyed, along with other vegetation, its root
20 structures survive the conflagration. That allows the grass to rapidly regenerate and expand into the surrounding space—cleared of competing vegetation by the flames.

3

Which choice best establishes the main idea of this paragraph?

A) NO CHANGE

B) One particularly problematic species is Saccharum Spontaneum, also known as wild sugarcane.

C) Even pests like mosquitos can make their way over, though they do little damage to the canal itself.

D) Some parts of the canal are inhabited by native organisms like the lesser capybara, a large rodent, but an invasive species is more prominent.

Question 4

Narwhal Tusks

Narwhal teeth are quite different from ours. The outer surface has millions of tiny channels which lead all the way to nerves in the center
Line of the tooth, and these nerves lead straight to
5 the whale's brain. This makes the tooth highly sensitive. Dr. Martin Nweeia, from the Harvard School of Dental Medicine, suggests that the tusk can taste, sense pressure, and distinguish temperatures in the surrounding seawater.

10   **4** We still don't know exactly why narwhal teeth are so sensitive. Perhaps the tusk helps the whales find food, but since most female narwhals don't have tusks, this seems unlikely. Others speculate that narwhals use their tusks to detect
15 changes in the weather—this would be valuable information for narwhal pods, who need access to holes in the ice in order to breathe. However, it will take many more years of dedicated study before we have a clear answer.

4

Which choice best establishes the main idea of this paragraph?

A) NO CHANGE

B) The most conspicuous difference between male and female narwhals is that males sport a distinctive tusk.

C) Narwhals live in Arctic waters and have a number of features that help them survive the cold.

D) The narwhal's distinctive tusk earned it the nickname "sea unicorn" from 16-century British sailors.

Question 5

My Favorite Career

[5] The most glamorous job I've ever had was reporting on the media for a local newspaper. Even when I'd been out until the wee hours enjoying the after-show parties with my celebrity buddies-for-the-day, I was expected to be in the office by 10 a.m. at the very latest. After all, someone had to open the press releases and stuff that arrived by the boxful every day. Someone had to answer the phone and conduct the interviews. Someone had to write the articles and compile the lists of coming attractions. Someone had to proofread those articles when it was time to publish that week's issue. That someone was me.

I admit that there were times I hid in my car for a nap. I admit that I fell asleep at my desk a few times. I even admit there were times when I thought about skipping a concert, or not going to the art opening, or maybe going to just one event in an evening instead of attending four. I never did, though, because it was too much fun. When I got promoted to features editor I was relieved that I could stay home occasionally.

5

Which choice best establishes the main idea of the passage as a whole?

A) NO CHANGE

B) No matter what section you write for, working at a newspaper means opening a tremendous amount of mail.

C) Sometimes my job kept me up so late that I found myself falling asleep at work.

D) Working as an Arts and Entertainment editor was thrilling—but it was also exhausting.

Question 6

The Pop Music Mastermind

[6] Few producers can claim to have worked with both Britney Spears and Taylor Swift. Like Dr. Luke, Stargate, RedOne, Greg Kurstin, and a few others, Martin is a "superproducer"— one of the handful of songwriters behind almost all of today's pop hits. Even in this elite group, Max stands out: he has written more number one songs than anyone in history except John Lennon and Paul McCartney of the Beatles.

Born Karl Martin Sandberg in Stockholm, Sweden, he started his music career in the late 1980's as a heavy metal singer. In 1993, his band came to the attention of Denniz PoP, a DJ who had recently founded a songwriting and recording studio called Cheiron. Impressed by Sandberg's gift for melody, Denniz brought him onto the Cheiron team, renaming him "Max Martin".

In 1997, Denniz paired Max with a new American boy band struggling to find an audience. That band was the Backstreet Boys, and on the strength of Martin's songs, their first album became one of the best-selling debuts of all time. Over the next few years, hits like Backstreet's "I Want It That Way" and Britney Spears' "...Baby One More Time" established Martin as the most successful composer in pop.

However, by 2004, Max's career was stalling. Teen pop, his specialty, had been replaced on the charts by guitar-driven indie rock. Looking for a new sound, Martin teamed up with Lukasz Gottwald, an underground producer wrapping up a ten-year stint as the lead guitarist for the Saturday Night Live band. "Since U Been Gone", the song they wrote together for Kelly Clarkson,

combined Max's melodic sensibility with Luke's
guitar drive; it became a massive hit, launching
Luke's career and re-launching Max's. Since
then, Martin's string of hits for Katy Perry, Taylor
Swift, Justin Bieber, Usher, Maroon 5, and many
40 more has cemented his status as pop's most
reliable hitmaker.

6

Which choice best establishes the main idea of the
passage as a whole?

A) NO CHANGE

B) Max Martin is one of the most successful
songwriters of all time, with a career spanning
multiple decades.

C) Music producers today often work under
pseudonyms, or assumed names, and Max
Martin is no exception.

D) A surprising proportion of American hit music
is produced by men from Sweden and Norway.

Question 7

Medical Illustrators Show Hidden Worlds

Have you ever marvelled at the detailed
drawings in a medical textbook like Gray's
Anatomy and wondered about the artists who
Line   made them? **7** Composed by Henry Gray and
5   illustrated by Henry Vandyke Carter, this famous
textbook was first published in 1858. Every
anatomy textbook, instructional animation, and
educational model of the human body requires a
medical artist's precision and knowledge. What's
10   more, as 3D modeling technologies improve,
the demand for such artists will likely increase
considerably.

7

Which choice best establishes the main idea of the
paragraph?

A) NO CHANGE

B) Have you ever admired the precision and
control of surgeons, or the grace under fire of
emergency responders?

C) It's striking to think that this landmark volume
was created without the benefit of modern
technology.

D) For those who love science and art, medical
illustration offers the exciting possibility of a
career in both.

Question 8

Velvet Ants

Hikers and gardeners in southern regions of
the United States may already be familiar with
the "velvet ant," a ground insect with a tough
Line   exoskeleton covered in thick tufts of fur-usually
5   red or orange-from which the "velvet" component
of its name is derived. The "ant" part is actually
just a misnomer, though: the velvet ant isn't an ant
at all. It's actually a wasp.

The sting of the velvet ant is so notorious that
10   they have another nickname: "cow killer." This
nickname arises from the myth that the sting of
the velvet ant is so painful that it could kill a
cow. Just like the name "velvet ant," though, this
moniker is more about how the insect is perceived
15   than what it actually is. The cow killer's sting
can't really kill a cow; in fact, the stings are not
even particularly dangerous to humans. They are,
however, quite painful.

8 The Wasps, a comedy by the ancient

²⁰ Greek playwright Aristophanes, does not feature any actual wasps: however, at one point, a group of old men attack one of the protagonists like a swarm of wasps. The wasps are solitary animals, and they're not aggressive, so even

²⁵ those people who spend a lot of time outside will only encounter them rarely. When they do have an encounter, the wasp will generally not sting. Wearing shoes outside will help people to avoid stepping on the wasps while barefoot, which is

³⁰ the most likely cause of stings. It's not usually necessary to eradicate the wasps; it's usually enough to give them a little bit of space, and let them go about their business.

8

Which choice best establishes the main idea of the paragraph?

A) NO CHANGE

B) Although Africanized bees, commonly known as "killer bees," are widely feared, they only kill one or two people per year on average.

C) The phrase "hornet's nest" is sometimes used as a metaphor to describe a dangerous or annoying situation.

D) Those who live or travel in places where velvet ants live should be wary of their painful sting, but only need to take simple precautions.

Question 9

Let's Go Fly A Kite

[9] The first kite may have been flown in about 200 B.C. by a Chinese general to measure the distance his troops would need to tunnel to

^{Line} get inside the walls of a city. There are a number

⁵ of factors that must be considered before sending a kite aloft. Naturally, the wind conditions need to be taken into account because a strong wind can batter a simple paper kite but winds that are too gentle won't be able to lift a fanciful box kite.

¹⁰ The best place to fly a kite is an open field with no power lines or trees and, remembering the lesson of Ben Franklin, the best time to fly a kite is when there are no thunderstorms in the area.

9

Which choice best establishes the main idea of the paragraph?

A) NO CHANGE

B) While flying a kite may seem like an easy skill to attain, the truth is that the process is relatively complex.

C) Famously, Benjamin Franklin flew a kite to prove the existence of electricity.

D) Modern kites range from the classic simple diamond shape all the way to complex box kites and dramatic dragon kites that feature long tails and spectacular designs.

1. (B) is the correct answer. (B) is correct because the whole paragraph discusses the dangers that rising seas pose to atolls: the sea level is rising "at a rate of 3.4 centimeters per year," which is "too rapidly for corals to keep up." (A) is incorrect because this paragraph is not about various natural features that develop slowly; it is specifically about the threat atolls face from the sea. (C) is incorrect because the only threat the paragraph discusses is the sea level, not pollution or a range of "other dangers." (D) is incorrect because neither the paragraph nor the passage suggests that rising sea levels are "naturally" dangerous to atolls. In fact, since atolls develop when the sea level sinks, one might think that rising sea levels will help atolls develop! As this paragraph explains, the problem is more specific: sea levels are rising much faster than coral can form.

2. (C) is the correct answer. (C) is correct because the paragraph discusses the spread of tropical insects like mosquitos and kissing bugs into North America. (A) is incorrect because, even though the paragraph mentions Chagas disease repeatedly, it does not focus on the effects of Chagas disease or any of the other diseases it mentions. (B) is incorrect because the paragraph as a whole is not only about malaria; it is about mosquitos, kissing bugs, and the various diseases they transmit. (D) is incorrect because the paragraph discusses the populations of insects in the present, not on historical insect-borne diseases.

3. (B) is the correct answer. (B) is correct because this choice effectively introduces the specific species that is the focus of this paragraph. Consider the next sentence, which begins with "it": what is the antecedent of "it"? It's something that is also called "canal grass." According to the last sentence of the paragraph, it is "taking over more and more terrain once occupied by dense jungles." (B) introduces us to a "particularly problematic" species of grass, which clearly establishes something that makes sense in the context of the rest of the paragraph. (A) is incorrect because it makes it seem as though the "it" could only be "the Panama Canal" itself. However, that's a large, man-made feature—not a species of grass. (C) is incorrect because it focuses on mosquitoes, which aren't mentioned anywhere else in the paragraph. (D) is incorrect because it focuses mainly on a native species, the capybara, which is not mentioned elsewhere in the paragraph.

4. (A) is the correct answer. (A) is correct because the paragraph presents a number of theories for what narwhal teeth are used to sense—in other words, why they are so sensitive. (B) is incorrect because, even though the second sentence notes that female narwhals don't have tusks, the paragraph as a whole is not about differences between male and female narwhals. (C) is incorrect because, even though the third sentence suggests that narwhals' teeth help them survive in winter, the other theory—about food—has nothing to do with the cold. (D) is incorrect because the paragraph does not otherwise discuss historical ideas about narwhals.

5. (D) is the correct answer. (D) is correct because the passage lists many exciting aspects of the narrator's job (the parties, the concerts, the art openings) but also describes how tiring it was (the narrator sometimes fell asleep at work). (A) is incorrect because, although the passage does describe many glamorous features of the narrator's job, the passage as a whole contrasts these with how tiring the job was. (B) is incorrect because, although the first paragraph does mention "the press releases and stuff" that the narrator had to read through every morning, it also describes many other responsibilities beyond opening mail. (C) is incorrect because, although the passage does describe how tiring the narrator's job was, the passage as a whole contrasts this with the exciting aspects of the job.

6. (B) is the correct answer. (B) is correct because the passage as a whole is about Max Martin and his long, successful career. (A) is incorrect because it doesn't establish who the passage is about. (C) is incorrect because the passage as a whole is about Max Martin's career, not his pseudonym. (D) is incorrect because the passage is about one specific producer from Sweden, not Swedish and Norwegian producers in general.

7. (D) is the correct answer. (D) is correct because the paragraph is about medical illustration in general, a profession that requires "precision and knowledge"—in other words, artistic skill and scientific expertise. (A) and (C) are incorrect because the paragraph only mentions Gray's Anatomy as an example of a textbook featuring medical illustrations; it is not the main idea of the paragraph. (B) is incorrect because the paragraph is specifically about medical illustrators, not surgeons, emergency responders, or other impressive medical professionals.

8. (D) is the correct answer. (D) is correct because the paragraph as a whole explains that velvet ants are "not even particularly dangerous" even though their sting is painful. (A) is incorrect because, even though this sentence discusses a play called The Wasps, it does not otherwise relate to the rest of the paragraph. (B) is incorrect because it is about Africanized bees, while the paragraph is focused on velvet ants. (C) is incorrect because the paragraph is about real-life wasps, not wasps or hornets in an expression or metaphor.

9. (B) is the correct answer. (B) is correct because the paragraph as a whole discusses various factors that make flying a kite fairly difficult. (A) is incorrect because the paragraph as a whole does not discuss the military uses of kites. (C) is incorrect because the paragraph is about the challenges of flying a kite, not about specific people who have flown kites in the past. (D) is incorrect because, even though the paragraph names two kinds of kites, it only does so to explain what kind of winds make flying them difficult.

Supporting Evidence
Part 2

Supporting Evidence questions ask you to change, insert, or delete supporting evidence for an idea. Sometimes the question will specify a particular idea to be supported, either by stating the idea in the question or by indicating where it appears in the passage.

However, in many cases you will need to recognize on your own that a sentence serves as supporting evidence for an important idea in the passage.

DIRECTIONS

Every passage comes with a set of questions. Some questions will refer to a portion of the passage that has been underlined. Other questions will refer to a particular location in a passage or ask that you consider the passage in full.

After you read the passage, select the answers to questions that most effectively improve the passage's writing quality or that adjust the passage to follow the conventions of standard written English. Many questions give you the option to select "NO CHANGE." Select that option in cases where you think the relevant part of the passage should remain as it currently is.

Question 1

How Atolls Are Formed

An atoll is a special type of coral reef, distinguished by its striking, ring-like shape. It forms in a complicated way. Have you ever heard of islands being formed by volcanic eruptions?
5 Atolls are also partly formed by volcanoes, but where volcanic islands are high and mountainous, atolls are low. How, exactly, do atolls come to be?

The English scientist Charles Darwin, who travelled in the South Pacific from 1831-1836,
10 developed a theory about atoll formation that is still generally accepted. Darwin suggested that an atoll takes the place of a mountainous volcanic island. When the volcano becomes extinct, it slowly sinks back into the sea. At the same time,

15 coral starts to surround the island in a circular reef. In time, the volcanic island disappears, leaving a ring of coral in its place. This is a long process, taking up to 30 million years.

Because atolls are made of coral, they can
20 only form in tropical and subtropical waters. The majority are in the Pacific Ocean, with a significant number in the Indian Ocean, too. The only Atlantic atolls are a group of eight in the Caribbean, off the coast of Nicaragua.

25 In some cases, atolls are large enough to support islands, vegetation, and even towns. For example, Malé, the capital of the Indian Ocean nation of the Maldives, is an atoll city with over 153,000 inhabitants. 1 A number of other island
30 nations, including Kiribati, Tahiti, and Micronesia,

also possess populated atolls. Because these atolls, along with other coral islands, are so low, many are in imminent danger from rising sea levels caused by climate change.

35   The process of atoll formation shows how coral and volcanoes, working in concert over millions of years, can create beautiful circular forms in the middle of the sea—forms which in some cases sustain thousands of people.

1

The writer is considering deleting the underlined sentence. Should the sentence be kept or deleted?

A) Kept, because it develops the paragraph's claim that atolls are large enough to support human communities.

B) Kept, because it gives further examples of atolls.

C) Deleted, because the passage's focus is on the development of atolls in general, not on specific atolls.

D) Deleted, because these atolls are at risk from climate change.

Questions 2 & 3

Narwhal Tusks

At the end of the 16th century, the English Queen Elizabeth I received a curious present. Sailors brought her a jeweled "unicorn horn"

Line valued at 10,000 pounds sterling—roughly the
5 price of a castle! The sailors said it came from a "sea-unicorn", but its true source was probably a narwhal, a type of small Arctic whale. Male narwhals—and about 15 percent of females— have long, spiralling tusks that really do look like
10 unicorn horns. Scientists have only just begun to understand how special narwhal tusks are.

It was once thought that narwhals used their tusks to fight each other or poke holes in the ice. **2** However, while narwhals do rub their tusks
15 together, they don't seem to be fighting. Nor has anyone ever observed a narwhal breaking the ice with its tusk. In fact, scientists now know that the tusks are not horns, but teeth. Not only are they teeth, they are unusually sensitive teeth, with large
20 numbers of nerve endings exposed through tiny holes on their surface.

We still don't know exactly why narwhal teeth are so sensitive. Perhaps the tusk helps the whales find food, but since most female narwhals don't
25 have tusks this seems unlikely. Others speculate that narwhals use their tusks to detect changes in the weather—this would be valuable information for narwhal pods, who need access to holes in the ice in order to breathe. **3** After all, the
30 name "narwhal" comes from an old Norse word meaning "corpse whale." However, it will take many more years of dedicated study before we have a clear answer.

At this point, the author is considering adding the following sentence:

The author Jules Verne even suggested that their tusks could sink ships!

Should the author make this addition here?

A) Yes, because it reports an early theory about the narwhal tusk, which later research proved to be true.

B) Yes, because it offers a vivid example of an old misconception about narwhal tusks.

C) No, because it merely reiterates the main point of the essay.

D) No, because it fails to explain why we used to know so little about narwhal tusks.

Which choice best supports the theory presented in the previous sentence?

A) NO CHANGE

B) Narwhals must swim away from the ice to the open ocean before the weather grows too cold and ice-holes freeze over.

C) Some scientists once thought that narwhal tusks serve as a navigational rudder, allowing the narwhal to change the direction of their swimming by tilting their tusk.

D) Shakespeare used the image of a unicorn getting its horn stuck in a tree in Timon of Athens.

Questions 4 & 5

Medical Illustrators Show Hidden Worlds

Have you ever marvelled at the detailed drawings in a medical textbook like Gray's Anatomy, and wondered about the artists who
Line made them? For those who love science and art,
5 medical illustration offers the exciting possibility of a career in both. Every anatomy textbook, instructional animation, and educational model of the human body requires a medical artist's precision and knowledge. What's more, as 3D
10 modeling technologies improve, the demand for such artists will likely increase considerably.

What kind of education do medical artists have? As undergraduates, they may take an art or a science degree, but either way it's very important
15 that they develop their drawing skills and prepare what's called a "portfolio," or a representative sample of their artwork. The next step for many aspiring medical artists is a specialized Master's degree: a small number of schools in the United
20 States offer such a program, as well as one each in Canada and the UK. However, not all medical illustrators study in such a program.

In addition to studying in formal degree programs, it's common for medical illustrators
25 to receive certification from The Board of Certification of Medical Illustrators. This credential requires artists to take a written exam and submit their portfolios for review. **4**

Medical illustrators put their skills to work in
30 a number of venues. Large research centers like the Mayo Clinic employ them, as do medical publishing companies, hospitals, and animation studios. Some companies even specialize in medico-legal art, creating images to aid in the

presentation of evidence in the courtroom. There are also many opportunities for freelance work.

Technology has greatly expanded the ways that medical artists can depict bodies, anatomies, and procedures. Medical artists still use traditional artistic techniques, like sketching and inking diagrams by hand, **5** just as Henry Vandyke Carter used in the 19th century to illustrate Gray's Anatomy. Some artists even help develop video-game style training tools to teach surgeons complicated procedures. One such example is GIST Explorer, a free iPad app which educates surgeons about a rare condition through the medium of a game.

Medical illustrators are at the cutting edge of developments in digital technology and medicine. While the field remains small—there are just 2,000 such artists working in North America today—the outlook for growth is promising. The next generation of medical innovators will depend on careful artists for their books, their animations, and even their apps.

4

At this point, the author wants to add a statement explaining the continuing obligations that certified medical illustrators have to their organization. Which choice best accomplishes this goal?

A) The Association holds annual meetings, which are open to members and non-members alike.

B) The group works to educate its members about intellectual property, so that artists know their rights as they relate to the ownership of their work.

C) Private sponsors can contribute to a fund that provides further education and training for artists.

D) Once certified, they must renew their certifications every five years by demonstrating their continuing professional development and growth.

5

Which choice best supports the statement made in the previous sentence?

A) NO CHANGE

B) to represent bodies and their parts in a wide range of states of health.

C) though the wood engravings that once dominated anatomical illustration have almost entirely fallen out of use.

D) but those techniques exist alongside 3D animations, computer simulations, and even 3D printing.

Questions 6 & 7

Salt-Rising Bread: A Delicious Mystery

A quick glance at one recipe for salt-rising bread reveals a glaring omission: there's no salt on the list of ingredients. Another recipe for multiple loaves requires only one teaspoon of salt. If there is little to no salt in it, why is it called "salt-rising bread"? No one knows for certain, though we do know that the bread was a staple on the American frontier during the 19th century, and the tradition has been kept alive in certain areas like western New York and Pennsylvania, little pockets of Michigan, and the southern and western portions of the Appalachians. [6]

The other missing ingredient in salt-rising bread is yeast, the usual leavener in bread recipes. Yeastless breads were common in the 1800s because, at that point, commercial yeast was not yet available, so home bakers had to create starters like sourdough and the mash typically used for what became salt-rising bread. [7] This doesn't explain the name, though. The main theory about that can be found in stories from the westward-traveling pioneer women who were known to keep their bread starters warm in the salt barrels of their family wagons. An alternative version is that housewives of the era kept their starter warm by placing it in a bed of heated rock salt. Regardless of the method, it's inspiring to think about how innovative these women were in their quest to provide food for their families.

6

At this point, the author is considering adding the following sentence:

It's also possible that the bread got its name from its high salt content.

Should the author make this addition here?

A) Yes, because it continues the list of theories of how salt-rising bread got its name.

B) Yes, because it develops the idea of pioneer women as innovative home cooks.

C) No, because it contradicts information earlier in the passage.

D) No, because the real reason for the name is revealed later in the passage.

7

At this point, the author wants to add further, specific detail about how salt-rising bread rises. Which choice best accomplishes this goal?

A) The bacteria in the mash is associated with food poisoning in other contexts, but is made harmless by baking.

B) Salt-rising bread does not rise because of salt or yeast.

C) In this mash, clostridium perfringens, a bacteria, produces gas, causing the dough to rise.

D) Conventional leavened breads rise due to yeast.

Question 8

Canal Grass: A Cautionary Tale

The Panama Canal is an engineering marvel. It stretches for 48 miles across the isthmus of Panama, including 21 miles through Gatun Lake,

one of the largest man-made lakes in the world.
The Canal was constructed over a thirty year
period spanning the end of the 19th century and
the dawn of the 20th. Today, the canal is a major
thoroughfare for maritime trade: more than 330
million tons of cargo pass through the canal
each year.

However, the canal has brought more than
trade to Panama: it has also been an entry point
for invasive species. Marine organisms cling to
the hulls of ships or swim in their ballast water,
rats come in with the cargo, and the people on
the ships 8 bring goods and merchandise from
around the world.

One particularly problematic species is
Saccharum Spontaneum, also known as wild
sugarcane. It is believed to have been imported to
Panama by Americans hoping to control erosion
along the banks of the canal in the 1920s, and it
has become so ubiquitous around the canal that it
is commonly known simply as "canal grass." Each
year, however, it spreads further beyond the banks
where it was first planted, taking over more and
more terrain once occupied by dense jungles.

Canal grass has a strange ally in its expansion:
fire. The grass easily ignites in the tropical nation's
long, hot dry-season. While the stalks of the grass
are destroyed, along with other vegetation, its root
structures survive the conflagration. That allows
the grass to rapidly regenerate and expand into
the surrounding space—cleared of competing
vegetation by the flames.

While canal grass prevents erosion as intended,
it does not retain moisture as effectively as the
forests that it replaces. As a result, the expansion
of canal grass has contributed to lower water
levels in Gatun Lake during the dry season.

Without adequate water in the lake, the Panama
Canal will not be able to operate. Thus, a species
imported to protect the canal has now become a
threat to its continued existence.

8

Which choice best supports the main point of the
paragraph?

A) NO CHANGE

B) often smuggle in undeclared goods.

C) bring along pets and exotic plants.

D) rarely appreciate the fragility of the local
ecosystem.

Question 9

Rising Temperatures, Spreading Fevers

Tropical diseases—malaria, dengue fever,
Chagas disease—are, in the American mind,
foreign threats. However, the insects that carry
these diseases used to be common in the United
States, and are still present. Cases of Chagas
disease are rare, and improvements in pest control
largely eliminated malaria and dengue from the
American landscape decades ago, but as global
temperatures rise, changing climate dynamics
enhance the threat posed by these diseases.

The range of the tropical insects that transmit
tropical diseases is expanding as the climate
grows warmer, and the populations are increasing
in some places where they already exist as year-
round conditions become more hospitable.
9 Malaria has been almost totally eradicated
in the United States since the 1950s, but small
outbreaks still occur, and the mosquitoes that

can transmit the disease remain common—so
the disease could re-emerge on a larger scale as
mosquito populations spread. Kissing bugs, which
transmit Chagas disease, already range across the
Southern states, and recent testing of kissing bugs
in Arizona and California showed that more than a
third had fed on human blood, and more than half
carried the parasite that causes Chagas disease.
While there are still only a few reported cases of
Chagas disease in the United States, cases may
rise as the insects spread northwards.

9

At this point, the author is considering adding the
following sentence:

This has consequences: there was an outbreak of
dengue in Florida in 2009, sickening 88 people
between 2009 and 2010.

Should the author make this addition here?

A) Yes, because it gives an example of the general
   trend described in the previous sentence.

B) Yes, because it provides a transition to the
   discussion of Chagas disease later in the
   paragraph.

C) No, because it interrupts the paragraph's
   discussion with irrelevant information.

D) No, because it repeats information that is
   already presented in the first paragraph.

Question 10

The Pop Music Mastermind

Max Martin is one of the most successful
songwriters of all time, but you've probably
never heard his name. Like Dr. Luke, Stargate,
RedOne, Greg Kurstin, and a few others, Martin
is a "superproducer"—one of the handful of
songwriters behind almost all of today's pop
hits. He has written more number one songs than
anyone in history except John Lennon and Paul
McCartney of the Beatles. 10 "Superproducers"
are often called in to help another songwriter
finish a particular piece.

10

Which choice best supports the main point of the
paragraph?

A) NO CHANGE

B) Another especially prolific songwriter is Diane
   Warren, who has written 32 top ten songs since
   1983.

C) When Taylor Swift or Katy Perry needs a song,
   these are the people who deliver—and no one
   delivers better than Max Martin.

D) Sometimes these "superproducers" collaborate
   with each other: Martin and Dr. Luke have
   made a number of successful songs working
   together.

Question 11

The Watery Adventures of Benjamin Franklin

Most often associated with his role as a
Founding Father of the United States, during
his lifetime Benjamin Franklin was involved in
a wide variety of pursuits. One surprising tidbit
about Franklin is that he was an avid swimmer
whose aquatic activities led to his induction into
the International Swimming Hall of Fame.

Like many people who grow up along the
coast, Franklin loved spending time near and
in the water. Though he was considered quite
an expert swimmer it seems Franklin was not

satisfied with his speed, which led to one of his first inventions: a set of swim fins or, as he called them, swimming paddles. Inspired by a painter's palette, the wooden paddles did make him go faster, but Franklin abandoned them after realizing that they made his wrists tired.

Franklin also combined his love of swimming and his well-known interest in kite flying. He wrote about having spent an afternoon being propelled across a pond while lying on his back and holding onto a kite string.

Known for his inquiring mind, Franklin actually studied "The Art of Swimming" by the French scientist Melchisedech Thevenot and applied what he'd learned from the book. He then added a few moves of his own, which he delighted in sharing with others. 11 He determined that the surface of water could be calmed by adding oil and that freezing water could eliminate its conductive properties.

Franklin taught a number of friends how to swim and was even offered the chance to open a swim school in London. Though he passed on the opportunity to become a professional swim coach, Franklin did advise others on water safety and was a proponent of universal swimming programs, believing that all children ought to know how to swim.

11

Which choice is most consistent with the main claim of the previous sentence?

A) NO CHANGE

B) This is only one of his physical feats, which also include cartooning and playing a number of musical instruments.

C) While living in England in the 1720s, he once took to the Thames River to demonstrate his swimming prowess for some companions, covering about 3 1/2 miles in the process.

D) In 1776, Franklin was dispatched to France as the Ambassador for the United States, a position he held until 1785.

Questions 12 & 13

Let's Go Fly A Kite

No one is certain when or where the first kite was flown but, given kite flying's modern reputation as a leisure activity, it is surprising to find that the first written record describing kites focused on the use of a kite in battle. It seems that in about 200 B.C. a Chinese general used a kite to measure the distance his troops would need to tunnel to get inside the walls of a city this general was attacking. By the 7th century,when Japanese monks began flying kites to ward off evil spirits, kites had been transformed from instruments of war to symbols of protection. 12

In the 18th and 19th century, kites were flown in the name of science. The story of Benjamin Franklin using a kite to prove the existence of electricity is among the most often-told tales, though few people have heard that kites were used to pull horseless carriages before combustion engines became the norm.

20   While flying a kite may seem simple, the truth is that the process is relatively complex. There are a number of factors that must be considered before sending a kite aloft. [13] Naturally, the wind conditions need to be taken into account

25   because a strong wind can batter a simple paper kite while but winds that are too gentle won't be able to lift a fanciful box kite. The best place to fly a kite is an open field with no power lines or trees and, remembering the lesson of Ben Franklin,

30   the best time to fly a kite is when there are no thunderstorms in the area.

12

At this point, the writer wants to add a statement about the historical spread of kites to Europe. Which choice best accomplishes this goal?

A) Kites didn't gain prominence in Europe until later, when 16th and 17th-century sailors brought them back from voyages in Asia.

B) The modern sport of kitesurfing has European roots; the first patent for a kitesurfing board was given to a Dutch inventor, and two French brothers further developed the idea.

C) Chinese immigrants brought kites to Guyana, in South America, in the 19th century.

D) Benjamin Franklin also used a kite to pull him when he went swimming.

13

The writer is considering deleting the underlined sentence. Should the sentence be kept or deleted?

A) Kept, because it explores one of the factors one should keep in mind when flying a kite.

B) Kept, because it sets up the mention of Ben Franklin later in the paragraph.

C) Deleted, because it interrupts the paragraph's advice about how to fly a kite with a list of kite varieties.

D) Deleted, because wind is only one of many factors to consider when flying a kite.

1. (A) is the correct answer. (A) is correct because this paragraph begins with the claim that some atolls "are large enough to support...towns." The second sentence gives one example, and this sentence gives more. (B) is incorrect because these are not examples of atolls: they are examples of nations that "possess populated atolls." (C) is incorrect because this paragraph is not about atolls in general: it is about atolls with human populations threatened by rising sea levels. (D) is incorrect because the danger these atolls are in does not change the fact that they are examples of nations with populated atolls.

2. (B) is the correct answer. The first sentence of this paragraph, beginning with "It was once thought that," shows that this paragraph will discuss ideas about narwhal tusks that are no longer believed. Verne's idea is a particularly dramatic example of an old, incorrect belief about narwhals. (A) is incorrect because there's no evidence in the passage that later research proved Verne's idea. (C) is incorrect because the main point of the essay isn't that narwhals sink ships. The final sentence of the first paragraph indicates that the essay will focus on recent discoveries related to narwhal tusks. (D) is incorrect because this paragraph suggests that contemporary scientists have increased our knowledge about narwhal tusks. We used to know less simply because these scientists had not done their research yet.

3. (B) is the correct answer. It supports the previous claim about narwhals using their tusks to detect changes in the weather by clarifying just how important the weather is to their migration patterns. (A) is incorrect because the origin of the word "narwhal" and the phrase "corpse whale" do not support the idea that narwhals need to reach the surface to breathe. (C) is incorrect because it presents a new theory rather than supporting the theory in the previous sentence. (D) is incorrect because a story about unicorns has nothing to do with the way narwhals breathe.

4. (D) is the correct answer. The stated goal is to show what "obligations" the "certified" artists have, and only (D) does this; the sentence describes what artists "must" do "once certified." Remember that an "obligation" is something you have to do. (A) isn't correct because there's no indication that the annual meetings are an obligation. (B) doesn't describe an obligation either; instead, it discusses something that the group does for its members. (C) describes something that sponsors "can" do, if they choose, rather than something the certified artists have to do.

5. (D) is the correct answer. The previous sentence says that technology has added ways that medical illustrators can do their work. The first half of this sentence lists some tradition methods; this underlined portion adds some new, technologically based methods. (A) is incorrect (B) is incorrect because the previous sentence is not about the range of bodies that illustrators can represent. (C) is incorrect because it only discusses another historical technique; it fails to mention any new, technologically based techniques.

6. (C) is the correct answer. The first paragraph states that there is "little to no salt" in salt-rising bread; therefore, salt-rising bread does not have a "high salt content." (A) is incorrect because this paragraph lists theories about how salt-rising bread got its name, given that it contains so little salt; since this theory claims that the bread contains a lot of salt, it does not fit into this list. (B) is incorrect because the salt content of this bread does not affect whether or not pioneer women were innovative cooks. (D) is incorrect because the passage does not present a "real reason" later on.

7. (C) is the correct answer. It offers the most specific explanation for why salt-rising dough rises. (A) also mentions bacteria in the mash, but doesn't link it to the bread's rising. (B) merely states what doesn't cause the bread to rise, and repeats information stated earlier. (D) only discusses other breads, not salt-rising bread.

8. (C) is the correct answer. The main point of the paragraph is that "the canal...has been an entry point for invasive species." Invasive species are foreign plants and animals, and "pets and exotic plants" are examples of both. (A) is incorrect because objects like "goods and merchandise" are not alive and therefore not "invasive species." (B) is incorrect because smuggled goods are not necessarily living "invasive species." (D) is incorrect because people's feelings or attitudes do not have a direct effect on the ecosystem: what matters is their actions, especially if they bring in foreign plants or animals.

9. (A) is the correct answer. The previous sentence makes the general claim that tropical diseases are spreading as the climate warms; the reappearances of dengue in the United States is an example of this trend. (B) is incorrect because this sentence only mentions dengue, not Chagas disease. (C) is incorrect because this information is relevant: it is a specific example of the spread of tropical diseases, which is the topic of this paragraph. (D) is incorrect because the first paragraph only mentions dengue in general terms; it does not give specific dates or numbers.

10. (C) is the correct answer. The main point of this paragraph is that Max Martin is one of the most successful producers in music; claiming that famous pop stars approach him for songs supports this idea. (A) is incorrect because this paragraph does not claim elsewhere that "superproducers" help other songwriters finish songs, so this sentence does not support anything else. (B) is incorrect because mentioning another successful songwriter does not support this paragraph's claims about Max Martin. (D) is incorrect because the main idea of this paragraph is not that "superproducers" sometimes work together; it is just that Max Martin is a very successful producer.

11. (C) is the correct answer. The previous sentence says that Franklin "delighted in sharing with others" his own "moves" as a swimmer. This sentence gives an example of Franklin showing other people how well he could swim. (A) is incorrect because, even though it relates to Franklin and water, it does not show him demonstrating his swimming abilities. (B) is incorrect because the previous sentence is about Franklin's abilities as a swimmer, not his physical abilities in general. (D) is incorrect because it is off-topic: even though a French scientist is mentioned earlier in the paragraph, Franklin's appointment as an ambassador to France is not related to his swimming.

12. (A) is the correct answer. The goal is to describe the "historical spread of kites to Europe," and this choice aptly shows how that happened in the 16th and 17th centuries. (B) is wrong because it describes the origins of a modern sport, not the "historical spread" of kites. (C) is wrong because it discusses kites in South America, not Europe. (D) is incorrect because it relates to the American figure Benjamin Franklin's swimming kite.

13. (A) is the correct answer. This paragraph is about "a number of factors that must be considered" when flying a kite, and this sentence discusses one of those factors: wind conditions. (B) is incorrect because this sentence doesn't mention Franklin or thunderstorms, so it doesn't set up the last sentence. (C) is incorrect because this sentence only mentions kite types as part of its discussion of wind conditions, which are "factors that must be considered" when flying a kite. (D) is incorrect even though the "because" part of this choice is true: this sentence is about only one factor, but it doesn't need to be about more than one.

Relevant Information
Part 3

Relevant Information questions ask you to evaluate information for its relevance and remove information that diminishes the focus of the passage or a part of the passage. You may need to recognize when information is irrelevant to any central idea in the passage and should be removed. You may also need to resist the option of leaving information in when it does support a key idea in the passage but still reduces its focus because the information is misplaced or redundant.

DIRECTIONS

Every passage comes with a set of questions. Some questions will ask you to consider how the writer might revise the passage to improve the expression of ideas. Other questions will ask you to consider correcting potential errors in sentence structure, usage, or punctuation. There may be one or more graphics that you will need to consult as you revise and edit the passage.

Some questions will refer to a portion of the passage that has been underlined. Other questions will refer to a particular location in a passage or ask that you consider the passage in full.

After you read the passage, select the answers to questions that most effectively improve the passage's writing quality or that adjust the passage to follow the conventions of standard written English. Many questions give you the option to select "NO CHANGE." Select that option in cases where you think the relevant part of the passage should remain as it currently is.

Questions 1 & 2

My Favorite Career

[1] Early in my career I was the arts and entertainment editor for a regional weekly newspaper. [2] For a person who loved talking to artists, musicians, actors, and writers, this job surpassed my most fervent hopes and wildest dreams of what a job could be. [3] Others might dream of being a pilot, a truck driver, or a herpetologist. [4] There were myriad perks that came with the gig, from free tickets for virtually any concert or play I wanted to see to getting advance copies of soon-to-be best sellers. [5] I got to interview major movie stars, famous musicians, and writers. [6] I was the envy of all my friends and a fair number of people who decided they would like to be friends once they found out about the free tickets. [7] To be honest, looking back, I even envy my younger self! ▢

There was just one problem with the job: it was exhausting. Even when I'd been out until the wee hours enjoying the after-show parties with my celebrity buddies-for-the-day I was expected to be in the office by 10 a.m. at the very latest. After all, someone had to open the press releases and other items that arrived by the boxful every day. ▢2

Someone had to answer the phone and conduct the interviews. Someone had to write the articles and compile the lists of coming attractions. Someone had to proofread those articles when it was time to publish that week's issue. That someone was me.

1

The writer is considering deleting one of the sentences in this paragraph in order improve its focus. Which sentence should be deleted in order to accomplish this goal?

A) Sentence 2

B) Sentence 3

C) Sentence 4

D) Sentence 6

2

Which choice best completes the description of the writer's morning responsibilities ?

A) There were review copies of newly published books, and letters to the editor, and all of it had to be opened and sorted.

B) The paper also covered regional sports and news events.

C) Weekly papers often offer a platform for more in-depth journalism and longer features than dailies.

D) The night before a paper goes to press is always a busy one.

Question 3

How Atolls are Formed

An atoll is a special type of coral reef, distinguished by its striking, ring-like shape. It forms in a complicated way. Have you ever heard of islands being formed by volcanic eruptions? Atolls are also partly formed by volcanoes, but where volcanic islands are high and mountainous, atolls are low. How, exactly, do atolls come to be?

The English scientist Charles Darwin, who travelled in the South Pacific from 1831-1836, developed a theory about atoll formation that is still generally accepted. Darwin suggested that an atoll takes the place of a mountainous volcanic island. When the volcano becomes extinct, it slowly sinks back into the sea. At the same time, coral starts to surround the island in a circular reef. In time, the volcanic island disappears, leaving a ring of coral in its place. This is a long process, taking up to 30 million years.

Because atolls are made of coral, they can only form in tropical and subtropical waters. The majority are in the Pacific Ocean, with a significant number in the Indian Ocean, too. The only Atlantic atolls are a group of eight in the Caribbean, off the coast of Nicaragua.

In some cases, atolls are large enough to support islands, vegetation, and even towns. For example, Malé, the capital of the Indian Ocean nation of the Maldives, is an atoll city with over 153,000 inhabitants. A number of other island nations, including Kiribati, Tahiti, and Micronesia, also possess populated atolls. Because these atolls, along with other coral islands, are so low, many are in imminent danger from rising sea levels caused by climate change. 3

The process of atoll formation shows how coral and volcanoes, working in concert over millions of years, can create beautiful circular forms in the middle of the sea—forms which in some cases sustain thousands of people.

At this point, the writer is thinking of adding the following sentence:

> This is just one of many imminent consequences of climate change, which also include heat waves that are particularly dangerous for elderly people.

Should the writer make this addition here?

A) Yes, because the paragraph in question is primarily about the elderly.

B) Yes, because it provides important context for the observation about rising sea levels.

C) No, because the focus of the paragraph is on atolls, not the effects of climate change in general.

D) No, because the author does not say whether there are any elderly people in Kirbati.

Question 4

Let's Go Fly A Kite

April is National Kite Month. Over the course of 30 days, countless kite flying events are held all over the U.S. to celebrate this momentous occasion. The skies fill with all manner of kites, from the classic simple diamond shape to complex box kites and dramatic dragon kites that feature long tails and spectacular designs.

No one is certain when or where the first kite was flown but, given kite flying's modern reputation as a leisure activity, it is surprising to find that the first written record describing kites focused on the use of a kite in battle. It seems that in about 200 B.C. a Chinese general used a kite to measure the distance his troops would need to tunnel to get inside the walls of a city this general

was attacking. By the 7th century, when Japanese monks began flying kites to ward off evil spirits, kites had been transformed from instruments of war to symbols of protection.

In the 18th and 19th century, kites were flown in the name of science. The story of Benjamin Franklin using a kite to prove the existence of electricity is among the most often-told tales, though few people have heard that kites were used to pull horseless carriages before combustion engines became the norm. **4**

While flying a kite may seem like an easy skill to attain, the truth is that the process is relatively complex. There are a number of factors that must be considered before sending a kite aloft. Naturally, the wind conditions need to be taken into account because a strong wind can batter a simple paper kite while but winds that are too gentle won't be able to lift a fanciful box kite. The best place to fly a kite is an open field with no power lines or trees and, remembering the lesson of Ben Franklin, the best time to fly a kite is when there are no thunderstorms in the area

At this point, the writer is considering adding the following sentence:

> Steam-powered cars also had a brief heyday in the years before the combustion engine achieved prominence.

Should the writer make this addition here?

A) Yes, because it contributes to the paragraph's focus on alternative car-propulsion methods.

B) Yes, because it relates to the essay's focus on the power of air and steam to move things.

C) No, because the essay's focus is on kite-powered cars, not steam-powered cars.

D) No, because the focus of the essay is on kites, not steam power.

Question 5

Canal Grass: A Cautionary Tale

The Panama Canal is an engineering marvel. It stretches for 48 miles across the Isthmus of Panama, including 21 miles through Gatun Lake, one of the largest man-made lakes in the world. The Canal was constructed over a thirty year period spanning the end of the 19th century and the dawn of the 20th. **5** At the time of its completion, the canal's lock system was the largest concrete structure in the world. Today, the canal is a major thoroughfare for maritime trade: more than 330 million tons of cargo pass through the canal each year.

However, the canal has brought more than trade to Panama: it has also been an entry point for invasive species, and serves as an example of how the introduction of exotic species can have unintended consequences. Marine organisms cling to the hulls of ships or swim in their ballast water, rats and ants come in with the goods, and pets and exotic plants are brought in as cargo. One particularly problematic species is Saccharum Spontaneum, also known as wild sugarcane, or canal grass.

This exotic species was imported by Americans hoping to control erosion along the banks of the canal in the 1970s, but since its importation it has spread far beyond the canal's banks. It has a strange ally in its expansion: fire. The grass easily ignites in the long, hot dry-season. While the visible grass is destroyed, its root structures survive the conflagration, allowing the grass to regenerate and expand into the surrounding space—cleared of competing vegetation by the flames.

Though canal grass does prevent erosion, it does not retain moisture as effectively as the native vegetation it displaces. As a result, its expansion has contributed to lower water levels in Gatun Lake during the dry season. Without adequate water in the lake, the Panama Canal cannot operate. Thus, a species imported to protect the canal has now become a threat to its continued existence.

5

The writer is considering deleting the underlined sentence. Should the sentence be kept or deleted?

A) Deleted, because the focus of the paragraph is on canal grass, not the Panama Canal itself.

B) Deleted, because it repeats information provided earlier in the paragraph.

C) Kept, because it contributes to the description of the Panama Canal as an "engineering marvel."

D) Kept, because it is consistent with the focus of the passage, which is on the building of the canal.

Question 6

Salt-Rising Bread: A Delicious Mystery

Salt-Rising bread was a staple on the American frontier during the 19th century and the tradition has been kept alive in certain areas like Western
Line New York State and Pennsylvania, little pockets of
5 Michigan, and the southern and western portions of the Appalachians.

A quick glance at one recipe for salt-rising bread, however, reveals a glaring omission: there's no salt on the list of ingredients. Another recipe
10 for multiple loaves requires only one teaspoon of salt. If there is little to no salt in it, why is it called "salt-rising bread"?

Pioneer women stored the starters for their bread in salt, though there are competing theories
15 about why they did so. The most popular theory is that the salt was heated and used to keep the starter warm. **6** Regardless of the method, it's inspiring to think about how innovative these women were in their quest to provide food for
20 their families.

Since the starter for salt-rising bread requires consistent warmth for as long as 18 hours and the smell has been described as being similar to the aroma of dirty socks, it's a bit of a surprise
25 to realize that home cooks and even professional bakers continue to make it. But devotees love the fairly dense, moist bread that has a distinctive cheese-like flavor. Perhaps that is why there has been a resurgence in the popularity of this
30 delicious and mysterious bread.

6

At this point, the writer is considering adding the following sentence:

Another theory suggests that starters were stored in salt because salt inhibited wild yeast growth, encouraging the growth of bacteria that give the bread its distinctive flavor.

Should the writer make this addition here?

A) Yes, because it maintains the paragraph's focus on how salt is a primary ingredient in this bread.

B) Yes, because an additional example contributes to the paragraph's focus on competing theories.

C) No, because it interrupts the paragraph with the addition of irrelevant information.

D) No, because it does not offer an explanation for the name "salt-rising bread."

Question 7

The Pop Music Mastermind

Max Martin is one of the most successful songwriters of all time, but you've probably never heard his name. Like Dr. Luke, Stargate, RedOne, Greg Kurstin, and a few others, Martin is a "superproducer"— one of the handful of songwriters behind almost all of today's pop hits. Even in this elite group, Max stands out: he has written more number one songs than anyone in history except John Lennon and Paul McCartney of the Beatles.

[1] Born Karl Martin Sandberg in Stockholm, Sweden, he started his music career in the late 1980's as a heavy metal singer. [2] Heavy metal, or "metal" as its devotees often call it, began in the late 1960s with bands like Deep Purple and Black Sabbath. [3] In 1993, his band came to the attention of Denniz PoP, a DJ who had recently founded a songwriting and recording studio called Cheiron. [4] Impressed by Sandberg's gift for melody, Denniz brought him onto the Cheiron team, renaming him "Max Martin". 7

In 1997, Denniz paired Max with a new American boy band struggling to find an audience. That band was the Backstreet Boys, and on the strength of Martin's songs, their first album became one of the best-selling debuts of all time. Over the next few years, hits like Backstreet's "I Want It That Way" and Britney Spears' "...Baby One More Time" established Martin as the most successful composer in pop.

7

To make this paragraph most logical, sentence 2 should be

A) placed where it is now.

B) placed before sentence 1.

C) placed after sentence 3.

D) DELETED from the paragraph.

Question 8

Medical Illustrators Show Hidden Worlds

Have you ever marvelled at the detailed drawings in a medical textbook like Gray's Anatomy, and wondered about the artists who made them? For those who love science and art, medical illustration offers the exciting possibility of a career in both. Every anatomy textbook, instructional animation, and educational model of the human body requires a medical artist's precision and knowledge. What's more, as 3D modeling technologies improve, the demand for such artists will likely increase considerably.

What kind of education do medical artists have? As undergraduates, they may take an art or a science degree, but either way it's very important that they develop their drawing skills and prepare what's called a "portfolio," or a representative sample of their artwork. The next step for many aspiring medical artists is a specialized Master's degree: a small number of schools in the United States offer such a program, as well as one each in Canada and the UK. However, not all medical illustrators study in such a program.

Medical artists put their skills to work in a number of venues. Large research centers like the Mayo Clinic employ them, as do medical publishing companies, hospitals, and animation studios. Some companies even specialize in medico-legal art, creating images to aid in the presentation of evidence in the courtroom. 8 Some medical artists, however, may prefer the freedom and variety of freelance work, accepting jobs from a variety of customers.

Technology has greatly expanded the ways

that medical artists can depict bodies, anatomies, and procedures. Medical artists still use traditional artistic techniques, like sketching and inking diagrams by hand, but those techniques exist alongside 3D animations, computer simulations, and even 3D printing. Some artists even help develop video-game style training tools to teach surgeons complicated procedures. One such example is GIST Explorer, a free iPad app which educates surgeons about a rare condition through the medium of a game.

Medical illustrators are at the cutting edge of developments in digital technology and medicine. While the field remains small—there are just 2,000 such artists working in North America today—the outlook for growth is promising. The next generation of medical innovators will depend on careful artists for their books, their animations, and even their apps.

8

At this point, the writer is considering adding the following sentence:

Other artworks that can be used in court include crime scene sketches, sketches of suspects based on witness testimony, and visual aids like flow charts.

Should the writer make this addition here?

A) Yes, because it fits with the paragraph's focus on art used for medical and legal purposes.

B) Yes, because it suggests that artists may also have a professional role outside of medical settings.

C) No, because this information is not relevant to the types of work that medical artists perform.

D) No, because it fails to develop ideas about the training medical illustrators require.

Question 9

The Watery Adventures of Benjamin Franklin

Though we remember him mainly as a Founding Father of the United States, during his lifetime Benjamin Franklin was involved in a wide variety of pursuits. One surprising tidbit about Franklin is that he was an avid swimmer whose aquatic activities led to his induction into the International Swimming Hall of Fame. **9**

Franklin's birthplace was the Atlantic port city of Boston. Like many people who grow up along the coast, Franklin loved spending time near and in the water. Franklin studied "The Art of Swimming" by the French scientist Melchisedech Thevenot, and applied what he'd learned from the book. He then added a few moves of his own, which he delighted in sharing with others. While living in England in the 1720s, he once took to the Thames River to demonstrate his swimming prowess for some companions, covering about 3.5 miles in the process.

Franklin was actually offered the chance to open a swim school in London. He passed on the opportunity to become a professional swim coach, but Franklin taught a number of his friends how to swim, advised others on water safety, and was a proponent of universal swimming programs, believing that all children ought to know how to swim.

Though he was considered quite an expert swimmer, Franklin's most enduring contribution to the art of swimming, and the achievement which likely did the most to spur his induction into the Swimming Hall of Fame, was one of his first inventions. At only 11 years of age, Franklin created a set of "swimming paddles." They were

wooden paddles, designed to sit in one's palm,
each with a small hole so that they could be held
with one's thumb. The wooden paddles did make
him go faster, but Franklin abandoned them after
realizing that they made his wrists tired. He also
40 experimented with paddles attached to his feet, but
abandoned those as well after observing that the
rigid foot paddles interfered with his stroke. While
Franklin abandoned his own efforts at engineering
effective swim paddles, later inventors would
45 pick up the thread and devise the modern fins and
hand paddles that divers, bodyboarders, and other
swimmers use today.

9

At this point, the author is considering adding the
following sentence:

> Franklin was also famous for his experiments
> with electricity.

Should the author make this addition here?

A) Yes, because it provides an effective transition
from Paragraph 1 to Paragraph 2.

B) Yes, because it supports the central idea of the
first paragraph.

C) No, because it contradicts information
elsewhere in the passage.

D) No, because it diminishes the focus of the
passage.

Question 10

Narwhal Tusks

At the end of the 16th century, the English
Queen Elizabeth I received a curious present.
Sailors brought her a jeweled "unicorn horn"
Line valued at 10,000 pounds sterling—roughly the
5 price of a castle! The sailors said it came from a
"sea-unicorn," but its true source was probably
a narwhal, a type of small Arctic whale. Male
narwhals—and about 15 percent of females—
have long, spiralling tusks that really do look like
10 unicorn horns. Scientists have only just begun to
understand how special narwhal tusks are.

It was once thought that narwhals used their
tusks to fight each other or poke holes in the ice.
The author Jules Verne even suggested that their
15 tusks could sink ships! However, while narwhals
do rub their tusks together, they don't seem to be
fighting. Nor has anyone ever observed a narwhal
breaking the ice with its tusk. In fact, scientists
now know that the tusks are not horns, but teeth.

20 [1] A narwhal tooth is quite different from
ours. [2] Our teeth are also very different from
rodent teeth, which continue to grow throughout
a rodent's life. [3] The outer surface has millions
of tiny channels which lead all the way to nerves
25 in the center of the tooth, and these nerves lead
straight to the whale's brain. [4] This makes the
tooth highly sensitive. [5] Dr. Martin Nweeia,
from the Harvard School of Dental Medicine,
suggests that the tusk can taste, sense pressure,
30 and distinguish temperatures in the surrounding
seawater. **10**

10

The writer is considering deleting one of the sentences in this paragraph in order to improve its focus. Which sentence should be deleted in order to accomplish this goal?

A) Sentence 1.

B) Sentence 2.

C) Sentence 4.

D) Sentence 5.

Question 11

Rising Temperatures, Spreading Fevers

Tropical diseases—malaria, dengue fever, Chagas disease—are, in the American mind, foreign threats. They're the sorts of things that we only worry about when we travel. ▢11 However, the insects that carry these diseases used to be common in the United States, and are still present. Cases of Chagas disease are rare, and improvements in pest control largely eliminated malaria and dengue from the American landscape decades ago, but as global temperatures rise, changing climate dynamics enhance the threat posed by these diseases.

The range of the tropical insects that transmit tropical diseases is expanding as the climate grows warmer, and the populations are increasing in some places where they already exist as year-round conditions become more hospitable. This has consequences: there was an outbreak of dengue in Florida in 2009, sickening 88 people between 2009 and 2010. Malaria has been almost totally eradicated in the United States since the 1950s, but small outbreaks still occur, and the mosquitoes that can transmit the disease remain common—so the disease could re-emerge on

a larger scale as mosquito populations spread. Kissing bugs, which transmit Chagas disease, already range across the Southern states, and recent testing of kissing bugs in Arizona and California showed that more than a third had fed on human blood, and more than half carried the parasite that causes Chagas disease. While there are still only a few reported cases of Chagas disease in the United States, cases may rise as the insects spread northwards.

These threats require action: preparing for a warmer world means preparing for the resurgence of tropical diseases and its arrival in new places. The CDC is already tracking the threat; we should also be aggressively expanding pest-control efforts, and launching campaigns to raise awareness about the dangers of mosquitos and other disease-carrying insects in places where people are not accustomed to dealing with them.

11

At this point, the author is considering adding the following sentence:

Carlos Chagas described the disease that bears his name in 1909.

Should the author make this addition here?

A) Yes, because it provides additional information about Chagas disease, which is a key idea in this paragraph.

B) Yes, because it relates to the passage's focus on important medical discoveries.

C) No, because the focus of the passage is on malaria, rather than Chagas disease.

D) No, because it distracts from the paragraph's focus on the return of tropical diseases to the United States.

1. (B) is the correct answer. Sentence 3 comes after a remark about how the job "surpassed" the author's "most fervent hopes" and "wildest dreams" and before an explanation of the "perks" of the job. It therefore disrupts the author's explanation with a statement about the dreams of other people. (A) is incorrect because it introduces the idea that the author loved this job, which the paragraph develops in the following sentences. (C) is incorrect because it begins the explanation of why the author loved this job. (D) is incorrect because the phrase "I even envy my younger self" in Sentence 7 is a reference to "I was the envy of all my friends" in Sentence 6.

2. (A) is the correct answer. The other choices aren't immediately related to the goal of elaborating on what items the paper received in the morning. (B) relates to other kinds of journalism done at the paper, and (C) discusses weekly papers more generally. (D) is also not related to the items the paper received in the morning.

3. (C) is the correct answer. Although the passage mentions the danger that rising sea levels pose to inhabited atolls, the focus of the paragraph is on atolls, not climate change. Mentioning other consequences of climate change is not relevant to that focus. (A) is incorrect because the passage does not otherwise mention the elderly at all. (B) is incorrect because, as the passage explains, sea levels have an effect on atolls regardless of any other impacts of climate change, so these other details do not add important or necessary context. (D) is incorrect because, whether or not there are any elderly people in Kirbati, the passage is about sea levels, not other effects of climate change.

4. (D) is the correct answer. The passage only mentions kite-powered cars as part of its general discussion of kites. Mentioning steam-powered cars only distracts from the focus on kites. (A) is incorrect because the paragraph is focused on the uses of kites in the 18th and 19th centuries, not alternative car-propulsion methods in general. (B) is incorrect because the essay is focused specifically on kites, not more broadly on air and steam power. (C) is incorrect because the essay is focused on kites in general, not kite-powered cars specifically.

5. (C) is the correct answer. The paragraph focuses on the extraordinary engineering of the Panama Canal, and the detail about the locks provides a specific example of the canal's exceptional engineering. (A) is incorrect because this paragraph focuses on the construction of the canal. Canal grass isn't introduced until the following paragraph. (B) is incorrect because, while we have already learned that Gatun lake is one of the largest artificial lakes, the information about the size of the lock system is new. (D) is incorrect because the passage as a whole is focused on canal grass; only the first paragraph is about the building of the canal.

6. (B) is the correct answer. The addition balances the information in a way that improves focus on the central idea. It might seem strange that adding an example of a competing idea can improve a paragraph's focus, but this paragraph begins with the claim that there are competing theories. Providing an example of only one theory makes the paragraph lopsided: it focuses too much on the detail of one theory at the expense of the central idea of competing theories. Adding another example improves the focus on the central idea of competing theories by balancing the supporting examples. (A) is incorrect because the passage makes clear that salt is not necessarily an ingredient in the bread. It may merely have gotten its name from the warm salt it rested on as part of the rising process. (C) is incorrect because an additional example of the "competing theories" already described in the first sentence is a relevant addition to the paragraph. (D) is incorrect because this example gives a possible reason for the name.

7. (D) is the correct answer. This paragraph focuses on the early days of Martin's career, and a remark about the origins of heavy metal distracts from that focus. (A), (B), and (C) are all incorrect because this sentence will be off-topic no matter where it is placed in the paragraph.

8. (C) is the correct answer. This paragraph only mentions courtroom evidence as one example of the ways medical illustrators can use their skills. Listing other kinds of courtroom evidence distracts from the focus on medical illustration. (A) is incorrect because the paragraph is not focused on medical and legal art in general; it is focused on opportunities for medical illustrators to use their skills. (B) is incorrect because the passage and the paragraph are about medical illustrators, not artists in general. (D) is incorrect because this paragraph is not about the training of medical illustrators; that is discussed in the previous paragraph.

9. (D) is the correct answer. The passage is focused on Franklin's swimming, not his experiments with electricity or any of his other interests. (A) is incorrect because this sentence does not introduce the topic of the next paragraph: Paragraph 2 is still about swimming, not Franklin's work on electricity. (B) is incorrect because the central idea of the first paragraph is that Franklin was "an avid swimmer"; his work on electricity is not related to this. (C) is incorrect because this sentence does not contradict information anywhere else in the passage, which does not bring up Franklin's electrical experiments at all.

10. (B) is the correct answer. The paragraph only mentions human teeth as part of its discussion of how unusual narwhal teeth are. It would be off-topic to talk further about human teeth, let alone rodent teeth. (A) is incorrect because it sets up the discussion of how unusual narwhal teeth are. Also, Sentence 2 depends on Sentence 1, so Sentence 1 can't be cut: the phrase "Our teeth are also very different from rodent teeth" refers back to "These teeth are quite different from ours." (C) is incorrect because Sentence 4 is not off-topic: it explains one of the unusual features of narwhal teeth. (D) is incorrect because it continues to explain how unusually sensitive narwhal teeth are.

11. (D) is the correct answer. This paragraph introduces the idea that tropical diseases are returning to the United States. Chagas disease is just one of these diseases, and explaining how it got its name is not relevant to the main idea of the paragraph. (A) is incorrect because Chagas disease is not mentioned until later in the paragraph; the key idea in these first few sentences is that tropical diseases can be contracted in the United States. (B) is incorrect because the paragraph is focused on the spread of tropical diseases, not on medical discoveries. (C) is incorrect because the passage is focused on tropical diseases in general; malaria and Chagas disease are both just examples of this category.

Graphic Analysis
Part 4

Graphic Analysis questions ask about information presented in charts and graphs. They may require you to revise information in the passage so that it is consistent with graphical information, add information to a passage based on a graph, or add or revise sentences that require you to synthesize information from a graph and a passage. Rarely, you may be required to choose between graphs and select the graph that is most consistent with information presented in the passage.

DIRECTIONS

Every passage comes with a set of questions. Some questions will ask you to consider how the writer might revise the passage to improve the expression of ideas. Other questions will ask you to consider correcting potential errors in sentence structure, usage, or punctuation. There may be one or more graphics that you will need to consult as you revise and edit the passage.

Some questions will refer to a portion of the passage that has been underlined. Other questions will refer to a particular location in a passage or ask that you consider the passage in full.

After you read the passage, select the answers to questions that most effectively improve the passage's writing quality or that adjust the passage to follow the conventions of standard written English. Many questions give you the option to select "NO CHANGE." Select that option in cases where you think the relevant part of the passage should remain as it currently is.

Question 1

Adapted from 2015 Cornelius, Mary L., and Erin M. Gallatin, "Task allocation in the tunneling behavior of workers of the Formosan subterranean termite, Coptotermes formosanus Shiraki"

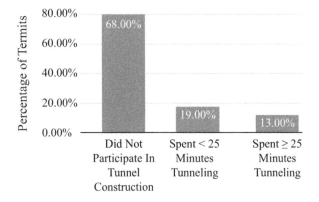

Average Time Spent on Tunnel Construction Over Two Days

The entomologist Mary L. Cornelius conducted an experiment to observe the tunneling behaviour of the formosan subterranean
Line termite—a species whose digging is particularly
5 harmful to wood-framed buildings. She observed the termites over two days, and calculated the average time the termites spent tunneling. Despite the considerable damage these insects deal, their digging habits are a little counterintuitive. 1
10 The majority of termites participated in tunneling, but did not do so for more than 25 minutes.

1

Which choice offers an accurate interpretation of the data in the graphs?

A) NO CHANGE

B) Less than 25% of the termites tunneled on both of the two days observed.

C) The majority of the termites who tunneled did so for less than 25 minutes.

D) Less than 30% of termites spent any time tunneling.

Graph A

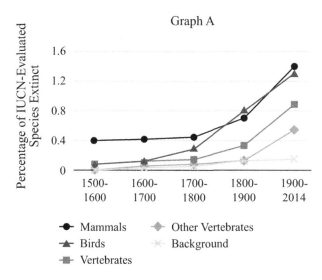

Question 2

Adapted from Ceballos et. al. "Accelerated modern human–induced species losses: Entering the sixth mass extinction"

A recent study of the rate of animal extinctions over the last five hundred years has confirmed that we are currently experiencing a mass

Line extinction event. The study compared the modern

5 rate of species extinctions to what's called the "background rate," or the number of species that would go extinct under ordinary circumstances. The team plotted species losses according to both conservative (Graph A) and less conservative

10 estimates (Graph B). In either case, the news is not good. **2** The projection in Graph A posits a rate of extinction substantially higher than the background rate, but the projection in Graph B does not.

2

Which choice offers an accurate interpretation of the data in the graphs?

A) NO CHANGE

B) Only the extinction rate for mammals is below the background rate in both graphs.

C) Graph B posits a less drastic rate of extinction for birds than Graph A.

D) Graph B posits a greater number of extinctions than A, but both are well above the background rate.

Graph B

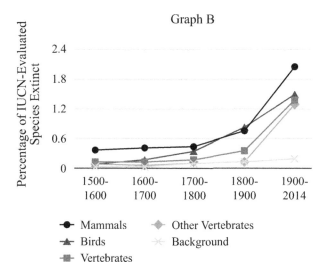

Question 3

US Chickpea Exports by Volume

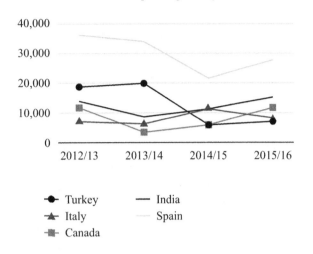

3

Which choice offers an accurate interpretation of the data in the graph?

A) Turkey received more chickpeas in 2014-2015 than Canada and Italy combined.

B) The amount of chickpeas exported to Spain was higher than that of any other country, even at its lowest point.

C) India received twice as many US chickpeas as Italy did in the 2014-15 year.

D) Canada never received an amount higher than 10,000 in a year.

Question 4

Figure 2: Yearly number (number of bars in each year) and duration (y-axis) of identified heat-wave events in Spain in the period of 2005–2014 (source: State Meteorology Agency (AEMET), [25]).

© 2016 M. A. Hernández-Ceballos et al.

A heat wave is a period of abnormally hot weather. As global temperatures increase, it's likely that countries around the world will
Line experience more heat waves. Climate scientists
5 in Spain measured the number of heat waves that occurred in the country each year from 2005-2014, and they also measured how long each heat wave lasted. Based on their data, they concluded that there were more heat waves in 2012 than
10 2013, **4** but the heat wave in 2013 lasted longer than any of the heat waves in 2012.

Yearly Number of Duration of Heat Waves

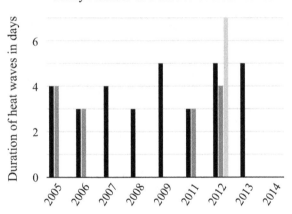

Number of bars indicates number of heat waves during year.

4

Which choice offers an accurate interpretation of the data in the graph?

A) NO CHANGE

B) in every year with multiple heat waves, each heat wave was the same duration.

C) of the years measured, there was only one heat-wave-free year.

D) years with only one heat wave always experienced more cumulative days of heat wave than years with multiple heat waves.

Question 5

Adapted from "Nematode diversity, abundance and community structure 50 years after the formation of the volcanic island of Surtsey"   [paper name?]

© 2014 K. Ilieva-Makulec, B. Bjarnadottir, and B. D. Sigurdsson

Surtsey, a volcanic island off the coast of Iceland, is one of the youngest places on earth. It formed from an eruption in 1963, and has served as a fascinating test-case for the ways in which uninhabited islands become populated by plant, animal, and microbial life. Scientists carefully monitor the island to make sure that no species are introduced with human assistance. When some boys tried to plant potatoes, the potatoes were swiftly removed; the same thing happened when an "improperly handled defecation" caused a tomato to grow. These practices allow the scientists to observe Surtsey's ecosystem under ideal conditions. One of the lifeforms they study are nematodes, a group of roundworm species with diverse eating habits. Some are omnivorous, some are carnivorous, some are plant feeders, and others are hyphal feeders who eat fungus. In a 2014 study of Surtsey's various soil biomes, scientists found that [5] omnivores were as common in the topsoil within the seagull colony as they were in the subsoil outside the seagull colony.

Line
5

10

15

20

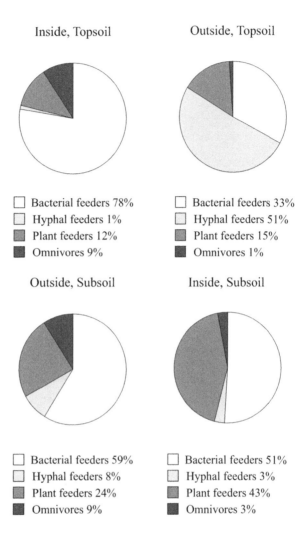

Inside, Topsoil

☐ Bacterial feeders 78%
☐ Hyphal feeders 1%
▨ Plant feeders 12%
■ Omnivores 9%

Outside, Topsoil

☐ Bacterial feeders 33%
☐ Hyphal feeders 51%
▨ Plant feeders 15%
■ Omnivores 1%

Outside, Subsoil

☐ Bacterial feeders 59%
☐ Hyphal feeders 8%
▨ Plant feeders 24%
■ Omnivores 9%

Inside, Subsoil

☐ Bacterial feeders 51%
☐ Hyphal feeders 3%
▨ Plant feeders 43%
■ Omnivores 3%

5

Which choice offers an accurate interpretation of the data in the graph?

A) NO CHANGE

B) plant feeders were as common in topsoil within the seagull colony as they were in subsoil outside of the seagull colony.

C) bacterial feeders were the most common type of nematode in every study plot except for the subsoil plot inside the seagull colony.

D) the percentage of hyphal feeders in the subsoil of the seagull colony was twice as high as the percentage of hyphal feeders in the subsoil outside of the colony.

Question 6

Percentage of Salmonella Infections by Month

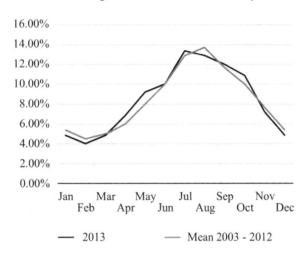

Adapted From CDC National Enteric Disease Surveillance: Salmonella Annual Report, 2013.

The Center for Disease Control monitors the rate of salmonella infections in the United States. More cases of salmonella are reported in some months than in others, with the greatest percentage of cases reported in the summer months and the smallest percentage of cases reported in the winter months. The pattern is quite consistent. If we compare the average percentage of infections per month from the years 2003-2012 to the rate of infections in one year, 2013, we can see that that 6 August saw the greatest percentage of Salmonella infections in both 2013 and as a mean percentage from 2003-2012.

6

What choice offers an accurate interpretation of the data in the graph?

A) NO CHANGE

B) there were no months in 2013 when the percentage of cases reported was even two percentage points different than the average rate for 2003-2012.

C) February saw a smaller number of infections in 2013 than on average for 2003-2012.

D) the number of cases reported each month in 2013 was very close to the average number of cases reported in the same month from 2003-2012.

US Greenhouse Gas Emissions from the Transportation Sector, 1990 - 2014

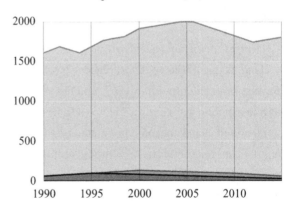

- Fossil fuel combustion
- Use of fluorinated gases
- Fossil fuel combustion and other transportion

Question 7

US Greenhouse Gas Emissions from the
Agricultureal Sector, 1990 - 2014

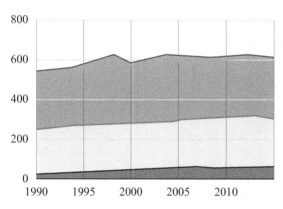

Livestock
Crop Cultivation
Fuel Combustion

Adapted from EPA Inventory of U.S. Greenhouse Gas
Emissions and Sinks

    The United States Environmental Protection
Agency measures the emission of greenhouse
gases from the various sectors of American

Line agriculture and industry. While methane emissions

5 from cattle farming are certainly a cause for
concern, the EPA's records show that in 2006,
7 the transportation sector's carbon dioxide
emissions were approximately three times greater
than the agriculture sector's livestock emissions in

10 the same year.

Which choice offers an accurate interpretation of
the data in the graphs?

A) NO CHANGE

B) the agriculture sector's significant spikes in
livestock and crop cultivation emissions in
1998 and 2004 are identical to the patterns of
fluorinated gas emissions in the transportation
sector.

C) the agriculture sector's total emissions in
2014 were more than half the amount of the
transportation sector's total emissions in the
same year.

D) the agriculture sector's total emissions in
2014 were less than half the amount of the
transportation sector's total emissions in the
same year.

Number of Cattle Marketed on 1,000+ Capacity
Feedlots - United States (Million head)

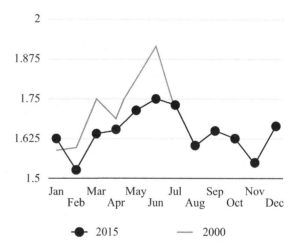

2015   —— 2000

Question 8

Number of Cattle Placed on 1,000+ Capacity
Feedlots – United States (Million head)

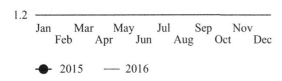

Source: USDA Cattle on Feed Report, August 2016

In July 2016, the United States Department of Agriculture measured the number of cattle placed and marketed on feedlots in both 2015 and 2016

Line up to the month of their study. They concluded
5 that in 2015, [8] the month which saw the greatest number of cattle placed on feedlots also saw the greatest number of cattle marketed.

8

Which choice offers an accurate interpretation of the data in the graphs?

A) NO CHANGE

B) the number of cattle placed on feedlots in October 2015 exceeds the number of cattle marketed in June 2016.

C) relative to March and May, April saw an increase in cattle placed on feedlots in both 2015 and 2016.

D) from December 2015 to January 2016, there was an increase in cattle placed on feedlots.

Question 9

Composition of Riverbed, 2005

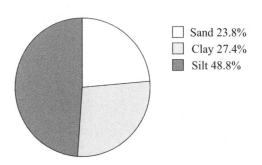

Composition of Riverbed, 2015

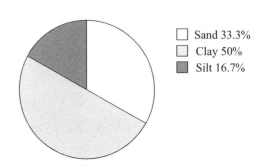

In 2005, workers began routinely dredging a river to increase and maintain its depth, so that commercial ships could easily pass through.

Line Scientists analyzed the composition of the
5 riverbed over a ten-year period of dredging, and compared the data at the start of their study to the data at the end. They concluded that [9] sand remained the dominant material on the riverbed at both the beginning and the end of their study.

9

Which of the following choices offer a correct interpretation of the charts?

A) NO CHANGE

B) silt maintained the most stable position as a percentage of the whole riverbed, neither losing or gaining any percentage points.

C) silt lost ground to clay, which became the most common material on the riverbed.

D) none of the materials on the riverbed gained or lost more than ten percentage points over ten years.

Multimedia Artists and Animators: Percent change in employment. projected 2014-24

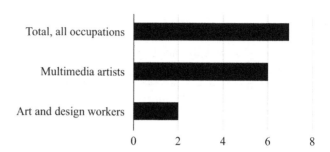

The Association of Medical Illustrators suggests that the job outlook is good for their profession, based on statistics from the U.S.
Line Bureau of Labor. Placing themselves in the
5 category of "multimedia artists," they point out that their field is projected to grow **10** nearly as much as that of art and design workers in general.

10

Which of the choices offers a correct interpretation of the material in the graph?

A) NO CHANGE

B) more than the total employment growth projected for all occupations.

C) by five percent in the next ten years.

D) nearly as much as the total employment growth projected for all occupations.

1. (C) is the correct answer. There are two columns for termites who actually tunneled, and the larger number (19%) tunnelled for under 25 minutes. (A) is wrong because the majority of the termites, 68%, did not tunnel at all. (B) is incorrect because the chart doesn't record which termites tunneled on each day; it merely presents an average over two days. (D) is incorrect because the two columns for active termites add up to 32%, which is over 30.

2. (D) is the correct answer. The lines in Graph B increase at a steeper incline, suggesting higher percentages of extinction, and all lines in both graphs are well above the background rate. (A) is incorrect because both graphs posit a rate higher than the background rate (indicated here by the dotted line). (B) is wrong because the mammal extinction rate is never below the background rate. (C) is wrong because the rate of extinctions in B is higher than that in A for all animal types.

3. (B) is the correct answer. The line indicating Spain's share of US chickpea exports, the simple medium grey, is always the highest on the graph; it's never exceeded. (A) is incorrect; Turkey's share of the exports actually decreased over the four years studied. Once you know this, you don't even need to confirm the other half of the statement. (C) is also incorrect. In 2014-15, India and Italy received nearly the same amount of American chickpeas. There are no white diamonds over 6000 ms. (D) is incorrect because Canada exceeded 10,000 in both 2012-13 and 2015-16.

4. (C) is the correct answer. 2014 is the only year of the nine represented which did not have a heat wave. (A) is incorrect because 2013's five-day heat wave was surpassed by the third, seven-day heat wave of 2012. (B) is incorrect because 2012's multiple heat waves were all of different durations. (D) is incorrect because the opposite is true: years with just one heat wave event never received more than 5 days of heat wave, and years with multiple events never received fewer than 6.

5. (A) Is the correct answer. Omnivores constituted 9% of nematodes in the topsoil in the seagull colony, and 9% of nematodes in the subsoil outside of the seagull colony. (B) is incorrect because plant feeders made up 12% of nematodes in the topsoil of the seagull colony, and 24% of nematodes in the subsoil outside of the seagull colony. (C) is incorrect because bacterial feeders were actually the most common nematode in every study plot except for the topsoil outside of the seagull colony. (D) is incorrect because hyphal feeders constituted only 3% of nematodes in the seagull colony subsoil, and 8% in the subsoil outside of the colony.

6. (B) is the correct answer. The biggest difference between any individual month in 2013 and any month's average rate occurs in May, with the 2013 rate at just above 9% and the average rate at just below 8%. Since this largest difference is less than 2 percentage points, there is never a time where the difference between 2013 and a 2003-2012 average is greater than 2 percentage points. (A) is incorrect because it claims that August was the month of greatest infections for both lines, which isn't true; it's only the greatest for the 2003-2012 mean. (C) and (D) can both be quickly ruled out because the graph actually doesn't measure the number of infections or reported cases at all; it simply charts the percentage of cases reported per month.

7. (D) is the correct answer. In 2014, the transportation sector emitted well over 1,500 million metric tons, while the agriculture sector emitted just over 600—in other words, less than half. (A) is incorrect because the agriculture sector's livestock emissions in 2006 were approximately 200 million metric tons, while the transportation sector's carbon dioxide emissions were just a bit under 2000—much more than three times the livestock amount. (B) is incorrect because the peaks in livestock and crop cultivation emissions simply don't match the pattern of fluorinated gas emissions emissions. (C) is wrong because the agriculture sector's approximately 600 million metric tons are not more than half of the transportation sector's approximately 1,500.

8. (B) is the correct answer. October 2015 saw over 2 million cattle placed on feedlots, and June 2016 saw less than 2 million marketed. (A) is wrong because the month in 2015 in which the most cattle were marketed was June, and the month in 2015 in which the most cattle were placed was October. (C) is incorrect because in both years April saw a decrease in cattle placed, relative to the neighbouring months. (D) is incorrect because January 2016's number of cattle placed on feedlots is higher than December 2015's.

9. (C) is the correct answer. Of the three materials, clay was the only one not to lose any percentage points. Instead, it gained points. (A) is incorrect because sand was never the most plentiful material on the riverbed. (B) is incorrect because silt actually saw a dramatic decrease in percentage points. (D) can be eliminated because both silt and clay changed by over ten points.

10. (D) is the correct answer. The growth rate for multimedia artists and animators is 6 percent, almost as much as that of the total growth rate for all occupations, which is 7 percent. (A) is incorrect because the employment rate for multimedia artists is actually projected to grow by four percent more than art and design workers. (B) is incorrect because the change in employment for multimedia artists is expected to be one percent less than the total growth for all occupations. (C) is not correct because the employment figures for multimedia artists actually grew by 6 percent.

Ivy Global

Section 2
Organization

Questions in the Development domain test your ability to improve the structure of ideas in the passage by changing the order of certain elements or by adding, deleting, or revising transitional words and statements. You'll need to pay attention to the logical and tonal relationships between sentences and paragraphs.

Organization questions contribute to the "Expression" subscore.

There are only 2 specific question types in this domain:

Organization			
OL	Logical Sentence Order	OT	Transitional Words and Sentences

Logical Sentence Order

Part 1

Logical Sentence Order questions ask you to reorganize elements of the passage. You may need to reorder sentences within a paragraph, but you may also need to reorganize paragraphs within a passage. Sometimes, you will need to decide where to add a new sentence. You will need to consider the logical sequence of events in a chronology, the development of information, the logical ordering of references to information and their referents, and the logical ordering of sentences by their function (for example, placing a sentence or paragraph that appears to be composed as an introduction early in the paragraph or passage).

DIRECTIONS

Every passage comes with a set of questions. Some questions will ask you to consider how the writer might revise the passage to improve the expression of ideas. Some questions will refer to a portion of the passage that has been underlined. Other questions will refer to a particular location in a passage or ask that you consider the passage in full.

After you read the passage, select the answers to questions that most effectively improve the passage's writing quality or that adjust the passage to follow the conventions of standard written English. Many questions give you the option to select "NO CHANGE." Select that option in cases where you think the relevant part of the passage should remain as it currently is.

Questions 1 & 2

Canal Grass: A Cautionary Tale

[1] The Panama Canal is an engineering marvel. [2] It stretches for 48 miles across the isthmus of panama, including 21 miles through Gatun Lake, one of the largest man-made lakes in the world. [3] Today, the canal is a major thoroughfare for maritime trade: more than 330 million tons of cargo pass through the canal each year. [1]

However, the canal has brought more than trade to Panama: it has also been an entry point for invasive species. Marine organisms cling to the hulls of ships or swim in their ballast water,

rats and ants come in with the goods, and pets and exotic plants are brought in as cargo. One particularly problematic species is Saccharum Spontaneum, also known as wild sugarcane, or—in Panama—"canal grass."

Though the canal grass prevents erosion as intended, it does not retain moisture as effectively as the forests that it replaces. As a result, the expansion of canal grass has contributed to lower water levels in Gatun Lake during the dry season. Without adequate water in the lake, the Panama Canal will not be able to operate. Thus, a species imported to protect the canal has now become a threat to its continued existence.

This exotic species was imported by Americans

hoping to control erosion along the banks of the canal in the 1970s, but since its importation it has spread far beyond the canal zone. It has a strange ally in its expansion: fire. The grass easily ignites in the long, hot dry-season. While the visible grass is destroyed, its root structures survive the conflagration, allowing the grass to regenerate and expand into the surrounding space—cleared of competing vegetation by the flames. 2

1

Upon reviewing this paragraph and realizing that some information has been left out, the writer composes the following sentence:

The Canal was constructed over a thirty year period spanning the end of the 19th century and the dawn of the 20th.

The most logical placement for this sentence would be:

A) before Sentence 1.

B) after Sentence 1.

C) after Sentence 2.

D) after Sentence 3.

2

For the sake of logic and cohesion, Paragraph 3 should be placed:

A) where it is now.

B) before Paragraph 1.

C) before Paragraph 2.

D) after Paragraph 4.

Medical Illustrators Show Hidden Worlds

[1] Every anatomy textbook, instructional animation, and educational model of the human body requires a medical artist's precision and knowledge. [2] Have you ever marvelled at the detailed drawings in a medical textbook like Gray's Anatomy and wondered about the artists who made them? [3] For those who love science and art, medical illustration offers the exciting possibility of a career in both. [4] What's more, as 3D modeling technologies improve, the demand for such artists will likely increase considerably. 3

What kind of education do medical artists have? As undergraduates, they may take an art or a science degree, but either way it's very important that they develop their drawing skills and prepare what's called a "portfolio," or a representative sample of their artwork. The next step for many aspiring medical artists is a specialized Master's degree: a small number of schools in the United States offer such a program, as well as one each in Canada and the UK. However, not all medical illustrators study in such a program.

Medical illustrators put their skills to work in a number of venues. Large research centers like the Mayo Clinic employ them, as do medical publishing companies, hospitals, and animation studios. Some companies even specialize in medico-legal art, creating images to aid in the presentation of evidence in the courtroom. There are also many opportunities for freelance work.

In addition to studying in formal degree programs, it's common for medical illustrators to receive certification from The Board of Certification of Medical Illustrators. This credential requires artists to take a written exam and submit their portfolios for review. Once certified, they must renew their certifications every five years by demonstrating their continuing professional development and growth.

40 [1] Technology has greatly expanded the ways that medical artists can depict bodies, anatomies, and procedures. [2] There's still a place for traditional medical illustration, but those techniques exist alongside 3D animations, computer
45 simulations, and even 3D printing. [3] Some artists even help develop video-game style training tools to teach surgeons complicated procedures. [4] One example is GIST Explorer, a free iPad app which educates surgeons about a rare condition through
50 the medium of a game. [5] The next generation of medical innovators will depend on careful artists for their books, their animations, and even their apps. 4

3

For the sake of the logic and coherence of this paragraph, Sentence 1 should be placed:

A) where it is now.

B) after Sentence 2.

C) after Sentence 3.

D) after Sentence 4.

4

For the sake of the logic and coherence of this paragraph, Sentence 4 should be placed:

A) where it is now.

B) before Sentence 1.

C) after Sentence 2.

D) after Sentence 5.

5

For the sake of logic and cohesion, Paragraph 4 should be placed:

A) where it is now.

B) after Paragraph 1.

C) after Paragraph 2.

D) after Paragraph 5.

Question 6

Rising Temperatures, Spreading Fevers

[1] The range of the tropical insects that transmit tropical diseases is expanding as the climate grows warmer, and the populations are increasing in some places where they already exist as year-round conditions become more hospitable. [2] This has consequences: there was an outbreak of dengue in Florida in 2009, sickening 88 people between 2009 and 2010. [3] Malaria has been almost totally eradicated in the United States since the 1950s, but small outbreaks still occur, and the mosquitoes that can transmit the disease remain common—so the disease could re-emerge on a larger scale as mosquito populations spread. [4] While there are still only a few reported cases of Chagas disease in the United States, cases may rise as the insects spread northwards. [5] Kissing bugs, which transmit Chagas disease, already range across the Southern states, and recent testing of kissing bugs in Arizona and California showed that more than a third had fed on human blood, and more than half carried the parasite that causes Chagas disease. 6

6

For the sake of the logic and coherence of this paragraph, Sentence 5 should be placed:

A) where it is now.

B) before Sentence 1.

C) after Sentence 3.

D) before Sentence 4.

Questions 7 & 8

Velvet Ants

[1] It's easy to understand why people might be confused: we usually think of wasps as flying insects, but velvet ants are wingless. [2] Velvet ants are extremely sexually dimorphic, meaning that the two sexes have very different forms. [3] At least, the females are. [4] It can be difficult even for experts to tell whether a male and female velvet ant are even of the same species. [5] The males have wings, are sometimes much larger than the females, and more closely resemble our traditional image of wasps--though they have no stingers. [6] The females, meanwhile, lack wings, but possess powerful stings. 7

The sting of the velvet ant is so notorious that they have another nickname: "cow killer." They name arises from the belief the sting is so painful that it could kill a cow. Just like the name "velvet ant," though, this moniker is more about how the insect is perceived than what it actually is. The cow killer's sting can't really kill a cow; in fact, the stings are not even particularly dangerous to humans. They are, however, quite painful.

Those who live or travel in places where velvet ants live should be wary of their painful sting, but only need to take simple precautions. The wasps are solitary animals, and they're not aggressive, so even those people who spend a lot of time outside will only encounter the wasps rarely. Even when people do encounter the wasps, the wasps generally will not sting. It's therefore not usually necessary to eradicate the wasps; it's enough to simply wear thick-soled shoes, and give the wasps a little space.

Hikers and gardeners in southern regions of the United States may already be familiar with

the "velvet ant," a ground insect with a tough
exoskeleton covered in thick tufts of fur-usually
red or orange-from which the "velvet" component
of its name is derived. The "ant" part is actually
40 just a misnomer, though: the velvet ant isn't an ant
at all. It's actually a wasp.

7

For the sake of the logic and coherence of this
paragraph, Sentence 3 should be placed:

A) where it is now.

B) before Sentence 2.

C) after Sentence 4.

D) before Sentence 6.

8

For the sake of logic and cohesion, Paragraph 4
should be placed:

A) where it is now.

B) before Paragraph 1.

C) after Paragraph 1.

D) after Paragraph 2.

Question 9

How Atolls are Formed

An atoll is a special type of coral reef,
distinguished by its striking, ring-like shape. It
forms in a complicated way. Have you ever heard
Line of islands being formed by volcanic eruptions?
5 Atolls are also partly formed by volcanoes, but
where volcanic islands are high and mountainous,
atolls are low. How, exactly, do atolls come to be?

Because atolls are made of coral, they can
only form in tropical and subtropical waters.
10 The majority are in the Pacific Ocean, with a
significant number in the Indian Ocean, too. The
only Atlantic atolls are a group of eight in the
Caribbean, off the coast of Nicaragua.

The English scientist Charles Darwin, who
15 travelled in the South Pacific from 1831-1836,
developed a theory about atoll formation that is
still generally accepted. Darwin suggested that an
atoll takes the place of a mountainous volcanic
island. When the volcano becomes extinct, it
20 slowly sinks back into the sea. At the same time,
coral starts to surround the island in a circular
reef. In time, the volcanic island disappears,
leaving a ring of coral in its place. This is a long
process, taking up to 30 million years.

25 In some cases, atolls are large enough to
support islands, vegetation, and even towns. For
example, Malé, the capital of the Indian Ocean
nation of the Maldives, is an atoll city with over
153,000 inhabitants. A number of other island
30 nations, including Kiribati, Tahiti, and Micronesia,
also possess populated atolls. Because these atolls,
along with other coral islands, are so low, many
are in imminent danger from rising sea levels
caused by climate change.

The process of atoll formation shows how coral and volcanoes, working in concert over millions of years, can create beautiful circular forms in the middle of the sea—forms which in some cases sustain thousands of people.

9

For the sake of logic and cohesion, Paragraph 3 should be placed:

A) where it is now.

B) before Paragraph 1.

C) after Paragraph 1.

D) after Paragraph 4.

Questions 10 & 11

My Favorite Career

-1-

Early in my career I was the arts and entertainment editor for a regional weekly newspaper. For a person who loved talking to artists, musicians, actors, and writers, this job surpassed my most fervent hopes and my wildest dreams of what a job could be. There were a myriad of perks that came with the gig, from free tickets to virtually any concert or play I wanted to see to getting advance copies of soon-to-be best sellers. I got to interview major movie stars, famous musicians, and writers.

-2-

I was the envy of all my friends and a fair number of people who decided they would like to be friends once they found out about the free tickets. To be honest, now even I envy my past self; I had the best job ever.

-3-

[1] There was just one problem with the job: it was exhausting. [2] Even when I'd been out until the wee hours enjoying the after-show parties with my celebrity buddies-for-the-day I was expected to be in the office by 10 a.m. at the very latest. [3] After all, someone had to open the press releases and stuff that arrived by the boxful every day. [4] That someone was me. [5] Someone had to answer the phone and conduct the interviews. [6] Someone had to write the articles and compile the lists of coming attractions. [7] Someone had to proofread those articles when it was time to publish that week's issue. 10

-4-

I admit that there were times I hid in my car for a nap. I admit that I fell asleep at my desk a few times. I even admit there were times when I thought about skipping a concert, or not going to the art opening, or maybe going to just one event in an evening instead of attending four. I never did, though, because it was too much fun. When I got promoted to features editor I was relieved that I could stay home occasionally. When I look back, however, I miss that job. It really was the best job ever. 11

10

For the sake of the logic and coherence of this paragraph, Sentence 4 should be placed:

A) where it is now.

B) after Sentence 1.

C) after Sentence 5.

D) after Sentence 7.

11

For the sake of logic and cohesion, Paragraph 2 should be placed:

A) where it is now.

B) before Paragraph 1.

C) after Paragraph 3.

D) after Paragraph 4.

Question 12

Let's Go Fly a Kite

-1-

In the 18th and 19th century, kites were flown in the name of science. The story of Benjamin Franklin using a kite to prove the existence of electricity is among the most often-told; less well-known is the story of the Charvolant, a kite-drawn horseless carriage patented in 1826.

-2-

April is National Kite Month. Over the course of 30 days, countless kite flying events are held all over the United States. The skies fill with all manner of kites, from the classic simple diamond shape to complex box kites and dramatic dragon kites that feature long tails and spectacular designs.

-3-

No one is certain when or where the first kite was flown, but, given kite flying's modern reputation as a leisure activity, it is surprising to find that the first written record focused on the use of a kite in battle. It seems that in about 200 B.C. a Chinese general used a kite to measure the distance his troops would need to tunnel to get inside the walls of a city this general was attacking. By the 7th century, kites had been

transformed from instruments of war to symbols of protection, as Japanese monks flew kites to ward off evil spirits.

-4-

Today, the most popular use for kites is recreation. That includes the popular pastime of flying a kite on a string held in the hand, but also high-action sports like kitesurfing, in which a person on a small board is pulled across the water at high speeds by a large kite. The Charvolant also has a modern descendent: the kite buggy, a small land vehicle pulled by a kite.

-5-

In April, as fanciful, colorful shapes fill the skies over parks and beaches—floating in the breeze, or racing through the air—keep a thought in mind for the long and winding tale of these elegant devices. 12

12

For the sake of logic and cohesion, Paragraph 1 should be placed:

A) where it is now.

B) after Paragraph 2.

C) after Paragraph 3.

D) after Paragraph 4.

Question 13

The Watery Adventures of Ben Franklin

[1] Like many people who grow up along the coast, Franklin loved spending time near and in the water. [2] Inspired by a painter's palette, the wooden paddles did make him go faster but Franklin abandoned them after realizing that

they made his wrists tired. [3] Franklin also combined his love of swimming and his well-known interest in kite flying. [4] He wrote about having spent an afternoon being propelled across a pond while lying on his back and holding onto a kite string. [5] Though he was considered quite an expert swimmer, it seems Franklin was not satisfied with his speed, which led to one of his first inventions: a set of swim fins or, as he called them, swimming paddles. 13

13

For the sake of the logic and coherence of this paragraph, Sentence 5 should be placed:

A) where it is now.

B) after Sentence 1.

C) after Sentence 2.

D) after Sentence 3.

Questions 14 & 15

The Pop Music Mastermind

-1-

Born Karl Martin Sandberg in Stockholm, Sweden, he started his music career in the late 1980's as a heavy metal singer. In 1993, his band came to the attention of Denniz PoP, a DJ who had recently founded a songwriting and recording studio called Cheiron. Impressed by Sandberg's gift for melody, Denniz brought him onto the Cheiron team, renaming him "Max Martin".

-2-

Max Martin is one of the most successful songwriters of all time, but you've probably never heard his name. Like Dr. Luke, Stargate, RedOne, Greg Kurstin, and a few others, Martin is a "superproducer"— one of the handful of songwriters behind almost all of today's pop hits. Even in this elite group, Max stands out: he has written more number one songs than anyone in history except John Lennon and Paul McCartney of the Beatles.

-3-

In 1997, Denniz paired Max with a new American boy band struggling to find an audience. That band was the Backstreet Boys, and on the strength of Martin's songs, their first album became one of the best-selling debuts of all time. Over the next few years, hits like Backstreet's "I Want It That Way" and Britney Spears' "...Baby One More Time" established Martin as the most successful composer in pop.

-4-

[1] Teen pop, his specialty, had been replaced on the charts by guitar-driven indie rock. [2] Looking for a new sound, Martin teamed up with Lukasz Gottwald, an underground producer wrapping up a ten-year stint as the lead guitarist for the Saturday Night Live band. [3] "Since U Been Gone", the song they wrote together for Kelly Clarkson, combined Max's melodic sensibility with Luke's guitar drive; it became a massive hit, launching Luke's career and re-launching Max's. [4] However, by 2004, Max's career was stalling. [5] Since then, Martin's string of hits for Katy Perry, Taylor Swift, Justin Bieber, Usher, Maroon 5, and many more has cemented his status as pop's most reliable hitmaker. 14 15

For the sake of the logic and coherence of this paragraph, Sentence 4 should be placed:

A) where it is now.

B) before Sentence 1.

C) after Sentence 2.

D) after Sentence 5.

15

For the sake of logic and cohesion, Paragraph 2 should be placed:

A) where it is now.

B) before Paragraph 1.

C) after Paragraph 3.

D) after Paragraph 4.

Question 16

Salt-Rising Bread

[1] The other missing ingredient in salt-rising bread is yeast, the usual leavener in bread recipes. [2] This doesn't explain the name, though the
Line main theory about that can be found in stories
5 from the westward-traveling pioneer women who were known to keep their bread starters warm in the salt barrels of their family wagons. [3] An alternative version is that housewives of the era kept their starter warm by placing it in a bed of
10 heated rock salt. [4] Regardless of the method, it's inspiring to think about how innovative these women were in their quest to provide food for their families. 16

16

Upon reviewing this paragraph and realizing that some information has been left out, the writer composes the following sentence:

Yeastless breads were common in the 1800s because, at that point, commercial yeast was not yet available so home bakers had to create starters like sourdough and the mash typically used for what became salt-rising bread.

The most logical placement for this sentence would be:

A) before Sentence 1.

B) after Sentence 1.

C) before Sentence 3.

D) after Sentence 4.

Questions 17 & 18

Narwhal Tusks

-1-

We still don't know exactly why narwhal teeth are so sensitive. Perhaps the tusk helps the whales find food, but since most female narwhals don't
Line have tusks this seems unlikely. Others speculate
5 that narwhals use their tusks to detect changes in the weather—this would be valuable information for narwhal pods, who need access to holes in the ice in order to breathe. However, it will take many more years of dedicated study before we have a
10 clear answer.

-2-

[1] At the end of the 16th century, the English Queen Elizabeth I received a curious present. [2] The sailors said it came from a "sea-unicorn", but

its true source was probably a narwhal, a type of
15 small Arctic whale. [3] Male narwhals—and about
15 percent of females—have long, spiralling
tusks that really do look like unicorn horns. [4]
Scientists have only just begun to understand how
special narwhal tusks are. 17

-3-

20   It was once thought that narwhals used their
tusks to fight each other or poke holes in the ice.
The author Jules Verne even suggested that their
tusks could sink ships! However, while narwhals
do rub their tusks together, they don't seem to be
25 fighting. Nor has anyone ever observed a narwhal
breaking the ice with its tusk. In fact, scientists
now know that the tusks are not horns, but teeth.

-4-

These teeth are quite different from ours. The
outer surface has millions of tiny channels which
30 lead all the way to nerves in the center of the
tooth, and these nerves lead straight to the whale's
brain.This makes the tooth highly sensitive. Dr.
Martin Nweeia, from the Harvard School of
Dental Medicine, suggests that the tusk can taste,
35 sense pressure, and distinguish temperatures in the
surrounding seawater. 18

17

Upon reviewing this paragraph and realizing that
some information has been left out, the writer
composes the following sentence:

Sailors brought her a jeweled "unicorn horn"
valued at 10,000 pounds sterling—roughly the
price of a castle!

The most logical placement for this sentence
would be:

A) before Sentence 1.

B) after Sentence 1.

C) after Sentence 3.

D) after Sentence 4.

18

For the sake of logic and cohesion, Paragraph 1
should be placed:

A) where it is now.

B) after Paragraph 2.

C) after Paragraph 3.

D) after Paragraph 4.

Answers & Explanations

1. The correct answer is (C). The information about when the Canal was built most logically follows the explanation about where it was built. (A) is incorrect because Sentence 1 introduces the subject, which logically precedes an explanation about when the Canal was built. (B) may be tempting because the length of time it took to build the Canal supports the claim that it is an engineering marvel, but it makes more sense to discus the time period in which the canal was built in order to transition to sentence 3, which describes the canal in the present. (D) is incorrect because it's illogical to jump back to the topic of the canal's construction after sentence 3 raises the topic of its current use.

2. The correct answer is (D). The effect of the grass being imported should logically follow the information about how the grass arrived. (A), (B), and (C) are all incorrect because the suggested order of information is not logical.

3. The correct answer is (B). This arrangement answers the rhetorical question in Sentence 2, showing that the "artists who made" drawings in books like Grey's Anatomy are specialized medical artists. Answer (A) is incorrect because it's not logical to explain the requirement that an artist be knowledgeable in order to create medical illustrations before establishing where those illustrations appear and who might be best qualified for a career as a medical illustrator. (C) is incorrect because this placement would disrupt the logical organization of ideas. (D) is incorrect because it doesn't make sense to explain where medical illustrations currently appear after introducing possible future expansions in the field.

4. The correct answer is (A). Sentence 4 offers examples of the type of training tools introduced in Sentence 3. (B), (C), and (D) are not correct because they disrupt the logical flow of information by separating an example from the sentence that introduces it.

5. The correct answer is (C). The information about certification and professional development most logically follows information about the education of medical illustrators. (A) is incorrect because the information in the paragraph interrupts the logical transition from the current state of the occupation described in Paragraph 3 and the future possibilities described in Paragraph 4. (B) is incorrect because it would be confusing to introduce certification information before explaining what profession is being discussed. (D) is incorrect because Paragraph 5 is clearly a conclusion that revisits the information provided throughout the passage and introducing new information after this is not logical.

6. The correct answer is (D). Sentence 5 is concerned with current conditions which should, logically, precede the predictions about the future stated in Sentence 4. (A) is not correct for the same reason. (B) is incorrect because Sentence 1 introduces the issue being explored in the paragraph and placing Sentence 5 before this would upset the logical order of ideas. (C) is incorrect because Sentence 3 explains both current conditions and a specific potential danger in the spread of tropical insects and placing Sentence 5 between Sentences 3 and 4 would create a lack of coherence.

7. The correct answer is (B). Sentence 3 clarifies information introduced in Sentence 1, explaining that only female velvet ants are wingless. (A) is incorrect because Sentence 2 offers a more detailed explanation of the differences between female and male velvet ants. (C) is incorrect because Sentence 4 builds on the information about the very different forms the two sexes of velvet ants take. (D) is incorrect because would create confusion because Sentence 6 and Sentence 3 are both concerned only with female velvet ants so comparing females to females is not logical.

8. The correct answer is (B). Paragraph 4 provides general introductory content about the velvet ant, without which the rest of the essay doesn't make as much sense. (A) places this introductory paragraph at the very end, which creates a confusing essay. (C) and (D) also fail to place the introduction at the front of the essay.

9. The correct answer is (C). Darwin's theory about how atolls are created logically follows the question posed in Paragraph 1 and logically precedes information about where atolls form. (A), (B), and (D) are incorrect because all of them disrupt the logical organization of information.

10. The correct answer is (D). Sentence 4 is the logical conclusion to the series of assertions made in Sentences 3, 5, 6, and 7 — someone had to complete all those tasks and that someone was the narrator. (A), (B), and (C) all disrupt the logic and coherence of the paragraph.

11. The correct answer is (A). The first paragraph serves to introduce the job discussed in the passage, and the third paragraph introduces the idea that it wasn't quite perfect. Paragraph 2 expresses strong positive sentiments about the job, and it makes sense to place it before a paragraph that notes an exception. (B) is incorrect because it is not logical for the writer to explain that she was the envy of her friends before describing the job. (C) is incorrect because it is not logical to suggest that the writer's friends envied her exhaustion and heavy workload. (D) is incorrect because Paragraph 4 is obviously a conclusion so it would disrupt the cohesion of the passage to place Paragraph 2 after the conclusion.

12. The correct answer is (C). Paragraph 1 explores the use of kites at a point following their earliest history as described in Paragraph 3 so this is the logical placement. (A) is incorrect because it is illogical to explore an historic use of kites before introducing the topic of kites. (B) and (D) are both incorrect because placing the paragraph at either of these points would disrupt the chronological order of information.

13. The correct answer is (B). It is logical to introduce the information about why Franklin invented his swim paddles before explaining the inspiration for the paddles' form and the connection between the paddles and his fascination with kites. (A) is incorrect because the information in Sentence 1 logically precedes the information that Franklin wanted to improve his swimming speed. (C) is incorrect because it makes no sense to explain the inspiration for the paddles' form before introducing the paddles. (D) is incorrect because it is illogical to explain the connection between Franklin's love of swimming and his fascination with kites before introducing the paddles.

14. The correct answer is (B). The information about when Max's career was stalled introduces the subject being explored in the paragraph; though "However," may seem like an awkward way to begin a passage, it is a perfectly acceptable way to transition into a paragraph within a passage. (A) and (C) are both incorrect because the information in Sentences 1 and 2 would logically follow the information about the state of Max's career in 2004. (D) is incorrect because concluding the paragraph that explains how Max turned his career around with the information that Max's career was stalling in 2004 makes no sense.

15. The correct answer is (B). Paragraph 2 relates to very general, introductory material about Max Martin, and makes the most sense as the essay's very first paragraph. (A) puts Paragraph 1 first. While Paragraph 1 does discuss the birth of Max Martin, since he hasn't been introduced under his pseudonym yet, Paragraph 1 is not a good introduction. (C) places the basic introductory material even further along in the passage, and (D) tries to make it the essay's conclusion.

16. The correct answer is (B). The information that yeast was not readily available so home bakers relied on yeastless starters logically follows the information that yeast is the common leavener of most breads. (A) is incorrect because explaining that yeastless breads were once common does not logically precede the point that yeast is missing from this particular bread. (C) is incorrect because Sentences 2 and 3 focus on the possible origins of this bread's unusual name, which logically follows the information in the proposed addition. (D) is incorrect because ending a paragraph that is focused on explaining some of the history of salt-rising bread with the information in the proposed addition is illogical.

17. The correct answer is (B). The placement that creates the most logical order is between Sentence 1, which tells us Queen Elizabeth I received a gift and Sentence 2, which tells us what claims about the gift were made by those bestowing the gift; both omit the detail about what the gift was and who gave the gift. (A) is incorrect because the new sentence explains who gave the gift of the jeweled unicorn horn but it does not specify to whom the gift was given. (C) is incorrect because it is not logical to explain that the queen got a gift, that certain claims were made about that gift, and that male narwhals have tusks that resemble unicorn horns before explaining what the gift was. (D) is incorrect because it repeats all the errors of logical order in the other incorrect answers.

18. The correct answer is (D). Paragraph 1 focuses on possible answers to the mystery of the narwhal tusk's sensitivity so it logically would follow the paragraph that introduces this fact. (A), (B), and (C) are all incorrect because the organization of information is not logical.

Transitional Words and Sentences
Part 2

Transitional Words and Sentences questions ask you to add, revise, or remove transitional words, phrases, or even sentences. You will need to consider the logical relationships between pieces of information, the likely goals of the author in the transition, and both the logical implications of transition words and the attitudes that they express. In addition to selecting appropriate transition words, you may need to remove extraneous transition words that are misleading or merely empty.

DIRECTIONS

Every passage comes with a set of questions. Some questions will ask you to consider how the writer might revise the passage to improve the expression of ideas. Some questions will refer to a portion of the passage that has been underlined. Other questions will refer to a particular location in a passage or ask that you consider the passage in full.

After you read the passage, select the answers to questions that most effectively improve the passage's writing quality or that adjust the passage to follow the conventions of standard written English. Many questions give you the option to select "NO CHANGE." Select that option in cases where you think the relevant part of the passage should remain as it currently is.

1

Last night I had a dream about a talking waffle-iron. As a result, I had eaten waffles the day before, but it was still really weird.

A) NO CHANGE

B) Instead,

C) Next,

D) Admittedly,

2

The first ever communication satellites—Telstar 1 and Telstar 2—are still orbiting the earth. In fact, they do not work anymore.

A) NO CHANGE

B) However,

C) Consequently,

D) For example,

3

Different universities will often have different names for their faculties. In contrast, if you study English at Brontosaurus University, you are part of the Faculty of Arts; if you study English at Diplodocus State, you are part of the Faculty of Arts and Social Science; and if you study English at Pterodactyl College of Art and Design, you are part of the Faculty of Post-Cretaceous Studies.

A) NO CHANGE

B) Yet,

C) For example,

D) Otherwise,

4

Last week, Paula wrote a magazine article about the history of the bagel. This week, she's going to write about the history of the donut, and next week she'll write about bundt cakes. Because of her stories' similar themes, her column is called "The Hole Story."

A) NO CHANGE

B) Instead of

C) Since

D) After a while

5

The mayor of this town skateboards to work. Similarly, on the weekends she prefers surfing to skateboarding.

A) NO CHANGE

B) However,

C) Likewise,

D) In the same way,

6

The camera fell out of the helicopter and into the crowded skating rink. Unfortunately, nobody was hurt and the camera was totally unscathed. What a relief!

A) NO CHANGE

B) Consequently,

C) Fortunately,

D) Alas,

Questions 7 - 10

Velvet Ants

[7] The family Mutillidae includes hundreds of species of insects commonly known as "velvet ants." The "velvet" part of their name derives from the colorful tufts of hair on the insects' bodies. The "ant" part is actually a misnomer, though: the velvet ant isn't an ant at all. It's actually a wasp.

[8] Both ants and wasps are insects: we usually think of wasps as flying insects, but velvet ants are wingless. At least, the females are. Velvet ants are extremely sexually dimorphic, meaning that the two sexes have very different forms. It can be difficult even for experts to tell whether a male and female velvet ant are even of the same species. The males have wings, are sometimes much larger than the females, and more closely resemble our traditional image of wasps--though they have no stingers. The females, meanwhile, lack wings, but possess powerful stings.

The sting of the velvet ant is so notorious that they have another nickname: "cow killer." This nickname arises from the myth that the sting of the velvet ant is so painful that it could kill a

cow. Just like the name "velvet ant," though, this
moniker is more about how the insect is perceived
than what it actually is. The cow killer's sting
can't really kill a cow; in fact, the stings are not
even particularly dangerous to humans. They are,
however, quite painful.

9 Velvet ants aren't exactly the ideal pet,
but they're not monsters, either. The wasps are
solitary animals, and they're not aggressive, so
even those people who spend a lot of time outside
will only encounter them rarely. When they
do have an encounter, the wasp will generally
not sting if it's able to get away. Wearing shoes
outside will help people to avoid stepping on the
wasps while barefoot, which is the most likely
cause of stings. If a homeowner does have a
problem with velvet ants in the yard, increasing
grass cover and clearing out anthills will make the
yard less appealing to velvet ants. It's not usually
necessary to eradicate the wasps, though; it's
usually enough to give them a little bit of space,
and let them go about their business.

So, as it turns out, the velvet ant, or cow killer,
is not an ant, not made of velvet, and not deadly
to cows. This notorious little insect isn't very
dangerous at all. 10 So much for that name!

7

Given that all of the choices are true, which one
most effectively introduces the essay as a whole?

A) NO CHANGE

B) Velvet ants come in a wide variety of colors,
including red, orange, yellow, and even blue
varieties.

C) Wasps can be annoying pests, but the velvet
ant is a wasp that parasitizes other wasps.

D) Wasps, including velvet ants, are feared for
their stings—but only the females actually
have stingers.

8

Which choice provides the best transition between
the two paragraphs?

A) NO CHANGE

B) It's not hard to see where the misunderstanding
comes from:

C) Wasps and ants are both from the suborder
Apocrita, and have a common ancestor:

D) It's not a bee, either:

9

Given that all of the choices are true, which one most effectively introduces the following paragraph?

A) NO CHANGE

B) Eliminating velvet ants can be a tricky affair, because they do not live in easy-to-locate hives like other wasps.

C) While the prospect of a painful sting may be frightening, the insects usually aren't a problem, and a few simple precautions can eliminate most risk.

D) Because they parasitize other wasps, some of which can be more aggressive, some velvet ants may actually be desirable.

10

Which of these choices provides the best concluding sentence for the essay?

A) NO CHANGE

B) Perhaps the lesson we should learn from the "velvet ant" is not to be fooled by names.

C) Further, while bees get all the good press, wasps actually pollinate flowers too.

D) Its latin name is Mutillidae.

Starting in 1818, William Blake drew a series of portraits, called the Visionary Heads, for his friend John Varley. They depict a number of historical and mythological figures who, Blake said, appeared to him in night-time visions. <u>While</u> Varley appears to have fully believed that Blake could actually "see" the true faces of these long-dead people, it's not clear what Blake believed.

A) NO CHANGE

B) Because

C) Provided that

D) Since

One of Kate's favorite pastimes is bowling. <u>However,</u> her team has won the rec league championship twice.

A) NO CHANGE

B) Conversely,

C) In fact,

D) That being said,

Cacti are well worth having in your home. For one thing, they're very easy plants to care for. <u>Nevertheless,</u> they're bright and attractive when they flower.

A) NO CHANGE

B) Consequently,

C) In addition,

D) However,

First, we filled the cement mixer with yellow roses. <u>Indeed,</u> we told the Superintendent of Schools that there was something wrong with our cement mixer. When he saw the roses, he gave us all suspensions.

A) NO CHANGE

B) Next,

C) On the other hand,

D) Nevertheless,

Question 15 - 18

Narwhal Tusks

At the end of the 16th century, the English Queen Elizabeth I received a curious present. Sailors brought her a jeweled "unicorn horn"

Line valued at 10,000 pounds sterling—roughly the

5 price of a castle! The sailors said it came from a "sea-unicorn", but its true source was probably a narwhal, a type of small Arctic whale. Male narwhals—and about 15 percent of females— have long, spiralling tusks that really do look like

10 unicorn horns. Scientists have only just begun to understand how special narwhal tusks are.

15 <u>It was once thought that narwhal tusks could be used to neutralize poison.</u> The author Jules Verne even suggested that their tusks could

15 sink ships! However, while narwhals do rub their tusks together, they don't seem to be fighting. Nor has anyone ever observed a narwhal breaking the ice with its tusk. In fact, scientists now know that the tusks are not horns, but teeth.

20 These teeth are quite different from ours. The outer surface has millions of tiny channels which lead all the way to nerves in the center of the tooth, and these nerves lead straight to

the whale's brain. This makes the tooth highly

25 sensitive. Dr. Martin Nweeia, from the Harvard School of Dental Medicine, suggests that the tusk can taste, sense pressure, and distinguish temperatures in the surrounding seawater. 16 <u>This is a remarkable range of sensory information</u>

30 <u>from an organ once thought to be a simple horn.</u>

17 <u>Modern science has dispelled superstitions about the magical powers of narwhal tusks.</u> Perhaps the tusk helps the whales find food, but since most female narwhals don't have

35 tusks this seems unlikely. Others speculate that narwhals use their tusks to detect changes in the weather—this would be valuable information for narwhal pods, who need access to holes in the ice in order to breathe. 18 <u>Who knew that narwhals</u>

40 <u>aren't actually unicorns after all?</u>

Given that all of the choices are true, which one most effectively introduces the following paragraph?

A) NO CHANGE

B) In the past, it was believed that narwhals used their tusks to fight over mates, as bucks do, or to rend holes in the ice.

C) Narwhal's bodies can grow to about 18 feet in length, and their horns can add nearly 9 extra feet.

D) Narwhal tusks were once believed to possess magical powers and could be sold for more than their weight in gold.

Which of the following choices provides the best conclusion to this paragraph?

A) NO CHANGE

B) Dr. Nweeia is a noted expert in narwhal studies.

C) If only human teeth were so sensitive!

D) This is only one of many important discoveries by the Harvard School of Dental Medicine.

Given that all of the choices are true, which one most effectively introduces the following paragraph?

A) NO CHANGE

B) Not all narwhals have tusks; males develop them, as well as a small number of females.

C) While we know that narwhal tusks are acute sensory organs, we still don't know exactly what they are used for.

D) There are millions of nerve endings in narwhal tusks, making them incredibly sensitive organs.

18

Which of the following choices provides the best conclusion to the essay?

A) NO CHANGE

B) Whatever the answer is, it will take many more years of study and research to discover.

C) Dr. Nweeia believes that when narwhals rub their tusks together, they are brushing their teeth.

D) As the recipient of a tooth with monetary value, Elizabeth I was somewhat like the tooth fairy.

1. The correct answer is (D). Using "Admittedly" means accepting a premise, but also offering up a contrasting idea after it. In other words, the speaker admits that she did eat waffles the day before, but that her dream was nevertheless really weird. (A) creates a causal connection that, in context, is back-to-front. Since the speaker had a dream "last night," it wouldn't make sense for this to cause her to eat waffles "the day before." As far as we know, time doesn't work that way. (B), "Instead," is incorrect because the word indicates the substituting out of one thing for another one. In context, the two sentences are connected, so it is wrong to use "Instead" here. (C) suggests a sequence of events, but, as with (A), it creates a mixed-up timeframe. "Next" means "afterwards," but the speaker ate the waffles "the day before."

2. The correct answer is (B). It appropriately indicates the contrast between the two sentences' ideas: first, that the two satellites are still in orbit, and, second, that they don't work anymore. (A), "In fact," is incorrect because it indicates addition and agreement, not contrast. (C) is incorrect because it suggests a causal link between the two ideas. The fact that the two satellites don't work isn't necessarily a consequence of their still being in orbit. (D) is incorrect because the phrase "For example" needs to follow something that requires an example—a general statement, for instance.

3. The correct answer is (C). The first sentence makes a general claim about universities. The second sentence is a long list of examples in support of this claim. This makes "For example" the clear winner. (A) is incorrect because the two sentences are not actually contrasted; the second sentence supports that statement made in the first. (B), "Yet," is also a word indicating a contrast. It's wrong for the same reason that (A) is. (D), "Otherwise," suggests a chain of cause and effect (ie "Take your umbrella, otherwise you'll get wet") which doesn't make any sense in context.

4. The correct answer is (A). The phrase "Because of" aptly establishes a causal connection between the themes of Paula's magazine articles and the name of her column. Paula writes about foods with holes in them, so her column's title reflects this. (B) is incorrect because "Instead of" doesn't make any sense here. (C) creates a clause error: you'd need a verb ("has," for instance) for this to be a complete clause. (D) doesn't make sense, and likewise creates a clause error; there's no verb present.

5. The correct answer is (B). The first sentence and the second sentence present two contrasting ideas: the mayor skateboards to work, but she surfs on the weekend. "However" appropriately indicates this contrast. (A) incorrectly suggests that the two ideas are the same, rather than a contrast. (C), "Likewise," makes the same mistake as (A). (D) also incorrectly indicates similarity.

6. The correct answer is (C). You can tell, in context, that the speaker is describing a fortunate outcome. The phrase "What a relief!" indicates that the speaker is happy that both the camera and the skaters were unharmed. (A) is wrong because the word indicates an unhappy outcome. If the speaker had intended to do harm to either the camera or the skaters, "Unfortunately" would make sense. However, the speaker expresses relief, so it doesn't make sense to pick "Unfortunately." (B) indicates a causal connection, but that doesn't make sense here. It's not clear how falling into the rink would cause the camera and skaters to be unhurt. (D), "Alas," is wrong for the same reason that (A) is; the word suggests an unfortunate outcome when, in context, the opposite is true.

7. The correct answer is (A). It opens the essay in the most general way, while still having a specific focus on velvet ants. The other choices are all either too general or too specific to be an introductory statement: (B) talks about the colors of velvet ants before any sentence has properly introduced the insects more generally. (C) similarly provides a specific detail rather than a general overview. (D) is too general, and relates to all wasps.

8. The correct answer is (B). It makes the most sense, linking a reader's likely confusion about the velvet ant after the first paragraph with a clarifying statement at the start of the second. (A) feels somewhat disconnected from what comes before and after. (C) similarly fails to provide a sensible segue between the paragraphs. (D) brings bees into the picture, which is perhaps most confusing of all.

9. The correct answer is (C). It introduces the idea that the risk of a velvet ant sting is low. (A) is close, but it's not specifically about stinging, and it introduces the idea of the velvet ant as a pet—an idea that isn't picked up again anywhere else. (B) isn't general enough as an introduction, and in any case the paragraph is mostly about avoiding stings rather than eliminating velvet ants. (D) is likewise a supporting rather than an introductory point.

10. The correct answer is (B). It sums up the points made in the body of the passage, and makes a concluding remark. (A) is incorrect because it doesn't clearly address any of the major points made in the passage, and doesn't connect very well with the previous sentence. The Velvet Ant has several names that don't accurately describe it. (C) introduces new information, so it's not a good conclusion. (D) also introduces a new fact.

11. The correct answer is (A). The sentence creates a contrast between Varley and Blake's beliefs about the Visionary Heads. "While" appropriately sets up this contrast. (B), "Because," is incorrect; it sets up a causal connection that doesn't make sense. There's no reason why Varley's belief would cause Blake's beliefs to be unclear. (C) is incorrect because it creates a comma splice later on in the sentence. Unlike "Because" and "While," "Indeed" is not a subordinating conjunction. Using it here turns the first clause into an independent clause, and makes the comma after "people" a comma splice. (D) is incorrect much like (B) is; it likewise suggests a causal connection that doesn't make sense in context.

12. The correct answer is (C). It's an additive transition word, which means that it adds emphasis to what was stated already. We learned in the previous sentence that bowling is one of Kate's favorite pastimes, and the point in the second sentence expands upon this idea. (A) is incorrect because it suggests a contrast; this doesn't make sense in context. If Kate loves bowling, it's not a contrasting idea for her to play on a team and win championships. (B) is wrong because it creates a sentence fragment. "Because" is a subordinating conjunction, and it turns the sentence into a dependent clause. (D), like (A), suggests a contrast that doesn't make sense in context.

13. The correct answer is (C). The second and third sentences serve as two examples in support of the claim in the first sentence. This makes "in addition" an appropriate way to link the two ideas. (A) is incorrect because it suggests that the cacti are bright and attractive in spite of being easy to care for. This doesn't make much sense; there's no necessary causal relationship between the two ideas. (B) also sets up a causal relationship that's not really there; being easy to care for doesn't cause the cacti to flower brightly. (D) suggests that the two ideas are contrasting, but that's not true.

14. The correct answer is (B). To answer it, think about the transition word used in the sentence preceding the underlined portion. It's "First," which means that what follows will be a sequence. "Next" appropriately indicates the next item in the sequence: first they filled the mixer with roses, and, next, they told the Superintendent there was something wrong with it. (A) is an additive transition word, which doesn't fit here. The second sentence advances a narrative sequence instead of emphasizing an idea. (C) uses a transition word that indicates a shift to a totally new idea, but that doesn't make sense here. (D) indicates a contrast, which is once again incorrect in context.

15. The correct answer is (B). It provides two early theories about the tusks, which the latter part of the paragraph disputes. (A) offers a belief which isn't addressed elsewhere in the passage, and is in any case a belief about what humans could use the tusks for, not how narwhals use them. (C) merely offers some information about the narwhal's body size. (D), just like (C), describes beliefs that aren't addressed elsewhere, and don't relate to the narwhal's own use of the horn.

16. The correct answer is (A). It wraps up the paragraph's focus on the tusk's function as a sensitive tooth with a simple, summarizing statement. (B) takes the focus away from the narwhal's tooth, narrowing in too much on Dr. Nweeia. (C) brings in speculation about human teeth that doesn't offer a relevant conclusion to the paragraph. (D) also shifts the focus to material that isn't relevant in context.

17. The correct answer is (C). It transitions from the discovery that the tusk is a tooth to the new paragraph's discussion of the latest theories about why the tusk is so sensitive. (A) is close, but it doesn't introduce the topic of current theories about the tusk's sensitivity with sufficient focus. (B) is even more clearly out of focus, returning to more basic facts about the tusks. (D) merely reiterates ideas presented earlier.

18. The correct answer is (B). It ends with a remark about the work that remains to be done before we know what narwhal tusks really do. (A) isn't a good choice because it doesn't sum up the main focus of the paragraph; it's not so much about disproving that narwhals are unicorns as it is about what their tusks do. (C) focuses too specifically on new details rather than a concluding statement. (D) calls back to the first paragraph, but doesn't sum up the body of the essay.

Section 3
Effective Language Use

Questions in the Effective Language Use domain test your ability to improve the language in a passage in contexts in which there are no grammatical errors, but the language used is tonally inappropriate, illogical, imprecise, or awkward. You'll need to replace individual words that don't have exactly the right meaning, make wordy sentences more concise, and make the style and tone of the passage more clear and consistent.

Effective Language Use questions contribute to the "Expression" subscore. They also contribute to the "Words in Context" cross-test score.

There are 4 specific question types in this domain:

Effective Language Use			
EP	Precise Word Choices	ET	Style and Tone
EC	Concise Sentences	ES	Clear Sentences

Precise Word Choices
Part 1

Precise Word Choices questions ask you to choose the vocabulary word that makes the most sense in context. You can't answer these questions with word knowledge alone. You always need to consider what idea the sentence is most likely trying to express: the answer choices will always have similar meanings, and you need to select the one that most precisely expresses the apparently intended meaning of the sentence. Look for words or phrases being compared to the underlined portion, or that would otherwise help you understand its meaning. Also consider the objects of descriptive words, and think about whether certain answer choices would typically be used to describe the objects they take in the sentence.

DIRECTIONS

Every passage comes with a set of questions. Some questions will ask you to consider how the writer might revise the passage to improve the expression of ideas. Other questions will ask you to consider correcting potential errors in sentence structure, usage, or punctuation. There may be one or more graphics that you will need to consult as you revise and edit the passage.

Some questions will refer to a portion of the passage that has been underlined. Other questions will refer to a particular location in a passage or ask that you consider the passage in full.

After you read the passage, select the answers to questions that most effectively improve the passage's writing quality or that adjust the passage to follow the conventions of standard written English. Many questions give you the option to select "NO CHANGE." Select that option in cases where you think the relevant part of the passage should remain as it currently is.

1

On display at the museum were several beautiful sculptures <u>shaved</u> out of soapstone.

A) NO CHANGE

B) coordinated

C) carved

D) culled

2

The library has a silent study room for anyone who <u>necessitates</u> a quiet space to work.

A) NO CHANGE

B) privileges

C) obliges

D) needs

3

I'm not sure that the statistics you've given me are <u>steady</u>. They're based on a very small, unrepresentative sample.

A) NO CHANGE

B) reliable

C) literal

D) faithful

4

Make sure that you <u>bashfully</u> mix your custard; if you aren't careful, it will turn into scrambled eggs.

A) NO CHANGE

B) sneakily

C) respectfully

D) carefully

5

I was really grateful that Erica wrote such a <u>brainy</u> get-well card. It made me feel good to know that she was thinking about me while I was in the hospital.

A) NO CHANGE

B) philosophical

C) thoughtful

D) studious

6

At one time, doctors would routinely <u>visit</u> patients in their own homes. Nowadays, that's a very rare level of service.

A) NO CHANGE

B) investigate

C) challenge

D) practice

7

When you listen to her records, you can tell that her work is <u>initiated</u> by disco music. It's probably her single biggest influence.

A) NO CHANGE

B) inspired

C) encouraged

D) bemused

8

I can't <u>replicate</u> exactly what this street corner looked like the last time I visited, but I'm sure that the donut shop is new, and that the other business are as well.

A) NO CHANGE

B) reclaim

C) recall

D) revoke

9

The car came around the corner at such a <u>large</u> speed that its wheels skidded, leaving the intersection streaked with rubber marks.

A) NO CHANGE

B) grand

C) high

D) big

10

After we had examined all of the bees, we <u>spilled</u> them back into the wild.

A) NO CHANGE

B) flushed

C) scooted

D) released

11

Hydroelectric dams, touted as a source of green energy, may actually <u>contribute</u> significantly to overall greenhouse gas emissions: they are now believed to be the single largest source of methane emissions from human activity.

A) NO CHANGE

B) donate

C) give

D) supply

1. (C) is the correct answer. We typically use "carved" to describe the forming of sculptures out of stone. (A), "shaved," suggests a different process, perhaps more appropriately used to describe the removal of a top layer or surface. (B), "coordinated," is also not precise enough; the word tends to describe more abstract actions like organizing a group of people. (D), "culled," is more commonly used to describe reducing the number of things in a group.

2. (D) is the correct answer. The word "needs" avoids the imprecise language of the other choices. (A), "necessitates," describes the effect of a cause (ie, "the rain necessitated a change of plans") rather than personal need. (B) is also imprecise as the word "privileges" suggests something closer to "prioritizes." (C), "obliges," has legal or moral connotations that aren't suitable here.

3. (B) is the correct answer. The statistics are based on "a very small, unrepresentative sample,", meaning that they don't appear to be "reliable," or in other words trustworthy or sufficient to draw conclusions from. (A) isn't precise enough, as the word "steady" refers to stable motion, which doesn't adequately capture the idea that the statistics can be trusted. It's true that "steady" can also more colloquially refer to a reliable person or relationship, but this sense isn't idiomatic when paired with a word like "statistics." (C) is incorrect because "literal" refers to a basic interpretation of a written statement; it doesn't have anything to do with numbers. (D) is incorrect because "faithful" is synonymous with "loyal," a personal quality that doesn't fit well with "statistics."

4. (D) is the correct answer. The other options aren't precise enough in context. (A) is incorrect because "bashfully" implies an attitude of shyness; it's not normally used to refer to one's cooking techniques. Here, the worst that could happen is scrambled eggs. (B) is wrong because you don't need to be "sneaky," or in other words tricky or stealthy, to mix custard. (C), "respectfully," does suggest gentleness, but not in the context of cooking.

5. (C) is the correct answer. This question tries to trick you by playing on two different meanings of the word "thoughtful." One means "kind" or "considerate," and the other means "absorbed in thought." In context, it makes the most sense for a get-well card to be "thoughtful" as in "kind." (A) is incorrect; the word "brainy" describes a smart act, but not necessarily a kind one. (B), "philosophical," indicates an attitude of intellectual inquiry that would make for a pretty strange get-well card. (D), "studious," also suggests that the card was intellectually oriented, but in context we know that the card made the author feel good while hospitalized.

6. (A) is the correct answer. It avoids the precision errors of the other choices. (B), "investigate," means to put something under close scrutiny; it suggests that the doctors are carrying out police work rather than practicing medicine. (C), "challenge," also doesn't fit well in context, as the word implies that the doctors confront or test their patients. (D) is very close, but the phrase "practice patients" isn't idiomatic. It would need to be phrased as "practice upon."

7. (B) is the correct answer. When we talk about musical influences, it's idiomatic to say that someone has been "inspired" by them. (A) isn't correct because "initiated," which simply means "begun" or "started," is too broad in its scope. (C) is incorrect because "encouraged" is not as suggestive of artistic influence as it is personal cheering-on. (D), "bemused," is synonymous with "confused," which wouldn't make sense here.

8.   (C) is the correct answer. The word "recall" is the most precise term for remembering what a place used to look like, of the options presented. (A), "replicate," means to repeat something again in the same way; it has scientific connotations that aren't a good fit here. (B), "reclaim," means to recover something, but it isn't normally associated with memory at all. (D), "revoke," refers to the ending of certain privileges or memberships.

9.   (C) is the correct answer. The word "high" is the most precise and idiomatic way to refer to a great speed. (A), "large," is incorrect; we don't usually refer to speed in terms of largeness. (B), "grand," is similar to, but not the same as "great," which would be another correct alternative; however, "grand" has an additional connotations of splendour that aren't an idiomatic way to refer to speed. (D), "big," likewise isn't precise or idiomatic in the context of speed.

10. (D) is the correct answer. When we let living things go back into the wild, the typical term is "release." The other words have similar, but not precisely identical meanings. (A), "spilled," isn't normally used in connection with living things; it's more often seen in connection with liquids. (B), "flushed," is likewise a word more appropriate when discussing liquids. (C), "scooted," does imply motion, but not in the specific and precise sense of creatures moving back into the wild.

11. (A) is the correct answer. In this context, the word "contributes" is the best fit. (B) incorrectly suggests that the dams are private individuals giving support to a cause. (C) is incorrect because it also suggests that the dam is a person with the ability to give things to someone else. (D) is incorrect because the word "supply" is imprecise in the context of gas emissions; we typically "supply" something good or useful, but greenhouse gas emissions are harmful.

Concise Sentences
Part 2

Concise Sentences questions ask you to revise sentences to eliminate empty phrases and repetitive words—but not key information. The shortest answer is often correct, but not always: look out for answer choices that eliminate important information and those that are short but still repeat information from elsewhere in the sentence.

DIRECTIONS

Every passage comes with a set of questions. Some questions will ask you to consider how the writer might revise the passage to improve the expression of ideas. Some questions will refer to a portion of the passage that has been underlined. Other questions will refer to a particular location in a passage or ask that you consider the passage in full.

After you read the passage, select the answers to questions that most effectively improve the passage's writing quality or that adjust the passage to follow the conventions of standard written English. Many questions give you the option to select "NO CHANGE." Select that option in cases where you think the relevant part of the passage should remain as it currently is.

1

With such a <u>large, big</u> budget, you'd think the movie would've had a better theme song.

A) NO CHANGE

B) lot of money and a big

C) big

D) large-sized

2

The Bet Giyorgis monolithic church, in Lalibela, Ethiopia, was <u>carved and shaped</u> out of a single block of limestone.

A) NO CHANGE

B) carved into a monolithic church

C) shaped from limestone

D) carved

3

When you look at a Pieter Breughel painting, you enter a busy world of detailed <u>paintings of</u> cities, fields, and villages.

A) NO CHANGE

B) and painted

C) Brueghel

D) DELETE the underlined portion.

4

Amy's favorite candy is licorice allsorts; her grandmother used to give <u>them</u> to her.

A) NO CHANGE

B) licorice allsorts

C) the licorice candy

D) these favorite allsorts

5

Shamir has loved music since he was <u>a very young person</u>; he wanted a guitar before he wanted a bike.

A) NO CHANGE

B) very young

C) young and a child

D) youthful and young

6

I've never seen such a multi-colored seahorse before. <u>Its many colors are</u> orange, yellow, green, and blue!

A) NO CHANGE

B) Its multiple colors include

C) It's

D) The colors it displays are

7

During a thunderstorm, sailors sometimes see St. Elmo's fire: <u>a glow of fiery fireballs</u> that appears at the ends of masts.

A) NO CHANGE

B) a glow that sailors see

C) a glow

D) seen on masts, it's a glow

8

The first appearance of the word "robot" is in a 1920 Czech play called R.U.R., which stands for "Rossum's Universal Robots." The author, Karel Čapek, wrote <u>the play R.U.R. ("Rossum's Universal Robots")</u> in response to society's increasing mechanization.

A) NO CHANGE

B) the play

C) the play in the year of 1920

D) the play, which is a performance to be acted in a theater,

9

Simone brings a paper fan with her on the subway because <u>the trains of the subway</u> often don't have air-conditioning.

A) NO CHANGE

B) the subway trains one encounters

C) the trains

D) on the subway the trains

10

The cartoon <u>is funny and makes people laugh.</u>

A) NO CHANGE

B) causes laughter and laughing.

C) creates much funniness

D) is funny.

1. (C) is the correct answer. It avoids the redundancy of the other choices. (A) uses both "large" and "big," but since the two words essentially mean the same thing, there's no need to use them both. (B) is redundant too; "a lot of money" is very close in meaning to "a big budget." (D) is redundant because the word "large" already refers to size.

2. (D) is the correct answer. It's the least redundant choice. (A) uses both "carved" and "shaped," but in context the two words express very similar ideas. (B) repeats the phrase "monolithic church" even though it was used already at the start of the sentence. (C) states that the church was "shaped from limestone" even though the sentence immediately repeats that it was made "out of a single block of limestone."

3. (D) is the correct answer. All of the other choices are redundant, meaning that you must omit the underlined portion. (A) is redundant because the sentence has already established that the "cities, fields, and villages" are in a painting. (B) is redundant for the same reason. (C) needlessly uses Brueghel's name as an adjective even though it's already been established that we're talking about "a Pieter Brueghel painting."

4. (A) is the correct answer. The pronoun "them" is the most concise choice. (B) repeats "licorice allsorts." (C) repeats two words, "licorice" and "candy," that were used already. (D) likewise repeats "favorite" and "allsorts" despite their appearance in the preceding clause.

5. (B) is the correct answer. The phrase "very young" is the most concise choice. (A) is too wordy, adding "a" and "person." (C) is redundant. While the two words are not exact synonyms, the ideas they express are still too similar to be expressed as a pair of adjectives joined by a conjunction. Note that the phrase "young child" would not be redundant, however; in that case, the word "young" modifies the word "child" (ie to stress that the subject was, for instance, five rather than twelve). (D) is very redundant,using two close synonyms.

6. (C) is the correct answer. It's the most concise option. It uses "It" to refer to the seahorse, and uses the contraction "'s" as well. (A) is redundant because "its many colors" repeats the idea that the seahorse is "multi-colored." (B) similarly uses "multiple colors" after "multi-colored" has already been used. (D)'s "The colors it displays are" is wordy, and also redundantly repeats a form of "color."

7. (C) is the correct answer. It describes St. Elmo's fire without redundancy. (A) uses a wordy "of" construction and the needlessly redundant "fiery fireballs." Since the phenomenon is already called "St. Elmo's fire," it's best not to repeat the word "fire" so much. (B) repeats information stated already; the first clause uses the words, "sailors sometimes see," so there's no need to use "that sailors see" in the second clause. (D) uses "seen on masts" even though the end of the sentence restates the information about masts. It also rather needlessly repeats the word "fire."

8. (B) is the correct answer; the other choices repeat information stated already. (A) repeats, verbatim, the play's abbreviated and full names. (C) is wordily phrased, and also redundant; we know that it was a "1920 play" already. (D) is very wordy and redundant; most plays are written as "performances to be acted in a theatre." While some plays aren't written to be performed, the majority are, so you'd probably only need to elaborate on a play's performance status if it wasn't meant to be acted.

9. (C) is the correct answer. It's the most concise choice of the four. In context, it's clear that "the trains" refer to subway trains. (A) uses a wordy "of the" construction and repeats "subway." (B) is too wordy and once again repeats "subway." (D) repeats "on the subway."

10. (D) is the correct answer. It's the only choice that isn't redundant or wordy. (A) is redundant because it states that the cartoon "is funny and makes people laugh." While these two ideas are not one hundred percent identical, they're quite similar. (B) is even more redundant; "laughter" and "laughing" are basically the same thing. (C), "creates much funniness," is very wordy.

Style and Tone
Part 3

Style and Tone questions ask you to pick the option that maintains the same style and tone as the rest of the passage. Many passages on the SAT are in a formal or journalistic style, but passages can appear in a variety of styles. Certain stylistic elements are usually undesirable: look out for phrases that use weak words and intensifiers, as a single strong word is usually preferable. Also look out for "colloquial" words: those are words that we often use in conversation, but rarely use in formal writing. Some passages on the SAT may be written in a colloquial style, but most will not be.

DIRECTIONS

Every passage comes with a set of questions. Some questions will ask you to consider how the writer might revise the passage to improve the expression of ideas. Other questions will ask you to consider correcting potential errors in sentence structure, usage, or punctuation. There may be one or more graphics that you will need to consult as you revise and edit the passage.

Some questions will refer to a portion of the passage that has been underlined. Other questions will refer to a particular location in a passage or ask that you consider the passage in full.

After you read the passage, select the answers to questions that most effectively improve the passage's writing quality or that adjust the passage to follow the conventions of standard written English. Many questions give you the option to select "NO CHANGE." Select that option in cases where you think the relevant part of the passage should remain as it currently is.

1

Maria has designed a machine-learning algorithm that greatly improves on older algorithms. Her code allows for greater leaps in inductive logic. Using her method, a computer can become <u>a real smartypants</u> in a given task in a short span of time.

A) NO CHANGE

B) really really good

C) super smart

D) highly proficient

2

Four of Shakespeare's most complex, poetically rich, and memorable tragedies—Hamlet, Othello, King Lear, and Macbeth—were written in the space of six years, between 1600 and 1606. However, Shakespeare also wrote an additional five plays during that time. <u>What a busy guy!</u> After 1606, his pace slowed.

A) NO CHANGE

B) I guess you could say he liked to "shake" things up!

C) Maybe the guy just wanted to be famous.

D) OMIT the underlined portion.

Cuttlefish have a somewhat deceptive name, as they are not actually fish. In fact, they are molluscs, closely related to octopuses, nautiluses, and squids. They have a <u>weird</u> shell inside their bodies called the cuttlebone. The cuttlebone helps them maintain their buoyancy.

A) NO CHANGE

B) wacky

C) unique

D) funny little

I haven't always liked trying new foods. When I was a kid, I knew this guy named Bill who liked to eat sunflower seeds while he was watching TV. They came in <u>an indubitably dizzying miscellany</u> of flavors, and he always had a few kinds around. When I went to his house, he wanted me to try them, too. I didn't really want to. I had never had them before, and I was a little bit grossed out by how Bill ate them. He would pop several of them into his mouth with the shells still on, then chew and squish them around for a minute before spitting the shells out into a little bowl.

A) NO CHANGE

B) myriad

C) all sorts of

D) a veritable cornucopia of

5

My friend Michelle likes to show up to things early. I, on the other hand, am usually fashionably late. This often makes it difficult for us to connect, because when I run late Michelle sometimes wanders off to find a nicer spot to wait than the place we planned to meet. Luckily, I can always tell when she has arrived at the beach before me. The soles of her shoes have a really distinct pattern, sort of like a cluster of crescent moons. By following her footprints in the sand, I can <u>determine her position.</u> Once I figured this out, we started meeting at the beach more often.

A) NO CHANGE

B) locate her final resting-place.

C) find where she's waiting.

D) divine her location.

Graphite, the soft, grey mineral used to make pencil leads, is actually a crystalline form of carbon. This means that graphite and diamond are made from the same element—despite their very different appearances and textures. Along with <u>a whole bunch of</u> other forms, graphite and diamond are known as carbon's allotropes. Other carbon allotropes include glassy carbon and the memorably-named buckminsterfullerene.

A) NO CHANGE

B) many

C) loads of

D) a pretty high number of

The main opposition party held about 40% of seats in the state legislature, while the majority party held about 55%, and members of other parties held the remaining seats. It was therefore very unlikely that the majority party would have the required two-thirds majority in order to pass contentious changes to election rules. However, the chairman, a member of the majority party, called for a voice vote instead of a roll-call vote—which meant that individual votes would not be counted. Instead, members of the legislature would be asked to shout "aye" or "nay," and the chairman would decide who won. When he claimed that he had heard a two-thirds majority for "aye," and that the measure would pass, members of the opposition party were absolutely <u>annoyed</u>. They claimed that the vote had been rigged.

A) NO CHANGE

B) miffed

C) ticked off

D) livid

8

Although the messenger hadn't eaten in two days of hard travel and must have been famished, etiquette did not permit him to express such strong feelings to a host of higher rank; when asked if he was hungry, he could only confess to feeling slightly <u>peckish</u>.

A) NO CHANGE

B) ravenous

C) dying of hunger

D) starved

As we ascended the last prominence and rounded the final curve, our formerly boisterous party fell suddenly into a reverent silence as we first observed the <u>pretty</u> spectacle of ancient stone walls rising from the earth, rainbows floating in mists thrown up from cliff-bound rapids, and frothing waters plunging into an abyss of unseen depths below.

A) NO CHANGE

B) lovely

C) awesome

D) very pretty

10

The paper's editorials were normally a little sarcastic, but most readers agreed that in the recent election cycle the tone of the editorials had gone from playful to <u>very mean</u>. They had become so unpleasant that some readers actually cancelled their subscriptions, while many others wrote letters to the editor to complain about the change.

A) NO CHANGE

B) somewhat cranky

C) caustic

D) just evil

1. (D) is the correct answer. The first sentence uses formal, technical language to describe Maria's project. Phrases like "machine-learning algorithm" and "greater leaps in inductive logic" contribute to the paragraph's formal and technical tone. This means that "highly proficient" is the most consistent option of the four. (A) is much too informal; the colloquial phrase "a real smartypants" fits better in more casual settings. (B) is likewise too informal for this passage. The intensifier "really" is not necessarily informal, but it is when it's doubled up as "really really." (C) is also too informal; the intensifier "super" fits best in more casual settings.

2. (D) is the correct answer. None of the other available options are a good idea. Each is too informal for the formal tone established in phrases like "complex, poetically rich, and memorable." (A) uses an informal exclamation and the casual term "guy." (B), with its truly embarrassing pun, is too bad to be believed. (C) also uses the informal term "guy," and makes a speculative claim about Shakespeare's desire for fame that doesn't follow from the preceding sentences.

3. (C) is the correct answer. It maintains the formal tone used elsewhere in the paragraph. We know the tone is formal because we can see long, complex words and phrases like "deceptive" and "maintain their buoyancy." The subject matter is also straightforwardly factual. (A), (B), and (D) are all too informal; they're words that would be more likely to appear in a conversation or an informal piece of writing.

4. (C) is the correct answer. The first sentence takes a very informal tone, referring to Bill as "this guy" and using colloquial phrases like "grossed out." (C), "all sorts," maintains the informality of the first sentence. (A) is much too formal, using language that you'd be more likely to find in an old book. (B) is similarly too formal, and is also much too long. (D) has the merit of being a bit shorter, but it's still too formal for this context.

5. (C) is the correct answer. The other sentences in the paragraph have a casual tone, using informal intensifiers like "really" and "sort of." This makes the simply-phrased "where she's waiting" the most consistent option. (A) uses the more complex multisyllabic phrase "determine her position." (B) is a term more closely associated with burial plots; we can quickly rule it out! (D) also expresses the activity in too stiff and formal a tone.

6. (B) is the correct answer. The passage takes a formal tone, consistent with what you'd expect from nonfiction writing. Note the scientific phrases like "a crystalline form of carbon." The word "many" is consistent with this tone. (A) is too informal; we're more likely to use "a whole bunch" in everyday speech or written dialogue. (C), "loads of," is also too informal. (D) is too informal because it uses the casual intensifier "pretty." It's also not very concise.

7. (D) is the correct answer. In this case your task is to find a word that conveys the appropriate tone in context. The content of the paragraph establishes a scenario in which a majority party appears to manipulate the vote in the legislature, a very serious infraction that would outrage the opposition. The phrase "absolutely livid" is a common and idiomatic way to describe serious rage. (A), "annoyed," understates the situation, as does (B), "miffed," which is additionally too informal. (C), "ticked off," is both too colloquial and an understatement in context.

8. (A) Is the correct answer. In this context, where due to "etiquette" the messenger is not permitted to express strong feelings, "peckish" has the right level of understatement. The (B), (C), and (D) options are all too strongly-worded in context; each word would express the "strong feelings" that the messenger can't voice.

9. (C) is the correct answer. Considering the very high-flown language of the passage as a whole (exemplified by words like "boisterous" and "reverent"), the word "awesome" (here used in its original sense of "awe-inspiring" rather than its more colloquial meaning) is the most appropriate. (A), (B), and (D) all use modest, conversational words that don't fully convey the magnitude of the situation.

10. (C) is the correct answer. It's the least colloquial choice for a passage that's written in a fairly formal voice. The paragraph does use less formal intensifiers like "a little," but in other cases the writer makes more formal choices like "unpleasant" and "sarcastic." (A) and (D) are too informal here because they use the colloquial intensifiers "very" and "just." (B) uses the intensifier "somewhat," which isn't strong enough to fit a context in which readers are cancelling their subscriptions in response to the tone of the editorials.

Clear Sentences
Part 4

Clear Sentences questions ask you to identify the best way of ordering and combining ideas in complex sentences. You will need to select appropriate conjunctions, reduce redundant phrases, and avoid overly-complex sentence structures where simpler sentences can effectively convey the same information. Look out for repeated subjects: when you combine two sentences that share the same subject, you don't necessarily need to name the subject twice.

DIRECTIONS

Every passage comes with a set of questions. Some questions will ask you to consider how the writer might revise the passage to improve the expression of ideas. Some questions will refer to a portion of the passage that has been underlined. Other questions will refer to a particular location in a passage or ask that you consider the passage in full.

After you read the passage, select the answers to questions that most effectively improve the passage's writing quality or that adjust the passage to follow the conventions of standard written English. Many questions give you the option to select "NO CHANGE." Select that option in cases where you think the relevant part of the passage should remain as it currently is.

1

 My grandpa use to love re-telling the same <u>old joke. The old joke was,</u> "You can tune a piano, but you can't tuna fish.".

Which choice most effectively combines the sentences at the underlined portion?

A) old joke:

B) old joke runs there

C) old joke that runs

D) old joke, and the old joke is

2

Members of the public have long been concerned about the potential effects of hydraulic fracturing <u>on water quality. A recent EPA report confirms</u> that wastewater and other byproducts of the process may indeed contaminate water supplies.

Which of the following choices most effectively combines the sentences at the underlined portion?

A) on water quality, a concern that a recent EPA report confirms by stating

B) on water quality, and recently there is a recent EPA report confirming

C) on water quality, confirming a recent EPA report

D) on water quality, and a recent EPA report confirms

The orator delivered a fifty-five minute speech on the importance of peace and respect. The audience devolved into an enormous fistfight.

Which of the following choices most effectively combines the sentences at the underlined portion?

A) peace and respect, yet then the audience devolved

B) peace and respect, but the audience devolved

C) peace and respect; this was followed by the audience's devolution

D) peace and respect, and the orator's speech caused the audience to devolve

4

I thought that was an old school friend walking down the street. When I waved and said hello, I realized it wasn't her.

Which of the following choices most effectively combines the sentences at the underlined portion?

A) street, but when i waved

B) street; I waved

C) street, when I waved

D) street, though it happened that when I waved

Ali gave his mother a new hiking backpack. She is very excited to try it out on the family's next vacation.

Which of the following choices most effectively combines the sentences at the underlined portion?

A) a new hiking backpack, she is very excited

B) a new hiking backpack, but therefore she is very excited

C) a new hiking backpack, when she is very excited

D) a new hiking backpack, and she is very excited

We thought the modem we'd used in Buffalo would also work in Seattle. We were wrong.

Which of the following choices best combines the sentences at the underlined portion?

A) in Seattle, we were wrong.

B) in Seattle, but we were wrong.

C) in Seattle, which was determined to be wrong.

D) in Seattle; in addition, we were wrong.

Last night, as Jan was driving his Stingray around town, a woman in a Jaguar pulled up beside <u>him. She dared him</u> to race her.

Which of the following choices best combines the sentences at the underlined portion?

A) him, and she was daring him

B) him and dared him

C) him, she dared him

D) his Stingray in her Jaguar

8

Jones pulled out his grappling hook and whirled it around his <u>head. He aimed</u> for a tree branch on the other side of the river.

Which of the following choices best combines the sentences at the underlined portion?

A) head as he was aiming

B) head, aiming

C) head and, desiring to hit a tree branch, aimed

D) head, but he aimed

There are several monsters in that <u>room. One of them</u> appears to have a fidget spinner.

A) room, and one of the ones

B) room, one

C) room who

D) room, and one of them

You have to be very careful when you prepare this <u>fish. Parts of it</u> are poisonous.

A) fish: they

B) fish, although its parts

C) fish, as parts of it

D) fish whose parts

1. (A) is the correct answer. It combines the two sentences using a colon in a way that avoids redundancy, an excess of language, or ungrammatical constructions. (B) is incorrect because "old joke runs there" isn't grammatical; it would need a word like "that" to be a complete construction, and even then "runs there" isn't idiomatic. (C) is incorrect because "old joke that runs," while not ungrammatical, is not concise. (D) is incorrect because it's especially redundant; it repeats the words "old joke" twice.

2. (D) is the correct answer. It avoids the errors found in the other choices, namely redundancy and incorrect interpretations of the relationship between the two sentences. (D) recognizes that the two sentences are best joined by a comma and the word "and." The ideas in the two sentences are that, first of all, the public is concerned about hydraulic fracturing, and that, second, the EPA report confirms the validity of those concerns. (A) is incorrect because it uses the word "concern" again and adds "by stating"; the result is both redundant and needlessly verbose. (B) is incorrect because it redundantly repeats a variation of the word "recent." (C) is incorrect because it mixes up the relationship between the two sentences, alleging that the concerns of the public concern the report, not the other way around.

3. (B) is the correct answer. It uses the appropriate conjunction and avoids redundancy or wordiness, The word "but" indicates a contrast, which in context make sense here. The speaker talked about peace and respect, so the audience's fighting is a contrasting idea. (A) is incorrect because "yet then" is needlessly wordy. "Yet" on its own would have been acceptable, though. (C) is incorrect because it is also too wordy. (D) is likewise too wordy.

4. (A) is the correct answer. It's the only option that doesn't contain grammatical errors or wordiness. The sentence needs a conjunction that shows a contrast, so "but" is the ideal choice. (B) is incorrect because it creates a comma splice; both "I waved and said hello" and "I realized it wasn't her" are independent clauses, meaning that they can't be joined with a comma alone. (C) is incorrect because it likewise creates a comma splice. Both "I thought that was an old school friend walking down the street" and "When I waved and said hello, I realized it wasn't her" are complete sentences, once again meaning that they can't be joined with a comma alone. (D) does use a conjunction, "though," but it is also very wordy, making it incorrect.

5. (D) is the correct answer. These sentences suggest a continuation of ideas, so "and" is correct. (A) is incorrect because it creates a comma splice; the two clauses are independent and thus need to be joined with something more than a comma.(B) is incorrect because it is needlessly wordy, but also confusingly begins to suggest a contrast using "but." (C) is incorrect because "when" doesn't suggest a continuation of ideas.

6. (B) is the correct answer. It uses "but" to indicate a contrast in ideas. (A) is incorrect because it creates a comma splice. (C) is incorrect because it is too wordy. (D) is likewise too wordy, needlessly using a heavy-duty semicolon and adding "in addition."

7. (B) is the correct answer. It combines the sentences concisely and without errors. (A) is incorrect because it is too wordy and removes the parallelism by adding "was" and using "daring." (C) is incorrect because it creates a comma splice. (D) is redundant because it repeats the makes of the cars.

8. (B) is the correct answer. It concisely makes clear what Jones aimed his grappling hook at. (A) is incorrect because it is too wordy. (C) is even wordier than A. (D) uses an illogical conjunction. "But" implies a contrast between ideas, but this sentence describes two parts of an action that occur in unison and make sense together.

9. (D) is the correct answer. It joins the two sentences using a comma and the word "and." (A) is redundant as it uses the words "one of the ones." (B) is incorrect because it creates a comma splice. (C) is incorrect because it creates an agreement error with "monsters...who appears."

10. (C) is the correct answer. It combines the sentences with a comma and "as," indicating that the second clause offers a reason for the first one. (A) is incorrect because it substitutes the pronoun "they" for "parts," suggesting all of the fish are poisonous and omitting important information. (B) is incorrect because it indicates a contrast in ideas rather than a continuation. (D) is incorrect because it fails to express the logical relationship between the two parts of the sentence. The idea that you need to be careful and the idea that some parts of the fish aren't just two things that both happen to be true: one is the reason for the other.

Ivy Global

Section 4
Sentence Structure

Sentence Structure questions test your ability to correct sentence-level grammatical errors. You'll need to recognize and correct fragments and run-ons, features of a sentence that should remain consistent or parallel in different parts of the sentence, and misplaced elements.

Sentence Structure questions contribute to the "Standard English Conventions" subscore.

There are 6 specific question types in this domain:

Sentence Structure			
SB	Making Whole Sentences and Avoiding run-ons	SM	Where to Put Descriptive Phrases
SS	Joining Sentences with Conjunctions	SV	Matching Verbs
SP	Matching Sentence Structures	SN	Matching Nouns

Making Whole Sentences and Avoiding Run-Ons
Part 1

Making Whole Sentences and Avoiding Run-Ons questions ask you to correct run-on sentences and sentence fragments by joining or dividing sentences and clauses, or by changing the way they're joined or divided

---

DIRECTIONS

Every passage comes with a set of questions. Some questions will ask you to consider how the writer might revise the passage to improve the expression of ideas. Some questions will refer to a portion of the passage that has been underlined. Other questions will refer to a particular location in a passage or ask that you consider the passage in full.

After you read the passage, select the answers to questions that most effectively improve the passage's writing quality or that adjust the passage to follow the conventions of standard written English. Many questions give you the option to select "NO CHANGE." Select that option in cases where you think the relevant part of the passage should remain as it currently is.

1

The chess coach explained how to set up the board. Also how to psyche out an opponent.

A) NO CHANGE

B) board, also

C) board. She also explained

D) board. And also how

2

The bandanas he makes can be used as napkins, they aren't napkins though, they are bandanas.

A) NO CHANGE

B) napkins; they aren't napkins, though, they

C) napkins. They aren't napkins, though; they

A) napkins, they aren't napkins though; they

3

Jack is great at video <u>games. Even though</u> he is blind in one eye.

A) NO CHANGE

B) games even though

C) games even, though

D) games, even though

4

My family has always lived on <u>the farm. Since those</u> first five acres were bought before the Civil War.

A) NO CHANGE

B) the farm, since those

C) the farm; since those

D) the farm since those

5

Last winter our teacher broke <u>her arm and</u> missed almost a month of school.

A) NO CHANGE

B) her arm; and she

C) her arm, and she

D) her arm, she

6

My favorite musical <u>is *The Sound of Music* it has</u> everything you want: romance, thrills, and a happy ending.

A) NO CHANGE

B) is *The Sound of Music*. It has

C) is *The Sound of Music*, it has

D) is: *The Sound of Music*; it has

7

We all loved playing that video <u>game—even the youngest kids, who</u> could barely understand what the controls actually did.

A) NO CHANGE

B) game. Even the youngest kids, who

C) game—and even the youngest kids who

D) game, even the youngest kids. Who

8

Steve argued with her even though she was agreeing with <u>him it</u> seemed like habit.

A) NO CHANGE

B) him, it

C) him and it

D) him. It

9

When she explained how to use the new <u>application; she</u> also taught us how to transfer data from the old application.

A) NO CHANGE

B) application. She

C) application, she

D) application she

10

It's safer to write in <u>complete sentences. Containing</u> subjects and verbs.

A) NO CHANGE

B) complete sentences containing

C) complete sentences; containing

D) complete sentences: containing

11

The CEO is a very nice <u>woman. Doesn't</u> stop her from making difficult business decisions.

A) NO CHANGE

B) woman; doesn't

C) woman, doesn't

D) woman. That doesn't

12

One of the first ads for the product <u>was launched on Sunday night and no one saw it,</u> because they were watching the shooting stars.

A) NO CHANGE

B) was launched. On Sunday night; no one saw it,

C) was launched on Sunday night, and no one saw it

D) was launched. On Sunday night, and no one saw it

13

It is hot <u>out. Over</u> 100 degrees, with the heat index.

A) NO CHANGE

B) out! Over

C) out; over

D) out. It is over

14

Harriet's mother <u>didn't work, unless one</u> could call belonging to the country club a job.

A) NO CHANGE

B) didn't work. Unless one

C) didn't work, one

D) didn't work! Unless one

15

The job was actually fairly simple. Examining and labeling the contents of abandoned suitcases.

A) NO CHANGE

B) fairly simple: examining and labeling

C) fairly simple. Examining, and labeling,

D) fairly simple; examining and labeling

16

Why should we spend time planting vegetables, we have: farmers markets and grocery stores.

A) NO CHANGE

B) vegetables? We have

C) vegetables we have:

D) vegetables we have;

17

My science class is amazing. Because our teacher allows us to do interesting experiments outside.

A) NO CHANGE

B) amazing because: our

C) amazing, our

D) amazing because our

18

It's tragedy when I fall down an entire flight of stairs, but it's comedy when you fall down an entire flight of stairs.

A) NO CHANGE

B) stairs but it's comedy

C) stairs, it's comedy

D) stairs: but it's comedy

19

My family loves all the S-word winter sports. Snowboarding Skiing Skating

A) NO CHANGE

B) sports: snowboarding, skiing, and skating

C) sports. Snowboarding, skiing, and skating

D) sports, snowboarding and skiing. And skating!

Answers & Explanations

1. (C) is the correct answer. In this case, the only way to correct the sentence fragment is by adding a subject and a verb. (A) is not correct because it contains the original error. (B) is not the correct option because merely inserting a comma creates a comma splice. (D) is not correct because the additional words do not correct the fragment.

2. (C) is the correct answer. This example is composed of three independent clauses; this choice uses a period to separate two of them and a semicolon to separate the other two, which are both correct punctuation marks to use for that purpose. Also, it correctly uses a comma to set off "though", an adverb modifying the phrase "they aren't napkins". (A) incorrectly connects all three clauses with commas, creating a long comma splice, and also leaves out the comma preceding "though". (B) correctly uses a semicolon to connect the first two clauses, but uses a comma after "though" to connect the second two, creating a comma splice. (D) flips that mistake and also leaves out the comma before "though".

3. (B) is the correct answer. It corrects the fragmented clause beginning with the phrase "Even though" by combining it with the rest of the sentence. (A) is not correct because the "Even though" is a subordinating conjunction, indicating that this is not a standalone sentence. (C) is not correct because the comma is inserted at the wrong point in the sentence. (D) is tempting, but it is incorrect because the comma is unnecessary.

4. (D) is the correct answer. It provides the best correction of the sentence fragment. (A) is not correct because the the phrase beginning with "Since" is a subordinating conjunction that lacks a subject so the phrase cannot stand alone as a sentence. (B) is not correct because the comma is unnecessary. (C) is incorrect because the phrase beginning with "Since" is not an independent clause so the semicolon is unnecessary.

5. (A) is the correct answer. When a sentence contains two clauses connected by "and", a comma is only appropriate before the "and" if the two clauses have different subjects. (B) and (C) both incorrectly add punctuation before "and," creating a comma splice and a fragment after the semicolon respectively. (D) adds a comma and omits "and," creating a comma splice.

6. (B) is the correct answer. It uses a period to separate two complete sentences. (A) does not separate these sentences at all, creating a run-on sentence. (C) incorrectly uses a comma to join the sentences, creating a comma splice. (D) incorrectly inserts a colon between a verb, "is", and its predicate, "The Sound of Music".

7. (A) is the correct answer. It correctly uses an em-dash to join an independent clause with a noun clause that expands on the independent clause's meaning. (B), by separating these clauses with a period, creates one complete sentence and one fragment. (C) adds "and" after the dash, which would only be correct if what followed "and" were an independent clause; since what follows is a noun clause, the sentence as a whole becomes ungrammatical. (D), by adding a period after "kids", creates a fragment after the period.

8. (D) is the correct answer. It correctly separates two independent clauses with a period. (A) does not use any punctuation to join these clauses, creating a run-on sentence. (B) incorrectly joins these two clauses with a comma, creating a comma splice. (C) is incorrect because, when joining two independent clauses with different subjects, a comma is necessary before the "and".

9. (C) is the correct answer. It correctly uses a comma to join a dependent and an independent clause. (A) incorrectly uses a semicolon, which can only be used to join two independent clauses. (B) incorrectly uses a period, which creates one fragment and one complete sentence. (D) does not use any punctuation at all, creating a run-on sentence.

10. (B) is the correct answer. It fixes the sentence fragment by joining all of the parts of the sentence without any unnecessary punctuation. (A) creates the sentence fragment, so it is not correct. (C) and (D) incorrectly attempt to fix the fragment by inserting incorrect punctuation marks.

11. (D) is the correct answer. It correctly inserts a pronoun as a subject to correct the sentence fragment. (A) creates the sentence fragment. (B) and (C) are not correct because neither corrects the problem of the missing subject in the subordinate clause.

12. (C) is the correct answer. It correctly uses a comma before "and" to join two complete sentences that have different subjects. (A) incorrectly omits the comma. (B) and (D) incorrectly insert a comma between the verb "was launched" and "on Sunday night," an adverbial phrase modifying it; this does not make sense and also creates a fragment after the period. (B) makes an additional error by inserting a semicolon after "On Sunday night" even though that phrase cannot stand on its own as a sentence.

13. (D) is the correct answer. The best way to repair the fragment is by revising to create two complete sentences. (A) is incorrect because the phrase starting with "Over" lacks a verb and a subject. (B) is incorrect because simply changing the punctuation for the first sentence does not fix the fragment. (C) is incorrect because inserting a semicolon does not fix the the fragment.

14. (A) is the correct answer. Here, the subordinate clause is correctly joined with the rest of the sentence. (B) and (D) are not correct because, in both cases, the punctuation turns the subordinate clause into a sentence fragment. (C) is not correct because the lack of punctuation creates a run-on sentence.

15. (B) is the correct answer. Because it lacks a subject and a verb, the phrase beginning with "Examining" is a fragment, not a sentence. (B) joins the fragment to the preceding sentence. (A) and (C) do not fix the fragment. (D) incorrectly uses a semicolon to join an independent clause and a phrase.

16. (B) is the correct answer. It uses a question mark at the end of a sentence and does not insert any inappropriate punctuation between the verb "have" and its predicate. (A) combines two independent clauses with a comma, creating a comma splice, and inserts a colon between "have" and its predicate. (C) and (D) both fail to use any punctuation to separate two independent clauses, creating run-on sentences, and both incorrectly insert punctuation between the verb "have" and its predicate.

17. (D) is the correct answer. There is no need to insert punctuation between "amazing" and "because." (A) and (B) are not correct because the punctuation creates sentence fragments. (C) is not the correct answer because the use of a comma creates a comma splice.

18. (A) is the correct answer. It joins two independent clauses with a comma and a coordinating conjunction (in this case, "but"). (B) incorrectly omits the comma, creating a run-on sentence. (C) omits the coordinating conjunction, creating a comma splice. (D) incorrectly uses a colon to join an independent clause and what is effectively a dependent clause (since it begins with "but").

19. (B) is the correct answer. It inserts a colon to introduce the list of S-word winter sports, thereby correcting the fragment in the original sentence. (A) is not correct because the list of sports is a series of sentence fragments. (C) is not the correct answer because introducing a list is a misuse of the semicolon. (D) is not correct because "Skating" is still a sentence fragment.

Joining Sentences with Conjunctions
Part 2

Joining Sentences with Conjunctions questions require you to recognize errors of subordination and coordination. They may require you to delete conjunctions between clauses when the first clause already includes a subordinating conjunction, determine whether a coordinating or subordinating conjunction is required to join two clauses, avoid creating run-on sentences by inserting subordinating conjunctions or relative pronouns, or avoid creating fragments by compounding coordinating and subordinating conjunctions.

DIRECTIONS

Every passage comes with a set of questions. Some questions will ask you to consider how the writer might revise the passage to improve the expression of ideas. Some questions will refer to a portion of the passage that has been underlined. Other questions will refer to a particular location in a passage or ask that you consider the passage in full.

After you read the passage, select the answers to questions that most effectively improve the passage's writing quality or that adjust the passage to follow the conventions of standard written English. Many questions give you the option to select "NO CHANGE." Select that option in cases where you think the relevant part of the passage should remain as it currently is.

1

There was a little too much going on this morning; the phone rang when I was just getting up to brew coffee. After the phone rang, before the doorbell rang.

A) NO CHANGE

B) After the phone rang, the doorbell rang.

C) After the phone rang, due to the fact that the doorbell rang.

D) Before the phone rang, after the doorbell rang.

2

After Ken's appearance on television, since everyone wanted his red sweater. It has has completely sold out at Izod.

A) NO CHANGE

B) Ken's appearance on television, since everyone

C) Ken's appearance on television, everyone

D) After Ken's appearance on television, everyone wanted

3

If <u>reaches</u> the island before the rainy season, Gilbert will sit on the beach all day.

A) NO CHANGE

B) reaching

C) reach

D) he reaches

4

<u>The French fries are finished frying</u>, we can share them. I'll even let you have the bigger plate!

A) NO CHANGE

B) As soon as the French fries are finished frying, once

C) Once the French fries are finished frying, so

D) As soon as the French fries are finished frying,

5

The rubber trees are growing <u>quickly we</u> tried that new fertilizer. It's much better than the fertilizer we used to use.

A) NO CHANGE

B) quickly since we

C) quickly, we

D) quickly, however, we

6

Luz put a long exposure on her camera so that <u>would capture</u> the stars appearing to move across the sky.

A) NO CHANGE

B) capturing

C) it would capture

D) captures

7

Where <u>smoking,</u> there's fire.

A) NO CHANGE

B) there's smoke,

C) smoke,

D) the smoking

8

Although <u>meeting</u> once at a dinner party, James Joyce and Marcel Proust did not exactly hit it off.

A) NO CHANGE

B) met

C) they met

D) their meeting

9

You can't go to the Museum of Natural History unless <u>clean</u> your room.

A) NO CHANGE

B) you clean

C) cleaning

D) cleaned

10

Noura's puppy is called Jake because <u>watching</u> *Adventure Time* when her father brought him home.

A) NO CHANGE

B) watched

C) was watching

D) she was watching

11

Even though <u>gets</u> on everybody's nerves, I am keeping this ringtone.

A) NO CHANGE

B) getting

C) get

D) it gets

12

Lex Luthor always blocks the way to the upstairs part of the bus, even <u>when fill</u> up with people.

A) NO CHANGE

B) when it fills

C) it fills

D) fill

13

Lex Luthor pushes the elevator's "close" button if <u>seeing</u> someone trying to get in.

A) NO CHANGE

B) he sees

C) see

D) OMIT the underlined portion

14

Because <u>has</u> such original ideas, Sara is a sought-after scriptwriter.

A) NO CHANGE

B) having

C) she has

D) has had

15

During Eisenhower's tenure at the White House, while he barbecued on the roof.

A) NO CHANGE

B) barbecuing

C) since he barbecued

D) he barbecued

16

Although the sailors were very tired, because the storm was finally over and no one was hurt.

A) NO CHANGE

B) when the storm

C) the storm

D) while the storm

17

While all locusts are grasshoppers, when not all grasshoppers are locusts.

A) NO CHANGE

B) even though

C) since

D) OMIT the underlined portion

18

Because it's unusually dark outside, because the sun goes down early at this latitude.

A) NO CHANGE

B) Since it's unusually dark outside,

C) It's unusually dark outside

D) The reason it's unusually dark outside

1. (B) is the correct answer. There are two clauses in this sentence, but only one of them should be subordinate. This choice correctly uses a single subordinating conjunction on the first clause. (A), (C), and (D) all use two conjunctions.

2. (D) is the correct answer. The phrase "Ken's appearance on television" doesn't contain a verb. (D) correctly uses the word "after" to subordinate this phrase to the following clause as a description of when it occurs. (A) incorrectly places a conjunction in front of the clause the phrase modifies. (B) only uses a conjunction before the second part of the sentence, but the first phrase can't actually stand as a clause on its own. (C) omits all conjunctions, which is incorrect for the same reason as (B).

3. (D) is the correct answer. It provides the dependent clause with a needed subject, "he." (A), (B), and (C) all lack a subject. Remember that every clause needs a subject and a verb.

4. (D) is the correct answer. The second clause of this sentence doesn't begin with a conjunction, so in order to join these with only a comma we need a subordinating conjunction in front of the first clause. (A) is incorrect because it creates a run-on sentence. (B) and (C) are incorrect because they use too many conjunctions.

5. (B) is the correct answer. It correctly uses a subordinating conjunction to connect the two clauses. (A) is incorrect because it is a run-on sentence. (C) is incorrect because it joins two independent clauses using only a comma. (D) is incorrect because it uses a conjunctive adverb in place of a conjunction.

6. (C) is the correct answer. It provides the clause with the required subject, "it" (that is, Luz's camera). (A), (B), and (D) all fail to provide the needed subject for the clause.

7. (B) is the correct answer. It provides the clause with its required verb, "is," and takes "smoke" as its subject. The other options fail to provide either a verb or a subject. (A) uses "smoking," which might seem acceptable, but remember that it's not a verb in that form; -ing words usually function as either adjectives or nouns. (C), "smoke," could function as a verb, but in that case you'd also need a subject. (D), much like (A), lacks a verb.

8. (C) is the correct answer. It gives the clause a subject, "they," and a verb, "met." (A)'s "meeting" doesn't function as a verb, and even if it were to be taken as a noun here, the clause lacks any other suitable verbs. (B)'s "met" is an appropriate verb, but the clause still lacks a subject. (D) also does not have a verb.

9. (B) is the correct answer. It gives the clause its required subject, "you." (A), "clean," lacks a subject. (C)'s "cleaning" could serve as a subject, but in that case you'd still need a verb. (D), "cleaned," lacks a subject.

10. (D) is the correct answer. It provides the clause with a subject, "she," and a verb phrase, "was watching." (A)'s "watching" doesn't function as a verb, and even if it did you'd still need a subject. (B) lacks a subject. (C) has an appropriate verb phrase, "was watching," but still needs a subject.

11. (D) is the correct answer. It provides a suitable subject, "it," and a verb, "gets." (A) lacks a subject; we can't tell who or what "gets on everybody's nerves." (B) lacks a coherent subject and verb; "getting" most frequently serves as part of an adjective or noun phrase. (C), "get," lacks a subject.

12. (B) is the correct answer. It includes the necessary subordinating conjunction "when" after "even." It also adds a required subject, "it," and verb, "fills." (A) lacks a subject, and it uses a form of "fill" that suggests a plural rather than a singular one. (C) lacks a subordinating conjunction. (D) likewise lacks such a conjunction, and it needs a subject too.

13. (B) is the correct answer. It provides a subject, "I," and a verb, "see." (A) doesn't have a coherent subject or verb; "seeing" almost always serves as part of an adjective or noun phrase. (C) lacks a subject. (D) is nearly acceptable, but "someone trying to get in" still lacks a verb.

14. (C) is the correct answer. The clause receives a subject from "she" and a verb from "has." (A) lacks a subject. (B)'s "having" doesn't provide an adequate verb or a subject. (D), "has had," also lacks a subject.

15. (D) is the correct answer. The sentence begins with a subordinating conjunction, so the first clause is a subordinate clause. No additional conjunction is necessary to join these clauses, so omitting the conjunction is correct. (A) and (C) are incorrect because they all add unnecessary conjunctions. (B) is incorrect because it uses the gerund form of "barbecue," which actually turns the sentence into a fragment.

16. (C) is the correct answer. The sentence begins with a subordinating conjunction, so the first clause is a subordinate clause. No additional conjunction is necessary to join these clauses. (A), (B), and (D) are all incorrect because they all add unnecessary conjunctions.

17. (D) is the correct answer. The sentence begins with a subordinating conjunction, so the first clause is a subordinate clause. No additional conjunction is necessary to join these clauses, so omitting the conjunction is correct. (A), (B), and (D) are all incorrect because they all add unnecessary conjunctions.

18. (C) is the correct answer. The second clause of this sentence begins with a conjunction. (A) and (C) are incorrect because they unnecessarily begin the sentence with a conjunction. (D) is incorrect because it removes the verb from the first clause, making the whole sentence a fragment.

Matching Sentence Structures
Part 3

Matching Sentence Structure questions ask you to make sure that different parts of a sentence or paragraph have the same structure when they need to. They may require you to match the grammatical structures of two clauses or phrases in a direct comparison or several items in a list. They may also require you to look out for correlative conjunction pairs like "not only … but also" and ensure that grammatical relationships match across the connected phrases and that there aren't any extra or missing pronouns or prepositions.

DIRECTIONS

Every passage comes with a set of questions. Some questions will ask you to consider how the writer might revise the passage to improve the expression of ideas. Some questions will refer to a portion of the passage that has been underlined. Other questions will refer to a particular location in a passage or ask that you consider the passage in full.

After you read the passage, select the answers to questions that most effectively improve the passage's writing quality or that adjust the passage to follow the conventions of standard written English. Many questions give you the option to select "NO CHANGE." Select that option in cases where you think the relevant part of the passage should remain as it currently is.

1

After a long vacation, Sharon likes <u>unpacking her bags, do her laundry, and sleeping</u> in her own bed.

A) NO CHANGE

B) unpacking her bags, does her laundry, and sleeps

C) unpack her bags, do her laundry, and sleep

D) unpacking her bags, doing her laundry, and sleeping

2

There are a number of ways to annotate a text, including: <u>highlighting, underline with a pen or pencil, and make notes</u> in the margins.

A) NO CHANGE

B) highlight, underlining with a pen or pencil, and make notes

C) highlighting, underlining with a pen or pencil, and making notes

D) highlighting, underlining with a pen or pencil, and make notes

3

When we went out for dinner, my grandmother loves to order a seafood tower, including mussels, oysters, shrimp, and clams.

A) NO CHANGE

B) loves to ordering

C) loved ordering

D) loved to ordering

4

Either we go to Europe or we don't go on vacation at all.

A) NO CHANGE

B) Europe nor

C) Europe but

D) Europe and

5

Not only did she lasso the goat on the first try but she also saves the rodeo clown!

A) NO CHANGE

B) but she will also save

C) and she also saved

D) but she also saved

6

For a team to be successful, teamwork is necessary; another requirement is individual effort.

A) NO CHANGE

B) individual effort is also required.

C) another requirement is individual effort.

D) individuals are also required to make an effort.

7

Whether you love sports or giving them a thumbs down, you must acknowledge that they are popular.

A) NO CHANGE

B) or give

C) or gives

D) or gave

8

Sadie realized that trying to plan the party was sort of like she tries to herd cats, so she gave up.

A) NO CHANGE

B) like she had tried to herd cats

C) like trying to herd cats

D) like trying to herding cats

9

Because Jerry couldn't afford to pay anyone, he made sure to provide lots of pastries, warm beverages, <u>and hand out ponchos.</u>

A) NO CHANGE

B) and that he handed out ponchos.

C) and handing-out of ponchos.

D) and ponchos.

10

Da Vinci was not only a prolific artist, <u>but also</u> a prolific inventor.

A) NO CHANGE

B) but he was

C) also being

D) he was also

11

Don't forget to <u>clean the tables, windowsills, and make the countertops clean.</u>

A) NO CHANGE

B) clean the tables, the windowsills, and make the countertops clean.

C) clean the tables, windowsills, and countertops.

D) clean the tables, clean the windowsills, and make the countertops clean.

12

Josephine <u>can pilot a ship, fly a plane, and she can drive a hovercraft.</u>

A) NO CHANGE

B) can pilot a ship, she can fly a plane, and drive a hovercraft.

C) can pilot a ship, fly a plane, and drive a hovercraft.

D) can pilot a ship, fly a plane, and a hovercraft.

13

We're <u>planning to grab a quick dinner and on dancing</u> at the Italo Disco Revival Night.

A) NO CHANGE

B) planning to grab a quick dinner and dance

C) planning on grabbing a quick dinner and to dance

D) planning to grab a quick dinner and then on dancing

14

The doctor <u>is a funny person, and who is good at making people feel relaxed.</u>

A) NO CHANGE

B) is funny and good at making people feel relaxed.

C) is funny, and whom is good at making people feel relaxed.

D) is funny and a person who is good at making people feel relaxed.

15

Shakespeare's plays draw from <u>classical, historical, and contemporary sources.</u>

A) NO CHANGE

B) classical sources, sources that are historical, and contemporary ones.

C) classical, historical, and sources that are contemporary.

D) classical sources, and historical and contemporary sources.

16

The main difference between dogs and cats is that dogs love you <u>and the feeling cats have for you is hate.</u>

A) NO CHANGE

B) and you are hated by cats.

C) and cats hate you.

D) and the difference is that cats hate you.

17

The benefits of the post-2008 recovery have been unequally distributed: most of the gains have gone to the highest earners, while <u>people who earn less</u> have seen next to no increase in income.

A) NO CHANGE

B) the lowest earners

C) earners on the low end

D) the other people who earn less

18

I've been having terrible internet problems lately: slow connections, long load times, and <u>laggy video calls.</u>

A) NO CHANGE

B) my video calls have been so laggy

C) lagginess in my video calls

D) video calls are also lagging

1. The correct answer is (D). It keeps each of the things Sharon does in the -ing form of the gerund phrase. (A) incorrectly uses two -ing words along with "do." (B) uses one -ing word along with two present-tense verbs; this doesn't preserve parallelism, and it also doesn't agree grammatically with "likes." (C) uses words that don't agree with "likes."

2. The correct answer is (C), because the ways of annotating are all expressed using the -ing form of the gerund phrase. (A), (B), and (D) do not not maintain the parallel structure.

3. The correct answer is (C) which maintains the use of the past tense, preserving the parallel structure. (A) incorrectly uses the present tense when referring to the grandmother's love of ordering the seafood tower. (B) repeats the error in (A) and creates a new error by using the gerund form with "to." (D) correctly uses the past tense, "loved," but creates an error by using the -ing form with "to."

4. The correct answer is (A) because it maintains the parallel structure of the paired correlative conjunctions of "either/ or." (B) incorrectly pairs "either" with "nor," disrupting the parallelism. (C) is incorrect because it pairs "either" and "but." (D) is incorrect because it pairs "either" with "and."

5. The correct answer is (D) which maintains the parallel structure by using the past tense throughout and the conjunction "but" which parallels the phrase "Not only did she". (A) is not correct because the present tense phrase "but she also saves" does not agree with the past tense "did she." (B) is not correct because the use of the future progressive "will also save" disagrees with the past tense. (C) is not correct because the conjunction "and" is not parallel with the phrase "Not only did she".

6. The correct answer is (B). Using "required" maintains the parallel structure begun by "is necessary"—both words are formed as adjectives. (A) turns "required" into the noun "requirement," as does (C). (D) does use "required," but next to "is another" this isn't grammatical.

7. (B) is correct. It maintains the parallel structure by forming "give" in the present-tense, second person form begun by "you love." (A) breaks the parallelism by forming "give" in the present-progressive tense, "giving." (C) doesn't agree grammatically with "you." (D) uses the past tense, so it's also incorrect.

8. The correct answer is (C) which maintains the parallel structure of verb tenses. (A), (B), and (D) are incorrect because each of them disrupts the parallel structure by mixing verb tenses.

9. The correct answer is (D) which maintains the parallel grammatical form for all the items in the series of things Jerry gave instead of money. (A) is not correct because the singular poncho is not parallel with the plural pastries and beverages. (B) is incorrect because it repeats the error created in (A) and "or" is the incorrect coordinating conjunction. (C) correctly creates a parallel between the plural pastries, beverages, and ponchos but it is incorrect because "but" is the incorrect coordinating conjunction.

10. The correct answer is (A) because the correlative conjunction "not only...but also" connects the two noun phrases: "a prolific artist" and "a prolific inventor." (B) is incorrect because the correlative conjunction is disrupted by mixing "not only" and "or also". (C) is incorrect because it mixes "not only" with "and also" to disrupt the parallel structure. (D) is incorrect because "but" is not a correlative conjunction.

11. The correct answer is (C). The verb "clean" applies to a list of several things that the sentence is reminding us to clean, so we don't need to repeat it. (A) is incorrect because adding the verb phrase "make the countertops clean" makes the list non-parallel. (B) is incorrect for the same reason. It just also includes an extra article. (D) is incorrect because, although it adds verb phrases to all three items, it uses identical verbs for the first two and unnecessarily uses a different verb to express the same idea in the third.

12. The correct answer is (C). This sentence requires several different verbs to describe the ways Josephine can use different vehicles, and (C) correctly uses a list of three parallel verb phrases. (A) is incorrect because the redundant phrase "she can" makes the list non-parallel. (B) is incorrect because using the phrase "she can" in the second item but not the third makes the list non-parallel. If the third item read "and she can drive a hovercraft," the sentence would be a little too wordy, but it would also be parallel. (D) is incorrect because it leaves out a verb in the third phrase in the list, making the list non-parallel. If we wanted to use a single verb, we could write "can pilot a ship, a plane, and a hovercraft," but if we want to use more than one verb then we have to use a verb for each item.

13. The correct answer is (B). The phrases "planning to" uses the word "to" to make two other phrases infinitive, and this choice places them both in forms that fit the phrase: "planning to grab a quick dinner" and "planning to ... dance". (A) is incorrect because the gerund "dancing" isn't in the right form to become an infinitive, so it isn't parallel with the other phrase. (C) and (D) are both incorrect because it mixes non-parallel prepositional and infinitive phrases.

14. The correct answer is (B). This sentence describes the doctor in two ways, and this option correctly uses forms that follow the verb "is" in logical and parallel ways: the adjectives "funny" and "good." (A) is incorrect because the phrase "who is good" isn't parallel with the phrase "is a funny person." (C) is incorrect for the same reason: replacing the word "who" with "whom" doesn't make the sentence parallel. (D) is incorrect because it uses a long, wordy noun modifier ("a person who is") that is not parallel with the adjective "funny."

15. The correct answer is (A). The words "classical, historical, and contemporary" are all adjectives describing different kinds of "sources." (B) is incorrect because it rearranges the syntax of the three phrases in non-parallel ways, shifting the adjective in the second item and replacing the word "sources" with a pronoun in only one out of the three phrases. (C) is incorrect because it makes the word "sources" part of the list, so the other two words in the list are on the same level, although they are supposed to describe "sources." (D) is incorrect because it turns what should be a simple three-item list into a list of a single item plus a compound item that includes two other items. This puts the items on different, non-parallel levels of organization.

16. The correct answer is (C). The phrase "dogs hate you" has a simple subject-verb-object structure. This choice uses the phrase "cats hate you," which has the same simple subject-verb-object structure. (A) is incorrect because it uses a passive-voice structure that makes "feeling" (not "cats") pragmatically parallel with "dogs." (B) is incorrect because it uses a passive-voice structure that makes "you" (not "cats") grammatically parallel with "dogs." (D) is incorrect because the phrase "the difference is" is both redundant and non-parallel.

17. The correct answer is (B). The phrase "the lowest earners" is grammatically parallel to "the highest earners." (A), (C), and (D) are all incorrect because they use non-parallel grammatical structures to express the same idea.

18. The correct answer is (A). Each item in this list is an adjective and a noun or noun phrase: "slow (adj.) connections (n.), long (adj.) load times (n. phrase), and laggy (adj.) video calls (n. phrase)." (B) is incorrect because it changes the last item to a whole independent clause, which doesn't fit in a simple adjective-noun list. (C) is incorrect because it changes the phrase to a form that starts with a noun ("lagginess"). (D) is incorrect for the same reason as (B): it turns the final item into an independent clause.

Where to Put Descriptive Phrases

Part 4

Where to Put Descriptive Phrases questions ask you to avoid and correct misplaced modifiers. You may need to move a modifying clause to a different location in the sentence or rearrange the words within a clause to ensure that modifiers are adjacent to appropriate objects, including cases in which you need to rearrange objects rather than modifiers.

DIRECTIONS

Every passage comes with a set of questions. Some questions will refer to a portion of the passage that has been underlined. Other questions will refer to a particular location in a passage or ask that you consider the passage in full.

After you read the passage, select the answers to questions that most effectively improve the passage's writing quality or that adjust the passage to follow the conventions of standard written English. Many questions give you the option to select "NO CHANGE." Select that option in cases where you think the relevant part of the passage should remain as it currently is.

1

While climbing the Empire State Building, the airplanes attacked King Kong.

A) NO CHANGE

B) The airplanes attacked King Kong while climbing the Empire State Building.

C) While being attacked by airplanes, the Empire State Building was being climbed by King Kong.

D) While climbing the Empire State Building, King Kong was attacked by the airplanes.

2

Following a strict color palette, Carol Ann's garden looked like a painting when she planted the annuals.

A) NO CHANGE

B) Carol Ann's garden looked like a painting when she planted the annuals following a strict color palette.

C) When she planted the annuals, Carol Ann's garden looked like a painting following a strict color palette.

D) Following a strict color palette when she planted the annuals, Carol Ann's garden looked like a painting.

Sunburnt, dehydrated, and tottering with exhaustion, the floorboards creaked in the old saloon as the cowboys staggered in.

A) NO CHANGE

B) Sunburnt, dehydrated, and tottering with exhaustion, the cowboys staggered into the old saloon, the floorboards creaking under them.

C) Sunburnt, dehydrated, and tottering with exhaustion, the cowboys' footsteps creaked on the old saloon floorboards as they staggered in.

D) The cowboys staggered into the old saloon, the floorboards creaking, sunburnt, dehydrated, and tottering with exhaustion.

A pillar of the community, we deeply admire Mr. Brent's neighborliness.

A) NO CHANGE

B) A pillar of the community, Mr. Brent's neighborliness is deeply admired.

C) We deeply admire Mr. Brent's neighborliness, a pillar of the community.

D) We deeply admire the neighborliness of Mr. Brent, a pillar of the community.

5

Carefully balanced on top of the door, she dumped the bucket of ice-cold water on herself when she walked in the room.

A) NO CHANGE

B) Carefully balanced on top of the door, the bucket of ice-cold water dumped over her when she walked in the room.

C) She dumped the bucket of ice-cold water on herself when she walked in the room, carefully balanced on top of the door.

D) The bucket of ice-cold water dumped over her when she walked in the room, carefully balanced on top of the door.

6

After driving for ten hours, the campground was still miles away. Dad pulled onto the shoulder and started to cry.

A) NO CHANGE

B) The campground was still miles away after driving for ten hours. Dad pulled onto the shoulder and started to cry.

C) After driving for ten hours, Dad pulled onto the shoulder and started to cry. The campground was still miles away.

D) Dad pulled onto the shoulder: after driving for ten hours, the campground was still miles away and started to cry.

7

Louise looked up at the new skyscraper looming over the city and sighed.

A) NO CHANGE

B) Louise looked up at the new skyscraper and sighed, looming over the city.

C) Looming over the city, Louise looked up at the new skyscraper and sighed.

D) Looming over the city, looking up at the new skyscraper, Louise sighed.

8

One of the hardest diseases to diagnose, medical TV shows often use lupus in their twist endings.

A) NO CHANGE

B) Medical TV shows often use lupus, one of the hardest diseases to diagnose, in their twist endings.

C) In their twist endings, lupus is often used by medical TV shows, one of the hardest diseases to diagnose.

D) One of the hardest diseases to diagnose, twist endings of medical TV shows often use lupus.

9

With a grunt of frustration, the crumpled sheet of paper flew from Igor's hand into the bin.

A) NO CHANGE

B) The crumpled sheet of paper flew from Igor's hand into the bin with a grunt of frustration.

C) With a grunt of frustration, Igor threw the crumpled sheet of paper into the bin.

D) Flying into the bin, Igor threw the crumpled sheet of paper with a grunt of frustration.

10

Twirling in endless pirouettes, we waltzed around the room, the antique chandelier shimmering above us.

A) NO CHANGE

B) Shimmering above us, we waltzed around the room, twirling in endless pirouettes under the antique chandelier.

C) Twirling in endless pirouettes, the antique chandelier shimmered above us, waltzing around the room.

D) We waltzed around the room, shimmering above us, the antique chandelier twirling in endless pirouettes.

11

An artistic lady with a moose head decorated the club's rear wall.

A) NO CHANGE

B) The club's rear wall with a moose head was decorated by an artistic lady.

C) By an artistic lady with a moose head, the club's rear wall was decorated.

D) An artistic lady decorated the club's rear wall with a moose head.

12

With an ear-piercing whinny, the jockey tried to
regain control of his horse as it reared up.

A) NO CHANGE

B) The jockey tried to regain control of his horse
   as it reared up with an ear-piercing whinny.

C) The jockey with an ear-piercing whinny tried
   to regain control of his horse as it reared up.

D) As it reared up, the jockey tried to regain
   control of his horse with an ear-piercing
   whinny.

13

Made out of cheesy snacks, Neal presented his
Cheesy Castle to the judges.

A) NO CHANGE

B) Neal, made out of cheesy snacks, presented his
   Cheesy Castle to the judges.

C) Neal presented his Cheesy Castle to the judges
   made out of cheesy snacks.

D) Neal presented his Cheesy Castle, made out of
   cheesy snacks, to the judges.

1. The correct answer is (D). It correctly places the modifying phrase "while climbing ..." next to its logical object, "King Kong." (A) and (B) incorrectly describe "the airplanes" as climbing. (C) incorrectly suggests that the Empire State Building was attacked by airplanes.

2. The correct answer is (B). This choice correctly places the phrase "following a strict color palette" so that it describes the fashion in which Carol Ann planted her annuals. (A) and (D) both incorrectly suggest that Carol Ann's garden itself followed a strict color palette. (C) is incorrect because it describes "a painting" as "following a strict color pattern."

3. The correct answer is (B). This choice correctly describes the cowboys as "sunburnt, dehydrated, and tottering with exhaustion" and correctly describes the floorboards as "creaking under them." (A) is incorrect because it describes the floorboards as "sunburnt, dehydrated, and tottering with exhaustion." (C) is incorrect because it incorrectly describes the cowoboys' footsteps as "sunburnt, dehydrated, and tottering with exhaustion." (D) is incorrect because it describes the floorboards as "sunburnt, dehydrated, and tottering with exhaustion."

4. The correct answer is (D). It correctly describes "Mr. Brent" as "a pillar of the community." (A) is incorrect because it describes "we" as "a pillar of the community." (B) and (C) are incorrect because they describe "Mr. Brent's neighborliness" as "a pillar of the community."

5. The correct answer is (B). It correctly describes "the bucket of ice-cold water" as "balanced on top of the door." (A) incorrectly suggests that "she" was "balanced on top of the door." (C) is incorrect because it suggests that either "she" or "the room" was "balanced on top of the door." (D) is incorrect because it's ambiguous: it might be modifying the bucket, in which case it suggests it was still "balanced on top of the door" after being "dumped over her," or it might be incorrectly modifying "the room."

6. The correct answer is (C). It correctly shows that "Dad" drove ten hours and started to cry, and indicates that "the campground" was miles away. (A) and (B) are incorrect because they suggest "the campground" was "driving for ten hours." (D) is incorrect for the same reason, and because it suggests the campground started to cry.

7. The correct answer is (A). It correctly indicates that the skyscraper was "looming over the city." (B), (C), and (D) are incorrect because they suggest that Louise was "looming over the city."

8. The correct answer is (B). It correctly describes "Lupus" as "one of the hardest diseases to diagnose." (A), (C), and (D) are all incorrect because they describe "medical TV shows" as "one of the hardest diseases to diagnose."

9. The correct answer is (C). It correctly describes the way that "Igor threw" the paper as being "with a grunt of frustration," and correctly indicates that "the paper" was thrown "into the bin." (A) and (B) are incorrect because they suggest that the paper flew on its own into the the bin and that the paper grunted with frustration. (D) is incorrect because it suggests that Igor flew into the bin.

10. The correct answer is (A). It correctly describes the way "we waltzed" as "twirling in endless pirouettes" and "the antique chandelier" as "shimmering above us." (B) is incorrect because it suggests that "we" were "shimmering above us." (C) is incorrect because it suggests that "the antique chandelier" was "twirling in endless pirouettes" and "waltzing around the room." (D) is incorrect because it suggests "we" were "shimmering above us" and that "the antique chandelier" was "twirling in endless pirouettes."

11. The correct answer is (D). It correctly indicates that "the rear wall" was "decorated … with a moose head." (A) and (C) are incorrect because they suggest that "an artistic lady" herself had "a moose head." (B) is incorrect because it modifies "the club's rear wall" with the phrase "with a moose head" as a restrictive clause. That illogically suggests that the club has multiple rear walls, and that the one with a moose head was decorated by an artistic lady.

12. The correct answer is (B). It correctly attributes the "ear-piercing whinny" to the "horse." (A), (C), and (D) all attribute the "ear-piercing whinny" to "the jockey."

13. The correct answer is (D). It correctly describes the "Cheesy Castle" as being "made out of cheesy snacks." (A) and (B) are incorrect because they suggest that "Neal" is "made out of cheesy snacks." (C) is incorrect because it suggests that "the judges" are "made out of cheesy snacks."

Matching Verbs
Part 5

Matching Verbs questions ask you to select verbs that maintain logical and consistent mood, tense, and voice across a sentence. You may need to ensure that the same tense is used in all verbs in a sentence, or that changes in tense follow the logic of a sequence of events. You may also need to ensure that the mood of verbs is consistent, especially when the verbs occur in the same sentence. You may also need to correct clauses that shift from the active to the passive voice, or, rarely, to match passive voice clauses.

DIRECTIONS

Every passage comes with a set of questions. Some questions will refer to a portion of the passage that has been underlined. Other questions will refer to a particular location in a passage or ask that you consider the passage in full.

After you read the passage, select the answers to questions that most effectively improve the passage's writing quality or that adjust the passage to follow the conventions of standard written English. Many questions give you the option to select "NO CHANGE." Select that option in cases where you think the relevant part of the passage should remain as it currently is.

1

Some patrons order coffee or espresso, and others are ordering tea.

A) NO CHANGE

B) others order

C) others ordered

D) others orders

2

If she had been born just two years later, she missed her chance.

A) NO CHANGE

B) was missing

C) has missed

D) would have missed

European immigrants arriving at Ellis Island still had a long way to go before they set foot on the mainland of the United States. They <u>will wait</u> in long lines to receive rapid-fire physicals, after which doctors chalked letters onto their clothes to indicate possible health problems.

A) NO CHANGE

B) are waiting

C) wait

D) waited

4

Immigrants who had certain diseases, or who were diagnosed with diseases during these perfunctory examinations, could be sent back to their country of origin. After passing a physical examination, immigrants <u>answer</u> a battery of questions about their beliefs, job prospects, and knowledge of the United States and its system of government.

A) NO CHANGE

B) answers

C) have answered

D) answered

5

Thanksgiving is a day of reflection, caring, and—most of all—overeating. The average American eats more than 4,500 calories on Thanksgiving Day; that's roughly twice the number of calories that an average person needs. After gorging on traditional Thanksgiving fare, most of us <u>felt</u> sleepy. We usually blame that drowsiness on turkey, which contains tryptophan, a drowsiness-causing amino acid.

A) NO CHANGE

B) had felt

C) are feeling

D) feel

However, the amount of tryptophan in turkey is simply too small to put us to sleep; egg whites contain about four times as much tryptophan per gram, and we eat those for breakfast. The truth is, our drowsiness probably <u>is having</u> much more to do with the sheer amount of food that we eat than with any particular dish.

A) NO CHANGE

B) has

C) will have had

D) had

In *The Odyssey*, Odysseus must navigate his ship between two sea monsters, Scylla and Charybdis. Scylla is a six-headed sea serpent, and Charybdis is a giant sea monster that opens its maw and swallows the sea. Odysseus <u>cannot avoid</u> them both; he must pass by one in order to avoid the other.

A) NO CHANGE

B) couldn't avoid

C) will not be able to avoid

D) cannot have avoided

8

Odysseus reasons that Scylla would certainly snatch and eat some of his men. He also realizes that he could chance Charybdis, and possibly escape with no losses--but that if Charybdis were to open her mouth while the ship was near, she <u>could have swallowed</u> his ship whole. Faced with this choice, Odysseus orders his men to avoid Charybdis and sail past Scylla.

A) NO CHANGE

B) would swallow

C) swallowed

D) swallows

9

As his ship passes by, Scylla strikes out at the ship with its six heads. It <u>had snatched</u> one man in each mouth, taking six men. However, the ship survives—and Odysseus is able to continue his journey.

A) NO CHANGE

B) snatched

C) will snatch

D) snatches

In 1976, Universal Studios asserted in court that they had the right to remake RKO General's 1933 movie "King Kong" because the character of King Kong was in the public domain. Then, in 1982, Universal <u>sues</u> the makers of the video game "Donkey Kong," asserting that the game infringed on their copyright of the "King Kong" character and franchise.

A) NO CHANGE

B) will sue

C) sued

D) is suing

1. The correct answer is (B). It maintains parallelism between the simple present verbs "order" and "order". (A) is incorrect because it shifts from the simple present, "order", to the present continuous, "are ordering". (C) is incorrect because it shifts to the simple past, "ordered". (D) is incorrect because it uses a singular verb, "orders", with a plural subject, "others".

2. The correct answer is (D). In a conditional sentence, if the verb in the dependent clause is in the past perfect (here, "had been"), then the verb in the main clause must be in the past conditional (here, "would have missed"). (A) incorrectly uses the simple past "missed". (B) incorrectly uses the past continuous "was missing". (C) incorrectly uses the past perfect "has missed".

3. The correct answer is (D). Since this story is taking place in the past (as indicated by the verb "still had" in the first sentence), a past-tense verb is required. "Waited" is a simple past form. (A), "will wait", is a future tense form; (B), "are waiting", and (C), "wait", are both present tense forms.

4. The correct answer is (D). The word "answered" maintains the use of past tense established in the passage. (A) is incorrect because of the shift to the present tense. (B) is incorrect because of the shift in tense, and "answers" is singular, not plural. (C) is incorrect because "have answered" is the present perfect tense, which expresses an action that began in the past and continues to the present, so it creates a shift from past tense.

5. The correct answer is (D). It maintains the present tense established earlier in the passage. (A) is incorrect because of the shift to the past tense. (B) is incorrect because of the shift to the past perfect tense which expresses an action that began before another time in the past. (C) is incorrect because of the shift to the present progressive tense that shows actions in progress.

6. The correct answer is (B). It maintains the present tense. (A) is incorrect because "is having" is the past progressive tense. (C) is incorrect because it is in the future perfect progressive tense. (D) is incorrect because it is the past tense.

7. The correct answer is (A). The phrase "cannot avoid" maintains the present tense established earlier in the passage. (B) is incorrect because "couldn't avoid" shifts to past tense. (C) is incorrect because it is the future progressive tense. (D) is incorrect because it is in the past perfect tense.

8. The correct answer is (B). It maintains the future tense established earlier in the passage. (A) is incorrect because "could have swallowed" shifts to the past perfect progressive tense. (C) is incorrect because it shifts to the past tense. (D) is incorrect because "swallows" is the plural present tense.

9. The correct answer is (D). It maintains the present tense. (A) is incorrect because "had snatched" is the past perfect tense that expresses an action that occurred before another time in the past. (B) is incorrect because it is the past tense. (C) is incorrect because it is the future tense.

10. The correct answer is (C). It maintains the past tense. (A) is incorrect because "sues" is the present tense. (B) is incorrect because "will sue" is the future tense. (D) is incorrect because "is suing" is the present progressive tense.

Matching Nouns
Part 6

Matching Nouns questions ask you to maintain consistent pronoun person and number across clauses and sentences. You may need to use logical and consistent pronouns with a known antecedent, or in cases in which the antecedent is unnamed, such as when the pronoun "one" is used to refer to a generic person.

DIRECTIONS

Every passage comes with a set of questions. Some questions will refer to a portion of the passage that has been underlined. Other questions will refer to a particular location in a passage or ask that you consider the passage in full.

After you read the passage, select the answers to questions that most effectively improve the passage's writing quality or that adjust the passage to follow the conventions of standard written English. Many questions give you the option to select "NO CHANGE." Select that option in cases where you think the relevant part of the passage should remain as it currently is.

1

You would be surprised at how many different ways you can roast a chicken. For starters, <u>you</u> can roast it with lemon, garlic, or even pistachio.

A) NO CHANGE

B) one

C) she

D) they

2

We saw deer from the window of the train. <u>It had white spots</u> and sturdy hooves.

A) NO CHANGE

B) You had white spots

C) She had white spots

D) They had white spots

3

Paulo taught his students to make masks out of paper plates, and asked them to create their own designs. They used crayons to draw one's designs.

A) NO CHANGE

B) their

C) her

D) our

4

Ellen was on a panel with two visiting professors. She liked Ellen's idea about the influence of Francis Bacon on Andrew Marvell.

A) NO CHANGE

B) You

C) They

D) He

5

I went to the grocery store looking for peach yogurt. She found that the only yogurt flavors in stock were blueberry and plain.

A) NO CHANGE

B) They

C) We

D) I

6

One always wonders just how seriously you should take the reviews of one's work.

A) NO CHANGE

B) one

C) we

D) they

7

Hoa is making a new sculpture. They resemble a silver tree with wavy, intricately-woven branches.

A) NO CHANGE

B) She resembles

C) It resembles

D) We resemble

8

This building has over a thousand windows in blue frames. It is blue because the architect is famous for using that color for window frames.

A) NO CHANGE

B) They are

C) He is

D) We are

9

James Baldwin left America for France when he was 24 years old. Baldwin first settled in Paris; later, <u>I</u> lived in the Provençal town of Saint-Paul-de-Vence.

A) NO CHANGE

B) one

C) you

D) he

10

There's a question I've been meaning to ask you: did <u>you</u> actually like the blueberry pie I gave you?

A) NO CHANGE

B) one

C) I

D) OMIT the underlined portion

1. The correct answer is (A). The first sentence consistently uses the generic "you" to address the reader(s). The second sentence maintains that consistent use. (B) shifts to "one," which, while conveying the same meaning, is not consistent with the convention established by the preceding sentence. (C), "she," breaks with the consistent "you" and is also confusing in context; we don't know who "she" is. (D) breaks the consistency and also causes confusion—it's not clear who "they" are.

2. The correct answer is (D). Remember that the plural of "deer" is "deer." You can tell that "deer" is plural in this case because the sentence begins, "We saw deer" rather than "We saw a deer." This means that the plural "They" is the correct pronoun. (A) incorrectly uses a singular pronoun, "it," when there are multiple deer. (B) makes things confusing by using the second-person "You." The speaker would need to be addressing the deer throughout for this to make any sense. (C) incorrectly uses another singular pronoun, "She."

3. The correct answer is (B). It uses the correct third-person-plural "their." It doesn't make sense to refer to the students' designs in the impersonal, as in (A); the students are referred to using the third-person-plural everywhere else in the two sentences. (C) is also incorrect; Paulo was referred to using "his," and there's no other individual mentioned in the sentences. (D), "our," uses a first-person-plural even though there's no clear group of people, including the speaker, for the "our" to refer to.

4. The correct answer is (C). In context, it makes the most sense for "the two visiting professors" to be the ones who liked Ellen's idea. Since they're two people, they need to be referred to using a plural "They." (A) is incorrect because it's not plural. The only individual referred to in the sentences is Ellen, and in context it wouldn't make sense for the singular pronoun "She" to refer to Ellen (it would imply that Ellen liked Ellen's idea). (B) uses "You," but there's no precedent for it in the sentences. (D), like (A), uses a singular pronoun and is incorrect for the same reason.

5. The correct answer is (D). The first sentence establishes an "I" narrative about going to the grocery store for peach yogurt. In context, it makes the most sense for the "I" to be the same person who finds out there's no peach yogurt in the second sentence. (A) uses a third-person pronoun, which makes a confusing shift in person. (B) shifts the person and number, using the third-person-plural "They." (C) shifts the number to the plural, but this doesn't make sense; the first sentence described a solitary person's quest for yogurt.

6. The correct answer is (B). It maintains the impersonal pronoun use at the start and end of the sentence. (A) incorrectly shifts to "you." (C) shifts to the first-person-plural "we." (D) incorrectly uses the third-person.

7. The correct answer is (C). In context, it makes the most sense for the subject of the second sentence to be the sculpture; since it's just one sculpture, the correct pronoun is "it." (A) is wrong because we know that the subject is the sculpture, and that there's only one. (B) is wrong because in context it's clear that the subject is the sculpture, not Hoa or any other person. (D) is likewise wrong because it doesn't fit with the sculpture.

8. The correct answer is (B). In context, it makes the most sense for the subject of the second sentence to be the window frames, not the building. The words, "They are blue," paired with "because the architect is famous for using that color for window frames" follow logically from the statement about blue frames in the first sentence. (A) causes an incorrect shift in number, from plural to singular. (C) introduces the idea of a blue person, which doesn't make sense in context. (D) introduces an unprecedented first-person-plural.

9. The correct answer is (D). The sentences set up a third-person narrative about James Baldwin, meaning that he should be referred to as "he" throughout. (A) is incorrect; the passage is not a first-person narrative by Baldwin about his life. (B) incorrectly shifts to the impersonal pronoun, "one." (C) incorrectly shifts to the second-person.

10. The correct answer is (A). The sentences address someone in the second-person, and it doesn't make sense for the underlined portion to deviate from that. (B), "one," incorrectly shifts to the impersonal pronoun. (C), "I," is incorrect because it would create a confusing question: "did I actually like the blueberry pie I gave you?" Since the speaker gave the pie to someone else, it makes sense for the question to be directed at the recipient of the pie. (D) is incorrect because the speaker's question needs some sort of pronoun to be grammatically complete.

Section 5
Conventions of Usage

Conventions of Usage questions test your ability to correct word-level grammatical errors. You'll need to recognize and correct pronouns with unclear antecedents, badly-formed possessive pronouns, verbs and nouns in forms that don't agree with other parts of the sentence, frequently confused words, and some cases of idiomatic word use.

Conventions of Usage questions contribute to the "Standard English Conventions" subscore.

There are 8 specific question types in this domain:

Conventions of Usage			
UPC	Clear Pronouns	UN	Noun Agreement
UD	Making Possessives	UF	Confusing Words
UPA	Pronoun Agreement	UL	Comparing Correctly
USV	Verb Agreement	UC	Appropriate Prepositions

Clear Pronouns

Part 1

Clear Pronouns questions require you to identify cases in which a pronoun has an ambiguous antecedent, meaing it isn't clear what noun the pronoun is supposed to refer to. Sometimes, you will need to select a clearer pronoun. Often, you will need to replace unclear pronouns with nouns that make the intended meaning of the sentence clearer.

DIRECTIONS

Every passage comes with a set of questions. Some questions will refer to a portion of the passage that has been underlined. Other questions will refer to a particular location in a passage or ask that you consider the passage in full.

After you read the passage, select the answers to questions that most effectively improve the passage's writing quality or that adjust the passage to follow the conventions of standard written English. Many questions give you the option to select "NO CHANGE." Select that option in cases where you think the relevant part of the passage should remain as it currently is.

1

Marisol gave Leslie a new snorkel for her birthday. She prefers snorkelling to scuba diving because it's less complicated.

A) NO CHANGE

B) Leslie

C) This avid snorkeler

D) This one

2

Once you've taken the jellies out of the molds, you have to throw them away. Next, decorate the jellies with lemon zest.

A) NO CHANGE

B) it

C) the molds

D) the jellies

3

The scientists and the aliens talked to each other on Skype. They sent them a cake emoji.

A) NO CHANGE

B) They sent

C) They received

D) The aliens sent the scientists

4

Brush the horses, polish the saddles, and stack them on the rack.

A) NO CHANGE

B) the horses

C) the saddles

D) it

5

Malik, Bill, and Bill's cousins are going to a movie on Thursday. He thinks they'll like the movie.

A) NO CHANGE

B) They think Malik will

C) They think they'll

D) Malik thinks Bill's cousins will

6

Cindy brought home-made potato wedges to the Smith family's party. She seasoned the wedges with paprika and allspice.

A) NO CHANGE

B) them

C) the Smith family

D) the party

7

Once you've cleaned the teapot and the kettle, put it away.

A) NO CHANGE

B) that thing

C) the teapot

D) this

8

Bruno and Tanisha gave a presentation to the class. They have been studying how plants grow in different climates.

A) NO CHANGE

B) Each has

C) The two have

D) Together they have

9

Philbert knitted a sweater and a scarf. Later, he sold <u>it</u> at the craft fair.

A) NO CHANGE

B) the sweater

C) the item

D) that

10

Dr. Martin Luther King Jr. was murdered on April 4th, 1968 by James Earl Ray. The murder came just one day after <u>he</u> had delivered his prophetic speech, "I have Been to the Mountaintop"

A) NO CHANGE

B) he himself

C) one

D) Dr. King

1. The correct answer is (B). It's the only choice that unambiguously identifies the recipient of the snorkel. (A), "She," is too vague; it might refer to Marisol or to Leslie. (C) is likewise too vague; the avid snorkeler could feasibly be either the giver or the receiver of the gift. (D) is also too vague.

2. The correct answer is (C). It takes away the ambiguity and also makes sense in context. (A) is too vague; it might refer to the molds, but it also might refer to the jellies. (B) is also very unclear; it could conceivably refer to everything—both the jellies and the molds. (D) removes the ambiguity, but in context it creates a silly meaning. If you need to decorate the jellies with lemon zest, it doesn't make sense to throw them away first.

3. The correct answer is (D). It's the only option that clears up who sent the emoji, and who received it. (A) is too vague. It's not clear which group did the sending, and which did the receiving. (B) is also too vague because it doesn't identify the sender or receiver, and (C) is vague for the same reason.

4. The correct answer is (C). It clears up the ambiguous pronoun reference, and it also makes the most sense in context. (A) is incorrect because it's not clear who, or what, is being stacked. (B) clears up the ambiguity but doesn't make sense; you can't stack horses on a rack! (D) is incorrect because "it" doesn't make a clear reference to anything.

5. The correct answer is (D). It's the least ambiguous option. (A) is unclear; we don't know who's thinking, or whom he's thinking about. (B) is likewise unclear; "They" could refer to either the cousins, or the cousins and Bill. (C) is especially unclear; the cousins could be thinking about Bill and Malik, or vice versa; either group could be thinking of themselves; finally, the entire group could be thinking of itself.

6. The correct answer is (A). It avoids ambiguity and also makes sense in context. (B) is unclear; you can't tell whether "them" refers to the wedges, the Smiths, or something else. (C) doesn't make sense in context. When you go to a party, you don't usually season the hosts. (D) likewise doesn't make sense in context.

7. The correct answer is (C). It's the only option without an ambiguous pronoun reference. (A) is unclear; you can't tell if it refers to that teapot or the kettle. (B) likewise doesn't make clear what needs to be put away. (D), too, fails to use pronouns clearly.

8. The correct answer is (C). It offers the least ambiguous reference to who's been studying how plants grow. Bruno and Tanisha are the only two named individuals, so it makes sense for "The two" to refer to them. (A) is too vague; it could conceivably refer to either the class, to Bruno and Tanisha, or to everyone present. (B), "Each has," could refer to Bruno and Tanisha, or to the members of the class. (D) similarly could refer to either the presenters, the class, or both.

9. The correct answer is (B). It makes clear that Philbert sold the sweater at the craft fair. (A) could conceivably refer to either the sweater or the scarf, and is therefore too confusing. (C), too, could refer to either of the items that Philbert knitted. (D) could refer to either the scarf or the sweater as well.

10. The correct answer is (D). It is the only option that precisely identifies who gave the speech. (A), "he", is insufficiently clear: since both Martin Luther King and James Earl Ray were named in the first sentence, "he" could refer to either of them. (B), "he himself", has the same problem. (C), "one", is even less clear; it might refer to either King or Ray or some undefined person.

Making Possessives
Part 2

Making Possessives questions ask you to distinguish between singular, plural, and possessive nouns, pronouns, and a special class of words called possessive determiners, and then to select the appropriate form for the context. Possessive determiners are descriptive words that we use to indicate possession. They look like pronouns, but they play a different grammatical role: the most common error involves confusing pronouns and possessive determiners.

DIRECTIONS

Every passage comes with a set of questions. Some questions will refer to a portion of the passage that has been underlined. Other questions will refer to a particular location in a passage or ask that you consider the passage in full.

After you read the passage, select the answers to questions that most effectively improve the passage's writing quality or that adjust the passage to follow the conventions of standard written English. Many questions give you the option to select "NO CHANGE." Select that option in cases where you think the relevant part of the passage should remain as it currently is.

1

He washes <u>he's</u> hands before he goes into the operating room.

A) NO CHANGE

B) he

C) his

D) the

2

Make sure that you check <u>yours</u> mailbox for anything from the school.

A) NO CHANGE

B) your

C) you're

D) you are

3

They've been selling <u>they're</u> crafts at the craft fair every year.

A) NO CHANGE

B) there

C) their

D) they are

4

Sylvia Plath worked at *Mademoiselle* as a guest editor in 1953; she had won <u>she</u> guest editorship in a contest.

A) NO CHANGE

B) she's

C) hers

D) her

5

<u>Its</u> a ferry you can take across the San Francisco Bay to Sausalito.

A) NO CHANGE

B) It's

C) Its'

D) Is it

6

I didn't realize that cake had been meant for <u>me</u>.

A) NO CHANGE

B) my

C) mine

D) I

7

If it's not James's turn to pay, then it's <u>us</u> turn.

A) NO CHANGE

B) we

C) you and my's

D) our

8

Since it rains so much in Tacoma, you must never wear <u>you are</u> shoes in the house.

A) NO CHANGE

B) you're

C) your

D) yours

9

I'd like Tina's help on my thank-you letter because <u>hers</u> ideas are always so good.

A) NO CHANGE

B) she's

C) her

D) she is

10

I see him walking <u>he is</u> dog every morning.

A) NO CHANGE

B) he's

C) he

D) his

1. The correct answer is (C). Since the subject of the sentence is a "He" figure, the possessive determiner needed in this sentence is "his"; "his" is both the possessive determiner and pronoun form of the "he" pronoun. (A) is incorrect because "he's" isn't the possessive form of "he"; it's a contraction of "he is." (B) is incorrect because "he" needs to be in the possessive form. (D) is incorrect because "the" makes it unclear whose hands the person is washing.

2. The correct answer is (B). The possessive determiner form of "you" is "your." You use "your" to modify an object, like "mailbox." (A) is incorrect because "yours" is the possessive pronoun form of "you," used to indicate the possession of an object, as in "that soap is yours." (C) is incorrect because "you're" is a contraction of "you are." (D) is incorrect because "you are" creates an ungrammatical construction.

3. The correct answer is (C). The word "their" is a possessive determiner; it indicates possession when the pronoun is "they." (A) is incorrect because "they're" is a contraction of "they are." (B) is incorrect because "there" is not a possessive. (D) is incorrect because "they are" creates an ungrammatical construction.

4. The correct answer is (D). The word "her" is the possessive determiner form of "she." (A) is incorrect because "she" does not indicate possession. (B) is incorrect because "she" does not indicate possession. (C) is incorrect because "hers" is a possessive pronoun, not a possessive determiner. You need an adjective here to modify "guest editorship."

5. The correct answer is (B). In this case a possessive determiner is not needed. Instead, you need a word that indicates "it is." "It's" is a contraction of "it is." (A) is incorrect because the possessive determiner "its" is not actually needed here. (C) is incorrect because "Its'" is never correct in any context; possessive determiners do not need apostrophes because they already indicate possession. (D) is incorrect because "Is it" would need a question mark at the end of the sentence to be grammatical.

6. The correct answer is (A). This sentence is fine as is, and doesn't need any modifications. (B) is incorrect because the possessive determiner "my" doesn't have anything to modify here; there'd need to be another noun after "my" for this to make sense. (C) is incorrect because "mine" is a possessive pronoun; in context it creates a confusing sentence. (D) is incorrect because when we discuss things that are "to" or "for" us we use "me," not "I."

7. The correct answer is (D). "Our" is the possessive determiner form of "we." (A) is incorrect because "us" is an object pronoun that doesn't indicate possession. (B) is incorrect because "we" likewise does not indicate possession. (C) is incorrect because "my's" is never correct in any context; as a possessive determiner, it doesn't need an apostrophe. Likewise, "you" would need to be replaced with "your" to indicate possession. The phrase "your and my turn" would be grammatically correct, but between us I think "our" still sounds better.

8. The correct answer is (C). The possessive determiner "your" is to modify "shoes." (A) is incorrect because it's ungrammatical and makes no sense. (B) is incorrect because "you're" is simply a contraction of "you are." (D) is incorrect because "yours" is a possessive pronoun rather than a possessive determiner, and is ungrammatical here.

9. The correct answer is (C). The word "her" is the possessive determiner form of "she," and modifies "ideas." (A) is incorrect because "hers" is a possessive pronoun rather than a possessive determiner, and can't modify "ideas" by coming before it. You'd need to express it as something like "ideas of hers." (B) is incorrect because "she's" is a contraction of "she is" and does not indicate possession. (D) is incorrect because "she is" creates a confusing ungrammatical sentence.

10. The correct answer is (D). The word "his" is both the possessive pronoun and possessive determiner form of "he." In this case you need the possessive determiner "his" to modify "dog." (A) is incorrect because "he is" doesn't indicate possession, and creates a confusing sentence. (B) is incorrect because "he's" is a contraction of "he is." (C) is incorrect because "he" doesn't indicate possession.

Pronoun Agreement
Part 3

Pronoun Agreement questions ask you to ensure that pronouns match their antecedents in person and number. You may need to correct pronouns that appear next to their antecedents or pronouns that are separated from their antecedents by another clause or long phrase. You may also need to ensure that personal pronouns are used for personal antecedents. While these questions generally avoid situations in which "they" might be regarded as an acceptable gender-neutral singular pronoun, they do require students to avoid the use of "they" to refer to a singular personal antecedent if it's already clear which gender should be used based on other pronouns.

DIRECTIONS

Every passage comes with a set of questions. Some questions will refer to a portion of the passage that has been underlined. Other questions will refer to a particular location in a passage or ask that you consider the passage in full.

After you read the passage, select the answers to questions that most effectively improve the passage's writing quality or that adjust the passage to follow the conventions of standard written English. Many questions give you the option to select "NO CHANGE." Select that option in cases where you think the relevant part of the passage should remain as it currently is.

1

All the students want to take the class trip, <u>so he and she</u> should sign up.

A) NO CHANGE

B) so they

C) so he or she

D) so it

2

The golfers finished <u>its</u> game and headed to the snack bar.

A) NO CHANGE

B) his

C) our

D) their

3

If the surfers want to catch the best waves, <u>them</u> should go to the beach in the morning.

A) NO CHANGE

B) he

C) she

D) they

4

Michael rowed his boat to shore while the crew sang <u>anyone's</u> favorite songs.

A) NO CHANGE

B) everything's

C) their

D) one's

5

Though Principal Harding requested full participation, none of the teachers accompanied <u>his</u> students to the assembly.

A) NO CHANGE

B) its

C) her

D) their

6

Our guests were all happy to help us with cleanup after <u>our</u> big dinner.

A) NO CHANGE

B) its

C) anyone's

D) her

7

My parents always used to tell me "better safe than sorry," and I have always followed <u>his</u> advice.

A) NO CHANGE

B) her

C) its

D) their

8

Robert gave me this copy of *The Catcher in the Rye*, and that's why <u>he's</u> my favourite book.

A) NO CHANGE

B) it's

C) they're

D) I'm

9

The fifth amendment of the U.S. Constitution prevents defendants from being forced to give testimony that would incriminate him.

A) NO CHANGE

B) him or her

C) them

D) oneself

10

The criminal syndicate known as "The Burning Enigma" fears none but Captain Codebreaker, the only superhero smart enough to destroy itself.

A) NO CHANGE

B) him

C) her

D) it

11

Ten ninjas leapt at once from the palace wall, both landing soundlessly on his feet.

A) NO CHANGE

B) all

C) them

D) each

1. The correct answer is (B). "All the students" is a plural noun phrase indicating more than two people, so it must be replaced with the plural pronoun "they". (A) is incorrect because "he and she" refers to two people, while "all the students" (as opposed to "both") must refer to at least three people. (C) is incorrect because "he or she" is a singular pronoun phrase. (D) is incorrect because "it" is singular.

2. The correct answer is (D). It correctly refers to "golfers" with a third-person plural pronoun. (A) and (B) are incorrect, because "its" (never appropriate for people) and "his" are singular pronouns, and "golfers" is plural. (C) is incorrect because, given the sentence, the speaker is not one of the golfers; therefore, a first-person pronoun is inappropriate.

3. The correct answer is (D). The phrase "the surfers" is a plural antecedent that refers to specific persons, and (D) is the correct form of a plural pronoun. While (A) may be tempting, it is not correct because the indefinite pronoun is wordy and refers to non-specific persons. (B) and (C) are not correct because the singular pronouns do not agree with the plural antecedent.

4. The correct answer is (C). This correctly expresses that the songs being sung are the favorites of the crew. (A), (B), and (D) are not correct because indefinite pronouns refer to non-specific persons or things and the crew is specified.

5. The correct answer is (D). When the antecedent is plural, the pronoun must be also. (A), (B), and (C) all offer a singular pronoun, which would not agree.

6. The correct answer is (A). In this case the sentence indicates that everyone shared the big dinner. (B), (C), and (D) are all singular and so do not agree with either "our guests" or "us."

7. The correct answer is (D). The phrase "my parents," a plural subject, must be referred to with the plural pronoun "they." (B) and (C) both suggest singular pronouns; so does (D), with the additional problem that "its" can only refer to objects and not people.

8. The correct answer is (B). The antecedent in this sentence is "The Catcher in the Rye," so "it's," the third-person singular inanimate pronoun, is needed. (A), "he's," is incorrect because the antecedent is an object rather than a male creature. (C) is incorrect because "they're" is plural. (D) is incorrect because The Catcher in the Rye is not the speaker of the sentence and therefore cannot be referred to using a first-person pronoun.

9. The correct answer is (C). The word "defendants", a plural antecedent, must be referred to with a plural pronoun. (A) and (B) both propose singular pronouns or pronoun phrases; so does (D), with the additional mistake of making the pronoun reflexive.

10. The correct answer is (D). The antecedent in this sentence is "The criminal syndicate," a singular noun referring to an entity; therefore, the singular impersonal pronoun "it" is appropriate. (A) is incorrect because Captain Codebreaker is doing the destroying and the The Burning Enigma is getting destroyed; since the subject and object are not the same, a reflexive pronoun is not appropriate. (B) and (C) are both incorrect because a criminal syndicate is an organization, not a creature with a gender, and therefore cannot be referred to with a gendered pronoun.

11. The correct answer is (D). The singular "his" in "landing soundlessly on his feet" indicates that the subject of "landing" must be singular, and "each" is the singular pronoun generally used to describe the members of a group. (A) is incorrect because "both" refers to two people or things, but there are ten ninjas. (B) is incorrect because the ten ninjas do not share a single man's feet and are probably not all landing on some singular eleventh person's feet. (C) is both plural, which is incorrect, and in the wrong form for the subject of a clause.

Verb Agreement
Part 4

Verb Agreement questions ask you to identify cases in which a verb doesn't match its subject in terms of number. Be careful to find the true subject of the verb, not just the nearest noun. Look out for questions that have a long phrase or clause in between the subject and the verb, especially if the phrase or clause includes any nouns with a different number than the verb.

DIRECTIONS

Every passage comes with a set of questions. Some questions will refer to a portion of the passage that has been underlined. Other questions will refer to a particular location in a passage or ask that you consider the passage in full.

After you read the passage, select the answers to questions that most effectively improve the passage's writing quality or that adjust the passage to follow the conventions of standard written English. Many questions give you the option to select "NO CHANGE." Select that option in cases where you think the relevant part of the passage should remain as it currently is.

1

The women at this restaurant smokes the best brisket in the entire region!

A) NO CHANGE

B) woman at this restaurant smoke

C) women at these restaurants smokes

D) women at this restaurant smoke

2

The bride and groom is in the limousine.

A) NO CHANGE

B) are

C) was

D) am

3

Both of the assistant managers <u>have a chance</u> to be promoted.

A) NO CHANGE

B) is having a chance

C) does have a chance

D) has a chance

4

Each of them <u>have a chance</u> to win the raffle.

A) NO CHANGE

B) have had a chance

C) having a chance

D) has a chance

5

Hydrogen peroxide and baking soda <u>creates</u> a volcano effect when mixed.

A) NO CHANGE

B) create

C) creating

D) to create

6

The dishes in the dishwasher <u>needs</u> washing.

A) NO CHANGE

B) has needed

C) is in need of

D) need

7

John's grandparents, who were very generous, <u>gives</u> his parents a trip to Venice for their anniversary.

A) NO CHANGE

B) giving

C) gave

D) has given

8

Mathematics <u>are</u> among my uncle's favorite hobbies.

A) NO CHANGE

B) am

C) is

D) was

9

Eddie is the only one of my cousins who <u>lives</u> close enough that he can come for dinner.

A) NO CHANGE

B) live

C) are living

D) have lived

10

Make sure to take a train that <u>arrives</u> two hours before the play.

A) NO CHANGE

B) are arriving

C) arrive

D) do arrive

11

Climate change is perhaps the most urgent of the many problems that <u>faces</u> the world today.

A) NO CHANGE

B) face

C) facing

D) is facing

12

Of all of my professors, Dr. Philomena Happenstance <u>are</u> my favorite.

A) NO CHANGE

B) is

C) were

D) am

13

Some of these hedges <u>looks</u> like cones, cylinders, or pyramids.

A) NO CHANGE

B) looking

C) look

D) was looking

14

One of the hedges <u>look</u> like a rhombus.

A) NO CHANGE

B) looking

C) looks

D) were looking

15

The chess grandmaster's brothers <u>prefers</u> to play checkers with her.

A) NO CHANGE

B) prefer

C) would prefers

D) preferring

16

The clouds <u>move</u> quickly over the water.

A) NO CHANGE

B) moving

C) moves

D) was moving

1. The correct answer is (D). The collective "women" are, in this case, treated as a single unit currently involved in an activity so the present singular verb form is correct. (A) is incorrect because the plural verb form doesn't agree with the singular subject. (B) is incorrect because the singular subject and plural verb form disagree. (C) may be tempting because the introduction of multiple restaurants makes it seem that the women can no longer be considered a single unit; however, the collective still stands and the plural verb form still disagrees.

2. The correct answer is (B). The word "and" joins the bride and groom to create a plural noun so the present tense plural form of "to be" is correct. (A) is incorrect because it mixes the plural noun and singular verb form. (C) is incorrect because it mixes the plural noun and the singular past tense of the verb. (D) is incorrect because it mixes the third person plural noun and the first person present tense of the verb form.

3. The correct answer is (A). The plural pronoun "both" requires a plural verb. (B), (C), and (D) all offer singular forms of the verb "have".

4. The correct answer is (D). The singular pronoun "each" requires a singular verb. (A) and (B) both offer plural forms of the verb "have". "Having", in (C), is a gerundive rather than a conjugated verb and therefore cannot agree with any subject.

5. The correct answer is (B). In this case, the compound subjects are joined with "and" to create a plural noun with which the plural verb form agrees. (A) is incorrect because it mixes the plural subjects and a third person singular verb form. (C) is incorrect because it mixes the plural subjects and the singular present progressive verb form. (D) is incorrect because the introduction of the word "to" creates a new error by making a sentence fragment.

6. The correct answer is (D). It correctly pairs "dishes", the plural subject of this sentence, with a plural form of the verb "need". (A), (B), and (C) all present singular forms of the verb "need".

7. The correct answer is (C). It correctly pairs "grandparents", a plural subject, with a plural form of the verb "give". (A) and (D) propose singular forms of "give". (B), a gerundive rather than a conjugated form of the verb, would make this sentence a fragment.

8. The correct answer is (C). Although the word "mathematics" ends with an "s," it is singular, and it requires a singular form of the verb "to be." (C), "is," is the singular form of that verb.

9. The correct answer is (A). It correctly pairs "the only one", a singular noun phrase, with "lives", a singular form of the verb "live". (B), (C), and (D) all propose plural forms of the verb.

10. The correct answer is (A). The singular subject "a train" requires a singular form of the verb "arrive". (B), (C), and (D) all offer plural forms of the verb, which do not agree with "a train".

11. The correct answer is (B). The subject of this verb is "problems," a plural verb, and this is the only form of the verb that agrees with that subject. If you mistakenly thought "climate change" was the subject, you might have picked (A). (C) is incorrect because it replaces an action verb with a gerund, and (D) is incorrect because "is" is a singular form of the verb "to be."

12. The correct answer is (B). The verb "is" is the form of "to be" that agrees with the singular subject "Dr. Philomena Happenstance." (A) is incorrect; it's for plural subjects. (C) is also for plural subjects. (D) is for the first-person.

13. The correct answer is (C). The verb "look" agrees with the plural "these hedges." (A) agrees with singular subjects, as does (D). (B) is the wrong tense.

14. The correct answer is (C). The word "looks" agrees with the singular "One of the hedges." (A) uses a form that agrees with a plural subject. (B) uses the wrong tense. (D) also agrees with plural subjects.

15. The correct answer is (B). The plural "brothers" needs "prefer" to be grammatical. (A) uses a word that agrees with singular subjects. (C) is not grammatical in any context. (D) uses the wrong tense.

16. The correct answer is (A). It uses the form of "move" that agrees with the plural subject, "clouds." (B) uses the wrong tense, and (C) also only agrees with singular subjects.

Noun Agreement
Part 5

Noun Agreement questions ask you to identify and correct cases where nouns are used in contexts that should logically require them to be either singular or plural when they are the opposite.

DIRECTIONS

Every passage comes with a set of questions. Some questions will refer to a portion of the passage that has been underlined. Other questions will refer to a particular location in a passage or ask that you consider the passage in full.

After you read the passage, select the answers to questions that most effectively improve the passage's writing quality or that adjust the passage to follow the conventions of standard written English. Many questions give you the option to select "NO CHANGE." Select that option in cases where you think the relevant part of the passage should remain as it currently is.

1

The scientists at this lab have developed an astonishing new treatment, and they hope to be <u>a prize-winner.</u>

A) NO CHANGE

B) the prize-winner.

C) prize-winners.

D) the recipient of prizes.

2

Yesterday Jim sold six cars; they were all <u>a sports car.</u>

A) NO CHANGE

B) sports cars

C) a sport car

D) the sports car

3

Pam and Ted are renowned for their <u>skill as a baker.</u>

A) NO CHANGE

B) skills as a baker.

C) skills as bakers.

D) skill as a bakers.

4

She prefers to wake up each morning to the sound of <u>many trumpet.</u>

A) NO CHANGE

B) trumpet.

C) a trumpets.

D) many trumpets.

5

The house will be fitted with a couple of <u>sliding door.</u>

A) NO CHANGE

B) slidings door.

C) a sliding doors.

D) sliding doors.

6

Most of the employees are <u>an engineer, but some are a designer.</u>

A) NO CHANGE

B) engineers, but some are designers.

C) engineers, but some are a designer.

D) an engineer, but some are designers.

7

The sky is full of stars, each one <u>a bright orbs of gas.</u>

A) NO CHANGE

B) a bright orbs of gases.

C) a bright orb of gas.

D) bright orb of gas.

8

Marie is lifting two <u>fifteen-pound weight.</u>

A) NO CHANGE

B) pound of weight.

C) fifteen-pounds weight.

D) fifteen-pound weights.

9

The forest is full of hundreds of <u>moose.</u>

A) NO CHANGE

B) the mooses.

C) a moose.

D) mooses.

10

Given that so few of us have ever been lucky enough to see a komodo dragon up close, I envy <u>the glimpse</u> caught by generations of fortunate visitors to Komodo Island.

A) NO CHANGE

B) a glimpse

C) the glimpses

D) glimpse

1. The correct answer is (C). It causes the plural subject "The scientists" to agree with the plural noun "prize winners." (A) is incorrect because it keeps "prize-winner" in the singular. (B) also incorrectly keeps "prize-winner" in the singular, merely adding the article "the." (D) is incorrect because, while it rephrases the idea of a person who gets a prize, it maintains the singular form.

2. The correct answer is (B). The plural "sports cars" agrees with "six cars." (A) is incorrect because "a sports car" is singular. (C) is incorrect because "a sport car" is also in the singular. (D), "the sports car," likewise incorrectly maintains the singular form.

3. The correct answer is (C). "Pam and Ted," being two people, must be matched with plural nouns. The phrase "skills as bakers" is in the plural. (A) is incorrect because "skill as a baker" is in the singular. (B), "skills as a baker," does make "skills" plural, but "baker" is still inappropriately in the singular. (D), "skill as a bakers," uses the ungrammatical "a bakers." Plural nouns need the article "the."

4. The correct answer is (D). Since there are "many" of the instrument, the noun "trumpet" needs to be plural, as "trumpets." (A) is incorrect because the word "many" indicates that "trumpet" must be plural. (B) is incorrect because "trumpet" lacks an article; it would need the article "a" to be grammatical. (C) is incorrect because "a trumpets" uses the singular article "a" with the plural noun "trumpets."

5. The correct answer is (D). The phrase "a couple" indicates two, and thus more than one of something. This means that "doors" needs to be plural. (A) is incorrect because it puts "door" in the singular despite the words "a couple." (B) is incorrect because "door" is once again in the singular. Note that while "slidings" is not any kind of door I know of, "slidings doors," in the plural, would not be inherently ungrammatical here. (C) is incorrect because it uses the singular article "a" with the plural noun "doors."

6. The correct answer is (B). The phrase "the employees" is in the plural, as is "some," meaning that both "engineers" and "designers" need to be plural too. (A) is incorrect because it puts both "engineer" and "designer" in the singular. (C) is incorrect because it puts "designer" in the singular despite the plural word "some." (D) is incorrect because it uses the singular "Engineer" despite the plural "most of the employees."

7. The correct answer is (C). It pairs the singular noun "orb" with the phrase "each one," which indicates the singular. (A) is incorrect because it uses the singular article "a" with the plural noun "orbs." (B) is incorrect because it also uses the singular article "a" with the plural noun "orbs." (D) is incorrect because it lacks any articles at all; "bright orbs of gas" would be grammatically, if not scientifically, correct without an article but since "orb" is in the singular it needs one.

8. The correct answer is (D). It correctly makes the "two" weights plural. (A) is incorrect because "two" weights need to be rendered in the plural, not the singular. (B) is incorrect because "pound of weight" is not in the plural despite the word "two." (C) is incorrect because it likewise does not pluralize "weight."

9. The correct answer is (A). The plural of "moose" is actually just "moose." (B) and (D) are therefore both incorrect because they use "mooses," which isn't the way to pluralize "moose." (C) is incorrect because the phrase "hundreds" indicates that there are multiple moose, but the article "a" is for singular nouns.

10. The correct answer is (C). The phrase "fortunate visitors" are in the plural and "generations" indicates that they didn't all go and see the komodo dragons at exactly the same time. This means the "glimpses" must also be in the plural. (A) is incorrect because it puts "glimpse" in the singular despite the multiple "visitors" seeing the dragons at multiple times. (B) is incorrect because it likewise puts "glimpse" in the singular. (D) incorrectly does that too, and also lacks an article.

Confusing Words
Part 6

Confusing Words questions ask you to identify the correct form of frequently-confused words to use in a certain context. You will need to distinguish between words that look or sound similar but have different meanings or grammatical roles.

DIRECTIONS

Every passage comes with a set of questions. Some questions will refer to a portion of the passage that has been underlined. Other questions will refer to a particular location in a passage or ask that you consider the passage in full.

After you read the passage, select the answers to questions that most effectively improve the passage's writing quality or that adjust the passage to follow the conventions of standard written English. Many questions give you the option to select "NO CHANGE." Select that option in cases where you think the relevant part of the passage should remain as it currently is.

1

There were things in their closets that they probably should've thrown out, like they're old bathrobes.

A) NO CHANGE

B) they are

C) their

D) there

2

She studied the affects of UV rays on the siding of buildings.

A) NO CHANGE

B) affects for

C) effects for

D) effects of

3

He found out that she was equally <u>adopt</u> at complex math and archery, which was a surprising combination of talents.

A) NO CHANGE

B) adapt

C) adept

D) adeptly

4

The <u>precedes</u> from the auction were contributed to the mayor's favorite charity.

A) NO CHANGE

B) proceed

C) precede

D) proceeds

5

Even though it's forbidden, the dog <u>lays</u> on the couch every chance he gets.

A) NO CHANGE

B) lies

C) lay

D) lie

6

The headmaster told the school's board that it was a matter of <u>principle</u>.

A) NO CHANGE

B) principals

C) principal

D) principally

7

She <u>quite</u> the next day, without giving the usual two weeks' notice.

A) NO CHANGE

B) quiet

C) quit

D) quiets

8

The old stable was <u>raised</u> to make way for a swimming pool.

A) NO CHANGE

B) risen

C) rised

D) razed

9

What she valued most about her great-aunt was the older woman's wise council.

A) NO CHANGE

B) counsel.

C) consul.

D) councils.

10

As she scanned the scene, she spotted Henry; he was a site for sore eyes.

A) NO CHANGE

B) cite

C) sight

D) sites

11

Each area of the resort has its own swimming pool.

A) NO CHANGE

B) its'

C) it's

D) it's very

12

They're taking the hobbits to Isengard.

A) NO CHANGE

B) there

C) their

D) there is

13

I didn't do it on propose.

A) NO CHANGE

B) porpoise.

C) purport.

D) purpose.

14

I feel as fresh as a blossoming floor today.

A) NO CHANGE

B) flour

C) flower

D) flow

15

Droughts affect everyone in the community, but they hurt the farmers most of all.

A) NO CHANGE

B) effect

C) affects

D) effects

1. The correct answer is (C). It indicates the bathrobes belong to them. (A) is not correct because "they're" is a contraction of "they are" which is a state of being rather than of possession. (B) is not correct for the same reasons (A) is not correct. (D) is not correct because "there" indicates a location, not possession.

2. The correct answer is (D). The word "effects," meaning the consequences or results of exposure to the UV rays on the buildings' siding. (A) and (B) are incorrect because to affect something means to act upon that thing, not the results of an action. (C) is incorrect because what is being studied is the multiple effects of the UV rays.

3. The correct answer is (C). The word "adept" expresses that she was proficient at both complex math and archery. (A) is incorrect because "adopt" means to take as one's own. (B) is incorrect because "adapt" means to adjust to different conditions. (D) is incorrect because "adeptly" means to perform an action in a proficient manner.

4. The correct answer is (D). The word "proceeds," in the context of this sentence, means the total amount derived from the auction. (A) and (C) are both incorrect because "precedes" and "precede" mean that one thing goes before another thing. (B) is incorrect because "proceed" means to go forward.

5. The correct answer is (B). The dog is reclining or resting on the couch. (A) is not correct because the dog is not placing things on the couch. (C) may be tempting because "lay" is the past tense of "to lie," but it is not correct because the dog is currently breaking the rules. (D) is not correct because "lie" is the plural form of the verb but there is only one dog who reclines on the couch

6. The correct answer is (A). The word "principle" means the guiding sense of the obligations of good conduct the headmaster is applying to whatever "it" is. (B) and (C) are incorrect because a principal or principals are the heads of an organization. (D) is not correct because of the singular "it" to which the principle relates.

7. The correct answer is (C). (A) is not correct because "quite" is an adverb, not an action. (B) is not correct because the adjective "quiet" describes a state of being, not an action. (D) is incorrect because "quiets" means a finishing stroke and though quitting may be seen as a finishing stroke, to quit is to take an action.

8. The correct answer is (D). The word "razed" means to have been torn down or demolished. (A) is incorrect because "raised" means to lift up which would be an unlikely method for making room for a swimming pool. (B) and (C) are both incorrect because the stable did not rise, it was removed.

9. The correct answer is (B). The word "counsel," which means the advice given by the great-aunt. (A) and (D) are not correct because a council is an assembly of persons and "councils" is the plural of council. (C) is incorrect because a "consul" is an official appointed by one country to oversee the commercial interests of that country and the welfare of its citizens in another country.

10. The correct answer is (C). In the context of this sentence, she was pleased to see Henry. (A) and (D) are incorrect because a site or sites refers to location. (B) is incorrect because to cite something means to reference it.

11. The correct answer is (A). The possessive pronoun "its" does not contain an apostrophe. (B) is not correct because there is no need to add an apostrophe to what is already a possessive pronoun. (C) is not correct because "it's" is a contraction for "it is." (D) is not correct because there is no need to add an apostrophe s to the singular possessive pronoun.

12. The correct answer is (A). It's a contraction of "they are." The other choices are commonly confused words with different definitions. (B), "there," is an adverb. (C) is a plural possessive. (D) doesn't make grammatical sense in this sentence.

13. The correct answer is (D). The phrase "on purpose" is an idiomatic expression meaning "intentionally" or "deliberately." (A) incorrectly uses "propose," which means "to offer" or "suggest." (B), "porpoise," is an aquatic mammal similar to a dolphin. (C) means "to appear" or "claim" to be something

14. The correct answer is (C). It makes the most sense for the speaker to feel like a flower, not a "floor," as in (A), a "flour," as in (B), or a "flow," as in (D).

15. The correct answer is (A). It uses the verb "affect", which means "to have an impact on". (B) uses the verb "effect", which means "to make [the direct object] happen"; this does not make sense in the context of the sentence, since droughts are not making everyone in the community happen. (C) and (D), "affects" and "effects", are both either singular forms of the verbs in question, which do not agree with the plural subject "droughts", or plural nouns, which make the sentence incoherent.

Comparing Correctly
Part 7

Comparing Correctly questions ask you to correct sentences in which unlike objects are compared. Most often, these errors occur where two complex phrases with modifiers are being compared. The phrases usually have some similar objects or properties, but the main words in the phrases are different kinds of objects.

DIRECTIONS

Every passage comes with a set of questions. Some questions will refer to a portion of the passage that has been underlined. Other questions will refer to a particular location in a passage or ask that you consider the passage in full.

After you read the passage, select the answers to questions that most effectively improve the passage's writing quality or that adjust the passage to follow the conventions of standard written English. Many questions give you the option to select "NO CHANGE." Select that option in cases where you think the relevant part of the passage should remain as it currently is.

1

Sharks have a special kind of scale called a dermal denticle, while most bony fish have leptoid scales. Sharks' dermal denticles differ from bony fish in that they are much more tooth-like. Under magnification, dermal denticles resemble rows of pointed teeth.

A) NO CHANGE

B) those of bony fish

C) leptoid scales

D) bony fish with leptoid scales

2

Scholars of law and ethics distinguish between "positive rights" and "negative rights." "Negative rights," like the right to be free from warrantless searches, protect you by specifying actions others aren't allowed to take against you; "positive rights," like confronting witnesses in criminal cases, protect you by specifying actions you must be allowed to take.

A) NO CHANGE

B) the right to confront witnesses

C) confrontation of witnesses

D) confronting the rights of witnesses

The main difference between an automatic transmission and a car with a manual transmission is the amount of control the driver is required to exercise.

A) NO CHANGE

B) manual transmission's

C) car's

D) manual transmission

Although Imani's paper on plant biology was accepted without revisions, Lou's paper on the life-cycle of earthworms was returned with extensive comments.

A) NO CHANGE

B) the life-cycle of earthworms

C) Lou, who wrote a paper on the life-cycle of earthworms,

D) the subject of Lou's paper was the life-cycle of earthworms, which

Sedimentary rocks are a better source of fossils than metamorphic rocks. The relatively gentle accumulation of sedimentary rocks can bury and preserve remains without destroying them, while metamorphic rock, formed under intense heat and pressure, destroys fossils.

A) NO CHANGE

B) the violent deformation of metamorphic rock

C) metamorphic rock

D) intense heat and pressure can form metamorphic rock and

1. The correct answer is (C). It correctly compares the "dermal denticles," the type of scales sharks have, to "leptoid scales," the kind that "most bony fish" have. (A) incorrectly compares "dermal denticles" to "bony fish," rather than their scales. (B) is close, because it corrects the issue of directly comparing shark scale and bony fish; however, this phrasing suggests a comparison between the "dermal denticles" of sharks and bony fish, and the context makes it clear that the intention is to compare two different kinds of scales—not the same scales on two different kinds of fish. (D) is incorrect because, although it mentions "leptoid scales," it still directly compares "dermal denticles" and "bony fish."

2. The correct answer is (B). It correctly completes a logical comparison between two specific examples of rights: "the right to be free from warrantless searches" and "the right to confront witnesses." (A), (C), and (D) all make comparisons between something specifically described as a right, and various descriptions of an action.

3. The correct answer is (D). The underlined phrase is being compared to the phrase "automatic transmission." (D) is the only option that completes the comparison with a parallel phrase, "manual transmission." (A) compares "automatic transmission," a part of a car, to "a car"—the whole object that a transmission is one part of. (B) unnecessarily makes the phrase possessive, making a comparison between a kind of transmission and some unnamed thing belonging to another kind of transmission. (C) uses a vague possessive that fails to complete a logical comparison.

4. The correct answer is (A). In this case, the sentence is actually correct as it is written. It correctly makes a logical comparison between "Imani's paper" and "Lou's paper." (B) is incorrect because it revises the sentence so as to create a comparison between "Imani's paper" and "the life-cycle of earthworms," which is the subject of Lou's paper—not a paper. (D) is incorrect for the same reason, although it uses wordier phrasing. (C) is incorrect because it illogically compares "Imani's paper" with "Lou," a person.

5. The correct answer is (B). It creates a direct comparison between two processes: "relatively gentle accumulation" and "violent deformation." (A) is incorrect because it draws a comparison between a process of "gentle accumulation" and "metamorphic rock," something formed by another process. (C) is incorrect for the same reason. (D) is incorrect because it makes a comparison between a process, "gentle accumulation," and the forces required to create another process, "intense heat and pressure."

Appropriate Prepositions
Part 8

Appropriate Prepositions questions ask you to select prepositions or phrases that are idiomatic in a given context. Sometimes, you can answer these questions by thinking about the meaning of the preposition and selecting the one that's most logical. Other times, the prepositions are part of abstract or metaphorical phrases. In those cases, you need to have a sense of what kinds of prepositions are typically used in those kinds of phrases.

DIRECTIONS

Every passage comes with a set of questions. Some questions will refer to a portion of the passage that has been underlined. Other questions will refer to a particular location in a passage or ask that you consider the passage in full.

After you read the passage, select the answers to questions that most effectively improve the passage's writing quality or that adjust the passage to follow the conventions of standard written English. Many questions give you the option to select "NO CHANGE." Select that option in cases where you think the relevant part of the passage should remain as it currently is.

1

Although he knew that Marisella had been working hard to keep Elizabeth's surprise party a secret, Diego still let the cat <u>out from the bag</u>. He didn't want to spoil the surprise, but he was afraid that Elizabeth would think that he had made a mistake and forgotten her birthday!

A) NO CHANGE

B) out of the bag

C) out by bag

D) out via bag

2

After an accident at the mine, investigators blamed management—pointing out that an employee had filed a safety complaint. Management responded by producing a large number of unsubstantiated safety complaints from the same employee, implying that it was reasonable to discount the complaint because the employee had a reputation <u>of</u> crying wolf.

A) NO CHANGE

B) for

C) at

D) in

3

People are influenced by the habits of those around them, especially those <u>from</u> authority. When managers set an example of diligence and hard work, it not only inspires confidence in their abilities, but also inspires their employees to go the extra mile.

A) NO CHANGE

B) at

C) upon

D) in

4

In the end, the failure of supersonic passenger flight was <u>chalked up</u> to economic factors. Maintaining supersonic jets was simply too expensive, and the ticket prices were too high for most consumers.

A) NO CHANGE

B) chalked out with

C) chalked into

D) chalked to

5

The housing project was a disaster: it ended up costing far more to house residents in the new building than it would have to subsidize their housing elsewhere. Local authorities agreed on the need to go back <u>to</u> the drawing board and figure out an entirely new approach to the housing problem.

A) NO CHANGE

B) at

C) with

D) by

6

All I did was forget to take my shoes off when I came inside, and Dave blew <u>out</u> at me! Talk about making a mountain out of a molehill.

A) NO CHANGE

B) through

C) away

D) up

7

I saw Kristin waving frantically <u>out across</u> the street, and I knew she was in a rush to hail a taxi.

A) NO CHANGE

B) by away

C) down over

D) from across

8

Martin swaggered <u>into</u> the stage, casting condescending looks at the competition. "Look at him," one of the other dancers whispered, "He thinks he's such a hotshot!"

A) NO CHANGE

B) within

C) onto

D) after

9

The terms "mushroom" and "toadstool" aren't exactly scientific. Some people believe that mushrooms are edible, while toadstools are poisonous, but that distinction doesn't really hold up. As a matter of fact, both terms simply refer to "the fruiting body of a fungus." Some toadstools are edible, and some mushrooms are poisonous; their names are more a matter <u>with</u> tradition and general appearance than scientific distinction.

A) NO CHANGE

B) to

C) for

D) of

10

It looked like she was talking to herself, but I suppose that she could've been <u>upon</u> the phone.

A) NO CHANGE

B) along

C) on

D) within

1. The correct answer is (B) because the preposition "of" is the idiomatic one to pair with the phrases including the words "let out." This means that the other choices, while not strictly grammatically incorrect, are simply not the conventional way to express this idea in English. (A), "out from the bag," is incorrect because it doesn't use the conventional preposition "of." (C), "out by bag," also does not use the idiomatic "of," and it also omits "the." (D), "out via bag," makes the same error.

2. The correct answer is (B) because "for" is the idiomatic preposition to pair with "reputation" in this context. (A), "of," is therefore incorrect—while we can still understand what the phrase means, it's simply not the conventional form. The same conditions apply to (C), "at," and (D), "in."

3. The correct answer is (D) because "in" is one of the idiomatic prepositions you can use in the phrase "those__ authority." It's not the only idiomatic preposition—"with" would also work—but it's the only one available to choose here. (A), "from," doesn't conventionally go between "those" and "authority"; neither do (B), "at," or (C), "upon."

4. The correct answer is (A) because "chalked up to" is an idiom meaning "explained by referring to" (the image is of people keeping track of points on a chalkboard). (B), (C), and (D) all present incorrect, unidiomatic variations on this phrase.

5. The correct answer is (A) because "to go back to the drawing board" is an idiom meaning "to come up with a brand new plan or design for something, usually after a failure" (the image is of designers having to draw a new plan). (B), (C), and (D) all present incorrect, unidiomatic variations on this phrase.

6. The correct answer is (D) because the idiomatic preposition to place after "blew," when describing someone getting mad, is "up." (A) is incorrect because "blew out" has a different meaning; it usually refers to a popped tire. (B), "through," isn't an idiomatic expression in any context. (C) creates a different idiomatic expression, "blew away," which typically describes objects swept up by a wind.

7. The correct answer is (D) because the idiomatic prepositions used to indicate that an action is taking place on the other side of a street are "from" and "across." (A), "out across," suggests that Kristin is waving her arms far over into the street, like a tree being out across a river. While that's an interesting mental image, it's not a very plausible interpretation of this sentence, so we should eliminate it for being illogical. (B), "by away," isn't an idiomatic combinations of prepositions. (C), "down over," is, like (A), not a pair of prepositions we can interpret in any logical way in this context.

8. The correct answer is (C) because "onto" is the idiomatic preposition to pair with "the stage" when we want to indicate that someone is entering such an area. (A) is incorrect because "into" would suggest that Martin bumped into the stage by accident. Since he "swaggered," or moved confidently, and the people around him call him a "hotshot," it doesn't seem likely that he was so clumsy. (B) is incorrect because "within" isn't the conventional preposition to describe someone moving onto a stage. (D) suggests that the stage was mobile and that Martin was following it.

9. The correct answer is (D) because the idiomatic preposition to place in "a matter__tradition" is "of." (A), (B), and (C) all present incorrect, unidiomatic variations on this phrase.

10. The correct answer is (C) because we conventionally use the preposition "on" to describe someone who's using a phone. (A), (B), and (D) use prepositions that aren't idiomatic. (D) also has the added error of suggesting that the person was literally inside the telephone—an illusion that most of us shed in early childhood.

Section 6
Conventions of Punctuation

Conventions of Punctuation questions test your ability to correct errors of punctuation. You'll need to recognize and correct problems with punctuation within or at the end of sentences, apostrophes with possessive nouns and pronouns, punctuation in lists, and punctuation around parenthetical elements. Sometimes, you may simply need to recognize when no punctuation is appropriate and remove unnecessary punctuation. Although the task gives away the answer, we've included a set of "Unnecessary Punctuation" drills so that you can get a feel for how the questions will look on the exam and review answer explanations to learn more about what makes punctuation inappropriate in certain places in a sentence.

Conventions of Punctuation questions contribute to the "Standard English Conventions" subscore.

There are 6 specific question types in this domain:

Conventions of Punctuation			
PE	Ending a Sentence	PL	Punctuating a List
PW	Punctuating a Sentence	PC	Extra Clauses
PP	Making Possessives	PU	Unnecessary Punctuation

Ending a Sentence
Part 1

Ending a Sentence questions ask you to select the appropriate punctuation to end a sentence. You should base your choice on the mood and tone of the sentence. If it is a simple declarative statement, you should select a period. If it's a question, you should select a question mark. If it's a strong, emphatic statement, you should select an exclamation mark.

DIRECTIONS

Every passage comes with a set of questions. Some questions will refer to a portion of the passage that has been underlined. Other questions will refer to a particular location in a passage or ask that you consider the passage in full.

After you read the passage, select the answers to questions that most effectively improve the passage's writing quality or that adjust the passage to follow the conventions of standard written English. Many questions give you the option to select "NO CHANGE." Select that option in cases where you think the relevant part of the passage should remain as it currently is.

1

The United States government has three branches. The executive branch is the office of the President. The legislative branch is Congress. The judicial branch is the Supreme Court!

A) NO CHANGE

B) Court?

C) Court.

D) Court

2

Are you going to the block party tomorrow?

A) NO CHANGE

B) tomorrow.

C) tomorrow!

D) tomorrow,

3

There were some questions about the way things were done, particularly the method used to hang the kitchen cabinets?

A) NO CHANGE

B) cabinets

C) cabinets!

D) cabinets.

4

Carol Ann asked, "Can we meet to discuss my concerns next week."

A) NO CHANGE

B) next week"

C) next week!"

D) next week?"

5

The excited cry went up among those gathered: "The prince is giving a ball."

A) NO CHANGE

B) giving a ball!"

C) giving a ball?"

D) giving a ball"

6

When school starts, you'll need to start going to bed earlier? That way you will have a better chance of getting enough sleep every night.

A) NO CHANGE

B) bed earlier, that way

C) bed earlier that way

D) bed earlier. That way

7

I really have nothing more to say about this subject …

A) NO CHANGE

B) about this subject.

C) about this subject?

D) about this subject,

8

There were some complications when the entire graduating class got involved in planning the party? In the end, we had three different styles of cup, ten bottles of only two kinds of soda, one snack platter, and no plates or ice.

A) NO CHANGE

B) planning the party

C) planning the party,

D) planning the party.

9

Why shouldn't we go on vacation right after <u>we move?</u>

A) NO CHANGE

B) we move!

C) we move.

D) we move,

10

I have just one question for you: are you Academy-Award-nominated director <u>Richard Linklater</u>.

A) NO CHANGE

B) Richard Linklater!

C) Richard Linklater?

D) Richard Linklater

11

As the perch sailed through the air, the captain shouted, <u>"Catch that perch."</u>

A) NO CHANGE

B) "Catch that perch?"

C) "Catch that perch"

D) "Catch that perch!"

12

Can any of us really know what the cat is <u>thinking?</u>

A) NO CHANGE

B) thinking!

C) thinking.

D) thinking

1. (C) is the correct answer. A period is the appropriate punctuation for this sentence, in context. (A) incorrectly uses an exclamation mark. Consider the three preceding sentences: they're a set of factual statements about the branches of the United States government. Since the final sentence doesn't relate anything all that different, in tone or in content, it wouldn't make sense to punctuate it with an exclamation mark. (B) uses a question mark even though the sentence isn't phrased as a question. (D) lacks any end-of-sentence punctuation at all.

2. (A) is the correct answer. The question starts with "Are you going," a clear interrogative statement. This means that you need to punctuate it with a question mark. (B) uses a period, which isn't the correct way to punctuate statements phrased as questions. (C) uses an exclamation mark—again, an inappropriate way to punctuate a question. (D) uses a comma which is also not the right way to punctuate a question.

3. (D) is the correct answer. Although the sentence mentions questions that some people have, the sentence is not itself a question. It is a declarative sentence, so it should end with a period. (A) is incorrect because it uses a question mark, even though the sentence is not itself a question. (B) fails to use any punctuation at all. (C) is not the correct answer because nothing in the sentence itself indicates that this is an exclamation.

4. (D) is the correct answer. The quotation is a direct question and the question mark should be placed inside the quotation marks. (A) is not the correct choice because a period is not the correct end of sentence punctuation for a direct question. (B) is not correct because it does not include any end-of-sentence punctuation. (C) is not the correct choice because an exclamation point is not the correct punctuation for a direct question.

5. (B) is the correct answer. The cry that went up is described as being excited, so the exclamation point provides necessary emphasis. (A) is not correct because the period is not emphatic enough. (C) is not correct because the quote is not a direct question. (D) is not the correct answer because it does not include any end-of-sentence punctuation

6. (D) is correct because the period punctuates the end of the first sentence. (A) is not correct because the first sentence is not a question. (B) is not correct because the use of a comma creates a comma splice. (C) is not the correct answer because no punctuation creates a run-on sentence.

7. (B) is the correct answer. A period is a simple way to end a complete declarative statement. (A) is not correct because ellipses are used to indicate material has been deleted from an otherwise word-for-word quotation, and the sentence is not a quote. (C) is not correct because the sentence is not a question. (D) is not correct because a comma is never used to punctuate the end of a sentence.

8. (D) is the correct answer. The period is the appropriate punctuation for the declarative sentence. (A) is not correct because the first sentence is not a direct question. (B) is not correct because a semicolon is not end-of-sentence punctuation. (C) is not correct because a comma is not end-of-sentence punctuation.

9. (A) is the correct answer. A question mark is an appropriate way to end a direct question. Though (B) may be tempting, the exclamation point is not the best punctuation here. (C) uses a period when the question mark is necessary. (D) incorrectly uses a comma, which is not the correct punctuation for the end of a sentence.

10. (C) is the correct answer. It uses a question mark to punctuate the question. (A) incorrectly punctuates the question with a period, (B) incorrectly uses an exclamation mark, and (D) lacks any end-of-sentence punctuation.

11. (D) is the correct answer. As a shouted exclamation, the best punctuation mark for the underlined portion is an exclamation mark. (A) uses a period, which is incorrect in context. (B)'s question mark is also out of place here, and (C) lacks any end-of-sentence punctuation at all.

12. (A) is the correct answer. It punctuates the question with a question mark. (B) uses an exclamation mark, which is not appropriate here. (C) incorrectly uses a period, and (D) lacks any end-of-sentence punctuation.

Punctuating a Sentence
Part 2

Punctuating a Sentence questions ask you to identify and correct a wide variety of punctuation errors that can occur between words or clauses within a sentence. You may need to select the appropriate punctuation to separate different kinds of clauses, remove punctuation that creates grammatical interruptions (like commas jammed between descriptive words and their objects), or correct a combination of errors involving different kinds of punctuation.

DIRECTIONS

Every passage comes with a set of questions. Some questions will refer to a portion of the passage that has been underlined. Other questions will refer to a particular location in a passage or ask that you consider the passage in full.

After you read the passage, select the answers to questions that most effectively improve the passage's writing quality or that adjust the passage to follow the conventions of standard written English. Many questions give you the option to select "NO CHANGE." Select that option in cases where you think the relevant part of the passage should remain as it currently is.

1

Near the river that ran through the farm Desmond found a canoe that had been hidden in the underbrush.

A) NO CHANGE

B) river, that ran through the farm, Desmond found a canoe

C) river that ran through the farm, Desmond found a canoe

D) river, that ran through the farm Desmond found a canoe

2

It's not enough to say that it's simple, you have to explain why exactly, it's simple.

A) NO CHANGE

B) it's simple you have to explain why exactly;

C) it's simple; you have to explain why, exactly,

D) it's simple you have to explain why, exactly,

3

On the morning of July 4, 1776, the territories that would become the United States were still British colonies. By that evening, 12 had declared their independence.

A) NO CHANGE

B) July 4, 1776 the territories

C) July 4 1776 the territories

D) July 4 1776, the territories

4

When baking, using a scale to weigh ingredients will improve the results using measuring cups isn't as accurate.

A) NO CHANGE

B) results, using measuring cups isn't

C) results; using measuring cups isn't

D) results using measuring cups. Isn't

5

"The only thing we have to fear, is fear itself." Said Franklin Roosevelt.

A) NO CHANGE

B) itself," said Franklin Roosevelt

C) itself." Said, Franklin Roosevelt

D) itself," said, Franklin Roosevelt

6

Otto's trucks have blue fenders; Harjit's trucks have blue and green ones.

A) NO CHANGE

B) fenders, Harjit's trucks

C) fenders Harjit's trucks

D) fenders Harjit's; trucks

7

We were going to drive to the restaurant together; however, it turned out Cathy needed to leave early.

A) NO CHANGE

B) together, however; it

C) together however, it

D) together, however, it

8

When we go camping, we always bring the same basic gear, like tents, sleeping bags, and air mattresses; we also usually bring some luxuries, like a French press coffee pot, a DVD player, and a solar charger.

A) NO CHANGE

B) mattresses we also usually bring;

C) mattresses, we also usually bring,

D) mattresses, we also usually bring:

9

Jenny got plenty of things at the grocery store. Root beer, ice cream, pretzels, and some cheese spread.

A) NO CHANGE

B) the grocery store: root beer,

C) the grocery store, root beer,

D) the grocery store root beer,

10

If you see Snoopy in the Thanksgiving Day Parade; be sure to ask him for an autograph.

A) NO CHANGE

B) Parade be; sure to ask him

C) Parade, be sure to ask him

D) Parade be sure to; ask him

11

That's not a bar of soap it's; a chocolate.

A) NO CHANGE

B) soap it's

C) soap; it's

D) soap and it's

12

Consider the words of that great philosopher, Homer Simpson: "All right, Brain. It's all up to you!"

A) NO CHANGE

B) Simpson "All right,

C) Simpson. Said "All right,

D) Simpson said "All right,

13

Students need to purchase a variety of materials before school starts: notebooks, computers, pens, and textbooks.

A) NO CHANGE

B) materials, before school starts, notebooks,

C) materials; before school starts, notebooks,

D) materials before school starts. Notebooks,

14

My grandpa told me that he attended the "School of Hard Knocks," and I asked if it was part of the UC system.

A) NO CHANGE

B) "School of Hard Knocks," and I asked: if

C) "School of Hard Knocks:" and I asked if

D) "School of Hard Knocks" and I asked if

15

When you're deciding on a mountain to climb, you should think about three important factors: length, width, and height.

A) NO CHANGE

B) factors;

C) factors,

D) factors

16

As a child, I was fascinated by the *Nannippus, an ancient species of* horse that had three toes.

A) NO CHANGE

B) *Nannippus*; an ancient species

C) *Nannippus*; an ancient species,

D) *Nannippus*, an ancient species;

17

There are three iconic Marx Brothers—Groucho, Harpo, and Chico—and a well-known fourth, Zeppo. However, few people know of a fifth, who never appeared on film Gummo.

A) NO CHANGE

B) film: Gummo.

C) film. Gummo.

D) film; Gummo.

18

We sure didn't expect to meet a bear in the kitchen; and the bear sure didn't expect to meet us!

A) NO CHANGE

B) kitchen, and

C) kitchen and

D) kitchen: and

19

We've narrowed down our search for a new sleep specialist to three candidates: Winkin, Blinkin, and Nod.

A) NO CHANGE

B) candidates

C) candidates;

D) candidates.

20

Evelyn decided to focus on what she wanted, a small ceremony, a simple tea party, and a plain gown.

A) NO CHANGE

B) she wanted. A small

C) she wanted a small

D) she wanted—a small

21

Casey took his place at bat and hit a—home run thus securing his place in the history books!

A) NO CHANGE

B) a home run thus

C) a home run thus—

D) a home run—thus

22

That motorcycle's not being <u>driven—it's driving</u> itself!

A) NO CHANGE

B) driven it's driving

C) driven it's—driving

D) driven it's driving—

23

I thought I saw Academy-Award-nominated <u>director Richard Linklater</u> in the subway, but it wasn't him.

A) NO CHANGE

B) director—Richard Linklater

C) director Richard—Linklater

D) director Richard Linklater—

24

There are a number of poets who also <u>write fiction as a matter of fact; some</u> fiction writers also write poetry.

A) NO CHANGE

B) write fiction; as a matter of fact, some

C) write fiction; as a matter of fact; some

D) write fiction as a matter of fact some

1. (C) is the correct answer. It inserts a comma after the introductory clause. (A) is not correct because the lack of punctuation creates a run-on sentence. (B) is not the correct option because "that ran through the farm" is a restrictive clause, and those do not need to be set off with commas. (D) is not correct because "Near the river" is not, in this case, an introductory clause.

2. (C) is the correct answer. It correctly uses a semicolon to connect two independent clauses and uses two commas to set off the parenthetical adverb "exactly". (A) is not the correct answer because it incorrectly uses a comma to connect the independent clauses and does not set off "exactly" with commas. (D) is not the correct answer because it uses no punctuation to link the independent clauses. (B) makes the same mistake; in addition, it does not set off "exactly" with commas and incorrectly inserts a semicolon between a verb and its predicate.

3. (A) is the correct answer. The year is set off from the rest of the sentence with commas. (B) incorrectly omits the necessary comma after the year. (C) incorrectly omits any punctuation. (D) incorrectly omits the comma needed between the day of the month and the year in which the action took place.

4. (C) is the correct answer. It correctly uses a semicolon to connect two independent clauses. (A) is incorrect because it uses no punctuation to connect the clauses, creating a run-on sentence. (B) uses a comma, which creates a comma splice. (D) incorrectly divides the sentences at the wrong point, creating a fragment.

5. (B) is the correct answer. A comma is the correct punctuation for a direct quote preceding an attribution to the speaker. (A) and (C) are incorrect because the use of a period to separate the quote from the attribution is incorrect. (D) incorrectly inserts a comma between "said" and "Franklin".

6. (A) is the correct choice. It uses a semicolon to join two independent clauses. (B) creates a comma splice, (C) a run-on sentence, and (D) an inappropriately-placed semicolon.

7. (A) is the correct answer. It correctly uses a semicolon to link two complete sentences and a comma to set off the introductory adverb "however". (B) incorrectly uses a comma to link the two sentences, creating a comma splice, and inserts a semicolon between "however" and the phrase it modifies. (C) fails to use any punctuation to link the two sentences. (D) incorrectly uses a comma to link the two sentences, creating a run-on sentence.

8. (A) is the correct answer. It correctly uses a semicolon to connect two complete sentences. (B) is not the correct answer because it does not use any punctuation to connect the two sentences, creating a run-on sentence. (C) incorrectly uses a comma to link the two sentences, creating a comma splice and incorrectly adds a comma between the verb "bring" and its objects. (D) also creates a comma splice and incorrectly adds a colon between "bring" and its objects.

9. (B) is the correct answer. It correctly uses a colon to introduce a list. (A) is not the correct answer because the period after "store" turns "Root beer…" into a sentence fragment. (C) is not the correct answer because the comma after "store" makes "the grocery store, root beer…" sound like a single list, which does not make sense. (D) is not the correct answer because it does not introduce the list with any punctuation at all, which creates the same problem as in (C) and also makes the first item in the list the nonsensical "grocery store root beer".

10. (C) is the correct answer. It uses a comma to join a dependent clause to an independent clause. (A) incorrectly uses a semicolon, which can only be used to join two independent clauses or complete sentences. (B) and (D) both insert the semicolon in the middle of a clause, which is never correct.

11. (C) is the correct answer. It uses the semicolon to join two independent clauses. (A) places the semicolon incorrectly, (B) is a run-on sentence, and (D) lacks a comma after "soap."

12. (A) is the correct answer. One of the functions of a colon is to introduce a clarification of something left undefined in the sentence before the colon. Here, "Consider the words…" sets up an undefined concept (the words) and what comes after the colon clarifies that concept (by stating the exact words). (B) is incorrect because it does not use any punctuation before the quotation mark; at least a comma would be necessary. (C) is incorrect because the second sentence it creates is an incoherent fragment. (D) incorrectly adds "said"; this creates a comma splice, since both "Consider...philosopher" and "Homer....you!'" are complete sentences.

13. (A) is the correct answer. It uses a colon to introduce a list of items, and includes a comma following the first item in the list. (B) is not the correct answer because a comma is not the correct punctuation. (C) is not correct because the semicolon cannot be used to introduce a list. (D) is not correct because this punctuation makes the list of materials a sentence fragment.

14. (A) Is the correct answer. A comma is the correct punctuation to use before "and" when connecting two complete sentences. (B) is incorrect, because it inserts a colon between a verb and its predicate. (C) is incorrect, because it inserts a colon inside a quotation; a colon is also not the right punctuation to use before "and" when connecting two sentences. (D) is incorrect because it does not use any punctuation to connect the two sentences, creating a run-on sentence.

15. (A) is the correct answer. The words "three important factors" suggest a list ("length, width, and height") is coming and indicate the necessity of a colon. (B) incorrectly uses a semicolon; remember that semicolons are only used to join two independent clauses. (C) uses a comma, but it's not the right punctuation for a list. (D) lacks any punctuation after "factor" and is thus also wrong.

16. (A) is the correct answer. It correctly uses a comma to separate the noun "Nannippus" from the appositive noun phrase "an ancient species... ". (B) incorrectly uses a semicolon to separate "Nannippus" from the appositive phrase associated with it. (C) makes the same mistake as (B) and also adds an inappropriate comma in the middle of a noun phrase. (D) incorrectly adds a semicolon in the middle of the noun phrase.

17. (B) is the correct answer. The colon is used appropriately as a way of setting off the word "Gummo." (A) lacks any punctuation, and is incorrect. (C) creates a sentence fragment out of "Gummo." (D) incorrectly uses a semicolon where it's not allowed (remember that semicolons join two independent clauses).

18. (B) is the correct answer. A comma is the correct punctuation to use before "and" when linking two independent clauses. (A) and (D) are incorrect because they use other, incorrect punctuation before "and." (C) is incorrect because it does not use any punctuation before "and," creating a run-on sentence.

19. (A) is the correct answer. It correctly uses a colon to set off a simple list. (B) lacks any punctuation after "candidates," and is incorrect. (C) uses a semicolon, which is not the right way to set off a list. (D) creates a sentence fragment.

20. (D) is the correct answer. The dash correctly introduces the parenthetical list explaining what Evelyn wanted. (A) is not correct because the comma after "wanted" suggests that "what she wanted, a small ceremony…" is all one list rather than a general term with a list explaining it. (B) inserts a period after "wanted," which turns "A small ceremony…" into a fragment. (C), like (A), suggests that all the noun phrases are part of a single list, and, by omitting any punctuation between "what she wanted" and "a small ceremony," creates the nonsensical noun phrase "what she wanted a small ceremony."

21. (D) is the correct answer. It uses a dash to link an independent and a dependent clause. (A) incorrectly inserts the dash between a noun and its article. (B) does not use any punctuation to link the two clauses, creating a run-on sentence. (C) inserts the dash at the wrong place, suggesting confusingly that "thus" describes how Casey hit the home run rather than the cause-and-effect relationship between the home run and Casey's place in history.

22. (A) is the correct answer. The em-dash sets off the exclamatory remark, "it's driving itself!" (B) creates a run-on sentence. (C) might almost work as a line of dialogue, but lacks punctuation between "driven" and "it's." (D) also lacks such punctuation.

23. (A) is the correct answer. In this case, the options using em dashes—(B), (C), and (D)—are all incorrect. They place needless dashes between parts of the noun phrase "Academy-Award-nominated director Richard Linklater."

24. (B) is the correct answer. It correctly inserts a comma before "as a matter of fact," which begins the second of two complete sentences, and uses a comma after "as a matter of fact" to set that adverbial phrase off from the phrase it modifies. (C) incorrectly inserts a semicolon between "as a matter of fact" and the phrase it modifies. (A) makes the same mistake and also does not use any punctuation to connect the two sentences. (D) fails to use any punctuation to connect the two sentences, creating a run-on sentence.

Making Possessives
Part 3

Making Possessives questions ask you to correctly create the possessive form of a noun or pronoun and avoid placing apostrophes or the letter 's' incorrectly on non-possessive forms. They often include a mix of plural and possessive nouns and pronouns, and you will need to distinguish between them.

DIRECTIONS

Every passage comes with a set of questions. Some questions will refer to a portion of the passage that has been underlined. Other questions will refer to a particular location in a passage or ask that you consider the passage in full.

After you read the passage, select the answers to questions that most effectively improve the passage's writing quality or that adjust the passage to follow the conventions of standard written English. Many questions give you the option to select "NO CHANGE." Select that option in cases where you think the relevant part of the passage should remain as it currently is.

1

There are times when <u>artists styles</u> undergo drastic changes; these are the times when those artists experience the most growth.

A) NO CHANGE

B) artist's styles

C) artists' styles'

D) artists' styles

2

It's a shame that tree fell on her <u>father-in-laws'</u> new camper.

A) NO CHANGE

B) father-in-law's

C) father-in-laws's

D) father-in-laws

3

Laura's hat was left behind on <u>the Swansons's</u> coat rack.

A) NO CHANGE

B) the Swansons

C) the Swansons'

D) the Swanson's

4

The four <u>honorees'</u> sat at the head table where everyone could see them.

A) NO CHANGE

B) honoree's

C) honorees

D) honorees's

5

<u>Kristin's and Elizabeth's offices'</u> are in different locations.

A) NO CHANGE

B) Kristin's and Elizabeths offices'

C) Kristins and Elizabeth's offices

D) Kristin's and Elizabeth's offices

6

<u>Some pedestrians'</u> forget to use the crosswalks.

A) NO CHANGE

B) pedestrian's

C) pedestrians

D) pedestrians's

7

Thank you for delivering the <u>childrens' lunch's.</u>

A) NO CHANGE

B) children's lunches.

C) children's lunch's.

D) childrens lunches'.

8

The <u>conductors' watches</u> were synchronized to make sure the orchestras all started at the same time.

A) NO CHANGE

B) conductors watches

C) conductor's watches

D) conductors's watches

9

Exercise is certain to have great benefits on almost <u>anyones's</u> physical health.

A) NO CHANGE

B) anyones'

C) anyone's

D) anyones

10

Some <u>author's</u> use pseudonyms, which means that they publish their work under another name.

A) NO CHANGE

B) authors

C) authors'

D) authors's

11

You stole a friend of <u>mines</u> pet bear!

A) NO CHANGE

B) mines'

C) mine's

D) mines's

12

This bus <u>seat's</u> sixty passengers.

A) NO CHANGE

B) seats's

C) seats

D) seats'

13

Loud <u>cheers greeted the dignitary's</u> plane when he landed in Moscow.

A) NO CHANGE

B) cheer's greeted the dignitaries

C) cheers' greeted the dignitaries'

D) cheers greeted the dignitarys

14

Some people believe, incorrectly, that a <u>deer's antlers</u> can be used to determine its age.

A) NO CHANGE

B) deers antler's

C) deers' antlers

D) deer's antler's

1. (D) is the correct answer. Here you must identify the best use of apostrophes to signify that the plural noun "artists" is possessive . (D) is the correct answer here because the styles belong to multiple artists. (A) is not correct because the apostrophe is omitted. (B) is not correct because the apostrophe indicates possession by a single artist. (C) is not correct because "styles" is not a possessive noun.

2. (B) is the correct answer because "father-in-law" is a compound noun and possession is properly indicated by using an 's with the last element. (A) is not correct because "father-in-laws" is not the correct way to indicate that the compound noun is plural (that would be "fathers-in-law"). (C) is not correct because the apostrophe is, once again, incorrectly used to try indicating that there are multiple fathers-in-law. (D) is incorrect because it omits the apostrophe required to indicate possession.

3. (C) is the correct answer. The correct way to indicate possession in the case of a plural noun that ends in -s is to add an apostrophe; therefore, (C) is the correct answer here because the coat rack belongs to all of the Swansons. (A) is incorrect because there is no need to add an -s after the apostrophe. (B) is not correct because it omits the apostrophe needed to indicate who possesses the coat rack. (D) is not correct because the apostrophe indicates possession by a single Swanson.

4. (C) is the correct answer. In this case the plural noun "honorees" is not possessive; the four honorees are the subject of the sentence. (A) is not correct because it unnecessarily creates a possessive construction. (B) is not correct for the same reason, and also because "honoree's" suggests there is only one honoree, while the sentence makes clear there are four. (D) is not correct because it unnecessarily creates a possessive and, in addition, does so incorrectly: because the noun is plural and ends in an -s, there is no need to add an additional -s.

5. (D) is the correct answer. In this case two individuals each possess an office. (A) is not the correct answer because there is no need to make the plural noun "offices" possessive. (B) is not correct because Elizabeth does, in fact, possess one of the offices in spite of the missing apostrophe, though the offices do not own anything. (C) is not correct because, in this case, Kristin does possess one off the offices, but the apostrophe that would indicate that is missing.

6. (C) is the correct answer. There is no need for an apostrophe in this sentence. (A) is not correct because it unnecessarily creates a possessive form. (B) is not correct for the same reason, and also because the singular "pedestrian" is incorrect. (D) is not correct because, even if there were a need for the apostrophe, there would be no need to add an -s following the plural possessive noun.

7. (B) is the correct answer. It's necessary to add an -'s to the plural noun "children" in order to indicate that it is possessive, while lunches are not possessive. (A) is not correct because "childrens" is not the correct plural noun and the singular "lunch" does not agree with the subject. (C) is not the correct choice because "lunch" is not possessive so there is no need for the apostrophe. (D) is not correct because "childrens" is not the correct plural noun and there is no need to make "lunches" possessive.

8. (A) is the correct answer. The watches belong to the multiple conductors. (B) is not the correct option because an apostrophe is necessary to indicate that the plural noun is possessive. (C) is not correct because it suggests there is only one conductor, which does not make sense in the sentence. (D) is not correct because there is no need to add an -s following the apostrophe when the possessive noun already ends with an -s.

9. (C) is the correct answer. It correctly forms the possessive of the singular pronoun "anyone". (A), (B), and (D) are incorrect because the pronoun "anyone" does not have a plural form "anyones," let alone possessive forms based on that plural. In addition, (A) makes the mistake of adding an extra -s after the apostrophe when the possessive noun already ends with an -s, which is never correct.

10. (B) is the correct answer. In this case, there's no need for an apostrophe because "authors" is simply a plural noun. (A) incorrectly punctuates the word as a singular possessive, (C) as a plural possessive, and (D) with a use of apostrophes that's incorrect in any context.

11. (C) is the correct answer. It punctuates the word "mine" as a possessive, as in "a friend of mine's." (A) isn't correct, as it fails to mark the word "mine" as a possessive. (B) suggests that the friend is a friend of multiple mines, which doesn't make sense in context. (D) uses apostrophes in a way that is never correct.

12. (C) is the correct answer. Here, "seats" is not a possessive noun, but a verb. (A) punctuates it as a possessive; (B) breaks the rules for apostrophes; (D) also punctuates it as a possessive.

13. (A) is the correct answer. It's the only option which uses appropriate punctuation. (B) misplaces an apostrophe in "cheers" and doesn't put in apostrophe in the possessive "dignitaries." (C) punctuates "dignitaries" as a possessive and places an inappropriate apostrophe after "cheers." (D) lacks the needed apostrophe in "dignitarys."

14. (A) is the correct answer. There is only one singular deer (indicated by the article "a"), plural antlers, and the deer is the only noun in "deer's antlers" that should be possessive (since the antlers do not possess anything). (D) is incorrect because it unnecessarily creates a possessive out of the (incorrectly singular) "antler's." (B) is incorrect for the same reason, and also because it does not create a possessive out of the (incorrectly plural) "deers." (C) is incorrect because it incorrectly pluralizes "deers'" before creating a possessive.

Punctuating a List
Part 4

Punctuating a List questions ask you to correctly punctuate lists of items. Usually, items should be separated with a comma following each separate item (but not necessarily each word). Sometimes, a complex list can include semicolons. Look out for answer choices that add commas in the middle of phrases that describe single items, answers that use different kinds of punctuation to do the same job, and answer choices that leave out necessary punctuation.

DIRECTIONS

Every passage comes with a set of questions. Some questions will refer to a portion of the passage that has been underlined. Other questions will refer to a particular location in a passage or ask that you consider the passage in full.

After you read the passage, select the answers to questions that most effectively improve the passage's writing quality or that adjust the passage to follow the conventions of standard written English. Many questions give you the option to select "NO CHANGE." Select that option in cases where you think the relevant part of the passage should remain as it currently is.

1

In this cupboard we have cereal flour pasta and other dry goods.

A) NO CHANGE

B) cereal, flour, pasta, and,

C) cereal flour pasta, and

D) cereal, flour, pasta, and

2

We need to have many things ready before tomorrow: our backpacks, which must be full of meat; our hats, which must be either blue, purple, or pink; and our mixtapes, which must sound good.

A) NO CHANGE

B) meat our hats

C) meat, our hats,

D) meat our hats,

3

The countries involved in the agreement <u>are Canada Mexico, and</u> the United States.

A) NO CHANGE

B) are, Canada Mexico and

C) are Canada, Mexico, and

D) are Canada, Mexico, and,

4

The instruments in an orchestra are classified according to several types: strings, such as cellos, violins, and violas; woodwinds, such as clarinets, <u>bassoons, and oboes, and</u> brass, which includes trumpets, trombones, and tubas.

A) NO CHANGE

B) bassoons, and oboes; and

C) bassoons and oboes and

D) bassoons and oboes, and

5

Laura has purchased many feet of <u>rayon nylon and polyester</u> for her costumes.

A) NO CHANGE

B) rayon nylon and, polyester

C) rayon, nylon, and, polyester

D) rayon, nylon, and polyester

6

<u>Without: cheese, lettuce, and meat</u>, my sandwich will just be bread.

A) NO CHANGE

B) Without cheese, lettuce, and meat,

C) Without cheese, lettuce, and meat:

D) Without cheese lettuce and meat

7

The film was <u>bad, boring, tasteless, unfunny, and</u> cheaply made.

A) NO CHANGE

B) bad boring, tasteless unfunny, and

C) bad; boring; tasteless; unfunny; and

D) bad, boring, tasteless, unfunny, and,

8

Here are my knee pads; <u>my helmet; and</u> my skates.

A) NO CHANGE

B) my: knee pads, my helmet, and

C) my knee pads, my helmet, and

D) my knee pads my helmet, my

Anjali has four <u>plants</u> a cactus, a jade plant, a bamboo plant, and a snake plant.

A) NO CHANGE

B) plants:

C) plants,

D) plants;

10

It's nice to visit an art museum <u>and look at paintings; sculptures; and</u> installations.

A) NO CHANGE

B) and look, at paintings sculptures and,

C) and look at paintings, sculptures, and

D) and look: at paintings, sculptures, and

1. (D) is the correct answer. It places a comma after each item in the underlined portion of the list: cereal, flour, and pasta. (A) is incorrect because none of the items in the underlined portion have commas. (B) is incorrect because it places an unnecessary comma after "and." (C) is incorrect because it neglects to add commas after "cereal" and "flour."

2. (A) is the correct answer. It uses a semicolon to separate items in a complex series. A complex series has punctuation within the items being listed, as well as between them. In this case, there are commas introducing the "which" phrases after "backpacks," "hats," and "mixtapes," meaning that these ideas must be kept apart using semicolons, not just commas. When solving this question, you can use the semicolon between "pink" and "and" as an example. (B) is incorrect because it doesn't use any punctuation between "meat" and "our" or after "hats." (C) is incorrect because, since this is a complex series, there must be a semicolon here instead of a comma. (D) is incorrect because, while it punctuates after "hats," it lacks punctuation after "meat."

3. (C) is the correct answer. It correctly punctuates each item in the series, placing commas after "Canada" and "Mexico" and leaving "and" unpunctuated. (A) is incorrect because it doesn't place a comma between "Canada" and "Mexico." (B) is incorrect because it also fails to place a comma between "Canada" and "Mexico," and also places an unneeded comma after "are." (D) is incorrect because it places an unneeded comma after "and."

4. (B) is the correct answer. This is a complex series, meaning that it has additional punctuation within its items. In this case the listed items are the types of instrument in an orchestra. There are commas within each item, listing some examples of each type of instrument, so the instruments themselves need to be set off with semicolons. (B) correctly places a semicolon after "oboes" and a comma after "bassoons." (A) is incorrect because it puts a comma after "oboes" instead of a semicolon. (C) is incorrect because it puts no punctuation in the underlined portion at all. (D) is incorrect because it puts a comma after "oboes" and nothing after "bassoons."

5. (D) is the correct answer. It places a comma after "rayon" and "nylon," appropriately punctuating the list. (A) is incorrect because it does not use any commas at all. (B) is incorrect because it doesn't put a comma after "rayon" and also puts an unneeded one after "nylon." (C) is incorrect because it places an unneeded comma after "and."

6. (B) is the correct answer. It places commas after "cheese," "lettuce," and "meat." In this case "meat" needs a comma because the list is part of the dependent clause "Without cheese..." (A) is incorrect because it places a colon after "Without." Colons should never come within a phrase—only at the end of an independent clause. (C) is incorrect because it places a colon after "meat," inappropriately coming at the end of a dependent, not an independent clause. (D) is incorrect because it uses no punctuation marks at all.

7. (A) is the correct answer. Each item in the series before "and" appropriately has a comma. (B) is incorrect because "bad" and "tasteless" lack commas. (C) is incorrect because it uses semicolons rather than commas; remember that semicolons are only used in lists that are complex, not simple. (D) is incorrect because it places a comma after "and."

8. (C) is the correct answer. It places commas after "knee pads" and "helmet." (A) is incorrect because it uses semicolons rather than commas; remember that semicolons are only used in lists when there is additional punctuation within the items. (B) is incorrect because it places a colon after "my." Colons must only appear after independent clauses. (D) is incorrect because it lacks an "and" and places a comma after "my."

9. (B) is the correct answer. It places a colon after "plants." The colon introduces the list of four plants. (A) is incorrect because it lacks any punctuation after "plants." (C) is incorrect because the comma after "plants," while grammatically correct, doesn't make sense in context. It suggests that Anjali has four plants as well as the four plants actually listed. It would be like saying, "I have three fruits, an apple, an orange, and a pear." (D) is incorrect because the list must be introduced with a colon, not a semicolon. Remember that semicolons are used to join independent clauses or punctuate items in complex lists.

10. (C) is the correct answer. It places commas after "paintings" and "sculptures." (A) is incorrect because it places semicolons after "paintings" and "sculptures." (B) is incorrect because it places unneeded commas after "look" and "and." (D) is incorrect because it places an unneeded colon after "look."

Extra Clauses
Part 5

Extra Clauses questions ask you to correct punctuation surrounding parenthetical information. Commas or em-dashes can be used to surround this kind of information and set it off from the rest of the sentence, but the same punctuation should be used on both sides of the information. There's an important exception to look out for: if a nonrestrictive or parenthetical element is at the beginning or end of an independent clause, only one side could have the kind of punctuation used to end or separate those clauses.

DIRECTIONS

Every passage comes with a set of questions. Some questions will refer to a portion of the passage that has been underlined. Other questions will refer to a particular location in a passage or ask that you consider the passage in full.

After you read the passage, select the answers to questions that most effectively improve the passage's writing quality or that adjust the passage to follow the conventions of standard written English. Many questions give you the option to select "NO CHANGE." Select that option in cases where you think the relevant part of the passage should remain as it currently is.

1

The Empire State Building, which was once the world's tallest building was featured in the movie King Kong.

A) NO CHANGE

B) Building, which was once the world's tallest building, was

C) Building which was once the world's tallest building was

D) Building which was once the world's tallest building, was

2

Please excuse me Aunt Mary for being late to the party.

A) NO CHANGE

B) me, Aunt Mary, for

C) me Aunt Mary, for

D) me, Aunt Mary for,

3

The <u>hoverboard, due to a design flaw, could</u> ultimately go in only one direction.

A) NO CHANGE

B) hoverboard due to a design flaw, could

C) hoverboard, due to a design flaw could

D) hoverboard due to a design flaw could

4

Once you have the <u>basics tent, sleeping bag, and a flashlight—then</u> you can start thinking about more camping gear.

A) NO CHANGE

B) basics—tent, sleeping bag, and a flashlight; then

C) basics—tent, sleeping bag, and a flashlight— then

D) basics: tent, sleeping bag, and a flashlight. Then

5

I've been following her work <u>she studies the effects of erosion in mountain valleys— because</u> it might answer my questions about our local stream system.

A) NO CHANGE

B) —she studies the effects of erosion in mountain valleys—

C) she studies the effects of erosion in mountain valleys

D) she studies—the effects of erosion in mountain valleys

6

Some of the muffins have cinnamon in <u>them—even, surprisingly, the cranberry one</u> but the blueberry one doesn't.

A) NO CHANGE

B) them even surprisingly—the cranberry one—

C) them even surprisingly, the cranberry—one

D) them, even—surprisingly—the cranberry one,

7

Some cities<u>—like the Belgian university town of Louvain-la-Neuve are</u> almost entirely car-free.

A) NO CHANGE

B) like the Belgian university town of Louvain-la-Neuve—are

C) like the Belgian university town of Louvain-la-Neuve are

D) —like the Belgian university town of Louvain-la-Neuve—are

8

During the terrarium craze of 2015-16, <u>Leah a glassblower—</u>saw an increase in sales.

A) NO CHANGE

B) Leah—a glassblower—

C) Leah—a glassblower

D) Leah a glassblower by trade

Answers & Explanations

1. (B) is the correct answer. It correctly identifies the boundaries of a parenthetical clause and uses parallel punctuation to set it off. (A) is not the correct answer because there is a comma missing at the end of the parenthetical phrase. (C) is not correct because commas are needed to set off the parenthetical phrase. (D) is not correct because it omits the comma at the start of the parenthetical phrase.

2. (B) is the correct answer. The commas set off the noun of direct address (Aunt Mary). In other words, they set off the name of the person that the comment is addressing. (A) is a run-on sentence, so it is not correct. (C) is not correct because it omits the necessary comma before the noun of direct address. (D) is not correct because it omits the necessary comma after "Aunt Mary."

3. (A) is the correct answer. The commas in the underlined portion set off the parenthetical phrase that explains the problem with the hoverboard. (B) is not correct because it omits the comma needed to properly begin the parenthetical phrase. (C) is not correct because it omits the comma needed to end the parenthetical phrase. (D) is not correct because it doesn't set off the parenthetical element at all.

4. (C) is the correct answer. The dashes correctly sets off the parenthetical list of the basic camping gear. (A) is not correct because it omits necessary punctuation. (B) incorrectly inserts a semicolon between an independent and subordinate clause. (D) creates a sentence fragment.

5. (B) is the correct answer. It uses two em dashes to frame a parenthetical remark. (A) is missing the first em dash, after "work." (C) lacks any em dashes, and (D) lacks the dash after "valleys."

6. (D) is the correct answer. It uses commas to set off the parenthetical phrase "even the cranberry one," which has the additional parenthetical "surprisingly" nested within it using em-dashes. (A) is close, beginning to set off the phrase "even the cranberry one" and setting off the word "surprisingly," but it doesn't finish punctuation around the first phrase. (B) sets off only "the cranberry one." (C) doesn't use parallel punctuation, and places the punctuation incorrectly.

7. (D) is the correct answer. It sets off the appositive statement with em dashes. (A) lacks an em dash after "Louvain-la-Neuve," and (B) lacks one before "like." (C) lacks any em dashes.

8. (B) is the correct answer. It sets off the parenthetical statement with em dashes. (A) lacks an em dash after "Leah." (C) doesn't fully enclose all of the parenthetical remark, "a glassblower by trade." (D) lacks any em dashes at all.

Unnecessary Punctuation

Part 6

Unnecessary Punctuation questions require you to identify and remove unnecessary punctuation that occurs inside a sentence.

DIRECTIONS

Every passage comes with a set of questions. Some questions will refer to a portion of the passage that has been underlined. Other questions will refer to a particular location in a passage or ask that you consider the passage in full.

After you read the passage, select the answers to questions that most effectively improve the passage's writing quality or that adjust the passage to follow the conventions of standard written English. Many questions give you the option to select "NO CHANGE." Select that option in cases where you think the relevant part of the passage should remain as it currently is.

1

Side <u>dishes, like, corn fritters and creamed spinach,</u> are an interesting way to experiment with new recipes.

A) NO CHANGE

B) dishes, like corn fritters and creamed spinach

C) dishes like corn fritters and creamed spinach

D) dishes like corn fritters, and creamed spinach

2

Driving through Edinburgh was more <u>interesting to us, than</u> any guided tour of the many castles in Scotland.

A) NO CHANGE

B) interesting, to us than

C) interesting to us, than,

D) interesting to us than

3

Would <u>you, be interested</u> in trying my home-made honey?

A) NO CHANGE

B) you be interested,

C) you be, interested

D) you be interested

4

Exploring <u>multiple works, by the same, artist</u> immediately gives one a broader sense of that artist's way of painting.

A) NO CHANGE

B) multiple works, by the same artist

C) multiple works by the same artist

D) multiple works by the same artist,

5

Our startup plans to launch apps that <u>will allow you to: track the</u> number of steps that your cats take during the day, customize ad content to include only products that you won't be tempted to purchase, and receive push notifications when your friends are tagged in photos with people who are cooler than you are.

A) NO CHANGE

B) will—allow you to track the

C) will: allow you to track the

D) will allow you to track the

6

Brenda made sure to double-check her book of <u>American:</u> finches, swallows, and starlings to confirm the identity of the bird in her photograph.

A) NO CHANGE

B) American,

C) American

D) American—

7

It's surprising how <u>many: apple</u> and orange trees you can see from this hill.

A) NO CHANGE

B) many, apple

C) many apple

D) many apple:

8

Billy doesn't know what he's <u>going—to do</u> with all these tricycles.

A) NO CHANGE

B) going to—do

C) going to do

D) going to do—

9

<u>The iguanas—must have been waiting</u> for us the whole time.

A) NO CHANGE

B) The iguanas must have been waiting

C) The iguanas must—have been waiting

D) The—iguanas must have been waiting

1. (C) is the correct answer. It removes the unnecessary commas from the underlined portion. (A) is not correct because it contains too many commas: the phrase could be set off as a parenthetical, but there should certainly not be a comma between the preposition "like" and its object. (B) goes half-way towards punctuating "like corn fritters and creamed spinach" as a parenthetical phrase. It would be correct to make the phrase parenthetical or not to do so, but it's not correct to use just one of the two required commas. (D) incorrectly inserts a comma between two noun phrases, "corn fritters" and "creamed spinach," that make a compound object for the preposition "like."

2. (D) is the correct answer. The underlined portion requires no punctuation. (A) is not correct because it inserts an unnecessary comma before the word "than." (B) is not correct because the comma incorrectly attempts to separate compound elements that are not independent clauses. (C) is not correct because it incorrectly attempts to create an unnecessary transitional expression.

3. (D) is the correct answer. It avoids the comma placement errors of the other choices. Neither (A), (B), nor (C) place commas in appropriate places.

4. (C) is the correct answer. There is no need for commas in this sentence. (A) is not correct because the commas around "by the same" separate the adjective "same" from the noun that it modifies, "artist." (B) places a comma in front of an essential phrase. The phrase "by the same artist" modifies "multiple works" in a way that specifies its meaning in this sentence, rather than just providing additional information, so it should not be set off with a comma. (D) inserts a comma that incorrectly separates the subject of the sentence from the main verb.

5. (D) is the correct answer. No punctuation is needed before the list in the original sentence. (A) is incorrect because, while colons are often incorrectly placed in front of lists in this fashion, it is incorrect to place a colon between a preposition and its object or objects. (B) is incorrect because, while it removes the colon, it incorrectly places a dash between the helping verb "will" and the main verb "allow," not only interrupting the sentence but also interrupting a verb tense. (C) is incorrect for the same reason: placing the colon between the helping verb and the main verb that it modifies interrupts the verb and the sentence.

6. (C) is the correct answer. In this case, "American" is an adjective modifying "finches, swallows, and starlings", so there's no need for any punctuation after it. (A) incorrectly places a colon after "American." (B) confusingly suggests that "American" is a part of the list, rather than an adjective modifying it. (D) places a confusing em-dash between "American" and the list.

7. (C) is the correct answer. There's no need for any punctuation between "many" and "apple." (A) uses an unnecessary colon, (B) uses an unnecessary comma, and (D) places an inappropriate colon after "apple."

8. (C) is the correct answer. In this case, there is no need for an em dash anywhere in the sentence. (A) is incorrect because it breaks up the phrase "going to do" with an unnecessary em dash, as does (B). (D) also uses a needless em dash.

9. (B) is the correct answer. There's actually no need for any em dash here. (A), (C), and (D) all place inappropriate em dashes that merely disrupt the sentence.

Made in the USA
Middletown, DE
25 January 2022

58710887R00230